Springer Texts in Business and Economics

Springer Texts in Business and Economics (STBE) delivers high-quality instructional content for undergraduates and graduates in all areas of Business/Management Science and Economics. The series is comprised of self-contained books with a broad and comprehensive coverage that are suitable for class as well as for individual self-study. All texts are authored by established experts in their fields and offer a solid methodological background, often accompanied by problems and exercises.

Andreas Krause

Theoretical Foundations of Investment Banking

Springer

Andreas Krause
University of Bath
Bath, UK

ISSN 2192-4333 ISSN 2192-4341 (electronic)
Springer Texts in Business and Economics
ISBN 978-3-031-58059-8 ISBN 978-3-031-58060-4 (eBook)
https://doi.org/10.1007/978-3-031-58060-4

This Springer imprint is published by the registered company Springer Nature Switzerland AG
The registered company address is: Gewerbestrasse 11, 6330 Cham, Switzerland

Preface

Investment banking, as we know it today, developed in London from the nineteenth century onward. Merchants engaged in the trading of valuable and, for the time, exotic commodities such as spices, tea, and coffee, or precious metals diversified their businesses, making use of their extensive trading network to obtain information about events in distant regions of the earth. Their information gave them an advantage when offering to finance trade and investments in these widely unknown regions. These businesses developed into what today we call investment banks. London, as the centre of the far-flung British Empire, became the leading financial centre in the world and the traditional British term 'merchant bank' for an investment bank refers to this origin of investment banking. London is today generally still seen as one of the most important financial centres globally, alongside New York, which is generally seen as having overtaken London in its importance.

Originally located in the City of London, also referred to as the 'Square Mile', many banks have relocated to Canary Wharf in the east of the City during the 1990s. Located in the former docks of London, the development into a financial hub signalled a shift from the trading of goods to that of financial services. Many banks, though, remain in the City, as it is commonly called, and are located near such iconic buildings as St Paul's Cathedral, the Tower of London, and the Bank of England in Threadneedle Street. The equivalent to the City and Canary Wharf in New York is Wall Street, often used as a term synonymous with investment banking.

Investment banks, in very simple terms, advise clients how to finance their companies and how companies or individuals may invest any funds they have available. They do not only provide advice, but facilitate their clients achieving these aims. They are involved in the merger of companies by providing advice, they help issuing securities such as stocks and bonds, and they enable investors to trade securities.

The aim of this book is to shed light on the advice investment banks provide their clients with. How do investment banks develop the advice they provide their clients with, and how do they facilitate the implementation of their advice? In order to arrive at the advice they give, investment banks rely mainly on two concepts from finance. The first concept is the valuation of securities—stocks, bonds, and derivatives. The second concept is the inference and anticipation of the behaviour by other market participants, such as shareholders or investors.

Valuing securities can be achieved using discounted cash flows and arbitrage, both well understood in theory as well as practice. The expertise of investment banks is mainly in their access to information, which goes beyond what most investors or companies could achieve. Inferring and anticipating the behaviour of other investors and shareholders requires more experience, as not only will investment banks need information, but they will also need to assess the information other people have and how they react to that information. Behavioural finance has made significant contributions in this area.

I am not taking this angle on investment banking here and do not discuss the valuation of companies or reactions by market participants. I am leaving these important aspects to contributions in corporate finance and financial markets, respectively. My focus will be on the advice investment banks give to their clients, assuming investment banks have analysed their information and obtained the best recommendation for their client from it. Will investment banks advise their clients according to these optimal recommendations? Or will they advise their clients differently? How can we ensure that investment bank give advice that is in the best interest of their clients? These are questions I will seek to address.

The focus of the analysis will be on the conflicts of interest between the investment bank and their clients. The best possible advice might not always be in the best interest of the investment bank. If they advise their clients differently, and their client follows this advice, this might generate more profit to the investment bank. I will investigate how the advice that is optimal for investment banks differs from the advice that would be in the best interest of their clients. How investment banks are rewarded for their advice will be critical in shaping the advice they give. Therefore, I will explore the contractual arrangements between investment banks and their clients and how these can be structured such that the advice given by investment banks is optimal not only for them, but also for their clients.

I will investigate in many settings the question of how the conflict of interest between investment banks and their clients manifests itself in, from their clients' perspective, suboptimal advice and how these can be reconciled. Covering all main business areas of investment banking, I will show how existing contractual arrangements are often optimal in minimising this conflict of interest. Investment banks cannot be relied on to provide clients with their best, unbiased advice. Conflicts of interest might bias such advice in the investment bank's favour, unless contractual arrangements are specifically set up to mitigate this effect. Understanding the incentives of investment banks will help us not only to understand the context in which advice is given, but also the often complex contractual arrangements that reduce conflicts of interest.

The models I use are in most cases highly stylised and seek to explore a single feature of the investment banking business. Such models, while often abstracting from the complexity of real situations, allow me to focus on the essence of the problem addressed and gain valuable insights that are often lost in more complicated settings. In addition, all models are, as much as feasible, consistent with each other, allowing me to compare and combine results for a more complete analysis of investment banking behaviour. Using a consistent notation across models will also help the reader to understand and interpret the models and their results.

Addressing many of the key characteristics of investment banking, we obtain an overview of the way investment banks operate and the challenges their clients are facing when seeking their advice. The business that is conducted in the glass towers of the City, Canary Wharf, Wall Street, and any other financial centre, is more than conducting valuations and second-guessing other market participants' decisions and reactions. Advice will be given, but such advice might serve the investment bank better than its recipient, their client. Knowing about these conflicts of interest and how they are mitigated will allow not only to understand investment banks better, but also assess the advice itself. Understanding that advice is driven not by a desire to solely benefit their clients, but investment banks themselves, will help to set the advice in context. Clients, acknowledging the context the advice is given in, will be able to make better informed decisions by questioning the investment banks' motifs.

Investment banks advise clients on often complex transactions, having to take into account a large range of information. The advice itself is the result of complex considerations. Understanding investment bank behaviour can also help us to understand company and investor decisions better.

Selection of Models Covered Having decided to focus on the economic incentives of investment banks and the consequences these have, I was able to exclude much of the models and theories that seek to explain how investment banks determine the best recommendations for their clients. Models of valuing stocks, bonds, or derivatives are excluded as are theories of portfolio selection and trading strategies. Instead, the focus is on models seeking to explain how investment banks make use of the results they obtain. Hence, I do not provide an overview of their expertise but their utilisation of their expertise when advising clients.

Although theoretical models on investment bank behaviour are not as widespread as in other areas of banking and finance, they cover the breadth of investment banking activities. Even the most comprehensive treatment of any subject will have to be selective in its scope and focus on what the author deems to be the essential elements of the topic, a selection that will necessarily be subjective. My goal in selecting models on investment banking was to provide an analysis of the key activities they engage in and do so using a consistent and accessible approach.

In most cases, the theoretical models selected allowed me to use similar frameworks across all investment banking activities. Common features of models include that a security will have two possible values—either a high or a low value, that investment banks receive an imperfect signal about this value, and that some market participants have superior information than others; this could be the issuer of securities, the investment bank, or investors. To achieve this goal, I have often used the ideas of published models and adjusted them to the framework I employ throughout this book. This has the consequence that many of the models have been altered considerably from the original models that served as inspiration. In this process, I might have altered assumptions, made simplifying assumptions, or changed the setting of model to suit my aims. The analysis of the results obtained from these (modified) models will in many cases also be much more limited and focus exclusively on aspects that serve the aim of analysing investment bank behaviour in the context of the activity analysed. I have on many occasions excluded assessments of social welfare, implications for regulatory interventions, or generalisations of the findings. While these points will be surely be of interest to an economist, I felt that unless they served a specific purpose in the context of the problem analysed, these considerations would not aid our understanding of investment bank behaviour. While I have provided detailed derivations of each model to allow readers to appreciate the results fully, I have in most instances not considered second-order conditions of optimisation problems; this was done as not to distract from the main derivation of the results.

Empirical models have not been included at all; the focus is exclusively on theoretical models. This is not because I regard empirical models as less valuable in understanding investment banks and their behaviour, they serve important roles in allowing to determine the relative importance of often conflicting incentives and of course discover many of the conflicts of interests and behavioural traits of investment banks. My aim here is to provide the theoretical foundations that may allow us to explain observed phenomena and sometimes make recommendation that enable an improvement of the outcomes for investment banks, their clients, or the general public.

Extent of Coverage The focus of this book is on the advice investment banks give to their clients and their interactions with them; this is often referred to as the front office of investment banks. It is the front office that generates the profits and is the part of the investment bank that has direct influence on the decisions made by their clients. I cover all the main business areas of investment banks, provide an overview of some of the key features of each activity, and highlight key problems in the advice investment banks give. Furthermore, I provide models to explain key characteristics of contractual arrangements and practices that are observed empirically. Depending on the state of the literature for a specific area, this coverage will be more or less extensive.

In addition to the front office, investment banks have so-called middle and back offices that support the functions of the front office. The middle office concerns itself with the running of the investment bank. It decides on the business strategy of the investment bank, such as which markets to enter, which services to provide, how to remunerate and develop employees; it operates internal controls, for example assessing and managing the risks investment banks take or managing the performance of the investment bank with its many business lines; finally, it manages the internal funds available by deciding how to invest these, commonly referred to as treasury management. The duties of the middle office will only be covered to the extent that it might affect front office activities, for example through incentives specific compensation strategies provide employees with.

Similarly, the back office of investment banks is not covered in this book. It is the back office that ensures information is available for those requiring access to advice clients, securities are allocated correctly to investors and monies collected as well paid, and trades in securities markets are executed correctly. With the advance in technology, the back office has become an ever more important part of investment banking, supporting the front office in advising clients and then allowing them to implement this advice. As with the middle office, I will concern myself with the back office only if this has direct implications for the advice given to clients.

The middle and back offices are providing the front office with the infrastructure to fulfil their roles. By focussing on the front office and the relationship of investment banks with their clients, I assume that the middle and back offices operate effectively and efficiently, but do not consider their roles in more detail.

Problem Sets Theoretical models provide valuable insights into investment bank advice and how this relates to the advice that would be in their clients' best interest. Such models are, however, by their very nature often abstract and seem far removed from the realities of the actual decisions that investment banks have to take. To show the relevance of the models I present here, each part of this book has a collection of problems that can be addressed using the models I present in this book. These problems are designed to provide realistic scenarios that investment banks, their clients, regulators, or other interested parties might face and where the models in this book provide a tool to assess possible outcomes or solutions. These problems are purely hypothetical and are not directly based on actual events in investment banking, although in some cases they might be inspired by such events and adjusted such that they can be solved using one of the models. In many cases, to solve a problem at all, or to solve it completely, two or more models need to be combined. The value of these problems is in deepening the understanding of the models and show how they are relevant in the actual decision-making of investment banks.

By bringing together the wide range of activities investment banks are engaged in into a single coherent framework, I hope that this book enhances not only our understanding of investment bank activities, the benefits they provide, but also the challenges that shortcomings in their advice entails.

Bath, UK
September, 2024

Andreas Krause

Contents

List of Figures

List of Table

1 Introduction

Investment banks are acting as intermediaries in securities markets, predominantly by providing information and advice to market participants rather than taking an active role; if an active role is taken, it is commonly only fleeting with the aim to convey information to market participants. While commercial banks provide loans to companies, individuals, and governments using mainly funds provided to them by others, generally called depositors, and to a much lesser extent their own equity, investment banks rarely use their own equity or funds provided to them by others; using a strict definition, investment banks do not obtain deposits and would operate only on equity or funds otherwise lent to them by other banks or the bond market. Instead, they seek to provide information to market participants that allows these market participants to negotiate any funding directly between them. For providing such information and advice, investment banks charge their clients a fee. Hence, the business model of investment banks is very different from that of commercial banks, whose profits rely on the difference of interest they charge on loans and the interest paid on deposits.

The Purpose of Investment Banks The traditional role of investment banks is the provision of advice to individuals, companies, and governments for one or more of the following types of transactions:

1. Raise funds from securities markets in the form of debt or equity
2. Purchase of equity securities of another company with the aim of gaining a controlling stake
3. Selling of equity securities to another entity seeking to gain a controlling stake
4. Negotiation of a company or government with security holders on restructuring equities and liabilities

The first type of transaction, the raising of funds from securities markets, concerns the issue of new or additional securities in what is generally referred to as the

A. Krause, *Theoretical Foundations of Investment Banking*, Springer Texts in Business and Economics, https://doi.org/10.1007/978-3-031-58060-4_1

primary market. If equity in the form of shares is issued to the general public and subsequently listed for trading on a stock exchange, it is commonly known as an initial public offering, while the increase in the number of issued shares already listed on a stock exchange is termed a secondary offering. However, equity does not have to be raised from the general public, but instead the investor base can be limited to those selected specifically by the company or investment bank, in which case this transaction is referred to as a private placement. In the same way, funds can be raised using debt instruments, such as bonds. Collectively, advice on such types of transactions to raise funds are known as securities underwriting.

The final three types of transactions are commonly referred to as mergers and acquisitions. Companies seeking to purchase another company will obtain advice on the price to offer, and the company being purchased will obtain advice on the price it should demand. The restructuring of companies will also require advice on appropriate exchange ratios between debt and equity, for example, or the price at which an investor might inject additional capital into a company. In all cases, the investment bank only provides advice, but would not purchase any equity or provide other forms of funding.

Business Lines of Investment Banks The purchase and selling of equity securities as outlined in the second and third type of transactions is commonly referred to as mergers and acquisitions. The investment bank will either advise the entity seeking to obtain a controlling stake in another company, or the entity which is targeted. The buyer of such a controlling stake can be another company, its own management, other individuals, or investment vehicles. If the buyer of the controlling stake is another company, this is either referred to as a merger or an acquisition. A merger is generally interpreted as two companies of comparable size that are combined such that both companies are seen as equal partners, often with senior management roles in the new company shared between those from the previous companies. In an acquisition, in contrast, the acquiring company, usually the larger of the two companies, does control all aspects of the acquired company, including taking over all senior management positions. The buyer of a controlling stake does not have to be another company, but could be the current senior management taking over the company from the current owners in a so-called management buy-out. Similarly, other individuals or investment vehicles could seek to obtain a controlling stake in a company. As usually such transactions are financed by debt, they are referred to as leveraged buy-outs.

A company in distress might seek to re-negotiate the terms of their debt, for example to swap debt for equity, to improve the balance sheet structure, and to ease the burden of interest payments on liquidity. They might also seek to extend the maturity of loans for the same reason. Such restructuring activities would be advised about by an investment bank.

The advice on the above transactions, mergers and acquisitions as well as underwriting, is often referred to *corporate finance* in an investment banking context. The advice investment banks give affects the issue of new securities and the purchase or sale of significant stakes in companies. As such, these transactions are different from trading activities in securities markets, where each transaction consists only of a very small fraction of the outstanding securities. While not part of corporate finance and not included in the traditional remit of investment banks, many investment banks expanded their business into the area of investment and trading. Firstly, by providing *research* about the prospects of companies and thereby of their securities, mostly shares; particularly in the case of countries and governments, investment banks will also assess the prospects of debt instruments. Investment banks employ financial analysts who provide investors with information about the future prospects of the company or the prospects of the repayment of debt instruments, often relative to benchmark securities or indices. Commonly, they combine this information with a recommendation to investors whether the security should be bought or additional units should be bought, the current holding be maintained, or the securities be sold if already held. Financial analysts providing such reports and recommendations can be seen as supporting the corporate finance advice investment banks provide. By giving investors access to information similar to what the company has access to when seeking advice, the informational asymmetry between companies and investors is reduced, improving the quality of securities markets. This should benefit the investor but also the issuer of the security as adverse selection is reduced.

A further expansion of the business of investment banks has been observed in what is often referred to as *trading and sales*. Investment banks often trade on their own account, called proprietary trading, to exploit the level of knowledge and expertise they have accumulated in their various lines of business. They commonly also provide brokerage services to their clients allowing them to access securities markets for trading and act as market makers by providing liquidity in markets. The latter will also allow them to support their clients from corporate finance by ensuring an orderly market for their securities is established. Wealthy individuals will often delegate their investment decisions to the asset management division of investment banks, who then will invest their wealth on their behalf. Finally, investment banks do not only underwrite securities for their clients, but might develop new types of securities to meet their clients' needs. Such financial innovations will often allow clients, whether they are companies, governments, or investors, to take advantage of regulatory loopholes, reduce tax burdens, or change the timing of paying or receiving funds. In many cases, investment banks developing such financial innovations will remain as the counterparty given that market acceptance will often be small. Once a financial innovation is more widely accepted, the role of investment banks in acting as the counterparty will reduce. Often the investment bank will seek to hedge any risk exposures the financial innovation caused through the use of existing financial instruments, such as options, futures, and swaps.

In addition, many investment banks also heavily invest their own funds into private equity, hedge funds, or direct investments into companies. Such investments are not considered in this book. Furthermore, the trading in capital markets also involves the need for the clearing and settlement of securities, an area often referred to as the 'back office', as well as the need for compliance with regulations and generally the management of risk, a risk management department, referred to as the 'middle office'. We do not cover these aspects in this book.

Most of the larger and well-known investment banks can best be described as "full-service investment banks" in that they offer all of the above services. In contrast, many smaller or "boutique" investment banks will focus on a small selection of services they offer. Some private banks focus on wealth management and therefore are mainly active in trading and sales only, and due to their lack of corporate finance services, they are often not classified as investment banks, although they fit within our definition of an investment bank. While clients in general might have demand for many of the services offered, their provision is to a large extent independent of each other. It is thus possible to treat them individually, and therefore, there is little difference in principle whether analysing the activities of full-service or boutique investment banks. In some instances, additional conflicts of interests might arise from the ability to cross-sell services, but these will be limited and not affect the overall results obtained.

By providing advice to clients rather than producing and selling a more tangible product or service, investment banks and clients have objective functions that are not always well aligned. Investment banks will seek to maximise their profits while clients would want to obtain the best possible advice. These two aims are generally not easily reconciled, even more so as investment banks rely on an informational advantage over their clients, making it difficult for them to make adjustments for the advice they receive. We will focus on this conflict of interest between investment banks and their clients and how this conflict of interest can be resolved at least partially through appropriate contracts between the two parties that align the interests as much as possible. These conflicts of interest also have implications for the compensation and employment of staff, how investment banks are organised, and which services they offer in the first place. We will explore these in the final part of this book.

Key Economic Aspects of Investment Banking The primary objective of investment banks is to maximise their own profits, rather than providing the best possible advice to their clients. With clients basing their decisions on the advice given by investment banks, this can lead to suboptimal decisions being made, whose origins can be seen in the distortion of advice given by investment banks, that is driven by their desire to maximise their own profits. For clients, it is difficult to take this conflict of interest fully into account as the informational asymmetry between the investment bank and their client does not allow them to infer the information investment banks hold fully, or, in cases where this might be possible, they are not able to convey such information to other market participants reliably. Analysing the incentives of investment banks using economic theories will allow us to identify the extent and causes of any biases in advice given by investment banks. This can then be extended to assess how clients and other market participants, being aware of the conflicts of interests between investment banks and their clients as well the implications for advice given, are reacting to the advice.

Being aware of these biases and the impact they will have on decisions, we can then evaluate the impact different contractual agreements between investment banks and their clients have on the advice given as well as the behaviour of clients and other market participants. If we recognise that advice is given by employees of investment banks, we can then look at the contractual arrangements between the investment bank and their employees, focussing on the impact of compensation and promotion policies. Employees will seek to maximise their own compensation in their current role, and might also take into account the possibility of promotions in the future, affecting the quality of work they provide and thus giving rise to another conflict of interest. In addition to the conflict of interest between investment banks and their clients, there is a conflict of interest between employees and investment banks.

The following models will address these aspects for the wide variety of business lines investment banks offer. The focus will be on identifying conflicts of interests and how they affect outcomes, usually assuming that clients follow the advice given by their investment bank, alongside the assessment of contractual arrangements to reduce such conflicts of interests and improve the outcomes for clients and possibly also investment banks and their employees.

Summary Investment banks advise on a wide range of capital market transactions by collecting relevant information and providing this to their clients as well as, in many instances, other market participants. Commonly, the aim of this information provision is to reduce the asymmetric information between market participants and thereby benefit their client by allowing transactions to be completed at more favourable conditions or even to be completed at all. The interests of the investment bank and their clients are not fully aligned, giving rise to conflicts of interests that can result in biased advice being given, that is advice that is not fully consistent with the information the investment bank holds. There exist contractual arrangements that address these conflicts of interest and seek to ensure that advice given is more aligned with the interests of their clients.

Prologue: Practices and Processes in Investment Banking

2

Before analysing the behaviour of investment banks and the implications this might have on their clients, it is important to gain an understanding of the role investment banks have in the different business lines they are active in. Besides the roles they play, I will also outline the way investment banks are commonly rewarded and how this might lead to conflicts of interest between them and their clients. It will be this conflict of interest that will be the focus of the subsequent analysis, and understanding its origin in the context of the role investment banks are playing is essential to understanding the advice they provide. As the way fees are determined to reward investment banks will be an important determinant of this conflict of interest, remuneration contracts will be investigated in more detail. This will then allow us to investigate how such contracts can be used to reduce the conflict of interest.

The key business lines of investment banks will be looked at in turn, focussing on essential facets that are of relevance from the perspective of analysing investment bank behaviour. The motivations of their clients are generally taken as given and not considered further here, nor will I consider the way investment banks analyse information on behalf of their clients; these aspects are left to the specialist literature in their respective fields of finance. Models that address issues mentioned in this overview of investment banking business are indicated by small superscripts referring to the relevant chapter.

A common characteristic across most business lines of investment banking is that investment banks are either better informed than other market participants or have the means to acquire such information in a way other market participants are not able to, in addition to having the expertise to analyse and interpret the obtained information. Of course, having obtained such information, investment banks could use this information directly, for example by trading securities. However, it is often more profitable to sell the information through providing advice to clients (Chap. 3). That way the benefits the information has to clients can be extracted by the investment bank through the fee charged for the advice, and if the information is more valuable to clients, or it can be sold to a large number of clients without

A. Krause, *Theoretical Foundations of Investment Banking*, Springer Texts in Business and Economics, https://doi.org/10.1007/978-3-031-58060-4_2

impacting the value of the information significantly, it is preferable for investment banks to provide such advice rather than act on the information themselves.

Being informed makes the role of investment banks as intermediaries different to that of many other intermediaries in markets. They are not only present in the market as a means to reduce transaction costs between market participants, but they have the ability to affect market outcomes directly. Using their superior information, they can signal to market participants the quality of a security (Sect. 4.1) and thereby even affect the quality of the security itself (Sect. 4.2). Therefore, investment banks cannot be seen as solely facilitating capital market transactions, their presence will have impact on the market outcome to an extent larger than the mere provision of information.

Of course, investment banks are not providing advice with the aim of benefitting their clients or other market participants, they foremost seek to maximise their own profits. As will become apparent in many of the models discussed, this will affect the outcome of their advice. In many cases, a higher profit to the investment bank will result in a lower surplus for their clients. If the investment banks' remuneration is linked to the benefits their advice provides clients with, investment banks will seek a balance between their own interests and that of their clients (Chap. 5). As we will see, the way this remuneration is determined, as well as other contractual features and commonly used processes, will limit the extent of any conflicts of interest. It is frequently observed that the contract specification that aligns the interests of investment banks and their clients closest, is the one dominating the market.

2.1 Mergers and Acquisitions Advice

One of the most profitable business lines for investment banks is mergers and acquisitions advice; it is also often seen as the most prestigious area to work within an investment bank, together with proprietary trading. Investment banks are involved in the negotiation of such transactions and work alongside lawyers and management consultants. Lawyers will advise on legal requirements within the process, and the role of management consultants is to ensure that the merger is beneficial for the company in the long run and that the integration of the two companies involved can be completed successfully. To this effect, they might provide information on the size of synergies, but also costs of integrating the two companies. The role of investment banks is mainly to analyse information provided to them and determine appropriate purchase prices that are acceptable to both sides.

The Scope of Mergers and Acquisitions In its pure meaning, mergers and acquisitions entail the combination of two companies into a single economic unit. In the case that both companies are of comparable status within the new organisation, this is commonly referred to as a merger, sometimes more specifically as a merger of equals. If one company will dominate the new organisation, this is commonly referred to as an acquisition of the dominated company. The way the resulting organisation is structured can vary, for example the acquired company or one of the merged companies might survive as a subsidiary of the acquiring company or the other merging company; alternatively, one of the companies might be fully absorbed into the other company, or both companies become subsidiaries of a newly formed company. Which format is chosen will depend to a large degree on legal considerations and tax implications, but also on the strategic outlook the joint companies have.

There are other transactions between companies that are similar to mergers and acquisitions and therefore similar considerations apply from the perspective of an investment bank. Rather than acquiring the company as a whole, the acquisition might only involve the assets of a company, leaving the company legally in the hands of the previous owners. Asset purchases have the same economic effects as purchasing the company itself. Again, the choice of such an agreement might be driven by legal and tax considerations. It is also not necessary that a company is bought completely, it is possible that previous owners retain a significant stake in the acquired company and the acquiring company only obtains a controlling stake or in some cases even a large minority stake.

Payment of the existing owners of a company acquired might be either in cash or in a stake of the acquiring company. As in many cases the companies involved are joint-stock companies, this involves providing the previous owners with shares of the acquiring company; of course, a stake in other legal forms is equally possible. We might also see a combination of cash and shares, or the use of bonds issued to previous owners. For mergers, it is common that shares are used as a means of payment. Which payment form is used will depend on the financial situation of all parties involved, the acquiring company's ability to pay cash, for example, as well as the requirement of the acquired company's owners for cash payment. The need to retain funds within the merged companies for future investment will also be an important determinant.

The scope of mergers and acquisitions in the context of investment bank advice can be extended even further than mergers and acquisitions as defined above. The purchase of a company, or of a significant stake in it, does not necessarily have to be made by another company. It could be that an investor seeks to purchase a company outright as a strategic long-term investment, this will often be private equity funds and similar constructs. In this case, the purchase is completed using cash and the requisite amount of cash is often obtained through a loan. Given the reliance on loans to finance the purchase price, such transactions are commonly referred to as a Leveraged Buy-Out (LBO). If the purchaser of the company is not an investor, but more specifically the management of the company, this would be referred to as a Management Buy-Out (MBO). An existing owner might also want to take a larger controlling stake by acquiring stakes from other owners. If the company has its shares listed at a stock exchange, this will often be referred to as Going Private.

While all these transactions might have very different motivations and also legal consequences, they all have in common that one entity, a company or group of individuals, seeks to obtain a significant stake in another company. The size of the stake usually goes beyond that of making investments through the stock market in listed companies. The aim is commonly to obtain full control by acquiring the full stake, a controlling stake, or in some cases obtaining a blocking minority. Despite the very different forms of these transactions might take, the essential role of investment banks is very similar, and for this reason, we consider them all under the umbrella of mergers and acquisitions.

The Role of Investment Banks Investment banks provide advice to the purchasers of companies, referred to as bidders, as well as sellers, known as targets. While the detailed roles of investment banks will differ depending on the nature of the proposed transaction, a common feature is to advise on the price that should be offered by bidders and which price targets should accept. The expertise of investment banks in valuing companies is at the forefront of this advice. Their expertise will be derived from employing specialists that have the knowledge and skills to conduct such valuations and that are commonly not recruited by companies as their expertise would only be used rarely. Given that investment banks provide such advice on many occasions, they will also have built-up experience that employees of companies would not have.

The involvement of investment banks might actually start before a bidder has identified a target. The owners of a target may wish to sell their stake and approach an investment bank with the aim not only of being advised on the price they should accept, but also in identifying a potential bidder and ensuring a bid is forthcoming. Investment banks would use their network of contacts with investors as well as other companies to identify suitable bidders and propose to them making a bid. Similarly, they might advise a potential bidder on suitable targets and approach them to assess their willingness to entertain a bid. Such investors would usually not be other companies that seek a merger for reasons of their core business strategy, but financial investors. Once a suitable bidder or target has been identified, investment banks will start to evaluate the companies in detail. If the transaction is friendly, meaning that the target agrees in principle to being purchased, they will disclose information to the bidder's investment bank, which is then evaluated by the investment bank to determine the value the company has to the purchaser. This would include any synergies that might arise from the purchase. Similarly, the investment bank advising the target will advise their owners on the value of their company, and if a stake in the bidding company is offered, also the value of that stake. These identified values then determine the maximum bidding price for the bidder and the minimum price the target would be willing to accept.

If the merger or acquisition is hostile, thus the target does not agree to the sale at all, the information on which investment banks will be able to work can only be based on publicly available information, the experience of the investment bank from previous deals, and the information that has been provided by the target due to legal requirements, as stipulated for many publicly listed companies. In all cases, however, the information provided by either party will seek to show the companies at its most advantageous, and it is the expertise of the investment bank to assess the information provided and, if necessary, seek the disclosure of additional information. This due diligence process aims to uncover any hidden negative aspects of a company, whether these are known to the company itself or not. Confidentiality of information is crucial at this stage as any disclosure will not only affect the bid price, but could affect the strategy of the companies if the transaction does not commence. A company might have obtained information about a competitor's strategy that might be valuable to them, or the pricing mechanism of a supplier that can be used in future negotiations. For this reason, it might well be that information is disclosed to the investment bank under the provision that it is not shared with their client. Negotiations on the purchase price might also be conducted only between investment banks as such confidential information would be used in the discussion of a suitable price; the companies will then only be presented with the results of the negotiation and the assurance by their respective investment banks that the agreed price takes into account all aspects fairly.

Investment banks therefore have a crucial role not only in obtaining and interpreting information to obtain a suitable price for their client, but also in the negotiations itself. The companies involved will lack information to assess the price that has been agreed on their part. It will therefore be difficult for them to reject a suggestion made by their investment bank. Nevertheless, from a legal perspective, the role of the investment bank is only to advise their clients, it is for their clients to accept or reject this advice. Any transaction will then be concluded between their clients directly, without an active involvement of the investment bank. Thus, neither investment bank would make the purchase on behalf of the bidder and then sell the company on to the bidder itself. While the role of investment banks is purely advisory, their access to information, beyond what is available to their clients, gives them a distinct advantage in assessing the transaction.

Selecting Investment Bank Advisors It is common for clients to approach several investment banks to advise on a transaction through what is often referred to as a beauty parade. For smaller transactions, clients might only approach a single investment bank they have worked with previously and the larger the transaction the more investment banks are approached. Clients will usually meet with a number of investment banks and seek out their experience of advising in comparable transactions, their assessment on possible purchase prices, as well as the estimated length of the process, alongside their fees. Based on such a pitch book, the client will then be able to select the investment bank that is most suitable to their needs. As the projected purchase price will be an important determinant of the choice for clients, experience with the bidder (for targets) or target (for bidders), respectively, can give assurances to the client that the projected conditions are feasible and realistic. In large and complex, often international transactions, multiple investment banks might be appointed as advisors with complementary experience, for example in different jurisdictions, or for mergers across different industries.

The Investment Banking Agreement The fees of investment banks in mergers and acquisitions advisory commonly consist of three components. Firstly, the direct costs investment banks face in evaluating the transaction. Such costs would include the travel and accommodation of the team conducting the evaluation in various locations of the target or bidding company. The second component is often referred to as the retainer fee; it is a fee that is either fixed for a transaction or based on the time period an investment bank is working on a transaction. Such fees are often charged on a monthly basis seeking to cover staff costs and ensure that if a transaction is not completed as no agreement between companies can be reached, the investment bank is rewarded for their efforts in providing the advice. The time period during which the retainer fee is payable would commence from the moment the investment bank starts working on behalf of their client, such as seeking to identify a suitable target or bidder, and ends with the completion of the transaction or the decision to abandon it. Although the retainer fee is paid regularly throughout the process, it can be interpreted as the cost of not going ahead with the merger and is hence akin to a break-up fee (Sect. 6.3).

The final component is the success fee, which is payable only if the transaction is completed. This fee is commonly calculated as a fraction of the value of the transaction. Such a contract imposes two conflicts of interest between investment banks and their clients. Firstly, for targets and bidder alike, it gives investment banks an incentive to ensure the transaction is completed, even if this is not in the interest of their client. It is only in this case that the success fee becomes due; the size of this fee, compared to the retainer fee, gives strong incentives to provide advice suggesting to complete the transaction (Sect. 6.2). A contract that pays a fee only if the transaction is completed is known as a conditional fee contract. The second conflict of interest arises from the fee being linked to the size of the transaction; a transaction at a higher price will increase the fee the investment bank obtains. This contract type in which the fee is payable only on the completion of the transaction and is dependent on the value of this transaction is called a contingent fee contract. It is therefore in the interest of the investment bank to increase the value of the transaction, and this implies that there are incentives for the investment bank advising the bidder to increase the purchase price beyond what a target might accept. From a target's perspective, this second conflict of interest does not arise as the seller will be interested in obtaining the highest possible price (Sect. 6.1.1).

While contingent fee contracts are common and widespread, they are not universally found; conditional fee contracts are also sometimes found. Their use has its advantages in situations where clients might be in a better position to assess the value of a merger due to their industry knowledge (Sect. 6.1.2). While these contract specifications create conflicts of interest, they are also able to align interests between investment banks and clients.

Reading Caselli et al. (2021, Chs. 9–12), Iannotta (2010, Chs. 7–9), Liaw (2012, Ch. 7), and Stowell (2018, Ch. 4).

2.2 Securities Underwriting

Securities can be issued by companies and subsequently be sold to investors directly. In most cases, however, investment banks are hired by the issuer to facilitate the sale to investors, a process that is referred to as underwriting. The role of the investment bank in this process is to advise the issuer on a suitable sale price and re-assure investors on the value of the securities that are offered. Thus, investment banks reduce the asymmetric information between issuers and investors on the qualities of the securities, while also informing issuers about appropriate prices for their securities. While investment banks have only the fee earned from underwriting to incentivise them to provide advice to issuers, this position changes for universal banks, whose profits from lending might be affected by the issuance of new securities (Sect. 7.6).

Depending on the type of issuer, the securities issued, as well as the investors the securities are offered to, procedures on underwriting securities will vary and see the involvement of lawyers at all stages to comply with regulatory requirements. The role of investment banks is, similar to their involvement in mergers and acquisitions, the provision and analysis of information to determine a fair value at which the security can be sold. However, as I will point out below, in most cases the involvement of investment banks is going beyond purely providing advice by actively soliciting demand for the security and purchasing the security with the aim of re-selling it to investors.

Security Types The range of securities that can be underwritten include shares, bonds, debt obligations based a wide range of securitised assets, as well as securities that are based on other securities (derivatives). The best-known form of underwriting is that involving an Initial Public Offering (IPO), where shares of a company are offered to the general public for the first time with the aim of listing these shares on a stock exchange. Rather than offering these shares to the general public, companies might only offer them to a selected group of investors in a private placement, without seeking to list them on a stock exchange. Such shares can be newly created by the company in a primary offering, or existing shares can be sold by current shareholders in a secondary offering; often a combination of both types of offerings can be observed in IPOs. Private placements are commonly in the form of shares being sold, but other legal forms of the company can be found in some jurisdictions. Seasoned Equity Offerings (SEOs) are shares being sold for companies that are already listed on a stock exchange and can be either primary or secondary offerings. Apart from shares and similar forms of equity, Seasoned Equity Offerings are not commonly found; only in some instances do we observe the increase of the outstanding amount of existing bonds and similar debt obligations.

Rights offers are to be distinguished from Seasoned Equity Offerings. Here existing shareholders have the right to purchase the newly issued shares at a given price, and are allocated a fixed fraction of their existing shareholdings. Commonly the purchase price will be below the current market price of the shares, and as new shares are offered, rights offers can only be primary offerings. If a shareholder does not want to purchase the newly issued shares, he can sell the rights to other investors. Given that the purchase price is below the current market price, such rights have a value and investors are willing to purchase these rights to buy shares at a discount. Depending on legal requirements, Seasoned Equity Offerings might not be possible, but rights issues are the only mechanism to increase the number of outstanding shares (notwithstanding stock-splits), although often shareholders can waive their rights to purchase the shares and a Seasoned Equity Offering can be made. While rights offers may benefit from the advice of investment banks, there is no formal underwriting process as the sale of the shares is guaranteed. For this reason, rights offers are not included into our assessment of security underwriting.

As mentioned above, other securities than shares and similar equity forms are issued. The most common security is that of a bond, issued by companies, banks, governments, and international bodies. In all but very few exemptions, bonds are primary offerings and they are offered to the general public and listed at an exchange or they can be privately placed with selected investors, often institutional investors such as insurance companies and pension funds. Bonds are also often issued by banks to their customers as an alternative to deposits, lacking any deposit insurance coverage, and commonly an inability to return the bond prior to maturity as these bonds may not be listed. With banks selling such bonds directly to their customers and thus there being no need for underwriting, we exclude these also from our considerations.

Apart from shares and bonds, many more debt instrument are issued, often by banks or larger companies. The latter are often combining debt and equity elements into a single security, for example convertible bonds or warrant bonds. Banks, and sometimes insurance companies, also issue bonds covered by other assets, such as mortgages (for example mortgage-backed securities) and loans (e.g. collateralised debt obligations). Often securities issued are also directly based on other securities, such as index certificates that seek to replicate the value of a stock market index and have a fixed time to maturity at which time they are repaid in accordance with the index level at the time. While the securities issued and the types of investors targeted are very different, the basic principles of underwriting are very similar.

The Underwriting Process After having decided to issue securities, the issuer will in most cases appoint underwriters, although it is not a requirement to do so. Investment banks will only be agreeing to act as underwriters if the security is of sufficiently high value to attract adequate interest by investors (Sect. 7.5). In cases of banks offering bonds or other securities directly to their own customers, their customer advisors will ensure the sale of the securities and the involvement of underwriters is not necessary. In most cases where securities are offered to the general public or selected investors in a private placement, underwriters are appointed in the way indicated below. Once an underwriter has been appointed, they will assess the issuer and the security in what is referred to as a due diligence process. Collecting all information that would be relevant for the current and future value of the security, investment banks then assemble a prospectus for potential investors. The degree of detail such a prospectus has to include will depend very much on the applicable regulation and can range from extensive disclosure requirements in the case of IPOs to very basic information if institutional investors in a private placement are targeted. If a security is to be listed on an exchange, there might be additional requirements imposed by the exchange itself such that a listing can be approved.

Once the due diligence process has been completed, the process of disseminating the information publicly commences. The main event in the provision of information to potential investors is the roadshow. The roadshow can be described as a marketing event that comprises of meetings with potential investors in which the security and the issuer is presented and interest in subscribing to the issue is raised. This period is commonly seen as central for obtaining a fair price for the security and selling all securities; investment banks will use their network of contacts to potential investors to invite them to such events and seek to solicit their interest. As part of the roadshow, they will also obtain indicative bids that will help the investment bank determine the offer price in the common book-building mechanism discussed below. While the amount of securities issued will usually be determined at the outset or the latest once the level of demand has become apparent during book-building, investment banks might be given the option of selling additional securities into the market to meet any excess demand in what is known as the Greenshoe option (Sect. 7.4).

After the roadshow has been completed and any indicative bids have been submitted, the investment bank would determine the offer price. It is common to set an offer price that is below the market clearing price. If securities are traded at an exchange after being issued, the market price will commonly revert to the market-clearing price and thus we observe a significant increase from the offer price once trading commences. Setting a price below the market-clearing price is referred to as underpricing. Underpricing implies that at the offer price there is excess demand and the security has to be rationed. This rationing will typically take the form that the investment bank, in cooperation with the issuer, decides which investors are allocated the security. There might be strategic aims by the issuer in the type of investors they seek, such as a combination of institutional and retail investors, a combination of long-term and short-term investors, or investors from different jurisdictions, all of which might help the issuer in any strategic corporate goals they might pursue. In addition, the investment bank can use the allocation of securities to reward their clients for loyalty, for example institutional investors using their brokerage services, managers of companies that are the investment bank's client, or their own asset management division to boost performance due to the underpricing of securities.

While the extent of underpricing varies considerably between securities, it is a common feature. Fixed income securities have usually the lowest underpricing, while they tend to be highest in IPOs. With underpricing, issuers receive less proceeds from their securities as they otherwise could have obtained, thus underpricing imposes a cost on issuers. The beneficiaries of this underpricing are, of course, those investors that have been allocated securities at a discounted price. As the underwriting spread charged by investment bank is commonly determined as a fraction of the issue price, investment banks are also obtaining less revenue than they could if selecting a market-clearing price. There are, however benefits of underpricing to investment banks that need to be balanced against these costs. Most notably we have a lower risk of not selling the issue in a firm-commitment contract (Sect. 7.1.1), reduced risk of litigation by investors if the market price falls below the initial market-clearing price (Sect. 7.3.3), increased trading by investors and the associated brokerage income (Sect. 7.3.4), or rewarding investors providing indicative bids during the book-building process (Sect. 7.1.2), and it provides incentives to such investors to become informed in the first instance (Sect. 7.3.2). As mentioned, there are costs to issuers from the lost revenue, but they will also benefit from an improved price finding process with more informed investors participating in the book-building mechanism (Sect. 7.1.2) and overcoming adverse selection in the form of the winner's curse that only those investors are allocated securities that value it too highly (Sect. 7.3.1). Furthermore, the allocation of securities to strategic investors might improve the performance of the issuer through monitoring (Sect. 7.3.5).

Once the security is issued, any securities that are listed will start to be traded on the exchange. While the formal involvement of the investment bank in the underwriting process will end at point, additional services after this point are commonly provided, as pointed out below.

Appointment of Underwriters The first step in the underwriting process is the appointment of an investment bank as an advisor, the underwriter. It is common for investment banks to appoint not only a single investment bank as their underwriter, but a group of investment banks, in what is commonly referred to as a syndicate. Syndicates are chosen to benefit from a wider range of contacts across investors to obtain a better price and be able to attract a wider range of investors subscribing to the issue (Sect. 7.2.2). Typically one of the underwriters is designated the lead underwriter, who has the most responsibilities and therefore the largest share of the fee paid by the issuer. Their roles include to complete the due diligence, organise the roadshow and book-building process as well as the allocation of shares to investors. In large and complex security issues, for example across multiple countries, more than one lead underwriter might be appointed that share these duties. Co-underwriters, together with the lead underwriter, are underwriting a share of the issue and support the lead underwriter in the book-building process as well as the roadshow by highlighting the security to their contacts.

Of course, issuers would want to appoint the syndicate that provides them with the highest net proceeds. It is common that a lead underwriter is appointed initially and then this lead underwriter appoints co-underwriters to complement their own investor base and skills. Rather than have a beauty contest of different potential lead underwriters, as in mergers and acquisitions advice, it is much more common for the issuer to appoint the lead underwriter directly without obtaining competing offers. The reason is that investment banks competing to be lead underwriter are less likely to be willing to become co-underwriters with another investment bank taking the role of lead underwriter. This will lead to the loss of expertise within the syndicate and access to investors associated with investment banks not appointed lead underwriter would be limited, giving rise to so-called trapped bidders. These are investors that would have been willing to subscribe to the issue, but, due to lack of access to them, did not obtain the information they required and hence do not subscribe, reducing overall demand for the issue and thus the price that can be obtained will be lowered. The losses arising from these trapped bidders need to be balanced against the losses from appointing a lead underwriter that might not be able to raise the highest proceeds (Sect. 7.2.1).

The Underwriting Contract Once a syndicate has been appointed, the contract between the issuer and the syndicate is drawn up. A common feature of most contracts in underwriting is that investment banks purchase the securities from the issuer and then sell them to investors. The reference price used in all contracts is the price the investment bank obtains from investors and it will buy the securities from issuers at a discount. This discount, known as the underwriting spread, is equivalent to a fee charged by the investment bank.

Investment banks often commit to the issuer in selling all shares at a certain price, thereby exposing themselves to the risk of having to purchase all securities, but not being able to re-sell these at the agreed price, and thus potentially making a loss. Such a contract is referred to as a firm-commitment contract. The term underwriting can be attributed to this contract specification as the investment bank guarantees (underwrites) to sell the securities at a stated price. In contrast, in a best efforts contract, the investment bank does not guarantee the sale of all securities, but only to attempt to do so. Of course, it would only earn the underwriting spread on those securities that have been sold. This imposes no risk on the investment bank, but as no guarantee to sell the securities is given to the issuer would also result in a lower underwriting spread. The optimal contractual format will have to balance these two aspects.

The price of the issue can be determined in three different ways. The first method is that the investment bank, or the syndicate as whole, collects all available information and determines a fixed issue price such that proceeds to the company or the investment bank are maximised. Using this mechanism, the importance of choosing between a firm-commitment and a best efforts contract becomes apparent as failure to sell all shares at the fixed price will impose losses on the investment bank in the case of a firm-commitment contract (Sect. 7.1.1). A more common methodology is book-building. Here the investment bank invites non-binding bids by institutional investors after the roadshow to indicate their interest in the security. Based on these bids, a price is then determined, often below the market-clearing price. This allows investment banks to create excess demand and allocate shares discretionarily, benefitting certain groups of investors. Such discretion might be used to obtain a specific investor profile on request of the issuer, but also as a measure to reward institutional investors having provided indicative bids. Using the book-building method then exposes the investment bank to a small risk between the determination of the price after having received the indicative bids and the binding bids are submitted (Sect. 7.1.2). In a firm-commitment contract, the investment bank at that point would guarantee the price to the issuer, but given the short time period between indicative bids and binding bids makes the emergence of material changes to investors' perceptions unlikely. It is also unlikely for investors to not submit bids as indicated as they will benefit from being invited to submit indicative bids.

It is very unusual to use an auction format, where only binding bids are submitted and the price determined as the market-clearing price. Here the investment bank has no discretion in allocating shares. Investment banks can use their discretion in the allocation of securities in the book-building mechanism to reward institutional investors for revealing their assessment of the security, making this mechanism preferred by issuers and investment bankers alike.

After-Market Roles While the formal involvement of investment banks in the issuance of securities might end after the security has been allocated to investors, there are often implicit or explicit agreements on further duties of the investment bank. In the case of IPOs, it is common for investment banks to provide analyst coverage after the shares have been listed. While legal constraints prevent the issue of analyst reports until the passing of a quiet period after the listing, subsequent updates on the prospects of the company are in many cases provided by the investment bank for a considerable period of time to allow the company to establish itself with investors and become more widely known. Investment banks are also ensuring that where the security is listed on an exchange, trading can commence with sufficient liquidity to allow buying and selling the security at low costs. To this effect, they might act as market makers in the security. The allocation process might also create at least temporary trading demands from investors that have not received their desired allocation, while other investors having received an allocation might want to sell their securities as the market price rises. In case the market price is at risk of falling below the issue price, the investment bank is often expected to support the price by buying up securities in the market. If the market price does not recover, the investment bank will make a loss from such an operation.

Reading Caselli et al. (2021, Chs. 4, 6–7), Iannotta (2010, Chs. 4–6), Liaw (2012, Chs. 8–9), and Stowell (2018, Ch. 3).

2.3 Financial Analyst Research

Financial analysts are part of the teams working on deals in mergers and acquisitions as well as underwriting securities. In that role they provide the analysis of information they have obtained from a variety of sources, including the company they advise, and ultimately determine an appropriate value for the security. This analysis is then incorporated into the advice given to the investment bank's client. Investment banks, however, also employ a different type of financial analysts that provide research on various markets and the wider economy, independent of the immediate need for the provision of advice to a client. Such financial analysts are commonly attached to the brokerage department of an investment bank, but will often operate quite independently.

In equity research, such financial analysts will report on individual shares, specific industries, or in some instances even the entire stock market. The emphasis of the research will be on the future prospect of the company, industry, or market from the perspective of on investor. In contrast, credit research focuses on the default risk of an issuer. For corporate issuers whose shares are also listed on an exchange, much of the analysis of that particular company would be identical, although the conclusions will focus on the ability to meet interest payments and the repayment of the debt and will be geared towards investors into such debt instruments. For government debt, there will be an overlap with economic research, which focuses on macroeconomic forecasts, like economic growth, inflation, interest rates, or exchange rates. The audience of economic research includes investors into equity and debt in those countries, but also companies engaging in business in these places, or seeking to expand into these countries. Finally, commodity research focusses on the likely supply and demand developments, with an assessment of the impact on prices, of a range of commodities, including precious and non-precious metals, oil, gas, and agricultural products. Such reports might be useful for traders in these products, but also companies producing or using any of these commodities.

Analyst Roles Financial analysts provide reports that give a summary of the information they have obtained and the conclusions they draw from this information. These reports can be used by investors and companies to inform their investment decisions. Equity research in particular has a prominent role in stock markets, and financial analysts provide not only information on the value of the shares if covering individual companies, but transform this value into an investment recommendation. If the value they assign the shares is above the current market price, they recommend to buy the shares, and if it is below the current market price, they recommend to sell the shares. If the deviation between the value and current market price is particularly large, they might issue a strong buy or strong sell recommendation to emphasise this difference; on the other hand, if the value they determine is approximately reflected in the current market price, they would issue a hold recommendation. Similar recommendations can be made for industries and the stock market as a whole. The analysis in other research areas is usually not combined with a direct investment recommendation as the audience reading these reports is much more heterogenous in their objectives.

Financial analysts provide such reports internally to their own asset managers and proprietary traders, which are then referred to as buy-side reports. Of more interest for our analysis of investment bank behaviour are sell-side reports that are provided to clients. Such sell-side reports are aimed at investors with the aim to provide information on their investment and trading decisions. Financial analysts obtain the relevant information from access to companies in analyst conferences, but also personal meetings with members of the senior management of a company, in addition to having access to published information through disclosures by the company and the wider (financial) press. Of course, companies have an interest in a positive coverage of their company and would be able to control access to information for individual financial analysts if they are not satisfied with the interpretation of the information a financial analyst provides. This may then lead to a conflict of interest between the desire of the financial analyst to obtain accurate information and being able to report its findings truthfully (Sect. 8.1).

Similarly, the investment bank may seek future business from a company that is covered by their financial analyst, for example when seeking advice in a merger. As long as companies are more likely to give such business to investment banks whose financial analysts provide a more positive coverage, the investment bank might have incentives to not publish their assessment truthfully, but publish an overly positive view of the company (Sect. 8.2). Overly positive assessments of companies' profits are not only the result of such conflicts of interest, but may also be driven in parts by a desire of financial analysts to further their careers by being seen as competent. Consequently, they prefer not to deviate from the consensus forecast of other financial analyst as they might be seen as less competent if their assessment is worse than that of other financial analysts. This is not being fully compensated if their assessment is better than that of their peers (Chap. 9). While most of these concerns apply to equity research foremost, similar considerations can also be made when assessing the credit risk of entities and the desire to avoid a large deviation from the consensus forecast is prevalent in all research areas.

Payment for Analyst Research Analyst reports are valuable for their clients as they provide additional information that might improve their decision-making. Rather than charging the investor directly for access to analyst reports, for example as a subscription, payment has traditionally been made through the brokerage commission an investment bank charges. Clients were paying an inflated brokerage commission and part of this commission was then allocated to those financial analysts covering the security (Chap. 13). This is often referred to as a soft commission. Many institutional investors prefer this arrangement to paying for analyst reports directly, as they might be able to charge any broker commissions to their clients, but directly paid costs have to be borne out of the management fees they charge, thus reducing their profits.

Regulatory efforts have commenced to abolish this practice of soft commissions by requiring that institutional investors have to pay for access to financial analyst reports directly. Such rules have been implemented in the European Union in 2018.

Regulation of Analysts Companies have an interest in obtaining positive analyst coverage and investment banks have an incentive to provide such positive coverage to ensure they obtain additional revenue from other investment banking business. On the other hand, investors have an interest in unbiased information. This has led to regulation that requires the organisational separation of financial analysts from the remaining investment banking business of mergers and acquisitions as well as underwriting. The aim is to eliminate the resulting conflict of interest between financial analysts and the other investment banking business. Financial analysts have to be physically separated from other investment banking business and these other businesses must have no influence on the decision which companies to cover with their research, how remuneration for financial analysts is determined, and financial analysts are not allowed to be involved soliciting investment banking business. This separation of financial analysts from the other parts of investment banks is often referred to as Chinese Walls (Chap. 10).

Regulation also addresses the influence companies might take on the assessment of financial analysts to provide a more positive coverage by providing financial analysts with more detailed information only if such positive coverage is assured. Regulation Fair Disclosure requires companies to disclose all material information publicly; thus, it is not possible to give access to information only to selected financial analysts in return for their positive coverage.

Reading Stowell (2018, p. 150–156).

2.4 Trading and Sales

While corporate finance with its main business lines of mergers and acquisitions advice and underwriting make a substantial part of the revenue of investment banks, they offer a wide range of other services that are sometimes collectively described as trading and sales. This rather heterogenous range of business lines consists of services and activities that facilitate the trading of securities by their clients as well as trading on their own account. Investment banks also contact clients with ideas of trading opportunities and trading strategies, with the aim to generate brokerage income and as a way to compensate informed investors for providing indicative bids in book-building. They also develop new financial products and services that will then subsequently be sold to clients, or developed on their request. For wealthy clients not willing or able to manage their own investments, many investment banks also offer a service to do so on their behalf, commonly called asset management or wealth management.

Compared to mergers and acquisitions, securities underwriting, and the provision of research, the activities of investment banks in trading and sales are very lightly regulated. Some restrictions apply in proprietary trading, such as the prohibition of insider trading using information on deals proceeding in the corporate finance division, but are not specific to investment banks; they apply similarly also to managers of such companies, their lawyers, and other advisors. A limitation on the extent of proprietary trading affects mainly universal banks, that is those investment banks that are part of a bank that is also engaged in commercial banking—the provision of loans and taking of deposits from the general public. This so-called Volcker Rule limits the amount of trading such banks can conduct relative to their capital but is not applicable to pure investment banks and universal banks that commonly have a large capital base to ease the effect of this rule. The way proprietary trading is conducted is not significantly affected.

Brokerage Investors cannot access exchanges directly, but have instead to go through a designated third party called a broker. The aim of requiring the use of a broker is to ensure that trades that are agreed on the exchange are then also subsequently honoured. A broker will commonly ensure that the client has the means to pay for the securities they purchase and that they can provide the securities they are seeking to sell. As such, a broker is a pure intermediary that charges a small fee for its services.

However, it is common for investment banks to not only act as such an intermediary, but also provide basic investment advice as part of the brokerage services. While this advice will not have the depth of analyst reports or the sophistication developed in asset management, it will allow the client to improve their decision-making. The suggested trading opportunities mentioned above might be part of this advice. Hence, brokerage is often accompanied with the provision of information and the broker fee charged will reflect this additional value (Chap. 13). Not all brokers follow this model and so called execution-only brokers can be found, mostly operating online only, that do not provide any advice to clients, although price information on listed securities is often given. Investment banks follow the full-service brokerage model that provides advice in addition to routing the client orders to the exchange.

Market Making It can be difficult to buy or sell some securities if there are no willing counterparties to trade with; in this case, a trader would have to wait until such an off-setting order arrives in the market. In thinly traded securities, the time until such an order arrives can be substantial and often the adverse effect an order has on the price in such a market can be considerable. To counter this effect, market makers have been established. A market maker has the obligation to quote a price at any time at which he is willing to buy and to sell the security. The price at which he is willing to buy the security is called the bid price, this is the price at which a trader can sell its security. The price at which the market maker is willing to sell the security, where the trader can buy it, is called the ask price. The difference between these two prices is referred to as the bid-ask spread. In market making, a key concern is how to set these two prices and thereby how big the resulting bid-ask spread will be.

Market makers have two concerns in this respect. Firstly, they have no interest in holding the security itself, their objective is to allow traders to trade immediately, thus to provide liquidity to the market. Hence, they will seek to set prices such that they do not build up large positions of the security (Sect. 14.1). They also, secondly, are generally seen as uninformed about the value of the security, but they are trading with informed traders, and if they set prices too low, they will continuously sell the security to such traders and build up a large negative position, and while if setting the price too high, traders will sell their securities and they build up a large positive position. In order to avoid these situations, they need to adjust prices such that buying and selling of securities is approximately balanced (Sect. 14.2).

Investment banks are engaged in market making often for historical reasons as it was common that brokers were also acting as market makers to allow their clients to trade more efficiently. Having acquired brokers or engaged in brokerage themselves, they often have retained market-making activities. In recent years, the importance of market making in securities markets has declined substantially as the advent of electronic trading made the submission of limit orders by traders much easier and their effect is similar to that of a market maker being present.

Proprietary Trading While most business lines in trading and sales are not very profitable, proprietary trading is the exemption. Having accumulated significant expertise in analysing securities and gained a good understanding of securities markets through contacts with traders and investors, investment banks are engaged in trading securities on their own account. While some smaller investment banks will specialise in the trading of only a selected range of securities, the major investment banks trade the full range of securities, in addition to trading in commodities, foreign exchange markets, and also crypto-assets. Given the potential profits to be made from trading, investment banks invest heavily into the expertise of their traders, not least due to the competition they will face from other investment banks (Sect. 15.1). This competition is also increasing from ever more sophisticated algorithmic trading.

As trading requires high efforts to be successful, apart from the requisite expertise, investment banks will seek to incentivise their traders by linking their salaries to their performance (Sect. 15.2). However, having such a performance-driven culture can easily lead to traders being tempted to misrepresent their trading success (Sect. 15.3), as many examples in history show. Repeatedly have we seen cases of traders making unauthorised trades that, once they turn out to be loss-making, are hidden from managers with the aim to recover these losses with more trading. While it is not known in how many cases such a strategy is successful, there are many cases where losses accumulated and were eventually discovered only once they reached significant sizes.

With a brokerage division, investment banks have access to information about traders that other market participants do not have. Knowing their clients, they will have some knowledge which trades are originating from informed traders and which trades are the result of uninformed traders that might trade for a variety of other reasons. Having access to this information, it will be possible for investment banks to infer much better the value of a security than it would be when relying only on their own information. If this information can be given to the trading desks of the investment bank, they can take this information into account when submitting their trades. This situation of a broker also engaging in proprietary trading and disclosing information in this way is known as dual capacity. Having dual capacity will affect the outcome in the security market (Sect. 15.4). With proprietary traders being informed, they will compete with informed clients for profits from trading, and being better informed due to access to information from the brokerage division, they will have an informational advantage.

Financial Innovations Clients always seek to optimise their own profits and investment banks can help them by creating securities that meet their needs better. Such developments might include the introduction of securities that allow clients to hedge risks, such as futures, options, and credit default swaps, but also securities that minimise tax liabilities of their clients or allow to circumvent regulatory constraints. Other innovations have included the creation of asset-backed securities, for example mortgage-back securities or collateralised debt obligations, that allowed banks to reduce their risk exposures, while opening up investment opportunities to their clients seeking exposure to such risks. Innovations are not only limited to the development of new securities, but can include the development of electronic trading or the use of artificial intelligence in extracting information from public sources.

While many innovations are desirable, many will never be introduced as their projected market does not justify the costs of their development (Sect. 11.1), while those innovations that are introduced can often easily be copied by other investment banks, eroding their competitive advantage. This might result in the strategic introduction of innovations over time or in cooperation with other investment banks (Sect. 11.2). Similarly, not every innovation that a competitor has introduced will be copied (Sect. 11.3).

Asset Management Investment banks have contacts to many institutional investors as well as wealthy individuals. The contact to institutional investors is fostered in part through their underwriting business if these investors are also issuing securities, most notably insurance companies, but also through their brokerage divisions for investors like pension funds. Access to wealthy individuals can similarly be obtained through brokerage and the provision of analyst reports, but also from contact with senior management in corporate finance. Many senior managers will obtain substantial salaries and have accumulated significant wealth, even though often only a small fraction of this is freely available and not invested into the company they are managing. Wealthy individuals often lack the time, but also the ability, to manage their own wealth. While institutional investors commonly have the expertise to manage their funds they seek to invest, they might want an outside management of their assets as a means of diversification from their own approach.

Tapping into this pool of wealth, many investment banks offer to manage assets on their clients' behalf. Using the expertise they have built up through advising companies and equity research, investment banks are often better informed than their clients about investment opportunities. This informational advantage of investment banks should result in better investment performance than what clients could achieve themselves. Of course, the fee investment banks charge to manage assets will erode some of this benefit. In addition, though, investment banks might not invest the assets in the best way from their client's perspective, but rather such that their own profits from the fees they charge are maximised. This can lead to a conflict of interest between the investment the client seeks and the investment the investment banks chooses (Chap. 12). Such a conflict of interest will reduce the benefits to clients from allowing investment banks to manage assets even further.

Reading Liaw (2012, Chs. 12–16) and Stowell (2018, Chs. 5–6).

2.5 Managing Investment Banks

Investment banks provide a wide range of services that, while often demanded by the same clients, require different expertise and will commonly be provided by different staff members working in separate departments with a wide range of varying expertise. As advice is based on information and the often subjective interpretation of information, assessing the quality of advice and the contribution of individuals is no easy task. The wide range of expertise present in investment banks makes it difficult for senior staff members to provide guidance to staff. To facilitate the operation of an investment bank in such an environment, they have developed a range of management methods that are often different to that of many other organisations. The key observations that distinguish investment banks from commercial banks and most industrial or service companies is a flat organisational structure, a reliance on bonuses to reward employees, and giving employees large degrees of autonomy in decision-making.

Organisation Investment banks can be seen as multi-product firms, where each product or service requires its own expertise and its own procedures. While information obtained in one area of the business can be re-used in another part, it often needs to be interpreted anew to suit the circumstances of the advice that is needed, making the different products and services less interdependent on each other than in many other organisations. As the needs of each client will also be different, the expertise required for the advice to be given will also be varying, making it necessary to assemble teams of experts specifically for the needs of each client. This makes working in set structures difficult, and investment banks have reacted to these challenges by forming teams for each client that combine the expertise required in that specific case.

Given the diversity of the business lines, it is difficult for senior managers to have the requisite knowledge to formulate specific strategies for each of these business lines and it is left typically to those divisions to formulate them based on their local knowledge. Given the lack of specialist knowledge across such a wide range of services, senior managers will generally be less able to contribute to advice or provide direction to more junior staff members. If senior managers are providing less benefits in the advice that clients receive, a flat structure will emerge, where only a small number of management layers are found (Sect. 18.1). With the lack of specific expertise among senior managers, decision-making at strategic, but also at operational level, is left much more in the hands of those staff members working directly with clients and who have the requisite specific expertise (Sect. 18.2). In investment banks, senior managers are mainly involved in managing the relationship with their clients, they maintain contact with the senior management of companies or investors and will commonly direct them towards services the investment bank can offer, leaving the provision of these services then to the less senior specialists in the respective divisions. In most other organisations, in contrast, senior managers are supervising the work of the staff members they have responsibilities for, with very limited contact to clients. The relationship management is conducted at much more junior levels. The level of expertise senior managers have in such much more focussed businesses allows them to direct and guide the work of their staff more effectively.

Salaries The remuneration in investment banks is commonly regarded as very generous, even when compared to similar roles in other industries (Sect. 15.2). Such high salaries are often associated with high levels of stress and pressure to deliver results, combined with long working hours. The reliance of investment banks on the knowledge and expertise of their staff members to provide advice to clients makes it difficult to assess the effort an employee has actually exerted. Whether advice was generating benefits to their clients will often only become known with long delays and can be subject to significant exogenous influences that affect their clients during such a prolonged period of time. There might also be a trade-off between effort put into any advice that has been generated and the knowledge and expertise staff have acquired, making assessing the work of staff members even more difficult for managers. For this reason, investment banks do not monitor their staff members closely to assess their performance, but instead link their salary to performance as measured by the profits generated to the investment bank (Sect. 16.1). Having such a link between remuneration and investment banking profits incentivises employees to exert high levels of effort and improves their level of expertise. Such a practice is reinforced through giving staff members high levels of autonomy at an early stage in their career allowing them to prove their ability as well as dedication to their role; staff members that are not performing well will then either not be promoted further, dismissed, or moved into other roles (Sect. 16.2). This practice is in contrast to many other organisations, where employees need to prove their ability to generate profits before being given substantial responsibilities. The difficulty in assessing the performance of individuals in investment banking makes such an approach less feasible.

With the ability to assess the work of employees being limited due to the nature of the business and the wide range of services requiring specialist knowledge making it more difficult for senior managers to effectively guide the work of more junior staff, partnerships have dominated investment banking for a much longer time period than in other businesses, including commercial banking. In a partnership, senior managers are also the owners of the business; thus, there is no separation of ownership and management. It is also common that particularly able staff members are invited to join the partnership and thus become co-owners, taking a much larger stake in the investment bank than is commonly possible with remunerations paid in the form of stocks or stock options. Partnerships provide incentives to junior staff to exert high levels of effort and acquire the requisite knowledge to become a partner and thus owner of the business (Sect. 17.1). As this puts strains on the partners themselves to train and mentor junior staff members, the increased demands on them, combined with the need for ever larger investment banks to meet all the demands of clients in an increasingly complex environment, partnerships have become difficult to sustain. As senior staff are the owners of the business and other staff members aspire to this position, the quality of services provided by such partnerships is usually higher than in investment banks that are incorporated and thus have a separation between owners and managers (Sect. 17.2).

Operating a large bonus pool, whose size depends on the performance of the investment bank as a whole, seeks to replicate this partnership structure. The bonuses of individual staff members are then allocated based on their individual performance, commonly assessed by their immediate manager. With the difficulty in assessing performance of individuals directly, given that most advice is developed in ever-changing teams, any such assessment will be subjective. However, given the local knowledge of the immediate superior, it is usually possible to provide a fair allocation of the bonus.

Strategy While the strategy pursued in each of the many business lines an investment bank is active in will be determined locally, some more general strategic aspects will be determined centrally by the most senior managers, often in collaboration with the specialists in each division. While many investment banks offer a wide range of services across the spectrum, so called bulge-bracket investment banks, others establish themselves as boutique investment banks by becoming a specialist in a small part of the market. Such specialisation might manifest itself in only offering selected services or to offer services only to specific types of clients. Both strategies have persisted for a long period of time, and their optimality will depend on the way business is conducted (Sect. 20.1). Some investment banks might seek to establish a relationship with clients and therefore offer a wider range of services, but at a slightly lower quality of service, while other investment banks might seek to provide only limited services to a wider range of clients. This allows them to specialise more and offer a higher quality of service in their field of specialisation.

While the choice of whether to establish a relationship with a specific client will be a decision made at the more local level, senior management might provide some guidance as towards the desirability of such a decision. Seeking to be able advising clients across a wide range of needs requires the bank to retain sufficient capacity to meet their demand. The demand of clients for any service cannot easily be foreseen and can also not be postponed to a point when capacity becomes available. Thus, building a relationship with clients is costly in that spare capacity must be retained, either in the form of excess staff during periods of less business or by requiring even longer working hours from staff members at times of high demand. These costs must be justified by the amount of revenue the client is likely to generate for the bank (Chap. 19). Of course, investment banks will seek to attract clients that provide them with the highest surplus and clients will seek an investment bank whose advice is most beneficial to them. This commonly leads to a situation in which the investment bank generating the highest absolute surplus for clients is also the most profitable and investments banks that generate lower surplus to clients are less profitable (Sect. 20.2). The result of such a match between investment banks and their clients is that the investment banks that attract the largest and most active clients, assuming they generate the most surplus due to their size and level of activity in capital markets, are the most profitable ones.

Reading Davis (2003, Chs. 4–6).

Part I

Investment Banks as Intermediaries

Investment banks are chosen as advisors for their superior knowledge and the additional information they might hold that could benefit their clients. These benefits could either arise directly for clients by allowing them to improve their decision-making using this additional expertise and information. However, any benefits might be indirectly accruing to clients from investment banks conveying information to other market participants, such as potential buyers of securities; this would allow for higher prices to be demanded when selling securities or other comparable benefits. It is common to view intermediaries in markets as being uninformed and merely passing through the products and services from suppliers to their ultimate clients. In this view, intermediaries are acting as a marketplace that allows suppliers and buyers to meet and conduct the transaction in a more efficient way. In the case of investment banks, this would be a too simplistic view as they provide information and thereby go beyond the mere facilitation of transactions.

When providing information and expertise to clients, investment banks seek to generate profits. With information not being verifiable by their clients at the point of sale, investment banks could exploit their position by selling information, even if they do not have obtained it. Even if an investment bank has acquired information and expertise, they could alternatively use this themselves directly, such as making investments using their own funds, and not sell it to clients. Chapter 3 shows when it is optimal for investment banks to sell information and that it can be ensured that the information sold is actually held by the investment bank. Providing such information will not only affect the information held by their clients or other market participants who this information is provided to but can have more widespread implications on market outcomes as we will see in Chap. 4. If the discrepancies of information between market participants are too large, especially between buyers and sellers of securities, transactions might not happen as no price can be agreed; the market collapses due to adverse selection. Providing information will reduce the asymmetric information between buyers and sellers in markets and thus might be sufficient to ensure transactions are completed. The additional information available will then in turn affect the sellers of securities and provide incentives to increase or reduce the value of their holdings. Returning to clients seeking advice, Chap. 5 will explore the incentives of investment banks to give biased advice that suits their own aims more than that of their clients.

These models show the importance of information in decision-making by clients and other market participants, as well as the potential effect on market outcomes. Of course, the varying roles of investment banks in specific capital market transactions cannot be captured by such generic settings and will have to be addressed subsequently.

3 Selling Information

Rather than use the information investment banks have acquired to make their own investment decisions, they might, in addition, sell this information and let their clients make their own decisions on the basis of this improved information. As it cannot easily be verified whether the investment bank has the information it is selling in the first place, as well as whether the information provided is accurate, a verification mechanism should be employed that allows any purchaser of this information to confirm the information provided.

Assume that a signal s can be observed by the investment bank, which for uninformed market participants has a mean of μ and variance σ_S^2. The return on a security is then given by $R = s + \varepsilon$, where ε is an error term with mean zero and variance σ_ε^2. With s and ε independent, we have that the variance of returns to an uninformed investment bank is given as $\sigma_R^2 = \sigma_S^2 + \sigma_\varepsilon^2$, and the expected return is μ. Assume an investment bank has total investment funds W_0 available, of which G is invested at the risk-free rate r into government securities and V into the security on which information might be provided, yielding a return of R. Thus, we have $W_0 = G + V$. After one time period, the bank then has wealth

$$W_1 = (1 + r)\, G + (1 + R)\, V = (1 + r)\, W_0 + (R - r)\, V, \tag{3.1}$$

where we replaced G using $W_0 = G + V$. Investment banks are assumed to have risk aversion z such that their expected utility is given by

$$U_B = E\,[W_1] - \frac{1}{2} z Var\,[W_1]\,. \tag{3.2}$$

We can now investigate the optimal investment bank behaviour in different scenarios: the presence and absence of actual information as well as the selling of information or not selling information.

A. Krause, *Theoretical Foundations of Investment Banking*, Springer Texts in Business and Economics, https://doi.org/10.1007/978-3-031-58060-4_3

Uninformed Investment Banks Uninformed investment banks do not obtain the signal s and thus rely on the common information regarding the expected return and variance of the security in question. We therefore have

$$\begin{aligned} E[W_1] &= (1+r)\,W_0 + (\mu - r)\,V, \\ Var[W_1] &= \sigma_R^2 V^2. \end{aligned} \tag{3.3}$$

Inserting these expressions into the expected utility of Eq. (3.2) and finding the optimal amount invested into the risky security, we get the first-order condition for the optimal investment into the security as

$$\frac{\partial U_B}{\partial V} = (\mu - r) - z\sigma_R^2 V = 0, \tag{3.4}$$

and hence obtain the optimal investment as

$$V^* = \frac{\mu - r}{z\sigma_R^2}, \tag{3.5}$$

resulting in expected utility

$$U_B^* = (1+r)\,W_0 + \frac{(\mu - r)^2}{2z\sigma_R^2}. \tag{3.6}$$

An uninformed investment bank would invest the amount of V^* into the security concerned and obtains a utility level of U_B^*. We will now see how this changes if the investment bank were to sell information in the form of a signal s, even though they have not obtained such a signal. This is possible due to the fact that information is not verifiable. Selling information at a price P, the expected utility of the investment bank will be

$$\hat{U}_B = (1+r)\,W_0 + (\mu - r)\,V + P - \frac{1}{2} z\sigma_R^2 V^2. \tag{3.7}$$

In order to prevent such an uninformed investment bank to sell information, a signal s they have not received, the expected utility of doing so must be less than the expected utility of not selling such information; hence $\hat{U}_B \leq U_B^*$, which when using Eqs. (3.6) and (3.7) becomes

$$P \leq P^* = \frac{(\mu - r)^2}{2z\sigma_R^2} - (\mu - r)\,V + \frac{1}{2} z\sigma_R^2 V^2. \tag{3.8}$$

Note that the amount of the security held, V, will in general not be identical to V^*. When selling information, the investment banks' incentives will take into account the revenue generated, which might well depend on the investment position V.

If the risk aversion z of the investment bank is unknown, we want to ensure condition (3.8) is valid for all possible risk aversions. The smallest possible value for P^* can be found if

$$\frac{\partial P^*}{\partial z} = -\frac{(\mu - r)^2}{2z^2\sigma_R^2} + \frac{1}{2}\sigma_R^2 V^2 = 0, \tag{3.9}$$

or

$$z^2 = \frac{(\mu - r)^2}{\sigma_R^4 V^2}. \tag{3.10}$$

If $V > 0$, then the price P^* is lowest if $z = \frac{\mu - r}{\sigma_R^2 V}$, as we assume that $\mu > r$. This gives us, after inserting into Eq. (3.8), that

$$P^* = 0. \tag{3.11}$$

Therefore, if the uninformed investment bank holds a positive amount of the security, it would be profitable to sell information at any positive price.

If $V < 0$, then the price P^* is lowest if $z = -\frac{\mu - r}{\sigma_R^2 V}$ and from Eq. (3.8), we have

$$P^* = -2(\mu - r)V > 0; \tag{3.12}$$

the price the investment bank could obtain from selling information needs to be sufficiently small in order to discourage such behaviour.

Inserting this expression for the maximum price the investment bank could obtain without actually selling information into the expected utility of the uninformed investment bank in Eq. (3.7), we get from the first-order condition $\frac{\partial \hat{U}_B}{\partial V} = 0$ the optimal investment into the risky security as

$$\hat{V}^* = -\frac{\mu - r}{z\sigma_R^2} \tag{3.13}$$

and thus

$$P^* = 2\frac{(\mu - r)^2}{z\sigma_R^2}. \tag{3.14}$$

Hence, if the optimal amount of the security held by the uninformed investment bank is positive, $V > 0$, it would sell information it does not own at any price, while for negative holdings, this would only be the case if the price obtained is sufficiently high; thus, $P > P^* = 2\frac{(\mu - r)^2}{z\sigma_R^2}$. This result on the willingness of uninformed investment banks to sell information can now be compared to that of informed investment banks.

Informed Investment Banks An informed investment bank will observe the signal s on the return of the security and use this information to revise their expectations on its risk and return. We have their expected utility given by

$$U_B = E\left[W_1|s\right] - \frac{1}{2}zVar\left[W_1|s\right] \tag{3.15}$$

with

$$\begin{aligned} E\left[W_1|s\right] &= (1+r)\,W_0 + (s-r)\,V, \\ Var\left[W_1|s\right] &= \sigma_\varepsilon^2 V^2 \end{aligned} \tag{3.16}$$

as $E\left[R|s\right] = s$ and $Var\left[R|s\right] = Var\left[\varepsilon\right] = \sigma_\varepsilon^2$. The first-order condition for the optimal investment into the security is then given by

$$\frac{\partial U_B}{\partial V} = (s-r) - z\sigma_\varepsilon^2 V = 0 \tag{3.17}$$

and hence,

$$V^{**} = \frac{s-r}{z\sigma_\varepsilon^2}, \tag{3.18}$$

such that the utility with the optimal investment into the security is obtained as

$$U_B^{**} = (1+r)\,W_0 + \frac{(s-r)^2}{2z\sigma_\varepsilon^2}. \tag{3.19}$$

Thus, investment banks, having received a signal s, will hold the amount V^{**} of the security relating to this information and achieve utility level U_B^{**}.

If the investment bank decides to sell information at a price P, its expected utility becomes

$$\hat{U}_B = (1+r)W_0 + (s-r)\,V + P - \frac{1}{2}z\sigma_\varepsilon^2 V^2. \tag{3.20}$$

The maximum price for the information, P, is P^* as given in Eq. (3.14) as the bank will charge the highest price possible while still deterring an uninformed investment bank from selling information. This way, the purchaser of information knows that the information is actually held by the investment bank. Optimising over the investment into the security, we obtain the same optimal investment V^{**} as the maximum price P^* is independent of the signal and other decisions of the informed investment bank. Choosing a price lower than P^* would not change this result. It is obvious that the expected utility from selling the information is increased, and hence, informed investment banks would always want to sell the information they hold.

When doing so, however, they need to ensure that buyers of the information can be assured that the information sold is actually held by the investment bank. To do this, they signal their information through the investment position V. As we have seen, uninformed investment banks would always sell information if $V > 0$, and hence, we will require that information is only sold if $V \leq 0$. Looking at the optimal investment of the informed investment bank in Eq. (3.18), we see that this is the case for $s \leq r$, implying that only negative information is sold. The size of the position V^{**} gives the buyer of the information assurance that the information sold is correct.

The reason for this result is that due to the absence of information, the uninformed investment bank would have to copy the behaviour of the informed investment bank and adjust its security holding to such an extent that its expected utility would reduce too much to be compensated for by the price obtained from selling this information. Therefore, we only observe the selling of negative information by informed investment banks. For positive information, $s > r$, the adjustment required by the investment bank would always be such that the additional revenue can be used to compensate for the loss in utility of this adjustment. In the case that information is negative, $s \leq r$, the adjustment required is much larger, namely, from V^* to $\hat{V}^* = -V^*$, and this large change in investment is not compensated if the price charged is sufficiently small.

After having considered the selling of information, we will now turn to the value of such information to buyers and explore the conditions under which this information is bought.

Purchase of Information An uninformed investor would make the same investment decision as an uninformed investment bank. Hence, in line with Eq. (3.6), their expected utility is given by

$$U_D^* = (1+r)\,W_0 + \frac{(\mu - r)^2}{2z\sigma_R^2}. \tag{3.21}$$

Let us now assume that the costs of information are equally shared between N buyers, each paying $\frac{P^*}{N}$. These investors will then act as being informed, and with Eq. (3.19) the utility of an informed buyer is identical to that of an informed investment bank, merely adjusted for the costs of obtaining this information. Hence,

$$\hat{U}_D^* = (1+r)\,W_0 + \frac{(s-r)^2}{2z\sigma_\varepsilon^2} - \frac{P^*}{N}. \tag{3.22}$$

For the acquisition of information to be profitable, we require that $\hat{U}_D^* \geq U_D^*$, which solves for

$$(s-r)^2 \geq \frac{\sigma_\varepsilon^2}{\sigma_R^2}\left((\mu-r)^2 + \frac{2z\sigma_R^2 P^*}{N}\right). \tag{3.23}$$

As we require that $s < r$ for the sale of information to commence and we assume that $\mu > r$, this solves for

$$s \leq r - \frac{\sigma_\varepsilon}{\sigma_R}\sqrt{(\mu-r)^2 + \frac{2z\sigma_R^2 P^*}{N}} < r. \tag{3.24}$$

Thus, purchasers of this information would only find their purchase profitable if it is sufficiently negative, otherwise not justifying the costs of acquiring this information. Of course, the investment bank selling information could reduce the price below P^*, but even reducing the price to zero will not eliminate the requirement for sufficiently negative signals to create such demand for information.

Summary It is only profitable for investment banks to sell negative information and for purchasers to buy such information only if it is sufficiently negative. As information is not easily verifiable, investment banks commit their investments such that it reflects the sold information. Nevertheless, investment banks can only commit investments when receiving information that suggests a return below the risk-free rate as then they will hold a short position to verify their information; for positive information, the difference in long positions between informed and uninformed investment banks does not allow for a clear distinction between these types of investment banks. Due to the cost of information, investors are only benefitting from its purchase if the information is sufficiently different from the current consensus, as otherwise the benefits of its use are too small.

Reading Allen (1990)

Informed Intermediaries 4

A characteristic of investment banks is that they can acquire information on securities and hence do not act as an uninformed intermediary but have to be treated as informed. Therefore, the actions taken by investment banks will in general contain information that other, uninformed, market participants can infer from their actions. In Sect. 4.1, we will see how investment banks can reduce the problem of adverse selection in capital market transactions and ensure transactions of high-quality securities can be completed. It is not only that investment banks affect the ability to trade existing securities, but they might also affect the quality of securities that are brought to the market in the first place, as Sect. 4.2 shows. In this way, they have the potential to change the composition of securities in the market.

These outcomes are achieved without investment banks giving advice directly to their clients or explicitly making information available to market participants, but it is merely their actions that reveal information to buyers of securities. While no contract with a client is necessary to achieve these outcomes as the actions by investment banks are profitable, they might well only be performed as part of a contract with a client, usually the issuer of the securities, with the aim of generating additional revenue.

4.1 Reducing Adverse Selection

The buyer of a security is often less well informed about its value than the issuer, which might be a company issuing shares or fixed income securities or a government agency issuing bonds. This informational asymmetry arises because either the buyer does not have the same access to the internal information the issuer might possess or the buyer has not the capacity to process all information that is available. The issuer of a security might now take advantage of this asymmetry and seek to sell securities of low value at a higher price. The buyers of the security will of course be aware of this possibility and take this scenario into account when determining whether

A. Krause, *Theoretical Foundations of Investment Banking*, Springer Texts in Business and Economics, https://doi.org/10.1007/978-3-031-58060-4_4

and at which price they are willing to buy the security. We investigate here how an investment bank can improve welfare through acquiring information about the value of the security and relaying this information through their actions to buyers.

Let us assume that there are two types of securities that could be issued; the type is known to the seller of this security, but not potential buyers. The seller might be the company issuing the security and the buyer a potential investor. The buyer only knows that the security is of high-quality H with probability p and of low-quality L with probability $1 - p$. The value of these securities to the buyer is V_i^B and to the seller of V_i^S. We assume that the buyer always values the security more highly than the seller, regardless of whether the security is of high or low quality, and therefore a trade between them would be desirable. Furthermore, the high-quality security is always more highly valued than the low-quality security, by buyers and sellers alike. There is, however, an adverse selection problem in that the expected value of the security to the buyer, $pV_H^B + (1-p)V_L^B$, is less than the value the seller puts on the high-quality security, V_H^S. This implies that if buyers have no indication of the type of the security, the price they are willing to pay would not induce the seller of the high-quality security to sell the security; consequently, only the low-quality security would be offered, and the high-quality security would never change hands, even though this would be welfare enhancing. The buyer, knowing the incentive of the seller to not sell the high-quality asset, will consequently not offer to pay more than V_L^B for the security, the value of the low-quality security to the buyer. This adverse selection problem would lead to the collapse of the market for high-quality securities.

The assumptions made can be formalised as follows:

$$\begin{aligned} V_i^B &> V_i^S, \\ V_H^j &> V_L^j, \\ V_H^S &> pV_H^B + (1-p)V_L^B. \end{aligned} \tag{4.1}$$

We will now consider a strategy by issuers that allows them to sell high-quality securities despite the adverse selection problem in at least some situations and then subsequently assess the impact investment banks might have on the ability to sell high-quality securities.

No Investment Bank Intervention To overcome the problem of adverse selection, we assume that sellers of high-quality securities delay the sale, while those of low-quality securities sell them instantly. This would allow the buyer to distinguish between the two securities. We assume that in this case, the seller receives the amount of V_H^S, as this is the reservation price of competitive sellers. A seller of low-quality securities could pretend to sell high-quality securities by also waiting and secure the higher price or sell the security instantly. If the seller receives a price of P_L for the low-quality security, he would sell immediately if

$$P_L \geq \rho V_H^S, \tag{4.2}$$

where ρ is the discount factor arising from the waiting for the future sale of the security. In this case, waiting to sell and pretend to hold a high-quality security is not beneficial as the price received instantly from the low-quality security is higher than the discounted value from waiting with the sale and pretending to sell high-quality securities. Thus, with this condition fulfilled, low-quality securities are sold immediately, and high-quality securities are held back for one time period.

The expected benefits of a buyer consist of delayed benefits from acquiring the high-quality security at price V_H^S, of which there is a fraction p in the market, and benefits from low-quality securities that have been acquired at price P_L instantly. Hence, we have the expected profits of the buyer given by

$$\Pi_C = p\rho\left(V_H^B - V_H^S\right) + (1-p)\left(V_L^B - P_L\right). \tag{4.3}$$

For the buyer to enter this market, we require that $\Pi_C \geq 0$, and with Eq. (4.2) defining the price as an equality as to minimise the surplus to sellers, we obtain the condition that

$$\rho \leq \rho^* = \frac{(1-p)\,V_L^B}{V_H^S - pV_H^B}. \tag{4.4}$$

If $V_H^S > pV_H^B$, we always find that $\Pi_C \geq 0$ as $\rho^* > 1$. If buyers are not too patient, they would want to participate in this market. The reason that patient buyers are not making profits is that the price of the low-quality security, P_L, is too high and the final term in Eq. (4.3) becomes too negative, offsetting the profits of the first term.

In the case that only the low-quality securities are offered, which might be the case if (4.4) is not fulfilled and we have $\rho > \rho^*$ or the market for the high-quality security breaks down due to adverse selection if the sale of the high-quality asset is not delayed, the total welfare is given by

$$\Pi_W^L = pV_H^S + (1-p)\,V_L^B, \tag{4.5}$$

where the first term shows the high-quality securities remaining with the seller and the second term the low-quality securities being sold to the buyer. In this case, the market for high-quality securities has broken down as only low-quality securities are sold.

Similarly, if Eq. (4.4) is fulfilled and both securities are traded, we find total welfare to be

$$\Pi_W^{HL} = p\rho V_H^B + (1-p)\,V_L^B, \tag{4.6}$$

where the high-quality securities are traded to the buyer at some delay, necessitating the discounting with a factor ρ. We now easily see that trading both securities is preferred if $\Pi_W^{HL} \geq \Pi_W^L$, which solves for $\rho V_H^B \geq V_H^S$. Thus, if the value of the high-quality security to the buyer is sufficiently more than to the seller, trading both securities is preferred, even if this happens with a delay for the high-quality securities.

Therefore, if $\frac{(1-p)V_L^B}{V_H^S - pV_H^B} \geq \rho \geq \frac{V_H^S}{V_H^B}$, the strategy of delaying the sale of high-quality securities is welfare enhancing and profitable to buyers. This constraint on the discount factor, representing the patience of buyers, is limiting the benefits of this arrangement. We will therefore evaluate whether the introduction of an investment bank might be beneficial.

Investment Bank Intervention Let us now introduce an investment bank that, at some cost C, can determine the quality of securities. There is no benefit from the existence of an investment bank for the low-quality securities. They can always be traded directly between buyers and sellers at a price $V_L^B \geq P_L \geq V_L^S$ as no seller has an incentive to misrepresent the high-quality security as being low-quality and thereby achieving a lower price. Any intermediary would increase costs to the buyer and/or seller and hence be less attractive than a direct trade. Hence, the investment bank will only be able to buy high-quality securities, if any, at a price $\hat{P}_H$ and sell it on at price P_H to buyers, where we need $V_H^S \leq \hat{P}_H < P_H \leq V_H^B$. This ensures that the price the ultimate buyer pays does not exceed the value of the security to it, the intermediary makes profits by selling the security at a higher price than buying it, and it pays at least the value of the security to the seller. The profits to the investment bank buying and selling the high-quality security only are then given by

$$\Pi_B = p\left(\rho P_H - \hat{P}_H\right) - C, \tag{4.7}$$

assuming the intermediary buys the security instantly and sells it again a time period later, thus requiring these future revenues to be discounted. As the investment bank only buys the high-quality security, any buyer knows that it is buying this type of security, while buying directly from a seller would give him the low-value security. As the investment bank pays the seller at least its reservation price V_H^S, it will be willing to sell their security.

If the investment bank correctly identifies the two securities as being of low and high quality, respectively, there would be no benefits from trading the low-quality security as outlined above, and we only need to consider the high-quality security. If the investment bank were not able to identify the security quality to a potential buyer, then the information provided would be of no use to a buyer, and the same situation as in the absence of investment banks would emerge. This implies that there would be no benefits of their existence and they would not be able to make profits as there are no benefits over direct trade. As we will see below, investment banks can make profits from acting as intermediaries for high-quality securities, and they will only trade in these. The welfare with an investment bank is then given by

$$\Pi_W^I = p\rho V_H^B + (1-p)\, V_L^B - C, \tag{4.8}$$

consisting of the delayed benefits to buyers obtaining the high-quality securities from the intermediary and the low-quality security directly from the seller. The prices paid are only having distributional effects between the buyer, seller, and investment bank. In addition, the costs C of the investment bank to identify the type of security needs to be borne as well.

Comparing the welfare of trading both securities in the absence of an investment bank and with an investment bank, Eqs. (4.6) and (4.8), we see instantly investment banks are not improving welfare, the costs of intermediaries identifying the security type reduce welfare by that amount, and investment banks should not be introduced. Comparing the welfare in the case that without investment banks only the low-quality security is traded with that of both being traded in the presence of an investment bank, Eqs. (4.5) and (4.8), we see that $\Pi_W^I \geq \Pi_W^L$ if

$$p\left(\rho V_H^B - V_H^S\right) \geq C \tag{4.9}$$

and the welfare is higher in the presence of an investment bank in the case the trading of the high-quality security is not feasible without an investment bank. As long as the costs to the investment bank is sufficiently low, they would therefore enhance social welfare by allowing high-quality securities to be traded.

If the investment bank would exploit its market power fully by setting $P_H = V_H^B$ and $\hat{P}_H = V_H^S$, then $\Pi_B \geq 0$, and using Eq. (4.7), this condition is identical to Eq. (4.9). Hence, investment banks make a profit and improve welfare.

Thus, investment banks are beneficial if the adverse selection problem is such that the market for high-quality securities would otherwise collapse. The investment bank allows trades to happen by buying the security itself and then selling it on, even if buyers are more patient than Eq. (4.4) would allow, as long as the costs of investment banks are sufficiently low as implied by Eq. (4.9). These conditions are fulfilled for low-costs C of identifying the security type, a large fraction of high-quality securities (p), or a low discount rate ρ. As $\frac{\partial \rho^*}{\partial p} = \frac{V_H^B - V_H^S}{\left(V_H^S - pV_H^B\right)^2} V_L^B > 0$, a smaller fraction of high-quality securities makes these benefits more widespread as it would require a lower discount rate for direct trades to be feasible.

We have thus seen that investment banks can overcome the adverse selection problem of markets for high-quality securities to break down. In order to achieve this outcome, they need to be able to identify the type of security being sold at sufficiently low costs. Investment banks would then buy high-quality securities and sell these on to buyers, who know that investment banks only offer high-quality securities. Low-quality securities would be bought directly off sellers.

Summary The introduction of investment banks can be beneficial if they can help identify the quality of securities through their expertise. If the quality of securities is not known by the buyer, then the price that can be achieved might not be high enough to meet the value of the seller of high-quality securities. Buyers know that investment banks only offer high-quality securities and are therefore willing to pay a price that meets the threshold of sellers, with the investment bank also able to make a profit. As buyers value the security more highly than sellers, this leads to an overall increase in welfare, as long as the costs of investment banks to identify the high-quality securities are sufficiently low.

Thus, the informational advantage of investment banks allows the issue of high-quality securities even in the presence of adverse selection. By enabling the sale of securities to buyers that value these higher than the seller, the total welfare is improved, even if the costs of investment banks are taken into account.

Reading Biglaiser (1993) and Spulber (1999, Ch. 7.4)

4.2 Quality of Securities Issued

Rather than assuming that the quality of securities is given, we might assume that issuers of securities can affect this quality. They might do so by increasing the effort level of managers or changing their strategy such that the interests of the security holders are taken into account better. This might impose costs on the issuer, such as increased efforts imposed on their management or reduced benefits to the management due to the changed strategy of the issuer. Both types of costs will affect the management's incentives to improve the quality of securities. If an investment bank is able to better identify the quality of securities, this will affect the price at which they can be sold, which in turn will determine the incentives to improve the quality of such securities.

We assume that securities are of either high or low quality, where the high quality occurs probability with p. The seller, such as the issuer, of the security is assumed to know its type, but the buyer can only rely on a signal s that has precision p_j, where $j = D$ for direct trades and the information available to the buyer and $j = B$ for the investment bank acting as an intermediary in the trade. We have $p_B > p_D > \frac{1}{2}$. With p_j indicating the probability that the signal received is correct, we set

$$Prob\,(s = H|H) = Prob\,(s = L|L) = p_j. \tag{4.10}$$

The signal the investment bank receives is more precise than that of the buyer, reflecting the assumption that investment banks have superior information.

With initial beliefs p on the likelihood of the security being of high quality, the signal allows the buyer and investment bank to update their beliefs such that for signals of a high-quality security, H, and low-quality security, L, respectively, we have when using Bayesian learning that

$$Prob\,(H|s = H) = p_j^H = \frac{pp_j}{pp_j + (1-p)\left(1-p_j\right)}, \quad (4.11)$$

$$Prob\,(L|s = L) = p_j^L = \frac{p\left(1-p_j\right)}{p\left(1-p_j\right) + (1-p)\,p_j},$$

with $p_B^H > p_D^H > p > p_D^L > p_B^L$. Depending on the type of security, i, the security has value V_i, where $V_H > V_L$ such that high-quality securities have a higher value than low-quality securities.

Within this framework, we can now analyse the optimal quality of securities that issuers will issue, firstly in the absence of an investment bank and then secondly in its presence.

Direct Trade Let us first assume that buyers and issuers trade directly with each other without the use of an investment bank. Depending on the signal s, we have the expected value to the buyer for a direct exchange between buyers and issuers, $E_D\,[V|s]$, given as

$$E_D\,[V|H] = p_D^H V_H + \left(1 - p_D^H\right) V_L, \quad (4.12)$$

$$E_D\,[V|L] = p_D^L V_L + \left(1 - p_D^L\right) V_H.$$

The first term in each expression denotes that the observed signal represents the quality of the security truthfully, while the second term that this signal is wrong.

Paying a price P_s, depending on his signal s, the buyer makes profits of

$$\Pi_C^s = E_D\,[V|s] - P_s \quad (4.13)$$

and perfect competition between buyers implies $\Pi_B^s = 0$ and hence $P_s = E_D\,[V|s]$. In a direct exchange, the issuer then obtains

$$\Pi_S = pP_H + (1-p)\,P_L - C, \quad (4.14)$$

where we assume that by incurring costs C, the issuer can affect the quality of the security through affecting the probability p of it being of high quality and hence receiving the higher price P_H. Ex ante, the buyer receives signal H with probability p and signal L with probability $1 - p$, giving rise to the respective prices.

We see from Eqs. (4.11) and (4.13) that

$$\frac{\partial p_j^H}{\partial p} = \frac{p_j \left(1 - p_j\right)}{\left(pp_j + (1-p)\left(1 - p_j\right)\right)^2}, \tag{4.15}$$
$$\frac{\partial p_j^L}{\partial p} = \frac{p_j \left(1 - p_j\right)}{\left(p\left(1 - p_j\right) + (1-p)\, p_j\right)^2},$$
$$\frac{\partial P_H}{\partial p} = \frac{\partial p_D^H}{\partial p} \left(V_H - V_L\right),$$
$$\frac{\partial P_L}{\partial p} = -\frac{\partial p_D^L}{\partial p} \left(V_H - V_L\right).$$

The first-order condition of maximising the issuer's profits by choosing the optimal probability of having a high-quality security, p, is given by $\frac{\partial \Pi_S}{\partial p} = 0$ and solves for

$$\frac{\partial C}{\partial p} = \left(P_H - P_L\right) + p\frac{\partial P_H}{\partial p} + (1-p)\frac{\partial P_L}{\partial p}. \tag{4.16}$$

The shape of the right-hand side of this equation can be analysed by inserting from Eqs. (4.11) and (4.15). At $p = 0$ and $p = 1$, this expression is zero and maximal at $p = \frac{1}{2}$. In general, the equilibrium p^* would be the solution to Eq. (4.16), and we assume that the marginal costs are increasing in the quality of the security, p. We can now compare this solution on the optimal quality of the security with that if an investment bank is present in the market.

Investment Bank Intermediation If investment banks are present, direct exchange between buyers and issuers remains available. Given the more precise information by the investment bank, their expected values for the security with signals H and L, respectively, are given by

$$E_B\left[V|H\right] = p_B^H V_H + \left(1 - p_B^H\right) V_L, \tag{4.17}$$
$$E_B\left[V|L\right] = p_B^L V_L + \left(1 - p_B^L\right) V_H.$$

and the price the investment bank would be willing to pay is $\hat{P}_s \leq E_B\left[V|s\right]$, with the relationship being an equality if investment banks compete for issuers. For the same signal s, we have due to $p_B^H > p_D^H > p > p_D^L > p_B^L$ that $E_B\left[V|H\right] > E_D\left[V|H\right] > E_D\left[V|L\right] > E_B\left[V|L\right]$. An investment bank would not buy securities for which they receive a low signal L as the price they would offer, $E_B\left[V|L\right]$, is below what could be realised in direct exchange, $E_D\left[V|L\right]$. Hence in order to attract sales of low-quality securities, investment banks would have to overpay, making a loss from the transaction, and instead, they prefer to not buy the security. On the other hand, for securities with the signal indicating high quality, H, the price they can offer is $E_B[V|H]$, which is higher than what direct exchange would yield, $E_D[V|H]$. Thus, investment banks will only buy securities for which they have received the high signal H.

An issuer with a high-quality security would not sell it below its value, which is given by $E_B[V|H]$; thus, if the signal of the investment bank is low (L) and the investment bank or the direct sale would require a sale below this value, the sale will not go ahead; the issuer retains the security at this value. Thus, the issuer obtains $\hat{P}_H = E_B[V|H]$ if the signal received is H, which happens with probability p. If the security is of low quality, the investment bank might incorrectly assess it as being of high quality, which happens with probability $(1-p)(1-p_B)$, and he is paid $\hat{P}_H = E_B[V|H]$. If the investment bank assesses the security correctly to be of low value, the bank would not offer to buy the security, and the issuer has to resort to direct sales. As he sells the security directly, the buyers know that the bank has assessed it as low-quality and thus will only pay $\hat{P}_L = E_B[V|L]$; this happens with probability $(1-p)p_B$.

Thus, the issuer now obtains total revenue of

$$\hat{\Pi}_S = p\hat{P}_H + (1-p)\left(p_B\hat{P}_L + (1-p_B)\hat{P}_H\right) - C, \tag{4.18}$$

where the first term denotes the high-quality security sold to the investment bank or held on to and the second term the security sold directly, identified correctly as low-quality by the investment bank or mis-identified as high-quality and subsequently bought by the investment bank.

The first-order condition $\frac{\partial\hat{\Pi}_S}{\partial p} = 0$ then solves for

$$\begin{aligned} \frac{\partial C}{\partial p} = {} & p_B\left(\hat{P}_H - \hat{P}_L\right) + p\frac{\partial\hat{P}_H}{\partial p} + (1-p)\frac{\partial\hat{P}_L}{\partial p} \\ & + (1-p)(1-p_B)\frac{\partial\hat{P}_H}{\partial p}, \end{aligned} \tag{4.19}$$

where we insert for $\hat{P}_s = E_B[V|s]$ from Eq. (4.17), p_B^s are given by Eq. (4.11), and $\frac{\partial\hat{P}_s}{\partial p}$ are given analogously to Eq. (4.15), replacing p_D with p_B.

We can now compare this first-order condition with that of direct trade from Eq. (4.16). We see that the first three terms are similar in that P_s is replaced with $\hat{P}_s$, and the first term shows the term p_B. The fourth term here is an additional positive expression. If the first three terms were larger in the presence of an investment bank, then the marginal costs of the issuer would be higher in equilibrium in the presence of an investment bank, and if we assume marginal costs to increase in the security quality p, the security quality is higher. This scenario will in general be observed if the signal quality the investment bank received, as measured by the precision p_B, is sufficiently high. Low precisions might well reduce these terms.

The more interesting case is the scenario that the first three terms are smaller in the presence of an investment bank than in direct trade. Then, depending on the size of this expression, the overall marginal costs can be higher or lower, and thus, security quality can be higher or lower. We easily see that $\hat{P}_H - \hat{P}_L > P_H - P_L$, but the term p_B may well make this term either smaller than with direct trade only. The next two terms similarly may decrease the expression relative to direct trade. We can show that the first three terms are zero for $p = 0$ and $p = 1$ and maximal at $p = \frac{1}{2}$, thus are having similar properties as in direct trade, but as per our assumption are smaller. In Fig. 4.1, these terms for direct trade are represented in blue and in green for the presence of an investment bank. The positive fourth term in Eq. (4.19) will distort this line and have a maximum at a value $p > \frac{1}{2}$. The resulting line is represented in red in the figure.

Given the complexity of the first order conditions, we will in the following analyse the equilibrium outcome graphically.

Comparing Direct Trade and Investment Banks Marginal costs to issuers of increasing security quality, $\frac{\partial C}{\partial p}$, are assumed to be increasing in p, i.e., the more effort the issuer makes, the higher the quality of the security, but these costs are increasing as the quality (p) increases. This relationship is represented by the highest line (black line in the online version) in Fig. 4.1. The marginal benefits of increasing security quality, represented by the right-hand side in the first-order conditions of Eqs. (4.16) and (4.19), for direct trade and investment bank intermediation, respectively, are shown by the top line (blue in the online version) and the middle line (red in the online version). As discussed above, the lowest line (green in the online version) represents the first three terms of the marginal benefits to the issuer in the presence of investment banks.

We observe that if the marginal costs of improving the security quality are high, as in Fig. 4.1a, the introduction of an investment bank reduces the average quality of securities by reducing p, the fraction of high-quality securities. On the other hand, if these marginal costs are low, having an investment bank intermediating the issue of securities increases the average security quality. We can separate two effects that drive this result. Let us write the difference between the first terms of Eqs. (4.17) and (4.19) as

$$
\begin{aligned}
&(P_H - P_L) - p_B\left(\hat{P}_H - \hat{P}_L\right) \\
&\quad = (1 - p_B)(P_H - P_L) + p_B\left((P_H - P_L) - \left(\hat{P}_H - \hat{P}_L\right)\right),
\end{aligned}
\tag{4.20}
$$

where the first term after the manipulation denotes the effect from mis-identifying low-value securities as high-value securities and hence giving issuers higher revenue. This reduces the overall efforts of issuers to maintain high quality as shown in Fig. 4.1a by the lowest line (green line in the online version) $p_B(P_H - P_L)$. The

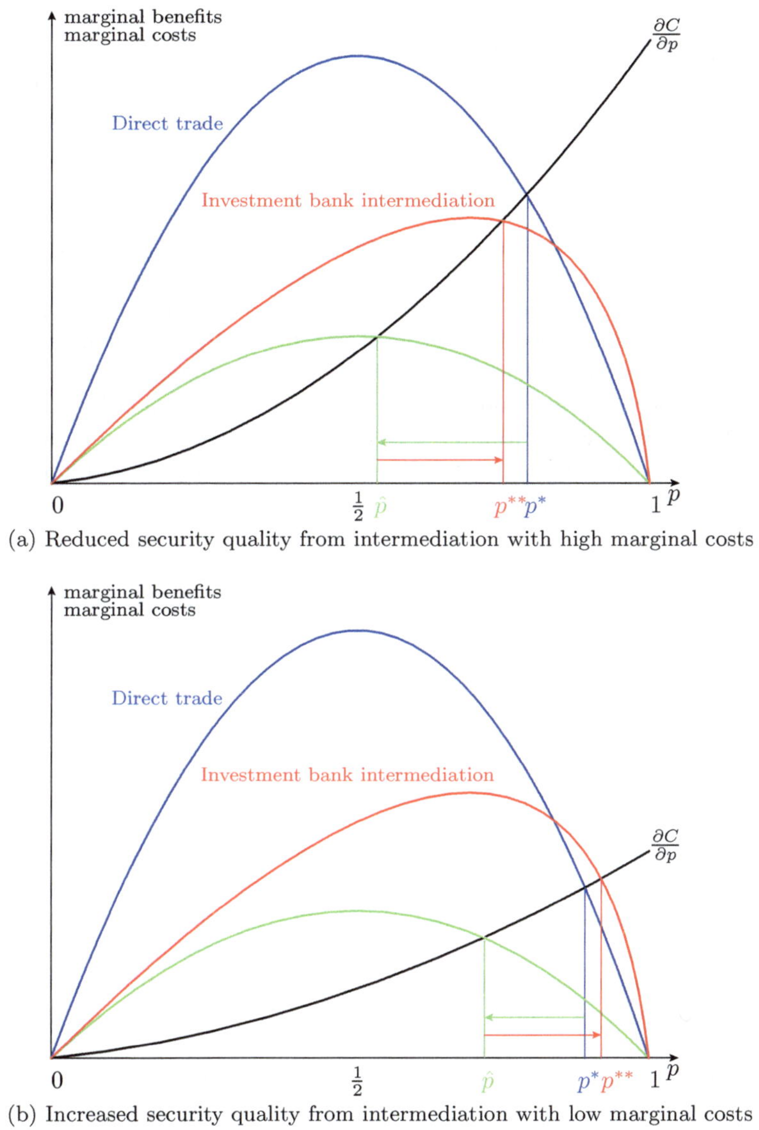

Fig. 4.1 Equilibrium security quality with direct trade and investment bank intermediation

second term captures the change in the prior belief of the quality of the security. The bank makes these differences more pronounced and thus induces more high-quality securities, (partly) offsetting the first effect. If marginal costs are high as in Fig. 4.1a, the first effect will dominate, but Fig. 4.1b shows that low marginal costs can increase the quality of securities as the second effect dominates. The remaining terms of the first-order conditions represent the marginal effects a change of the security quality will have on the price the issuer can obtain, and the rationale for the effect these have is similar to those for the first terms.

We thus see that while the profits of issuers increase in the presence of investment banks, the quality of securities might actually fall if the marginal costs of increasing security quality are high.

Summary Banks are assumed to have superior skills in identifying the quality of securities correctly. If issuers of securities, such as companies, can affect the quality of the securities they are selling, this increased ability to identify high-value securities provides them with incentives to increase the quality of securities to increase the revenue. On the other hand, a better ability to identify the security quality will increase the difference in the beliefs about different securities, reducing incentives to increase the quality of securities. If the marginal costs of increasing the quality of securities are low, the incentives to increase the quality of securities dominate, while with high marginal costs, the effects of increased information on security quality through banks dominate.

Here, the introduction of an investment bank can have a positive effect on the average security quality in the market, if the costs of improving security quality are not too high for their issuers. Otherwise, the introduction of an investment bank reduces the security quality.

Reading Biglaiser and Li (2018)

Conclusions

Being able to acquire information on the quality of securities, investment banks can relay this information to other market participants. They do so by only buying high-quality securities and reselling them to buyers, something that doing so for low-quality securities is not profitable. Thus, a buyer noticing that a security has been bought by an investment bank and is now resold to them will allow them to infer that this security is of high quality. Having made this inference, the asymmetric information between buyers and sellers is reduced. If in absence of an investment bank adverse selection prevents any transactions involving high-quality securities as the achievable price does not cover the costs of these securities, the reduced adverse selection, due to the information inferred by buyers, may well allow high-quality securities to be exchanged. The information provided will increase the price that buyers are willing to pay for high-quality securities and would allow sellers more easily to make a profit from selling. Thus, the presence of investment banks will allow markets to be established that otherwise would not exist due to high adverse selection costs.

Not only do investment banks affect the quality of securities traded in markets, but they can also affect the quality of securities that are offered in the first place. The fact that the quality of securities can be distinguished better in the presence of investment banks can provide an incentive for issuers of securities to ensure they are of higher quality. The higher price they can obtain, due to the better information on their quality being inferred by buyers, could induce increased efforts in improving this quality even further, as long as the costs of doing so are not too high. It might, on the other hand, be that this clearer distinction between security qualities allows issuers to reduce costs and lower the security quality, even though the lower quality will result in a lower price being obtained for the security.

The presence of investment banks, therefore, does affect the market outcome in two ways. Firstly, it enables the ability to complete transactions in high-quality securities in many situations where this would not have been possible without their presence. But secondly, they also affect the quality of securities offered in the first place. Therefore, investment banks are not only acting as intermediaries facilitating transactions between market participants, but also their ability to obtain and make available information to market participants will affect the market outcome itself.

5 Independent Financial Advice

Banks often advise clients on suitable products for investment, such as investment into mutual funds or insurance. Using their knowledge of the financial situation of their clients as well as their understanding of the market, they help clients choose the most suitable product for their needs. This advice can extend to specific capital market transactions as recommended by investment banks, such as pursuing a merger or acquisition, issuing securities, or taking significant stakes in other companies.

Let us assume that a client has the choice of two products, and given their knowledge, financial advisors in an investment bank assess that product 1 is most suitable to a client with probability p. Ex ante, this probability has a distribution function $G(p)$ with $E[p] = \frac{1}{2}$, and the density $g(p)$ is symmetric around this mean such that $G\left(\frac{1}{2}\right) = \frac{1}{2}$. If the advice is correct, the benefits to the clients are V_H; otherwise, it is $V_L < V_H$, and the advisors receive a commission of F_i from product provider i. We further assume that the advisor obtains a fraction f of the benefits the client obtains, as a fee.

We can now analyse the optimal recommendation given to the client if the commissions are not disclosed to clients.

Commissions Not Disclosed If recommending products 1 and 2, respectively, the advisor makes profits of

$$\begin{aligned} \Pi_A^1 &= f\left(pV_H + (1-p)V_L\right) + F_1, \\ \Pi_A^2 &= f\left((1-p)V_H + pV_L\right) + F_2. \end{aligned} \tag{5.1}$$

With probability p, product 1 is the appropriate choice, and if this product is recommended, the benefits are V_H; otherwise, they are V_L. If product 2 is recommended, it is appropriate with probability $1-p$, and the benefits obtained are V_H, while with probability p, the benefits are only V_L as product 2 is not

A. Krause, *Theoretical Foundations of Investment Banking*, Springer Texts in Business and Economics, https://doi.org/10.1007/978-3-031-58060-4_5

appropriate. Product 1 will be recommended if $\Pi_A^1 \geq \Pi_A^2$; hence,

$$p \geq p^* = \frac{1}{2} - \frac{F_1 - F_2}{2f\left(V_H - V_L\right)}. \tag{5.2}$$

We see that those products with a higher commission F_i are more often recommended, but this is balanced by the interest of the client; the larger the difference between the two products is, $V_H - V_L$, the less the impact of the differences in commissions, amplified by the fee the investment bank earns on their client's benefits.

The value derived by the client, who is charged a price P_i by product provider i, is then given by

$$\begin{aligned} \Pi_C^1 &= (1-f)\left(pV_H + (1-p)\,V_L\right) - P_1 \\ &= (1-f)\left(V_L + p\left(V_H - V_L\right)\right) - P_1, \\ \Pi_C^2 &= (1-f)\left((1-p)\,V_H + pV_L\right) - P_2 \\ &= (1-f)\left(V_H - p\left(V_H - V_L\right)\right) - P_2, \end{aligned} \tag{5.3}$$

where the benefits to the client are determined as above and they retain a fraction $1 - f$ of these benefits, less the price paid. We find that product 1 is preferred if $\Pi_C^1 \geq \Pi_C^2$; thus, if

$$p \geq p^{**} = \frac{1}{2} + \frac{P_1 - P_2}{2\left(1-f\right)\left(V_H - V_L\right)}. \tag{5.4}$$

The products are priced such that any client surplus is extracted, and if clients follow the advice given, then they will choose product 1 if $p \geq p^*$, as this is recommended, and product 2 otherwise. Hence, we set prices such that $E\left[\Pi_C^1 | p \geq p^*\right] = E\left[\Pi_C^2 | p < p^*\right] = 0$, which we can easily solve for

$$\begin{aligned} P_1^* &= (1-f)\left(V_L + \frac{V_H - V_L}{1 - G\left(p^*\right)} \int_{p^*}^{1} p dG\left(p\right)\right), \\ P_2^* &= (1-f)\left(V_H - \frac{V_H - V_L}{G\left(p^*\right)} \int_{0}^{p^*} p dG\left(p\right)\right). \end{aligned} \tag{5.5}$$

The profits of the suppliers with costs C_i are then given by the revenue arising from the sale, P_i, less the costs C_i and any commission F_i paid. This gives us

$$\begin{aligned} \Pi_S^1 &= \left(P_1^* - F_1 - C_1\right)\left(1 - G\left(p^*\right)\right), \\ \Pi_S^2 &= \left(P_2^* - F_2 - C_2\right) G\left(p^*\right), \end{aligned} \tag{5.6}$$

where we consider the respective market shares of $1 - G(p^*)$ and $G(p^*)$ for each of the suppliers.

Noting that $\frac{\partial p^*}{\partial F_1} = -\frac{1}{2f(V_H - V_L)}$ and $\frac{\partial p^*}{\partial F_2} = \frac{1}{2f(V_H - V_L)}$, we get the first-order conditions for maximising profits, $\frac{\partial \Pi_S^i}{\partial F_i} = 0$, to solve for

$$F_1 = P_1^* - C_1 - 2f(V_H - V_L)\frac{1 - G(p^*)}{g(p^*)}, \tag{5.7}$$
$$F_2 = P_2^* - C_2 - 2f(V_H - V_L)\frac{G(p^*)}{g(p^*)}.$$

Inserting this expression into Eq. (5.2), we can rewrite the determination of p^* as

$$\begin{aligned}\Psi = &\left(P_1^* - P_2^*\right) - (C_1 - C_2) \\ &-f(V_H - V_L)\left(\left(1 - 2p^*\right) + 2\frac{1 - 2G(p^*)}{g(p^*)}\right) = 0.\end{aligned} \tag{5.8}$$

From Eq. (5.5), we have with the Leibniz integral rule that

$$\frac{\partial P_1^*}{\partial p^*} = (1 - f)\frac{V_H - V_L}{1 - G(p^*)}\frac{g(p^*)}{1 - G(p^*)}\int_{p^*}^{1}\left(p - p^*\right)dG(p) > 0, \tag{5.9}$$
$$\frac{\partial P_2^*}{\partial p^*} = -(1 - f)\frac{V_H - V_L}{G(p^*)}\frac{g(p^*)}{G(p^*)}\int_0^{p^*}\left(p^* - p\right)dG(p) < 0,$$

where the sign of the integral arises from $p > p^*$ in the first case and $p < p^*$ in the second case. We also used that

$$p^*G\left(p^*\right) = \int_0^{p^*} p^*dG(p),$$
$$p^*\left(1 - G\left(p^*\right)\right) = \int_{p^*}^{1} p^*dG(p).$$

With Eq. (5.9), we easily see that $\frac{\partial\left(P_1^* - P_2^*\right)}{\partial p^*} > 0$. Hence, we get that

$$\begin{aligned}\frac{\partial \Psi}{\partial p^*} = &\frac{\partial\left(P_1^* - P_2^*\right)}{\partial p^*} \\ &-f(V_H - V_L)\left(-2 + 2\frac{\partial \frac{1 - G(p^*)}{g(p^*)}}{\partial p^*} - 2\frac{\partial \frac{G(p^*)}{g(p^*)}}{\partial p^*}\right) > 0,\end{aligned} \tag{5.10}$$

using the assumption that for the hazard rate and inverse hazard rate

$$\frac{\partial \frac{1-G(p^*)}{g(p^*)}}{\partial p^*} < 0,$$

$$\frac{\partial \frac{G(p^*)}{g(p^*)}}{\partial p^*} > 0,$$

together with our result that $\frac{\partial(P_1^*-P_2^*)}{\partial p^*} > 0$. Thus, any solution p^* to Eq. (5.8) is unique.

Let us now assume that $p^* = \frac{1}{2}$. Using that $G\left(\frac{1}{2}\right) = \frac{1}{2}$ and $E[p] = \int_0^1 pdG(p) = \frac{1}{2}$, we get using Eq. (5.5) that

$$\begin{aligned} P_1^* - P_2^* &= (1-f)(V_L - V_H) + 2(1-f)(V_H - V_L) \\ &\quad \times \left(\int_{p^*}^1 pdG(p) + \int_0^{p^*} pdG(p)\right) \\ &= -(1-f)(V_H - V_L) \\ &\quad + 2(1-f)(V_H - V_L)\int_0^1 pdG(p) \\ &= 0 \end{aligned} \tag{5.11}$$

as $\int_0^1 pdG(p) = E[p] = \frac{1}{2}$, and hence $\Psi = -(C_1 - C_2)$. If $C_1 = C_2$, then the solution is $p^* = p^{**} = \frac{1}{2}$, optimal for the advisor and the client.

If, however, $C_1 < C_2$, that is, product 1 has lower costs than product 2, then at $p^* = \frac{1}{2}$, we have $\Psi > 0$, and as from Eq. (5.10) we had that $\frac{\partial \Psi}{\partial p^*} > 0$, the optimal solution is $p^* < \frac{1}{2}$. With $p^* < \frac{1}{2}$, we have $1 - 2p^* > 0$ and $1 - 2G(p^*) > 0$, the latter as $G(p^*) < \frac{1}{2}$; we then have the final bracketed term in Eq. (5.8) as positive, implying that in order to obtain $\Psi = 0$, we need $P_1^* > P_2^*$. From Eq. (5.4), this implies that $p^{**} > \frac{1}{2}$, and hence the low-cost product 1 is more often recommended than is optimal for the client. This is because the client would like the investment bank to recommend product 1, the low-cost product, only if assessment of their needs shows that $p \in \left[p^{**}; 1\right]$. However, they recommend product 1 if $p \in \left[p^*; 1\right]$, including the area of $p \in \left[p^*; p^{**}\right]$.

The lower costs of product 1 would lead to higher profits for its supplier, allowing it to pay a higher commission to the investment bank without reducing profitability. This will induce the investment bank to recommend product 1 more often due to the lower threshold p^*, which in turn allows the price P_1 to increase from Eq. (5.9) as its market share is increased, and hence F_1 increases further as the supplier can divert a larger amount to the commission paid to the investment bank, thus reducing p^* even more in Eq. (5.2). The higher commission of the more costly product from the higher market share incentivizes the investment bank to recommend product 1 again, even if it is less likely to be suitable ($p^* < \frac{1}{2}$), thus reinforcing the stronger market position of product 1. The opposite is true for product 2.

Thus, we find that only if products have the same costs is the advice given to clients optimal for them. In general, clients get advised more frequently to obtain the lower-cost product that however sells at a higher price to accommodate the higher commission of the investment bank. We can now see whether the disclosure of any such commissions will improve the advice clients obtain.

Disclosed Commissions Thus far, we assumed that the commissions F_i were not known to clients and hence p^* was not known but had to be inferred by suppliers to determine their market share. Such a situation might arise if the costs of the products are not known to the clients or investment bank, and therefore they cannot infer F_i perfectly or are even unaware of the existence of any such commissions. Let us now assume that commissions have to be made known to clients; then the threshold for investment banks to recommend product 1, p^{***}, can be inferred from Eq. (5.2). In this case, the price can be set at this value by the client, and thus, extracting all surplus from the client yields prices

$$
\begin{aligned}
P_1^{**} &= (1-f)\left(V_L + p^{***}\left(V_H - V_L\right)\right), \\
P_2^{**} &= (1-f)\left(V_H - p^{***}\left(V_H - V_L\right)\right).
\end{aligned} \tag{5.12}
$$

If we again assume that $p^{***} = \frac{1}{2}$, we have as before that prices are equal, $P_1^{**} = P_2^{**}$. We then easily also obtain that if $C_1 = C_2$, we find $p^{***} = p^{**} = \frac{1}{2}$, unchanged from before. Thus, the disclosure of commissions does not make a difference if the two products have identical costs.

Let us now assume that $C_1 < c_2$ and the threshold is set as $p^{***} = p^*$, the same value as without disclosing commissions; then using Eqs. (5.5) and (5.12), we can obtain that

$$
P_1^{**} - P_1^* = (1-f)\frac{V_H - V_L}{1 - G(p^*)}\int_{p^*}^{1}\left(p^* - p\right)dG(p) > 0, \tag{5.13}
$$

$$
P_2^{**} - P_2^* = -(1-f)\frac{V_H - V_L}{G(p^*)}\int_{0}^{p^*}\left(p^* - p\right)dG(p) < 0
$$

and therefore $P_1^{**} - P_2^{**} > P_1^* - P_2^*$.

Let us now assume that from Eq. (5.8), we have $\Psi = 0$ in the case of non-disclosure of the commission. Then in the case with disclosure, still assuming the same $p^{***} = p^*$, we find that the same function $\hat{\Psi}$ is given by

$$
\begin{aligned}
\hat{\Psi} = {} & \left(P_1^{**} - P_2^{**}\right) - \left(C_1 - C_2\right) \\
& - f\left(V_H - V_L\right)\left(\left(1 - 2p^*\right) + 2\frac{1 - 2G(p^*)}{g(p^*)}\right)
\end{aligned} \tag{5.14}
$$

$$= \left(P_1^{**} - P_1^{*}\right) - \left(P_2^{**} - P_2^{*}\right)$$
$$> 0$$

as we use the results in Eq. (5.13) and used Eq. (5.8). Hence, as $\frac{\partial \hat{\Psi}}{\partial p^{***}} > 0$ as before, we have chosen a too high threshold p^{***}; therefore, if commissions are disclosed, the low-cost product 1 is even less often recommended as $p^{***} < p^{*}$. As $P_1^{**} - P_2^{**} > P_1^{*} - P_2^{*}$, we see from Eq. (5.4) that the optimal advice would be to recommend the low-cost product more often, increasing the difference between the advice given and the advice that is optimal for clients. If the differences between the two products are bigger, $V_H - V_L$, price changes will be larger as we can see from Eq. (5.13) and hence adjustments to p^{***} more pronounced. The removal of uncertainty about the threshold for recommending product 1 has the effect that its price can increase even more, while that of the high-cost product 2 would reduce more. This arises because the uncertainty about the commission, causing uncertainty in the price to the client, and hence his benefits, have been eliminated and can now extracted fully, rather than on the basis of its expected value. This generates more income to the supplier, who in turn can pay a higher commission to the investment bank, incentivizing it to recommend product 1 more often.

Summary We have seen that commissions to advisors provided by suppliers of products distort the advice such that low-cost products are more frequently suggested by advisors than would be optimal for their clients. This distortion arises from the higher commissions earned on these products, which are then sold to clients at a higher price to accommodate the commission. Companies seek to recover the commission they pay to investment banks through a higher market share, which they obtain if their product is more often recommended, resulting in even more increased commissions for this product and more distorted recommendations. The disclosure of commissions aggravates this situation as any surplus the clients might have from purchasing the products are extracted more efficiently, given the full knowledge clients have on commissions and hence prices. It is thus not in the interest of clients to require the disclosure of the commission investment banks obtain.

Reading Inderst and Ottaviani (2012)

Review of Part I

Investment banks provide advice and support to their clients on major capital market transactions. This advice will be based on information the investment bank holds about their clients' securities as well as the market as a whole, while support can take the form of providing information to other market participants about their client and the securities they issue. The information investment banks use to advise is not readily verifiable by their clients nor is any information provided to other market participants. It is hence essential that any such information is reliable, and while the reputation of investment banks would prevent the release of wrong or nonexistent information in the long term, investment banks can take steps to reassure anyone receiving information that its content is reported truthfully. By taking actions consistent with the information provided, such as making investments using their own funds, that would otherwise be detrimental to their profits, clients and market participants know that an investment bank holds the information it releases. However, this is only a distinguishing characteristic if this action cannot be copied by investment banks not holding the same information without reducing their profitability. As long as the information is negative, the adjustment in the actions by an investment bank not holding the corresponding information is too large to be profitable, and we therefore find that only negative information can be communicated effectively. Of course, the absence of negative information can then be interpreted as a confirmation for the existence of positive information as long as it is known that information is available. The additional revenue obtained from selling this negative information makes it profitable to not only use the information to increase the profits from their own actions but also sell the information, even if the actions need to be adjusted to convey the validity of the information provided.

Not only are investment banks providing information, but they can affect the outcomes of capital market transactions through their provision of information. Adverse selection can have the consequence of making capital market transaction of high-quality securities impossible. If buyers of such securities do not know the quality of securities, they would not be willing to pay the full price for high-quality securities, and if the provision of such securities is more costly, these might not be offered at all, and the market will only consist of low-quality securities. If investment banks can learn the qualities of securities, they can signal to potential buyers that a security has high quality by buying it themselves with the aim of reselling it to buyers. With the acquisition of information being costly, an investment bank could not recover these costs from selling low-quality securities as a direct sale between buyers, and sellers would not incur these costs. Hence, investment banks would only buy and resell high-quality securities, which implies that any security offered by an investment bank is of high quality. This way, investment banks can reduce adverse selection and ensure a market exists for such securities. Being able to command higher prices for their high-quality security due to the identification as such by investment banks could on the one hand provide an incentive to increase the quality even further, but on the other hand, it might induce the issuer of the security to exert less effort and reduce the quality of their security. If the costs of increasing the quality of a security are sufficiently low, the increased price from higher quality induces an increase in quality, but if these costs are sufficiently high, it might be more profitable to reduce the costs and accept a slightly lower price for the security. It is thus not only that investment banks allow markets to operate more effectively by reducing adverse selection, but they can also affect the quality of securities offered in the first place.

Advice given to clients is structured such that it maximises the profits of the investment bank, rather than serves best the interests of their client. This is especially relevant if the investment bank receives commission from the supplier of a service or product when a client chooses a specific product. While the investment bank might not completely ignore the interests of their client in providing advice, it will bias the advice towards the product or service with the higher commission paid. This means that the product or service offering higher commissions will increase their market share as they are recommended more often, which in turn allows them to pay higher commissions from the increased revenue. In addition, the supplier can raise the price of their product or service to recover the higher commission. While this will reduce their market share, such a strategy will generally be optimal to maximise overall profits. The process of being able to offer a higher commission than another product or service might arise if the costs are lower than for competing offerings. We would therefore expect to find products and services that face low costs to offer high commissions and sell at higher prices than those with higher costs and advice being biased towards them. In this way, investment banks are steering their clients not towards the products and services that are most suitable to them, but the suitability to clients will be balanced against the profits the advice will generate to investment banks. Requiring investment banks to disclose these commissions to clients will increase the bias in advice given. This is because knowing the commissions, clients can determine the bias in the advice given by investment banks, and this in turn allows suppliers to price their products and services more accurately as the surplus of clients is known to them and can be extracted more effectively, leading to higher prices and even more biased advice. Thus, there exists an even more pronounced conflict of interest between investment banks and their clients seeking advice.

Considering these aspects, it has become clear that investment banks play a significant role in capital market transactions. Investment banks are best placed to provide negative information to clients and the market, even though such advice might well be biased. In addition, due to their presence, they will also affect market outcomes, allowing all securities to be traded by reducing adverse selection and affecting the type of securities offered in the first place. The heterogeneity of the different business lines of investment banks requires a detailed assessment of each specific role to analyse in more detail how clients using investment banks affect the outcomes in these situations. This analysis will then also be able to determine contractual terms between investment banks and their clients that can be used to reduce any conflicts of interest that may arise.

Part II

Corporate Finance

Under the term corporate finance in investment banks, we find two very different business lines. One, mergers and acquisitions (M&A), involve the advice to companies seeking to acquire another, usually smaller, company, merge with another company on more equal terms, or being acquired by another company. The other, securities underwriting, is concerned with the raising of new funds for their clients, in the form of equity or debt instruments. These two business lines are the most prestigious in an investment bank, where M&A advisory is usually seen as the more prestigious of them, and in most cases they are the most profitable areas of investment banks. Only in some investment banks and during specific time periods might proprietary trading be more profitable, although this often requires a larger investment of resources, in particular capital, than is necessary in corporate finance.

In both business lines, investment banks act as advisors to their clients, but their active involvement in underwriting is much more prominent. Nevertheless, they have significant influence on the decisions made by the senior management of their clients in M&A as well. Here, investment banks advise on the conditions that should be attached when making an offer, whether to accept an offer that is made to them or even whether to abandon the plan for the acquisition or merger altogether. The formal decisions will always be taken by the senior management, taking into account the advice by investment banks, but it is not common for decisions to be made that go against the advice given by investment banks. The main focus in M&A advice is the senior management, and any engagement with investors will be limited to a small number of key investors, in addition to assessing the wider market reaction. In securities underwriting, however, taking into consideration investors is an essential part of the role investment banks have. They will contact potential investors to gauge the interest in the securities to be sold and use this information to determine a suitable offer price. Subsequently they are also heavily involved in the marketing of the issue (road show) and are in close contact with investors. A common contractual arrangement, firm commitment contracts, even sees investment banks buying the securities and then selling them on to investors. They are then involved in the allocation of securities to investors, deciding who receives their full demand, a partial fulfillment of their demand, or no allocation at all. Thus, while investment banks are advising senior management and act in cooperation with them, their scope to influence the outcome is significantly higher than in M&A.

Of course, as advisors to their clients, the advice they provide should be in the best interest of their client. However, often the interests of the investment bank in maximising their own profits are not fully compatible with providing unbiased and honest advice. Given that investment banks are sought as advisors due to the superior information they hold or can access, it will be difficult for their clients to challenge the advice they have been provided with. To this effect, contracts are drawn up that seek to align the interests of clients, and investment banks and competition between investment banks should ensure that only the most efficient contracts survive. The resulting contracts can be complex, such as the contingent contract commonly used in M&A or the book-building mechanism used in securities underwriting. How these contractual arrangements will benefit clients and investment banks and what the consequences are is the subject in the following chapters: Chap. 6 addresses the optimal contract in mergers and acquisitions and Chap. 7 contractual aspects in securities underwriting. In both cases, we will also identify remaining conflicts of interest between investment banks and their clients.

6 Mergers and Acquisitions Advisory

When advising clients, investment banks evaluate both companies involved in the merger. They will evaluate their client as well as the their merger partner, exploring the strength and weaknesses of each company, and determine a fair valuation for both. Based on their analysis of both companies, they will then also seek to determine the possible benefits from this merger, such as economies of scale, the strengthening of market positions, or the ability to enter new markets. Another aspect to consider in their advice is the reaction of shareholders and other market participants, including regulators and other stakeholders. Shareholders or private owners of a target company might be reluctant to agree to a merger or alternatively might be very willing to dispose of their holdings. Similarly, the shareholders or private owners of the client company might be more or less positively inclined to the proposed merger. The market reaction to a merger is also important; it might be that markets react positively or negatively to a proposed merger, depending on how they evaluate the prospects of the merged company, which might well differ from the assessment of the current owners. Regulators might interfere by imposing constraints on a merged company, for example, to ensure sufficient competition, and other stakeholders, such as consumers, might also view the merger differently. Taking all these aspects into account, the investment bank will propose a price that they regard as fair, as well as a suitable payment form, commonly cash payment or shares in the acquiring company. If the investment bank advises the target company, they would advise their client on whether an offer should be accepted or rejected. They might suggest to reject an offer as the price is too low and they assess the value of their client to be higher than what has been offered or because they are sufficiently confident that a better offer will be made. Such a better offer might be made by the same acquirer improving their offer after a rejection, or a new acquirer might emerge that is willing to offer better conditions. If advising the acquirer, investment banks would suggest an offer to be made to the owners of the target company, which they think will be accepted. Alternatively, they might want to advise their client to abandon the merger if there is no prospect of its success.

A. Krause, *Theoretical Foundations of Investment Banking*, Springer Texts in Business and Economics, https://doi.org/10.1007/978-3-031-58060-4_6

In this whole process, investment banks only act as advisors with decisions taken by their client. However, they will normally follow the advice of the investment bank, in particular as the view of their client has been included in the overall evaluation of the companies. Investment banks will also hold conversations with shareholders or private owners that are reluctant to support the merger, either because they see the conditions as not acceptable or because they do not support the merger at all. Again, investment banks have a purely advisory role, and their active involvement is not in acquiring the target company but, if at all necessary, will be limited to provide support in financing the transaction. This may take the form of a bridge loan that is provided directly by the investment bank or arranged by them with another bank or lender. Such bridge loans are short-term and in place to allow the acquirer to raise the funds necessary for any cash payments that are required. Bridge loans are repaid once a permanent financing of the transaction has been established, such as a long-term loan or the issue of securities. If securities are used to pay for the transaction, the investment bank could also be managing their issue.

While investment banks in mergers play no or only a very limited active role through bridge loans, their involvement is nevertheless important. They bring in their knowledge in assessing companies and their knowledge of market reactions using their extensive network of contacts. Based on information that companies either do not have access to or their access is limited, they can improve the position of their client and support them through the process of the merger.

While advising their clients on the merger, investment banks do not necessarily act in the interest of their clients. The advice they provide, which they can reasonably assume to be followed by their client, will be structured such that it maximises the profits of the investment bank, rather than their clients. This might well result in a conflict of interest between the investment bank and their client. The mechanism to address this conflict of interest is the fee investment banks charge. As part of the contract with their client detailing the advice investment banks are supposed to provide, the fees that are to be paid will be determined. Agreements can include fixed fees that are payable regardless of the outcome of the merger, fixed fees that are only payable if the merger is completed (conditional fee contracts), or fees that increase with the value of the merger and are only paid if the merger is completed (contingent fee contract). The terms of the fee payment may also include a typically smaller payment to the investment bank if the merger is not completed (breakup fee). These different forms of fees will affect the advice given by investment banks; some will amplify the conflict of interest, while others will align the incentives of investment banks and their clients more closely.

The following models will explore the consequences of different fee contracts for this conflict of interest between the advice given by investment banks and the preferences of their clients. Contingent fee contracts are those that in most situations align the interests of investment banks and their clients best. This result is consistent with the observation that contingent fee contracts are dominating in mergers and acquisitions advisory. Having explored them in Sect. 6.1, Sect. 6.2 will explore the incentives on abandoning a merger and Sect. 6.3 the optimality of breakup fees.

6.1 Contingent Fee Contracts

Fees that dependent on the size of a deal and are only payable on completion of a merger are a common feature of most contracts companies agree with investment banks. Such a contract is used to minimise the conflicts of interest between investment banks and their customers. Investment banks are focused on the fee income that a deal will generate, while their customers will seek to maximise the benefits from the mergers, net of any fees that are paid to the investment bank for their advice. If customers follow the advice of the investment bank as they believe in the superior knowledge of the investment bank about the best deal that is possible, these two objectives are commonly not aligned. While contingent fee contracts are not optimal in all situations, they cover a wide range of scenarios. We will show their optimality in the presence of moral hazard and adverse selection, respectively.

6.1.1 Eliminating Moral Hazard in Merger Advice

Investment banks advise clients on whether to accept or decline a merger offer from another company if working for the target company. When working for the acquirer, the investment bank would advise on whether to make a specific offer or not. They would have to take into account the surplus any such offer would generate for their client, as well as the likelihood of such an offer being accepted or, in the case of advising a target, another better offer being made in the future.

Let us now assume that the merger surplus can be either V_H or V_L. If an offer generating a surplus of V_i is made, the merger will be completed with probability π_i. We assume that making an offer V_H is giving a higher expected surplus than making an offer V_L; hence, $\pi_L V_L < \pi_H V_H$. The lower surplus V_L is more likely leading to completion of the merger; thus, $\pi_L > \pi_H$, but we also assume that $V_H > V_L$. We might interpret this as a scenario where a high surplus V_H to the bidder might be resisted by the shareholders of the target company and for this reason not be completed, while a lower surplus V_L will meet less resistance, but the overall benefits of an offer V_H will be higher for the bidder.

Conditional Fee Contract If the investment bank uses a conditional fee contract that pays the investment bank a fixed fee F upon completion of the merger, then with investment banks facing costs C, we have their expected profits given by

$$\Pi_B^i = \pi_i F - C \tag{6.1}$$

and hence $\Pi_B^L > \Pi_B^H$ as $\pi_L > \pi_H$. Thus, if the conditional fee contract is chosen, the bank would always prefer the less risky strategy and propose an offer generating surplus V_L. Competitive investment banks imply that we have $\Pi_B^L = 0$, and hence the investment banking fee is given by

$$F = \frac{C}{\pi_L}. \tag{6.2}$$

The outcomes from investment banks offering a conditional fee contract can now be compared to an investment bank offering a contingent fee contract.

Contingent Fee Contract With a contingent fee contract, the payment to the investment bank is not only conditional on the merger proceeding but also the value V_i generated, on which it charges a fee of f if the deal is completed, such that

$$\hat{\Pi}_B^i = f\pi_i V_i - C. \tag{6.3}$$

As $\pi_L V_L < \pi_H V_H$, we now immediately see that with contingent fee contracts, $\hat{\Pi}_B^L < \hat{\Pi}_B^H$, and hence investment banks will advise to make an offer generating surplus V_H. Competition between investment banks, again, requires that $\hat{\Pi}_B^H = 0$, and hence, the fee is set such that

$$f = \frac{C}{\pi_H V_H}. \tag{6.4}$$

For convenience, we here look at the fee being determined in relation to the surplus added by a merger, while in most contracts, this is specified as a fraction of the merger value. Assume a merger generates additional value $V_i = \overline{V} - P_i$ from the perspective of a buyer, with the post-merger value being $\overline{V}$ and the price paid is P_i. Then a fee on the merger value P_i, $\overline{f}$, can be determined such that $fV_i = \overline{V} - \left(1 + \overline{f}\right) P_i$, or $f = \frac{\overline{V}}{V_i} - \left(1 + \overline{f}\right) \frac{P_i}{V_i}$. From a target's perspective, we have similarly with the value pre-merger at $\overline{V}$ that $fV_i = \left(1 - \overline{f}\right) P_i - \overline{V}$, giving $f = \left(1 - \overline{f}\right) \frac{P_i}{V_i} - \frac{\overline{V}}{V_i}$. Hence, the fee as defined here has its equivalent in the fee defined as a fraction of the merger value.

Knowing that with contingent fee contracts, banks will advise on offering V_H, and with conditional fee contracts they advise V_L, we can now see which contract type their clients prefer.

Client Choice Assuming the client follows the advice of the investment bank, the profits for the client of the investment bank are then given by

$$\Pi_C^L = \pi_L (V_L - F) = \pi_L V_L - C, \tag{6.5}$$
$$\hat{\Pi}_C^H = (1 - f)\pi_H V_H = \pi_H V_H - C,$$

for the conditional and contingent fee contract, respectively, where we inserted the investment banking fees from Eqs. (6.2) and (6.4). With $\pi_L V_L < \pi_H V_H$, we see that clients prefer contingent fee contracts as they rule out advice to make or accept a the low-surplus offer, which the investment bank will suggest to them with a conditional fee contract.

If the client would pursue an offer giving surplus V_H with a conditional fee contract, and thereby go against the advice of the investment bank, the profits would be

$$\Pi_C^H = \pi_H (V_H - F) = \pi_H V_H - \frac{\pi_H}{\pi_L} C. \tag{6.6}$$

We now get that $\Pi_C^L \geq \Pi_C^H$ if $\pi_L V_L - \pi_H V_H > \frac{\pi_L - \pi_H}{\pi_L} C$. As $\pi_L > \pi_H$, the right-hand side is positive, while our assumption that $\pi_L V_L < \pi_H V_H$ makes the left-hand side negative. Thus, we cannot have $\Pi_C^L \geq \Pi_C^H$, and therefore with conditional fee contracts, the client would prefer the offer generating surplus V_H, while the bank advises their client on an offer generating surplus of only V_L, giving rise to moral hazard in their advice. Investment banks do not provide advice in the interest of their client.

In the contingent fee contract, the profits to a client pursuing an offer generating a surplus of V_L, going against the advice of the investment bank, obtains profits of

$$\hat{\Pi}_C^L = (1 - f) \pi_L V_L = \pi_L V_L - \frac{\pi_L V_L}{\pi_H V_H} C. \tag{6.7}$$

We now find that $\hat{\Pi}_C^H > \hat{\Pi}_C^L$, and therefore the advice of the investment bank leads to the higher profits for their client if $\pi_H V_H > C$, which should easily be fulfilled as otherwise seeking investment banking advice would lead to a loss for the client due to a too high fee being charged by the investment bank. Thus, with contingent fee contracts, no moral hazard can be found, and the advice of the investment bank is consistent with the preferences of their client.

Summary If investment banks use conditional fee contracts, they will advise their client to make or accept an offer with low surplus that is more likely to be accepted than an offer with a higher surplus but a lower acceptance rate. This changes with a contingent fee contract, in which the investment bank benefits from the higher merger value through a higher fee income. With a contingent fee contract, the incentives of the client and the investment bank are fully aligned, while with a conditional fee contract, the investment bank will not advise what is best for their client, leading to a moral hazard problem. Thus, choosing a contingent fee contract eliminates this moral hazard. Furthermore, the contingent fee contract is preferred by their clients over a conditional fee contract as well.

Reading Emons (2006)

6.1.2 Merger Advice with Adverse Selection

Investment banks might not always be better informed than their clients about all aspects of a merger. Two key components are the surplus a merger generates for the client and the probability of this merger commencing, and we assume that the client has better information on one of these components. We consider the impact of two types of contracts. When using a conditional fee contract, the investment bank is paid fixed fee F if the merger commences, which happens with probability π, and the investment bank has costs C. With a surplus of V if the merger is completed, the expected profits of the client and the investment bank are then given by

$$\begin{aligned} \Pi_C &= \pi (V - F), \\ \Pi_B &= \pi F - C. \end{aligned} \tag{6.8}$$

The other possible contract is a contingent fee contract that pays, if the merger commences, a fraction f of the surplus V. In this case, the expected profits of clients and investment banks are given by

$$\begin{aligned} \hat{\Pi}_C &= (1 - f) \pi V, \\ \hat{\Pi}_B &= f \pi V - C. \end{aligned} \tag{6.9}$$

For convenience, we here look at the fee being determined in relation to the surplus added by a merger, while in most contracts, this is specified as a fraction of the merger value. Assume a merger generates additional value $V = \overline{V} - P$ from the perspective of a buyer, with the post-merger value being $\overline{V}$ and the price paid is P. Then a fee on the merger value P_i, $\overline{f}$, can be determined such that $f V_i = \overline{V} - \left(1 + \overline{f}\right) P_i$ or $f = \frac{\overline{V}}{V} - \left(1 + \overline{f}\right) \frac{P}{V}$. From a target's perspective we have similarly with the value pre-merger at $\overline{V}$ that $f V = \left(1 - \overline{f}\right) P - \overline{V}$, giving $f = \left(1 - \overline{f}\right) \frac{P}{V} - \frac{\overline{V}}{V}$. Hence, the fee as defined here has its equivalent in the fee defined as a fraction of the merger value.

Size of Merger Benefits Unknown Let us first assume that investment banks do know the likelihood of a merger, π, but not the surplus generated, V. This might be the situation if a target or buyer has not yet been identified, but the investment bank knows from experience how likely a merger is going to succeed. The investment bank will form expectations on the surplus, $E[V]$, which can be used in Eqs. (6.8) and (6.9) to replace V. With our assumption that the client has superior knowledge about the merger, we assume that it would know the value of the surplus to be generated.

A client prefers the conditional fee contract if $\Pi_C \geq \hat{\Pi}_C$, or

$$V \geq \frac{F}{f}. \tag{6.10}$$

Competition between investment banks implies $\Pi_B = 0$ and hence

$$F = \frac{C}{\pi}. \tag{6.11}$$

Investment banks could offer a contingent fee contract if, after inserting for C from solving Eq. (6.11), we have

$$\hat{\Pi}_B = f\pi E[V] - C = \pi (fE[V] - F) \geq 0, \tag{6.12}$$

or

$$E[V] \geq \frac{F}{f}. \tag{6.13}$$

As the investment bank will only attract those clients to a conditional fee contract that are not meeting the condition in Eq. (6.10) and those with $\Pi_C \geq 0$ or $V \geq \frac{C}{\pi}$, we have

$$\begin{aligned} E[V] &= \int_{\frac{C}{\pi}}^{\frac{F}{f}} V dG(V) \leq \int_0^{\frac{F}{f}} V dG(V) \\ &\leq \int_0^{\frac{F}{f}} \frac{F}{f} dG(V) = \frac{F}{f} G\left(\frac{F}{f}\right) \leq \frac{F}{f}, \end{aligned} \tag{6.14}$$

which contradicts Eq. (6.13), and hence no contingent fee contract can be offered. Here $G(\cdot)$ denotes the distribution function of the surplus V as surmised by the investment bank.

Merger Probability Unknown Let us now instead assume that π, the probability to complete the merger, is not known to the investment bank but they know the expected merger surplus πV. This allows us to focus on the probability alone without the effect of the value generated. We might face such a situation if the client is well informed about the willingness of the other company to merge but finds it difficult to value the transaction. From Eq. (6.9) we can get that the contingent fee contract is preferred by the client if $\hat{\Pi}_C \geq \Pi_C$ and hence

$$\pi \geq \frac{f\pi V}{F}. \tag{6.15}$$

Competition between investment banks requires $\hat{\Pi}_B = 0$ and thus

$$f = \frac{C}{\pi V}. \tag{6.16}$$

An investment bank offering a conditional fee contract would obtain

$$\Pi_B = E[\pi] F - C = E[\pi] F - f\pi V \geq 0, \tag{6.17}$$

having inserted for C from solving Eq. (6.16) and replaced π with $E[\pi]$ for the investment bank. This now solves for

$$E[\pi] \geq \frac{f\pi V}{F}. \tag{6.18}$$

As only those clients violating Eq. (6.15), and $\hat{\Pi}_C \geq 0$, or $V \geq \frac{C}{\pi}$ after inserting for f from Eq. (6.16), will seek a conditional fee contract, we have with $H(\cdot)$ denoting the distribution of the likelihood of a merger from the investment bank's perspective that

$$\begin{aligned} E[\pi] &= \int_{\frac{C}{\pi}}^{f\pi V} F\pi dH(\pi) \leq \int_0^{\frac{f\pi V}{F}} \pi dH(\pi) \qquad (6.19) \\ &\leq \int_0^{\frac{f\pi V}{F}} \frac{f\pi V}{F} dH(\pi) = \frac{f\pi V}{F} H\left(\frac{f\pi V}{F}\right) \leq \frac{f\pi V}{F}, \end{aligned}$$

violating the condition in Eq. (6.18), and hence no conditional fee contract will be offered, but a contingent fee contract is chosen.

Summary We find that with their clients having better information on the size of the surplus, investment banks optimally offer conditional fee contracts, while if the superior information is about the likelihood of accepting a merger offer, contingent fee contracts are chosen. In conditional fee contracts, investment banks are not exposed to the risks arising from the size of the merger benefits and thus do not face adverse selection when dealing with better informed clients, making this contract specification more attractive. If the uncertainty is about the likelihood of a merger being completed, the conditional fee contract exposes investment banks to adverse selection. With our assumption that πV was known, the expected fee income $f\pi V$ would be known, while for conditional contracts, the expected fee income πF would be subject to adverse selection; hence, investment banks find contingent fee contracts more attractive. Thus, investment banks select contract forms that eliminate adverse selection and determine the contract conditions (fees) such that alternative contract forms are not attractive to clients. Clients will accept the contract, provided the projected merger surplus is sufficiently large.

Reading Emons (2007)

Resumé

Merger contracts are chosen such that they minimise the impact of moral hazard in the advice given by investment bank as well as adverse selection if the client is better informed than the investment bank about some aspects of the merger. Selecting such contracts will reduce the overall costs as the investment bank does not have to be compensated for adverse selection costs if clients choose the contract that allows them to pay lower fees and clients do not need to take into account the more moral hazard in the investment bank advising them on mergers, hence improving overall welfare. Contingent fee contracts are dominating in mergers as the alternative, a conditional fee contract, is only preferred if clients have better information on the merger surplus. This scenario is not frequently observed as clients are commonly unsure about the valuations of companies and hence the surplus a merger can provide.

6.2 Accepting Merger Offers

Investment banks commonly advise clients whether to accept an offer of a merger made by another company or what conditions to attach to an offer to merge if their client is making an offer. Clients will seek to maximise their surplus, taking into account the fees paid to the investment bank, while investment banks will seek to maximise their profits. These different objective functions may cause the advice given by investment banks to differ from the best interests of their client.

Let us assume that in a merger an offer with surplus V_L has been received. If the offer is accepted, the merger commences; if it is rejected, it may be concluded at a surplus of $V_H > V_L$ with probability π or not be completed at all. A new, improved offer might be obtained, if the original offer is rejected by the client, either from the same acquirer or a new bidder. If the client is making offers, the current offer can be interpreted as an offer that the target client would certainly accept, while the new offer might be an alternative offer that may not be accepted by the target client. Investment banks face costs C^* if the current merger offer is accepted and $C > C^*$ if it is rejected, and the process continues, giving rise to more costly effort by the investment bank.

We can now investigate a range of different contract specifications between the investment bank and their client to assess the impact this has on the incentives of the client to accept or reject the original offer, as well as the advice of the investment bank.

Fixed Fee Contracts Let us assume that, regardless of the outcome of the merger, the investment bank charges a fixed fee of F. The client would want to accept the initial offer V_L if its net surplus exceed that of waiting for an improved offer; thus,

$$V_L - F \geq \pi V_H - F. \tag{6.20}$$

This easily solves for

$$\pi \leq \pi_C^* = \frac{V_L}{V_H}. \tag{6.21}$$

Thus, if the likelihood of an improved offer is sufficiently low, it is better to accept the current offer.

Banks would advise the offer to be accepted if their profits from their client doing so exceeds that of advising them to hold out for a better offer, giving us

$$F - C^* \geq F - C \tag{6.22}$$

and as $C^* < C$, the investment bank advises that the current offer should always be accepted as this minimises the investment bank's costs. They do not gain additional revenue from suggesting to reject the initial offer but only incur additional costs, leading to this result. If $\pi_C^* < \pi \leq 1$, the advice of the bank is not in the interest of their client, and a conflict of interest between investment banks and clients emerges.

Conditional Fee Contract With conditional fee contracts, a fixed fee F is only payable if the merger is completed; thus, the clients would accept the initial offer V_L if

$$V_L - F \geq \pi \left(V_H - F\right). \tag{6.23}$$

Here we take into account that if V_L is accepted, the merger goes ahead with the surplus guaranteed and the fee F having to be paid. If, however, the initial offer is rejected, a better offer is only made with probability π, and only then is the fee F payable. This condition easily solves for

$$\pi \leq \pi_C^{**} = \frac{V_L - F}{V_H - F} < \pi_C^* \tag{6.24}$$

Using a conditional fee contract, the initial merger offer is less readily accepted than with fixed fee contracts. This is because the client only has to pay the fee if a better offer is received, lowering its cost of rejecting the initial offer as no fee is payable if no improved offer materialises. Alternatively, if the client is making the offer, then no fee is payable if the alternative offer were to be rejected by their target.

The investment bank would suggest that the offer is accepted with the conditional fee contract if

$$F - C^* \geq \pi F - C. \tag{6.25}$$

If the initial offer is accepted, it is guaranteed the fee income F, but if the offer is rejected, it faces higher costs C due to the additional work to secure a better offer, which only materialises with probability π, but would nevertheless earn the same fee. This condition solves for

$$\pi \leq \pi_B^* = 1 + \frac{C - C^*}{F} \tag{6.26}$$

and hence $\pi_B^* > 1$, making sure that the investment bank advises that any initial offer is accepted. Thus, when entering a conditional fee contract, there is a conflict of interest between the investment bank and their client if $\pi_C^{**} < \pi \leq 1$. Using a conditional fee contract increases the range of this conflict of interest compared to a fixed fee contract as $\pi_C^{**} < \pi_C^*$.

Contingent Fee Contract With a contingent fee contract, the investment bank receives a fraction f of the surplus if the merger is completed. Hence, the client would accept the offer if

$$V_L - fV_L \geq \pi \left(V_H - fV_H \right). \tag{6.27}$$

Again, if the initial offer V_L is accepted, the surplus V_L less the fee to the investment bank fV_L is guaranteed, while when holding out for an improved offer V_H, this materialises only with probability π. The condition solves for

$$\pi \leq \pi_C^{***} = \frac{V_L}{V_H} = \pi_C^*. \tag{6.28}$$

Clients therefore have the same threshold of accepting the initial offer as with the fixed fee contract.

The investment bank will advise their client to accept the initial offer if their profits are higher than if they advise them to hold out for a better offer; thus,

$$fV_L - C^* \geq \pi f V_H - C. \tag{6.29}$$

If the initial offer is accepted, the fee is received with certainty, while if their client holds out for a better offer, it is only obtained if such an offer is made, while incurring higher costs. This condition can be solved for

$$\pi \leq \pi_B^{***} = \frac{V_L}{V_H} + \frac{C - C^*}{fV_H}. \tag{6.30}$$

If $f \left(V_H - V_L \right) > C - C^*$, then $\pi_B^{***} < 1$, and the investment bank would not always advise their client to accept the initial offer. This threshold for accepting the initial offer takes into account that the additional revenue of the bank from the improved offer has to exceed its increase in costs. Thus, with a contingent fee contract, the conflict in interest is reduced to the area $\pi_C^{***} = \pi_C^* < \pi < \pi_B^{***} < 1$ as the threshold above which the investment bank advises to hold out for a better offer is lowered, although not fully to the level of their client. A conflict of interest could only be avoided if $C = C^*$ and no additional costs are incurred by the investment bank if an offer is rejected. Using a contingent fee contract gives the least distortion of all considered contracts with the investment bank.

We can rearrange Eqs. (6.28) and (6.30) in terms of the minimum offer V_L^i required and for a given π we get for clients and investment banks, respectively, that

$$V_L \geq V_L^C = \pi V_H, \tag{6.31}$$
$$V_L \geq V_L^B = \pi V_H - \frac{C - C^*}{f}.$$

We thus see that the investment banks would advise to accept lower offers than would be optimal for their clients. This result is driven by the fact that holding out for a higher offer makes it less likely for the investment bank to obtain their fee income, in addition to facing higher costs. This must be balanced against the higher fee income if the improved offer is realised. However, this compares favourably with fixed and conditional fee contracts, where investment banks would advise to accept any offer that is made.

The surplus V_i can be interpreted as the difference between the value of the merged client and the purchase price for acquires, $V_i = \overline{V} - P_i$, while for a target, it might be the difference between the purchase price and the current value, $V_i = P_i - \overline{V}$. Hence, V_i^j denotes the highest price at which on offer should be made by acquirers and the lowest to be accepted by a target. If following investment bank advice, acquirers will overpay for their target, and targets accept offers that are too low, compared to their optimal decision. Contingent fee contracts retain a conflict of interest between investment banks and their clients, but this is less pronounced than with fixed or conditional fee contracts.

For convenience, we here look at the fee being determined in relation to the surplus added by a merger, while in most contracts, this is specified as a fraction of the merger value. Assume a merger generates additional value $V_i = \overline{V} - P_i$ from the perspective of a buyer, with the post-merger value being $\overline{V}$ and the price paid is P_i. Then a fee on the merger value P_i, $\overline{f}$, can be determined such that $fV_i = \overline{V} - \left(1 + \overline{f}\right) P_i$, or $f = \frac{\overline{V}}{V_i} - \left(1 + \overline{f}\right) \frac{P_i}{V_i}$. From a target's perspective, we have similarly with the value pre-merger at $\overline{V}$ that $fV_i = \left(1 - \overline{f}\right) P_i - \overline{V}$ giving $f = \left(1 - \overline{f}\right) \frac{P_i}{V_i} - \frac{\overline{V}}{V_i}$. Hence, the fee as defined here has its equivalent in the fee defined as a fraction of the merger value.

Summary Contingent fee contracts minimise the conflicts of interest between investment banks and their clients regarding the advice on whether to accept a merger offer or hold out and hoping for a better offer. While these incentives are not fully aligned, the distortions of fixed and conditional fee contracts are higher as in both cases, the investment bank would advise to accept any offer that was made. The reason for contingent fee contracts causing less conflicts of interest is that the investment bank does have benefits from waiting for a better offer and their revenue increases if a better offer is forthcoming. However, this is limited by the fact that obtaining the fee becomes uncertain and their costs increase, resulting in the conflict of interest not being fully eliminated. Fixed and conditional fee contracts do not provide the investment bank with any benefits from an improved offer, but their costs increase, and in the case of conditional fee contracts, the obtaining of the fee becomes uncertain, making it optimal for the investment bank to advise to accept any offer that is made. Contingent fee contracts are a mechanism to minimise the conflicts of interest between investment banks and their clients.

Reading Gravelle and Waterson (1993)

6.3 Break-up fees

Let us assume that at the time the contract between the investment bank and the customer is negotiated, the likelihood of the merger succeeding and the size of the surplus are unknown. This would be the case if the investment bank has to conduct a more detailed due diligence to assess the value of the merger and its likelihood of succeeding. The merger commences with probability π, having distribution $H(\cdot)$, and generates value V with distribution $G(\cdot)$. The investment bank has fixed due diligent costs C_0, and if working on the merger properly, they face additional costs C. They charge a fee of F_1 if the merger succeeds, and if it is abandoned after they have done their due diligence and advised their client accordingly, they receive F_0.

Let us assume the investment bank knows the characteristics π and V after conducting their due diligence investigation, then, if taking the merger beyond the due diligence stage, their profits are given by

$$\hat{\Pi}_B = \pi F_1 + (1 - \pi) F_0 - C, \tag{6.32}$$

consisting of the fee F_1 if the merger commences, which happens with probability π, and the fee F_0 if they recommend to abandon the merger at some point, which occurs with probability $1 - \pi$. As they proceed beyond the due diligence stage, they face the additional costs C.

Once working on the merger after having completed the due diligence assessment, the investment bank learns π and V. It will at that point only continue if $\hat{\Pi}_B \geq 0$ or

$$\pi \geq \pi^* = \frac{C - F_0}{F_1 - F_0}. \tag{6.33}$$

Ex ante, when negotiating the contract without having completed the due diligence assessment, the values for π and V are not yet known. Including their due diligence costs C_0, total investment bank profits are then determined from

$$\Pi_B = \int_0^{+\infty} \int_{\pi^*}^1 \hat{\Pi}_B dH(\pi) dG(V) - C_0 \tag{6.34}$$

and in perfect competition we have $\Pi_B = 0$. We note that the investment bank only advises the merger to commence if $\pi \geq \pi^*$, and hence only in this case will they be able to generate any profits.

After the due diligence assessment of the investment bank and learning the values of π and V, the client has expected profits of

$$\hat{\Pi}_C = \pi (V - F_1) - (1 - \pi) F_0 \tag{6.35}$$

and when negotiating the contract prior to the due diligence assessment by the investment bank, and thus not knowing π and V, this is

$$\Pi_C = \int_0^{+\infty} \int_{\pi^*}^1 \hat{\Pi}_C dH(\pi) dG(V), \tag{6.36}$$

where again only for $\pi \geq \pi^*$ profits are generated, as only then the merger is advised to be pursued further.

Customers seek to maximise their profits Π_C from the contract, subject to the bank offering a contract, i.e., $\Pi_B = 0$. Hence, our objective function is

$$\mathcal{L} = \Pi_C + \zeta \Pi_B \tag{6.37}$$

where ζ is the Lagrange multiplier. Noting that from Eq. (6.33) we easily get

$$\begin{aligned} \frac{\partial \pi^*}{\partial F_0} &= \frac{C - F_i}{(F_1 - F_0)^2}, \\ \frac{\partial \pi^*}{\partial F_1} &= -\frac{C - F_0}{(F_1 - F_0)^2}, \end{aligned} \tag{6.38}$$

and inserting Eqs. (6.32), (6.34), (6.35), and (6.36) into Eq. (6.37), noting Eq. (6.38) and applying the Leibniz integral rule, we get the first-order conditions for the optimal fees as

$$\begin{aligned} \frac{\partial \mathcal{L}}{\partial F_0} = &- \int_0^{+\infty} \frac{C - F_1}{(F_1 - F_0)^2} \left(\frac{C - F_0}{F_1 - F_0} V - C \right) g(\pi^*) dH(V) \\ &- (1 - \zeta) \int_0^{+\infty} \int_{\pi^*}^1 (1 - \pi) dG(\pi) dH(V) = 0, \end{aligned} \tag{6.39}$$

$$\frac{\partial \mathcal{L}}{\partial F_1} = -\int_0^{+\infty} \frac{C - F_0}{(F_1 - F_0)^2} \left(\frac{C - F_0}{F_1 - F_0} V - C \right) g\left(\pi^*\right) dH\left(V\right)$$
$$- \left(1 - \zeta\right) \int_0^{+\infty} \int_{\pi^*}^1 \left(1 - \pi\right) dG\left(\pi\right) dH\left(V\right) = 0,$$

where $g(\cdot)$ denotes the density function of π. One solution is to set $\zeta = 1$, and then the last term in both expressions can be eliminated. Choosing $\zeta = 1$ implies that joint profits are maximised as we maximise the expression $\mathcal{L} = \Pi_C + \Pi_B$. The integral will then be zero if each integrand is zero; hence,

$$\frac{C - F_0}{F_1 - F_0} V - C = 0$$

in both conditions. This easily solves for

$$F_1 = F_0 + \frac{C - F_0}{C} V. \tag{6.40}$$

Requiring the profits of the clients to be non-negative, $\hat{\Pi}_C \geq 0$, to continue with the merger, we get after inserting Eq. (6.40) into Eq. (6.35) that

$$\pi \geq \pi^{**} = \frac{C}{V}. \tag{6.41}$$

Inserting Eq. (6.40) into Eq. (6.33), we see that $\pi^* = \pi^{**}$. This implies that investment banks and their clients want to proceed with the merger under the same conditions, and hence there is no conflict of interest between the preferences of the client and the advice of the investment bank.

We can now solve for the breakup fee F_0 by using the requirement that banks break even, i.e., $\Pi_B = 0$. Inserting Eq. (6.40) into Eq. (6.32), we get, when using Eq. (6.34), that

$$\left(C - F_0\right) \int_0^{+\infty} \int_{\pi^*}^1 \left(\frac{\pi V}{C} - 1 \right) dG\left(\pi\right) dH\left(V\right) - C_0 = 0, \tag{6.42}$$

which we can rewrite as

$$F_0 = C + \frac{C_0}{\int_0^{+\infty} \int_{\pi^*}^1 \left(1 - \frac{\pi}{\pi^*}\right) dG\left(\pi\right) dH\left(V\right)}, \tag{6.43}$$

using the definition of π^* and noting that $\pi^* = \pi^{**}$. Noting that $\pi > \pi^*$, we see that $F_0 < C_0$ if $C < C_0 \left(1 - \frac{1}{\int_0^{+\infty} \int_{\pi^*}^1 \left(1 - \frac{\pi}{\pi^*}\right) dG(\pi) dH(V)} \right)$. In the case that the additional costs after having conducted the due diligence assessment are not too high, noting that the term in brackets is above 1, investment banks will not recover their full due diligence costs from breakup fees. If these costs are higher though, the breakup fee will fully cover the due diligence costs, and given that $\Pi_B = 0$, this fee will partly subsidise the full costs of the investment bank if the merger is taken further. This way, the investment bank will not prematurely advise their client to abandon a merger to avoid not being able to recover the costs the investment bank faced, aligning their incentives with that of their clients. Similarly, if the full costs C are small, the investment bank might advise their client to proceed with a merger too often, hoping to obtain the higher fee F_1, and the smaller breakup fee balances this incentive.

Summary If we assume that investment banks only learn about the key properties of a merger, the probability of success, and the deal value, after conducting a due diligence assessment, contracts with a breakup fee are optimal. The breakup fee is used to align the incentives of the customer and the investment bank to continue or abandon the merger after learning the relevant information. Hence, breakup fees are a mechanism to ensure clients receive unbiased advice in mergers and acquisitions, although such a contractual arrangement makes it more costly for their clients to abandon a merger that turns out to be too low value or too unlikely to proceed.

Reading Dana and Spier (1993)

Conclusions

The optimal fee contracts from the perspective of clients are those that generate advice most closely aligned to their own interests. As such contracts are providing the most value to clients, they also allow investment banks to charge the highest fees, thus making the highest profits. In a competitive market, it would not be more profitable for an investment bank to offer an alternative contract specification that provides clients with more biased advice.

The conflict of interest is that if investment banks might advise to not proceed with a merger, then with conditional and contingent fee contracts, the investment bank would not earn any revenue. This would induce investment banks to advise their clients to proceed with the merger, even if this is not in their clients' interest. On the other hand, in a contingent fee contract, the higher fee arising from a higher merger value might induce investment banks to reject an offer and hope for an improvement to emerge. Again, this might not be in the best interest of their client. When rejecting an offer and holding out for a better offer, this will increase the costs to investment banks as the new offer needs to be evaluated, providing incentives to advise accepting an offer. Contingent fee contracts balance these aspects best and in most cases are the contract form that mostly closely aligns the interests of investment banks and their clients.

Such a contingent fee contract retains an incentive for investment banks to advise clients to proceed with a merger, even if this might not be in the best interests of their client. The reason is that the loss of revenue if no improved offer is made will reduce the profits of the investment bank substantially. Including a breakup fee, where the investment bank is paid a certain fraction of the fee if the merger does not proceed, can align the interests of investment banks and their clients further. The existence of the breakup fee allows the investment bank to advise rejecting an offer while still ensuring they receive some revenue, even if reduced compared to the full fee of proceeding with the current offer. Indeed, contingent fees with breakup clauses are the dominant contract form in mergers and acquisitions advisory.

It is not only the contract form chosen to align the interests of investment banks and their clients that prevents investment banks from providing advice that is too much catering towards their own objectives. Investment banks have to maintain a reputation for the quality of their advice in order to secure future business. Clients and prospective clients would be reluctant to rely on advice given by an investment bank that is known to provide advice that serves more their own interests than that of their clients. Such a reputation would not remain limited to mergers and acquisitions advisory but spill over into other business areas such as securities underwriting and investment advice. Hence, it will be a combination of contractual arrangements and the need to retain a reputation for good advice that ensures clients are provided with advice that is (mostly) aligned with their interests.

7 Securities Underwriting

The underwriting of securities encompasses the support for the issue of new securities to members of the public (public placement) or a wider, but selected, investor base (private placement). The types of securities underwritten can be very varied. It is most common in underwriting research to consider the issuing of shares to the general public for a subsequent listing on a stock exchange, a so-called Initial Public Offering (IPO). Shares by companies already listed on a stock exchanged may also be offered in a Seasoned Equity Offering (SEO), which will usually form part of raising additional capital for the company. In the case of both IPOs and SEOs, it is common for new shares to be created that are then sold, but we might well see the sale of shares already held by other investors. Another common security to be issued is a bond, either by companies, governments, or comparable public bodies. A wide variety of other securities are underwritten by investment banks, such as convertible bonds, warrant bonds, asset backed securities, collateralized debt obligations, or catastrophe bonds.

The role of the investment bank is to evaluate the security to be issued and assign a fair value to it. This evaluation will in general be conducted with the help of potential investors who provide the investment bank with information on their opinion about the security. Such information might be sought informally by contacting selected investors to which the investment bank has established a suitable relationship, or it may be enhanced by a more formal, but still non-binding, expression of interest in the securities (book building), on whose basis the value can be established.

Having determined the value of the security, it will then be offered to either the general public or the selected investor base. The investment bank will at this point support the issuer of the security in marketing (road shows) to solicit bids for the security. At this point the investment bank's role might be either limited to providing this support (best efforts contract) or the involvement will go further in that the investment bank actually purchases the securities and sells them on to investors (firm

A. Krause, *Theoretical Foundations of Investment Banking*, Springer Texts in Business and Economics, https://doi.org/10.1007/978-3-031-58060-4_7

commitment contract). The optimality of such contractual arrangements is assessed in Sect. 7.1.

Given the central role of information in determining the value of securities, which will then subsequently form the basis for the offer price, it is essential that investment banks have incentives to obtain such information and make use of their network of potential investors to obtain a thorough understanding of the market perception and attract the most widespread interest in the security. To this effect, Sect. 7.2 will investigate whether it is optimal to tender bids by investment banks for the underwriting business or approach an investment bank directly. We will also assess whether it is optimal to appoint more than one investment bank to underwrite the issue (syndicate formation).

Once the value of the security has been determined, the investment bank, in collaboration with the issuer, will determine the actual offer price and allocate the security to investors. At this point, it is common to underprice the security, which means that the offer price is below the value of the security, which is assumed to be reflected in the price once trading in the security commences. Such underpricing is particularly prominent in IPOs but can be found in most securities. Such underpricing reduces the proceeds the issuer obtains and also the fee the investment bank charges. We will discuss in Sect. 7.3 how underpricing can be used to cover a wider range of possible costs investment banks face but also how it can contribute to additional profits for the investment bank. Section 7.4 will explore how underpricing is increased to allow investment banks to sell more securities than originally planned and generating additional profits for investment banks. Other aspects to consider in underwriting is the choice of the underwriter, which securities to actually underwrite (Sect. 7.5), and the impact any additional benefits the issuing of securities might have on other areas of business of the bank, most notably the lending of universal banks as we consider in Sect. 7.6.

When underwriting securities, investment banks are more involved than acting as advisors; they interact with potential investors and seek to obtain information from them to facilitate the valuation of the security and thus determine the offer price. Investors providing such information can also be rewarded with the allocation of securities, which should provide them with instant profits as investment banks routinely recommend offer prices that are below the value they have obtained. The costs of underwriting to issuers are therefore not only limited to the underwriting fee charged by the investment bank directly but will include the lost revenue due to underpricing. The following models will analyse the possible motivations for such decisions by investment banks, the extent of any conflicts of interest, as well as the possible benefits to issuers.

7.1 Underwriting Contracts

When underwriting securities, investment banks seek to help issuers in selling their securities. A central aspect is the underwriting contract, which basically comes in two forms. In a best efforts contract, investment banks seek to advise issuers and promote their securities to investors, but whether all securities can be sold and at which price is not guaranteed. In contrast to that, the firm commitment contract requires the investment bank to buy the security from the issuer at an agreed price and will then in turn seek to sell these securities to investors. In the former case, the investment bank will charge a fee for their services, while in the latter case, the difference in the price the investment bank pays the issuer and the price obtained from investors compensates the investment bank. Section 7.1.1 will investigate which of these contracts is optimal.

Investment banks need information on the value of a security to advice the issuer accordingly and, in the case of firm commitment contracts, to determine the price they are paying the issuer for their securities. Such information the investment bank can accumulate through their own research, exploring documents supplied by the issuer, their general knowledge of the market, and discussions with potential investors. However, such an analysis will always be limited and the full market opinion difficult to obtain. In order to gather information more reliably, a book-building mechanism has been developed, which seeks to extract information from investors more reliably. Section 7.1.2 will analyse how book-building is beneficial not only for the investment bank but primarily to the issuer itself.

7.1.1 Firm Commitment and Best Efforts Contracts

Firm commitment contracts offer the issuers of a security the certainty of selling all their securities at a set price. It is the investment bank buying these securities, and it is then them who seek to re-sell them to investors. Hence, the risk of selling the securities to investors has been shifted from the issuer to the investment bank. The price the bank pays the issuer of the security will be below the price it expects to sell the securities at. This difference is referred to as the underwriting spread and provides the compensation for investment banks in issuing these securities; no additional fee is payable. In contrast, with a best efforts contract, investment banks only advise the issuer on the process, determine the pricing, and facilitate the marketing of the issue, but do not buy the securities themselves. The issuer sells the securities directly to investors and is thus not guaranteed a price for them, nor is it guaranteed that all securities are actually sold. For their advice, investment banks will charge a fee, usually expressed as a fraction of the total proceeds from the issue. Given these two contractual forms, neglecting any possible conflicts of interest, we will investigate which type of contract is preferred by investment banks and issuers.

Let us assume that the true value of the securities issued is unknown, but the value has a mean of V and the issuer determines a variance of σ_C^2 from the assessment of the securities, while the variance is σ_B^2 based on the assessment of the investment bank, where we assume that $\sigma_B^2 < \sigma_C^2$. Hence, investment banks are better at evaluating securities. In a firm commitment contract, the issuer receives a pre-determined amount S, while for a best efforts contract, they receive a fraction $1 - f$ of the value of the securities, with f being the fee charged by the investment bank.

Preferred Contract Form With investment banks and issuers having risk aversion z, we have the expected utility of the investment bank and issuer, respectively, for a best efforts contract given as

$$U_B = fV - \frac{1}{2}zf^2V^2\sigma_B^2, \tag{7.1}$$

$$U_C = (1-f)\,V - \frac{1}{2}z\,(1-f)^2\,V^2\sigma_C^2.$$

The investment bank obtains an expected revenue of fV while facing the risks on this amount, which has a variance of $f^2V^2\sigma_B^2$. The issuer receives the amount of $(1-f)\,V$ after paying the fee fV to the investment bank, and for this amount, the variance is $(1-f)^2\,V^2\sigma_C^2$, reducing their utility.

For a firm commitment contract, we similarly have

$$\hat{U}_B = V - S - \frac{1}{2}zV^2\sigma_B^2, \tag{7.2}$$

$$\hat{U}_C = S,$$

and investment banks indirectly charge the underwriting spread $V-S$, as they resell the security at a higher value V after obtaining them from the company at a price S. With the investment bank buying the whole issue, they are now exposed to a variance of $V^2\sigma_B^2$. Issuers receive a fixed payment of S and are not exposed to any risks, nor are there any fees to be paid as the investment bank is compensated by the underwriting spread $V-S$.

The investment bank prefers a firm commitment contract over a best efforts contract if their expected utility is higher, $\hat{U}_B \geq U_B$, which solves for

$$S \leq S^* = (1-f)\,V - \frac{1}{2}z\left(1-f^2\right)V^2\sigma_B^2. \tag{7.3}$$

Similarly, issuers prefer firm commitment contracts if $\hat{U}_C \geq U_C$; hence, we require that

$$S \geq S^{**} = (1-f)\,V - \frac{1}{2}z\,(1-f)^2\,V^2\sigma_C^2. \tag{7.4}$$

For a firm commitment contract to be optimal for both the issuer and the investment bank, we require that the price the issuer obtains is chosen such that $S^{**} \leq S \leq S^*$. For a possible solution, we need to ensure that $S^* \geq S^{**}$, which is the case if $\frac{\sigma_C^2}{\sigma_B^2} \geq \frac{1+f}{1-f}$. Hence, if the valuation uncertainty of the investment bank, σ_B^2, is sufficiently small compared to the valuation uncertainty of the issuer, a firm commitment contract will be optimal for issuers and investment banks. In all other cases, they will not be able to agree on a contract that is jointly optimal.

Of course, a contract does not only have to be better than another contract; it must also be profitable in its own right. Thus, we will investigate next under what conditions best effort and firm commitment contracts are feasible in the sense that they are profitable.

Feasibility of Underwriting Contracts For best efforts contracts to be viable, we need that it is profitable for both the investment bank and the issuer; hence, we require that $U_B \geq 0$ and $U_C \geq 0$, which implies that the fee f needs to be selected such that

$$1 - \frac{2}{zV\sigma_B^2} \leq f \leq \frac{2}{zV\sigma_C^2}, \tag{7.5}$$

which only has a possible solution if $1 - \frac{2}{zV\sigma_B^2} \leq \frac{2}{zV\sigma_C^2}$, which can be solved for

$$\frac{1}{\sigma_B^2} + \frac{1}{\sigma_C^2} \geq \frac{1}{2}zV. \tag{7.6}$$

Only if the valuation of the security can be done sufficiently precisely by either the company itself or the investment bank is a best efforts contract feasible. We also note that a larger issue, a high V, requires a more precise valuation to overcome the high risks the issuer as well as the investment bank are exposed to.

For the firm commitment contract, these viability constraints are $\hat{U}_B \geq 0$ and $\hat{U}_C \geq 0$, giving us that the price the investment bank pays the issuer must fulfill the condition that

$$0 \leq S \leq V - \frac{1}{2}zV^2\sigma_B^2, \tag{7.7}$$

and thus for a possible solution, we require $0 \leq V - \frac{1}{2}zV^2\sigma_B^2$, or

$$\frac{1}{\sigma_B^2} \geq \frac{1}{2}zV. \tag{7.8}$$

Compared to the restriction on best efforts contracts as shown in Eq. (7.6), this restriction is tighter as the term $\frac{1}{\sigma_C^2}$ is not present. Hence, investment banks need to be able to value the security even more precisely than with a best efforts contract. For securities that investment banks can value sufficiently precisely, firm commitment contracts are feasible, while for securities that cannot be valued precisely enough, only best effort contracts can be used. If neither the company issuing the securities nor the investment bank can value the security precisely, it will not be underwritten by an investment bank.

Underwriting Spread If the firm commitment contract is optimal for the investment bank, Eq. (7.3) implies that the underwriting spread $V - S$ is restricted by S^*, and hence

$$V - S \geq V - S^* = fV + \frac{1}{2}z\left(1 - f^2\right)V^2\sigma_B^2, \tag{7.9}$$

which is increasing in the uncertainty of the valuation of the security by the investment bank, σ_B^2, as this reflects the risk the investment bank is exposed to when seeking to sell the securities to investors. Thus, securities that are more difficult to value should have a larger underwriting spread.

If the firm commitment contract is chosen by the issuer, then we get from Eq. (7.4) that the underwriting spread of the firm commitment contract must fulfill

$$V - S \leq V - S^{**} = fV + \frac{1}{2}z\,(1 - f)^2\,V^2\sigma_C^2, \tag{7.10}$$

where the upper limit of the underwriting spread is increasing in the valuation uncertainty of the issuer, σ_C^2. The issuer is willing to accept an underwriting spread as this eliminates the valuation risk. Therefore, an underwriting spread can be chosen that fulfills $fV + \frac{1}{2}z\left(1 - f^2\right)V^2\sigma_B^2 \leq V - S \leq fV + \frac{1}{2}z\,(1 - f)^2\,V^2\sigma_C^2$. This spread will be strictly positive and can be set at the lower end if investment banks are acting competitively and at the upper end if investment banks can extract all surplus from issuers.

The relative underwriting spread, $\frac{V-S}{V}$, is generally increasing in the value of the issue, V, to compensate for the higher risks investment banks and issuers are taking. It is, however, often that with larger issues, the valuation can be done more precisely due to more information being available about the securities, reducing the underwriting spread through a reduction in σ_B^2 and σ_C^2.

Summary Companies issuing securities and the underwriting investment bank will agree on firm commitment contracts if the investment bank can reduce the valuation uncertainty sufficiently; otherwise, the best efforts contract is preferred. This arises from the higher risk an investment bank takes in firm commitment contracts by buying the securities directly, while in best efforts contracts, the exposure is limited to the fee income; in contrast, issuers reduce their risk exposure in firm commitment contracts as the investment bank buys the entire issue as an agreed price. As investment banks can value securities more precisely, this increases the overall welfare. The resulting underwriting spread compensates the investment bank for the additional risk it takes on, and the issuer is willing to accept this amount as its risk is reduced.

However, firm commitment contracts are only feasible if the investment bank can value the security with sufficient precision, while this constraint is less binding for best efforts contracts, where the ability of the company to assess their own securities is also considered. Thus, where the firm commitment contract is not feasible, the issuer and investment bank may settle for a best efforts contract. The dominance of firm commitment contracts in the issue of securities suggests that these conditions for their feasibility are commonly met.

Reading Mandelker and Raviv (1977).

7.1.2 Book-Building

It is common that investment banks approach selected potential investors in a security and invite them to submit bids indicating their interest. Such bids are non-binding, but it is generally expected that investors will honour these in the subsequent formal bids. These bids by selected investors are then used to determine a pricing range for the security before formal bids by any investors are invited; it is at this stage that investors previously approached are expected to submit similar bids again. The allocation of the security will then be based on the bids received from all investors, where it is common that previously approached investors are given priority in the allocation. This process is called book-building. We will be analysing the impact book-building has on the offer price of securities and compare this with mechanisms that allocate securities directly.

Let us assume that we have N informed investors, each receiving either a high (H) or low (L) signal on the value of the security, V, which is uniformly distributed over $\left[\underline{V}; \overline{V}\right]$. Normalising this variable for convenience, we define

$$\hat{V} = \frac{V - \underline{V}}{\overline{V} - \underline{V}}, \tag{7.11}$$

which is uniformly distributed on [0; 1]. Let h denote the number of high signals H that are received from the N investors, where obviously $0 \leq h \leq N$. Using Bayesian learning we obtain, when following the derivation in Welch (1992), that

$$\begin{aligned} E\left[\hat{V}|h\right] &= \frac{h+1}{N+2}, \\ Prob\,(h|H) &= \frac{2\,(h+1)}{N\,(N+1)}, \\ Prob\,(h|L) &= \frac{2\,(N-h)}{N\,(N+1)}. \end{aligned} \tag{7.12}$$

In obtaining these result, we assume that $Prob\left(H|\hat{V}\right) = \hat{V}$, and hence, the probability of obtaining a high signal if the true value of the security is $\hat{V}$ is given by $\hat{V}$. This allows us to transform the discrete observation of a high or low signal into a continuous value. Furthermore, assume that all numbers h of high signals are equally likely; hence, $Prob\,(h) = \frac{1}{N+1}$, such that $Prob\left(h \geq \hat{h}\right) = 1 - \frac{\hat{h}}{N+1}$. The second (third) expression in Eq. (7.12) denotes the probability that h high signals are observed by the other investors, if the current trader receives a high (low) signal himself, and the first expression provides us with the expected value of the normalised value of the security if h high signals are received.

We will now first evaluate as benchmarks the efficient pricing and then the price resulting out of a standard bidding process, before modelling the book-building process in more detail.

Efficient Pricing We assume that the issue price S is set such that it reflects the information of the market; thus, with h^* high signals, we set

$$S = E\left[\hat{V}|h^*\right]. \tag{7.13}$$

The issuer will sell its Q securities if at least h^* positive signals are received, indicating that at price S, the full issue can be sold. Thus, the issue is only sold if $h > h^*$, and then the issuer obtains $E\left[\hat{V}|h^*\right]$ for each of the Q securities, given total expected proceeds to the issuer of

$$\begin{aligned}\Pi_C &= Prob\left(h \geq h^*\right) E\left[\hat{V}|h^*\right] Q \\ &= \left(1 - \frac{h^*}{N+1}\right) \frac{h^*+1}{N+2} Q,\end{aligned} \tag{7.14}$$

when inserting from Eq. (7.12). If $h < h^*$, the issue will be withdrawn, and the issuer receives no proceeds at all. The issuer will select a threshold h^* such that its expected proceeds are maximised, requiring that

$$\frac{\partial \Pi_C}{\partial h^*} = \frac{N - 2h^*}{(N+1)(N+2)} Q = 0, \tag{7.15}$$

or

$$h^* = \frac{N}{2}. \tag{7.16}$$

The issuer would want half the informed investors to provide positive signals in order to maximise its proceeds. Inserting this result into Eqs. (7.13) and (7.12), we easily get

$$S = \frac{1}{2} \tag{7.17}$$

which is the unconditional expected value of $\hat{V}$, which as a normalised variable was uniformly distributed on [0; 1]. Thus, the offer would be priced fairly. Furthermore, we get from Eq. (7.14) that the total proceeds are given by

$$\Pi_C = \frac{1}{4}\frac{N+2}{N+1}Q, \tag{7.18}$$

which, for large a large number of informed investors, N, simplifies to $\Pi_C \approx \frac{1}{4}Q$.

It has to be noted that the price $S = \frac{1}{2}$ is only obtained if the issue is sold, as we assumed the issue has to be sold fully or it will be withdrawn; thus, obtaining any proceeds is not assured.

Bidding Process The signals investors have obtained are not directly observable, and while it might be efficient to base the pricing on obtaining at least h^* high signals, it is more common to let investors use their information to make a bid for the security. If investors submit bids to buy the security, they will do so based on their own signal, but they will also seek to infer the likelihood of h other investor obtaining high signals. $Prob\,(h|H)$ and $Prob\,(h|L)$ denote that h investors, including themselves, do obtain high signals, if they have obtained high and low signals themselves, respectively. The expected values of the security, depending on their own signal, are then given by

$$\begin{aligned} V_H &= \sum_{h=1}^{N} Prob\,(h-1|H)\,E\left[\hat{V}|h\right] \\ &= \sum_{h=1}^{N} \frac{2h}{N\,(N+1)}\frac{h+1}{N+2} \\ &= \frac{2}{N\,(N+1)\,(N+2)}\sum_{h=1}^{N}\left(h^2+h\right) \\ &= \frac{2}{3}, \\ V_L &= \sum_{h=1}^{N-1} Prob\,(h|L)\,E\left[\hat{V}|h\right] \\ &= \sum_{h=0}^{N-1} \frac{2\,(N-h)}{N\,(N+1)}\frac{h+1}{N+2} \\ &= \frac{2}{N\,(N+1)\,(N+2)}\sum_{h=1}^{N}\left(N+(N-1)\,h-h^2\right) \\ &= \frac{1}{3}, \end{aligned} \tag{7.19}$$

where we used that

$$\sum_{h=1}^{N} h = \frac{N(N+1)}{2},$$

$$\sum_{h=1}^{N} h^2 = \frac{N(N+1)(2N+1)}{6},$$

and we note that in Eq. (7.19) for V_H only $h-1$ other H signals are needed as the investor itself has an H signal and for V_L only $N-1$ signals H are possible as the investor has signal L.

Thus, investors value the stock at either $\frac{2}{3}$ if receiving signal H or $\frac{1}{3}$ if receiving signal L. An issue priced at $S \leq \frac{1}{3}$ would be fully sold as all investors value it higher. However, an offer price below $\frac{1}{3}$ would reduce the proceeds available to issuers, and hence, the lowest offer price that would be chosen is $S=\frac{1}{3}$. At $S>\frac{2}{3}$, no security would be sold as it is higher than any investor values it. Maximising revenue would either see $S=\frac{1}{3}$ or $S=\frac{2}{3}$, but at $S=\frac{2}{3}$, the issue might not be sold fully, and if we impose the constraint that all securities have to be sold, this constraint will require $S=\frac{1}{3}$. In this case, we easily obtain that

$$\Pi_C = \frac{1}{3}Q \tag{7.20}$$

which is higher than the efficient pricing in Eq. (7.18) for $N \geq 2$, while the offer price is lower at $\frac{1}{3}$ compared to $\frac{1}{2}$ with efficient pricing. The lower price here is compensated for by the certainty of selling the issue completely. Hence, the expected proceeds with bidding are higher, even though the price at $S=\frac{1}{3}$ is lower.

Using these results, we can now continue to analyse the book-building mechanism and compare its results with that of efficient pricing and the bidding process.

Book-Building Mechanism In book-building, investors submit their non-binding bids for the security, and by indicating the price they are willing to pay, they reveal whether the signal they received was high or low. However, we need to induce investors to reveal their information truthfully. If an investor receives signal H and reports this, we get his profits, consisting of the difference between the value defined by $E\left[\hat{V}|h+1\right]$ and the price at issue of the security, S_i^h, for h positive signals by other investors, as

$$\Pi_D^{HH} = \sum_{h=0}^{N-1} Prob(h|H)\left(E\left[\hat{V}|h+1\right] - S_H^h\right) Q_H, \tag{7.21}$$

where upon revealing the high signal, the investor will be allocated the quantity Q_H in the final allocation after the formal bids have been received. We take into account his own positive signal in the expected value and hence that $h + 1$ positive signals have been received in total, h, by other investors. If instead he reveals a low signal L, even though receiving the high signal, then his profits are given by

$$\Pi_D^{HL} = \sum_{h=0}^{N-1} Prob\,(h|H) \left(E\left[\hat{V}|h+1\right] - S_L^h\right) Q_L, \tag{7.22}$$

where he is allocated a quantity Q_L in the final allocation. The expected value of the security remains still being based on $h+1$ positive signals as the investor is well aware of the additional positive signal they have received, even if not disclosed. The offer price applied in this case will be S_L^h.

To induce the investor to reveal his signal truthfully, we need to ensure that $\Pi_D^{HH} \geq \Pi_D^{HL}$. Comparing the expressions in Eqs. (7.21) and (7.22), we see that $\Pi_D^{HH} \geq \Pi_D^{HL}$ if $S_H^h \leq S_L^h$ and $Q_L = Q_H$. In order as to not reduce the revenue by lowering the issue price and avoid a situation in which the offer price is reduced in response to a high signal, we set $S_H^h = S_L^h$ but instead set $Q_L \leq Q_H$ and thus obtain $\Pi_D^{HH} \geq \Pi_D^{HL}$, ensuring high signals are revealed truthfully. An investor having received a signal L would not claim to have received H as this in aggregate would increase the offer price without increasing the value of the security, reducing the investors profits.

Using Eq. (7.12) to obtain

$$E\left[\hat{V}|h+1\right] - E\left[\hat{V}|h\right] = \frac{1}{N+2}, \tag{7.23}$$

we can rewrite Eq. (7.22) as

$$\Pi_D^{HL} = \sum_{h=0}^{N-1} Prob\,(h|H) \left(E\left[\hat{V}|h\right] - S_L^h + \frac{1}{N+2}\right) Q_L. \tag{7.24}$$

The investment bank, on behalf of the issuer, now seeks to maximise the proceeds of the issue. Selling the whole issue Q, we need

$$Q = hQ_H + (N-h)\,Q_L \tag{7.25}$$

and the losses from selling the issue below its true value are identical to the profits of the investors buying the issue; hence

$$\hat{\Pi}_C = \sum_{h=0}^{N} Prob\,(h) \left(E\left[\hat{V}|h\right] - S_h\right) Q \tag{7.26}$$

$$= \sum_{h=0}^{N-1} \left(Prob\,(h+1) \left(E\left[\hat{V}|h+1\right] - S_{h+1}\right)(h+1)\,Q\right.$$

$$\left. + Prob\,(h) \left(E\left[\hat{V}|h\right] - S_h\right)(N-h)\,Q_L\right),$$

where we used that if $h = 0$, then no H signals are received and hence $Q_H = 0$ and if $h = N$, then no L signals are received and $Q_L = 0$. S_h here denotes the price applied if h signals are high.

We can now easily show that

$$Prob\,(h+1) = \frac{1}{N+1} = \frac{N}{2\,(h+1)} \frac{2\,(h+1)}{N\,(N+1)} \tag{7.27}$$

$$= \frac{N}{2\,(h+1)} Prob\,(h|H)\,,$$

$$Prob\,(h) = \frac{1}{N+1} = \frac{N}{2\,(N-h)} \frac{2\,(N-h)}{N\,(N+1)}$$

$$= \frac{N}{2\,(N-h)} Prob\,(h|L)\,.$$

Using these results, we can rewrite Eq. (7.26) as

$$\hat{\Pi}_C = \frac{N}{2} \sum_{h=0}^{N-1} \frac{Prob\,(h|H)}{N+2} Q_L \tag{7.28}$$

$$+ \frac{N}{2} \sum_{h=0}^{N-1} \left((Prob\,(h|H) + Prob\,(h|L)) \left(E\left[\hat{V}|h\right] - S_h\right)\right) Q_L$$

Minimising this expression can be achieved by setting $Q_L = 0$, or if $Q_L > 0$, then $S_h = E\left[\hat{V}|h\right]$, as $S_h \leq E\left[\hat{V}|h\right]$, and the price set cannot be set above the fundamental value, because this would impose losses on investors. If $hQ_H \geq Q$, then all securities can be allocated to investors with the high signal, and hence we would be able to set $Q_L = 0$ and $Q_H = \frac{Q}{h}$. If $hQ_H < Q$, then those investors with high signals will get their full allocation $Q_H = \overline{Q}$, and the remaining securities are allocated to investors with signal L, $Q_L = \frac{Q-h\overline{Q}}{N-h} > 0$ at price $S_h = E\left[\hat{V}|h\right]$. We focus on this more realistic case in the below analysis.

We thus have either $Q_L = 0$ or $S_h = E\left[\hat{V}|h\right]$, such that in Eq. (7.28), the second line vanishes, and the expression becomes

$$\hat{\Pi}_C = \frac{N}{2(N+2)} \sum_{h=0}^{Q-\overline{Q}} Prob(h|H) \frac{Q - h\overline{Q}}{N-h} \tag{7.29}$$

for the case that $Q_L > 0$ and $\hat{\Pi}_C = 0$ if $Q_L = 0$. The profits made for each security allocated are $E\left[\hat{V}|h\right] - S_h$, and with the profits given by $\hat{\Pi}_C$, these profits for each security will then be $\frac{\hat{\Pi}_C}{Q}$. Obviously, these two expressions for profits have to be identical; hence,

$$E\left[\hat{V}|h\right] - S_h = \frac{\hat{\Pi}_C}{Q} \tag{7.30}$$

and with $E\left[E\left[\hat{V}|h\right]\right] = E\left[\hat{V}\right] = \frac{1}{2}$, we find from solving Eq. (7.30) for S_h and taking expectations that the expected offer price is given by

$$E[S_h] = \frac{1}{2} - \frac{\hat{\Pi}_C}{Q}. \tag{7.31}$$

We now see from Eq. (7.29) that

$$\begin{aligned} \frac{\partial \hat{\Pi}_C}{\partial N} &= -\frac{1}{2(N+1)^2} \sum_{h+0}^{Q-\overline{Q}} \frac{2(h+1)}{N(N+1)} \frac{Q-h\overline{Q}}{N-h} \\ &\quad - \frac{N}{2(N+1)} \sum_{h=0}^{Q-\overline{Q}} \frac{2(h+1)\left(Q-h\overline{Q}\right)}{N^2(N+1)^2(N-h)^2} \\ &\quad \times \left(3N^2 + 2N - (2N-1)h\right) \\ &< 0 \end{aligned} \tag{7.32}$$

as the last term is positive due to $h \leq N < \frac{3N^2+2N}{2N+1}$. Hence, the more informed investors are available for an issue, the higher the offer price. The smallest possible number of investors, N, is such that $N\overline{Q} = Q$, i.e., if all investors have positive signals and just manage to buy the issue fully. In this case, we have $h = N = \frac{Q}{\overline{Q}}$. Inserting this expression into Eq. (7.29) gives us the highest possible profits as

$$\hat{\Pi}_C = \frac{Q}{2(N+2)} \tag{7.33}$$

and hence from Eq. (7.31), the lowest expected offer price is

$$E\left[S_h\right] = \frac{1}{2} - \frac{1}{2\left(N+2\right)} \geq \frac{1}{3}, \tag{7.34}$$

where the latter is the price emerging in the bidding process. Hence, the offer price in book-building is higher than in a bidding process, and as in both cases, the issue is guaranteed to be fully sold, and the proceeds obtained will be higher. The more informed investors, the higher the offer price will become as we see from Eq. (7.29) that $\lim_{N\rightarrow+\infty} \hat{\Pi}_C = 0$, and hence, $\lim_{N\rightarrow+\infty} E\left[S_h\right] = \frac{1}{2}$ and thus approaches the efficient pricing, while guaranteeing the issue to be sold, something which cannot be guaranteed in efficient pricing. The remaining lower offer price for a finite number of informed investors emerges as an incentive device to ensure they reveal their high signals correctly. The revealed information increases the offer price. Therefore, issuers would prefer book-building over a bidding process as this increases the proceeds they can obtain from the issue.

Using Eq. (7.23), we can write

$$\frac{1}{N+2} = E\left[\hat{V}|h+1\right] - E\left[\hat{V}|h\right] = \frac{E\left[V|h+1\right] - E\left[V|h\right]}{\overline{V} - \underline{V}}, \tag{7.35}$$

using that $\hat{V}$ is normalised and reverting back to the original value of the security, V. Using this expression, Eq. (7.29) becomes

$$\hat{\Pi}_C = \frac{N\left(\overline{V} - \underline{V}\right)}{E\left[V|h+1\right] - E\left[V|h\right]} \sum_{h=0}^{Q-\overline{Q}} \frac{2\left(h+1\right)}{N\left(N+1\right)} \frac{Q - h\overline{Q}}{N-h} \tag{7.36}$$

and we see immediately that as $\overline{V} - \underline{V}$, measuring the uncertainty about the value of the security, increases, the profits of investors increase, and hence, the offer price reduces. This is the result of the incentives to reveal information; if information asymmetry is higher, such as a from a wider range of possible values of the security, the potential benefits to informed investors concealing this information are higher. The lower offer price compensates them for giving up their higher benefits and ensures they are revealing their high signals truthfully.

Summary We have seen that the proceeds received by issuers are highest with book-building, which incentivises investors to reveal any high signals in order to ensure a higher allocation of securities and thus allows for a higher offer price while ensuring all securities are sold. Book-building is, however, only successful if the investment bank identifies a sufficient number of informed investors to obtain a sufficient number of high signals. Applying book-building as part of the underwriting process can help the investment bank reduce their and the issuer's uncertainty about the value of the security, ensuring it is sold at a fair price, compared to a bidding process. Of course, book-building will be part of the underwriting contract, which will be supplemented by either a best efforts contract for firm commitment contract. In the latter case, the results of book-building will inform the price the investment bank will pay the issuer prior to the public bidding for the security.

Reading Benveniste and Busaba (1997).

Resumé

If a book-building mechanism is employed in the underwriting of securities, it ensures issuers receive the highest proceeds while still selling all their securities. The reason is that informed investors are induced to reveal the information they hold truthfully, which allows the offer price to be based on the full and true information obtained from informed investors. It is most common that underwriting contracts are firm commitment contracts, where the bank pays the issuer a fixed amount for their securities. This amount will be determined mostly on the basis of the book-building process, reducing the risks to the investment bank substantially, which will also reduce the underwriting spread that is charged. Of course, any such spread will also have to cover the costs the investment bank faces in administering the issue of the security, including the use of their network of investors to solicit bids in the book-building process. These costs will also be included into the underwriting fee of a best efforts contract and thus will be taken into account when setting up any firm commitment contract. Of course, best efforts contracts can also include a book-building process; it is merely that the investment bank does not offer a fixed price to the issuer for the securities sold.

The choice of underwriting contract itself will depend on the investment bank's ability to reduce the valuation uncertainty of the security sufficiently, compared to the issuer itself. If the bank has a high enough ability in this regard, a firm commitment contract is optimal. A book-building process should reduce the valuation uncertainty substantially for both the investment bank and the issuer, reducing the advantage of investment banks. This in turn should result in firm commitment contracts being less commonly used. It might be, however, that investment banks are better at interpreting the results of book-building, retaining, or even increasing their advantage over issuers, making firm commitment contracts more likely to be agreed. Furthermore, it might be that when using their network of investors to obtain indicative bids in the book-building process, investment banks prefer to retain control over the sale of the securities to investors and therefore impose firm commitment contracts such that with the issuer having obtained their proceeds from the investment bank, and they are more able to react to market developments.

7.2 Appointing Underwriters

A key task of underwriters is to identify potential investors and induce them to subscribe to the securities issued and thereby obtain the highest possible offer price for their client. In doing so, investment banks will rely on their network of investors with whom they maintain contact for this purpose, besides other reasons arising from different business lines of the investment bank. Of course, an issuer should appoint an investment bank that has the most suitable network for their specific purpose, that is, an investment bank with contacts to the types of investors that would generally be interested in the security. However, identifying such investment banks might be problematic for issuers with limited experience, and the common approach by companies seeking to purchase products or services of significant value would be to put the purchase out to tender and then select the most suitable of the bids that are received. This practice seems to be uncommon when it comes to the appointment of underwriters, and Sect. 7.2.1 will argue that the efforts investment banks put into making their bids will be lower than when an underwriter is appointed directly without a tendering process, resulting in lower proceeds for the issuer even if the investment bank appointed might not be the best possible underwriter for them.

Given that investment banks rely on their network of investors to induce a high uptake of the underwritten security, it can be beneficial to appoint more than one investment bank in a syndicate as we will discuss in Sect. 7.2.2. Appointing more than one underwriter with the success depending on the efforts to identify potential investors of all investment banks jointly, individual underwriters might seek to free-ride on the efforts of other underwriters. We will see how the structure using a lead underwriter will allow for a syndicate size that is optimal for issuers of securities but that also avoids the free-riding problem.

7.2.1 Underwriter Selection

Issuers seek to appoint an investment bank as underwriter for their security issue. This can be done by direct appointment of an investment bank, where the issuer contacts a single investment bank and negotiates an underwriting contract with this specific investment bank. Alternatively, the issuer could invite a number of investment banks to provide them with offers, and they would select the offer that provides them with the highest net proceeds from the issue. A key element of such a bid by an investment bank would be the offer price they expect to achieve. In order to ascertain the offer price, investment banks have to gather information from potential investors on their willingness to buy the security. It is a common belief that competition between service providers improves the outcome for those using these services, here competition between investment banks to gain the underwriting business from the issuer.

Let us assume that the investment bank does not know the value V of the security but is aware that it is uniformly distributed in the interval from $\underline{V}$ to $\overline{V}$.

In order to sell the entire issue, the price must be chosen such that at least M investors are willing to buy the security. In order to gain an understanding of the market perception of the issue, the investment bank contacts $N \geq M$ investors and establishes the price at which they are willing to buy the security, assuming that this willingness will result in an actual purchase if the issue proceeds. The price that is determined will be that of the Mth highest submission by investors. As M investors believe the security to have a value at or above this price, they will purchase it, thus ensuring the issue is sold. At the same time, the proceeds available to the issuer is maximised as this is the highest price that can be chosen to sell the entire issue.

Issuers can now select an underwriter either by directly approaching an investment bank and agreeing terms with them or alternatively they can approach multiple investment banks and invite them to submit offers on the proceeds they would raise and then select the investment bank with the highest such offer.

Direct Appointment Let us first assume that the issuer appoints its underwriter directly. The investment bank will charge a fee f on the proceeds S that are raised. This fee might be an actual underwriting fee in the case of best efforts contracts, or it might be the underwriting spread in firm commitment contracts. In order to establish the offer price S, the investment bank will contact N potential investor, where each contact costs the investment bank C. Its profits are then given by

$$\Pi_B = fS - NC, \tag{7.37}$$

The issue price S will be given by expected value of the Mth highest valuation of those investors the investment bank contacts. We can employ the $(N - M + 1)$ th order statistic, and with the value of the security V being uniformly distributed, we know that the Mth highest valuation follows a beta distribution with parameters $N - M + 1$ and M. We then have the expected value of this beta distribution given by

$$S = \underline{V} + \left(\overline{V} - \underline{V}\right) \frac{N + 1 - M}{N + 1} = \overline{V} - \left(\overline{V} - \underline{V}\right) \frac{M}{N + 1}. \tag{7.38}$$

The investment bank seeks to maximise their profits in Eq. (7.37) by approaching the optimal number of investors N such that $\frac{\partial \Pi_B}{\partial N} = 0$. Inserting Eq. (7.38) for the offer price, this first-order condition solves for

$$N^* = \sqrt{\frac{Mf}{C}\left(\overline{V} - \underline{V}\right)} - 1. \tag{7.39}$$

We see that search efforts, as measured by the number of potential investors approached, are increasing in the number of required investors (M), the fees charged (f), and the uncertainty about the valuation, $\overline{V} - \underline{V}$, but decreasing in the search costs C. If more investors are required to purchase the issue, the investment bank needs to search for more potential investors in order to avoid having to accept some very low bids. Similarly, with a wide range of possible values for the security, the number of high bids will be limited, making it necessary to obtain additional bids to ensure a high offer price and hence a high fee income. A higher fee will act as a motivation to search more intensely as the revenue that a higher offer price generates will be higher, while higher costs will deter additional search.

Inserting Eq. (7.39) into Eq. (7.38), we get the expected proceeds to the issuer as

$$S^* = \overline{V} - \sqrt{\frac{CM\left(\overline{V} - \underline{V}\right)}{f}}. \tag{7.40}$$

The proceeds are reducing, and the more investors are required (M) as the investment bank has to accept lower offers to meet the requirements for the minimum number of investors, despite a higher search effort. Higher search costs (C) will reduce the search efforts and hence the offer price that can be achieved, as does an increased uncertainty about the value of the security ($\overline{V} - \underline{V}$), because a wider range of bids will be obtained, and this will lower the offer price that can be obtained, despite higher search efforts. A higher fee will increase the search efforts of investment banks and hence increase the offer price. The net proceeds the issuer obtains would be $(1 - f)\, S^*$.

Inserting Eqs. (7.39) and (7.40) into Eq. (7.37), we get the profits of the investment bank as

$$\Pi_B = f\overline{V} - 2\sqrt{Mfc\left(\overline{V} - \underline{V}\right)} + C. \tag{7.41}$$

Of course, underwriting needs to be profitable for investment banks, and we require that $\Pi_B \geq 0$; consequently, we need

$$M \leq \frac{\left(f\overline{V} + C\right)^2}{4fC\left(\overline{V} - \underline{V}\right)}. \tag{7.42}$$

Hence, if too many investors need to be found, which might be the case if potential investors are small, the issue will not be taken on as the investment bank will need to contact too many investors, and with each contact being costly, these costs exceed the underwriting fee that can be earned. Also, issues with a high degree of high valuation uncertainty, $\overline{V} - \underline{V}$, are less likely to be taken on due to the difficulty of finding sufficient numbers of investors assigning a high value to the security and securing sufficient revenue for the investment bank. On the other hand, large issues, $\overline{V}$, are more likely to be accepted due to the amount of fees this generates.

We can now compare the proceeds an issuer can obtain from appointing their investment bank directly to a situation where investment banks have to compete in order to be appointed as underwriters.

Competitive Bidding Let us now consider an issuer that does not directly appoint the investment bank but instead asks for bids by K investment banks and then chooses the one offering the highest proceeds. Only those investors that are with the chosen bank can get an allocation of the issue, and other investors cannot obtain shares, even if their valuation is higher, leading to so-called "trapped bidders". The reason for this assumption is that investment banks would prioritise the investors they have contacted and would not want to provide benefits to investors associated with competitors.

The profits of the investment bank now has to take into account that the revenue is only obtained if the investment bank is actually appointed as underwriter. We assume that all investment banks are identical, and therefore the probability of being appointed is $\frac{1}{K}$. The costs of contacting investors will have been incurred regardless whether the investment bank is appointed as underwriter or not. The profits of the investment bank change from Eq. (7.37) for direct appointments to

$$\hat{\Pi}_B = \frac{fS}{K} - NC. \tag{7.43}$$

The offer price will remain the Mth highest bid by those investors contacted, and thus Eq. (7.38) can be applied here as well. After inserting this expression, the optimal number of investors to contact is then obtained by solving the first-order condition $\frac{\partial \hat{\Pi}_B}{\partial N} = 0$, which gives us

$$N^{**} = \sqrt{\frac{Mf}{Kc}\left(\overline{V} - \underline{V}\right)} - 1 < N^* \tag{7.44}$$

and the proceeds for the issuer are

$$S^{**} = \overline{V} - \sqrt{\frac{K\left(\overline{V} - \underline{V}\right)Mc}{f}} < S^*. \tag{7.45}$$

The only difference to the direct appointment of underwriters is the effect of the competition (K) on search efforts, where the lower likelihood of gaining the underwriting contract reduces the search effort and subsequently the proceeds and offer price to issuers.

As the issuer now selects the bank with the highest proceeds, the expected proceeds promised by each investment bank, S^{**} are not relevant for its decision-making. Instead, the issuer will obtain the expected value of the maximum of the proceeds that are actually obtained from obtaining bids by potential investors. This is achieved by obtaining the Kth order statistic of the proceeds, which itself are an order statistic on a uniform distribution, which we know to follow a beta distribution. While in this case an analytical solution is not available, we know that this value is given by

$$S^{**}_{max} = \underline{V} + \left(\overline{V} - \underline{V}\right) K \int_{\underline{V}}^{\overline{V}} VG\left(V\right)^{K-1} dG\left(V\right), \tag{7.46}$$

where $G(\cdot)$ denotes the distribution function of the beta distribution with parameters $N^{**} - M + 1$ and M that arises from the $(N^{**} - M + 1)$ th order statistic of the proceeds as obtained by each investment bank. From Eq. (7.45), we see that S^{**} decreases with $\sqrt{K}$, and the increase in Eq. (7.46) from K is limited by the decrease from $G\left(V\right)$, such that overall numerical analysis shows that $S^{**}_{max} < S^{*}$. It is thus that issuers prefer to appoint underwriters directly rather than going through a tendering process.

Issuers prefer to appoint underwriters directly, because in competitive bidding, each investment bank will have a lower estimate of these proceeds because their search efforts are reduced due the uncertainty about them being appointed as underwriters, and thus they identify less investors that are willing to pay a high price for the security. Despite being able to choose the highest offer price from among competing investment banks, this does not fully compensate for the lower search effort and thus each, on average, providing a lower offer price.

Summary If issuers were to put the underwriting contract out for tender between investment banks and then decide on the offer with the highest proceeds, they will be worse off than if appointing an investment bank directly. The reason is that the uncertainty for the investment bank whether it will obtain the underwriting contract reduces the efforts to find investors valuing the issue highly, leading to a lower price being offered. This lower price is not compensated for by the issuer selecting the bank with the highest of these so-determined proceeds. This leads to the issuer being better off approaching an investment bank directly.

A key assumption for this result is that of "trapped bidders". Investors are typically cooperating with a small number of investment banks and might be contacted to give their assessment of a security, followed up with an undertaking to buy the security if the price is below the value they assign it. Once an investor has been contacted by an investment bank and given this undertaking, he is bound to only purchase the security through this investment bank. The reason can well be that the investor does not want to be seen as disloyal to the investment bank and not be contacted in future security offerings. Similarly, other investment bank might not want to benefit investors that have not been contacted initially for their opinion and thus not contributed to identifying the offer price, avoiding free-riding. It is therefore that an investment bank having obtained the underwriting contract cannot re-run the determination of the offer price by using a broader investor base and is thus unable to raise the offer price beyond their initial bid.

Reading Hansen and Khanna (1994).

7.2.2 Underwriting Syndicates

Investment banks seek to provide information to potential investors with the aim of enticing their interest in subscribing to securities that they plan to offer to the public on behalf of an issuer. Each investment bank will have their own network of potential investors from which they seek to solicit bids for the security they underwrite. Of course, the network for each investment bank is of limited size, and no single investment bank will be able to reach all potential investors. In order to expand the investor base, issuers could appoint more than one investment bank as their underwriters and ask them to form a syndicate. Having such a syndicate, however, will give rise to the potential of moral hazard among the appointed investment banks as the success of the issue depends on the overall effort of all syndicate members, with each investment bank making only a small contribution, but facing often substantial costs; they have an incentive to not exert any effort in selling the issue. Therefore, a mechanism needs to be established that seeks to overcome the moral hazard between investment banks and induce all to exert the requisite effort. The mechanism that is commonly found is that one investment bank is appointed the lead underwriter, taking a coordinating role and often also underwriting a larger fraction of the issue, in return for a disproportionate fraction of the fee income.

The more intense the search for potential investors valuing the security highly, the higher the proceeds to the company will be and thus the closer the security will come to realising its maximum value V. If investment banks are looking for potential investors more efficiently, more proceeds should be raised, although as the number of investment banks increases, an overlap of potential investors they have contacts with will decrease this efficiency. Having N investment banks contacting potential investors, we assume that the fraction of the maximum value V being realised is given by

$$\gamma = 1 - \frac{\eta}{N}, \tag{7.47}$$

where $0 < \eta < 1$ represents the effectiveness of search. If $\eta = 0$, the efficiency is very high, and no value is lost due the inability of investment banks to identify potential investors, while for $\eta = 1$, the losses can be substantial as the ability of investment banks to identify such investors is not very good.

Optimal Syndicate Size for Issuers The issuer, receiving a fraction γ of the value of the security, then agrees to pay a fee f to each of the N syndicate members, and hence, the net proceeds to the issuer are given by

$$\Pi_C = \gamma V - Nf\gamma V, \tag{7.48}$$

from which we can insert for γ from Eq. (7.47), and the optimal syndicate size from the issuer's perspective balances the higher proceeds against the higher fees. The solution of this optimisation problem is determined by solving the first-order condition $\frac{\partial \Pi_C}{\partial N} = 0$, which gives us the relationship that

$$fN^2 = \eta. \tag{7.49}$$

Using such a syndicate must be profitable to the issuer; thus, we require $\Pi_C \geq 0$, or $f \leq \frac{N-\eta}{N^2}$, which is fulfilled when using the relationship from Eq. (7.49) if $N \geq 2\eta$, and as we assumed that $\eta < 1$, we can reasonably suppose this condition to be met.

Inserting Eq. (7.49) into Eq. (7.48), we obtain

$$\Pi_C = \left(1 - 2\frac{\eta}{N}\right) V. \tag{7.50}$$

Thus, the optimal syndicate size would be as large as possible. This is because from Eq. (7.49), the fee that can be charged is decreasing in the syndicate size N.

Co-underwriters Let us now assume that the issuer appoints a syndicate in which one of the N investment banks is designated the lead underwriter and the remaining $N - 1$ investment banks take the role of co-underwriters. We here assume that these two types of underwriters only differ in the share of the total fees $Nf\gamma V$ they receive. Co-underwriters receive a share λ each, and the lead underwriter receives a fraction of $1 - (N - 1)\lambda$, i.e., the remaining fee. While in reality the lead underwriter will usually take a larger fraction of the underwriting task, we abstract from this aspect here in order to focus on the disproportionate fraction of fees that lead underwriters will receive.

If all co-underwriters provide efforts in finding potential investors, they obtain profits that are derived from the fraction λ of the total fees Nf on the proceeds of the issue, γV, while facing costs c_H for exerting this effort and other costs associated with underwriting. Thus

$$\Pi_B^H = \left(\left(1 - \frac{\eta}{N}\right) \lambda Nf - c_H\right) V. \tag{7.51}$$

If all other underwriters exert effort, but one underwriter does not, then this is equivalent to having only $N - 1$ banks identifying potential investors. Not exerting effort will reduce the costs of this underwriter to $c_L < c_H$. Hence, the profits when not exerting effort will be given by

$$\Pi_B^L = \left(\left(1 - \frac{\eta}{N-1}\right) \lambda Nf - c_L\right) V. \tag{7.52}$$

In order to induce efforts in co-underwriters, we need to ensure that $\Pi_B^H \geq \Pi_B^L$, or

$$\lambda f \geq \frac{c_H - c_L}{\eta} (N - 1) . \tag{7.53}$$

We also require that $\Pi_B^H \geq 0$ to ensure joining the syndicate and exerting effort is profitable. This condition then easily becomes

$$\lambda f \geq \frac{c_H}{N - \eta} . \tag{7.54}$$

If the constraint in Eq. (7.53) is more binding than the constraint in Eq. (7.54), thus if exerting efforts is always profitable, then, given the left-hand side of these two equations are identical, the right-hand side in Eq. (7.53) will be higher than in Eq. (7.54). This then implies

$$(N - 1) (N - \eta) \geq \frac{\eta c_H}{c_H - c_L}, \tag{7.55}$$

which solves for

$$N \geq N^* = \frac{1}{2} (1 + \eta) + \sqrt{\frac{1}{4} (1 + \eta)^2 + \frac{\eta c_L}{c_H - c_L}} \tag{7.56}$$

This scenario is the only one relevant because underwriters are only joining a syndicate if it is profitable for them to do so, and we are interested only in syndicates where underwriters exert effort. We have thus established a minimum syndicate size that is compatible with co-underwriters being both profitable and exerting effort. A too small syndicate would not raise sufficient proceeds due to the limited identification of potential investors and thus limit the fee income available to syndicate members; despite having to share this fee income with less syndicate members, a larger syndicate would be preferred. Of course, from Eqs. (7.53) and (7.54), we see that the fraction of the fee income obtained must be sufficiently high.

Having established the requirements for co-underwriters to be profitable and exerting profits, we will turn to the lead underwriter next.

Lead Underwriter The lead underwriter obtains a share $1 - (N - 1) \lambda$ of the fee income, and we assume they face the same costs as co-underwriters. Thus, the profits of exerting effort and not exerting effort, respectively, are given similarly to Eqs. (7.51) and (7.52) by

$$\hat{\Pi}_B^H = \left(\left(1 - \frac{\eta}{N} \right) N f \left(1 - (N - 1) \lambda \right) - c_H \right) V, \tag{7.57}$$

$$\hat{\Pi}_B^L = \left(\left(1 - \frac{\eta}{N - 1} \right) N f \left(1 - (N - 1) \lambda \right) - c_L \right) V$$

and to induce effort in lead underwriters, we require that $\hat{\Pi}_B^H \geq \hat{\Pi}_B^L$, which implies

$$f\left(1-(N-1)\lambda\right) \geq \frac{c_H - c_L}{\eta}(N-1). \tag{7.58}$$

The requirement that lead underwriters are profitable implies $\hat{\Pi}_B^H \geq 0$, which then solves for

$$f\left(1-(N-1)\lambda\right) \geq \frac{c_H}{N-\eta}. \tag{7.59}$$

The right-hand sides in Eqs. (7.58) and (7.59) are identical to those in Eqs. (7.53) and (7.54), respectively. We thus obtain the same condition for lead underwriters to be profitable and be exerting profits as for co-underwriters. Equations (7.54) and (7.55) apply to lead underwriters equally. We can now insert Eq. (7.49), which established the relationship in a syndicate that is optimal for issuers, into Eqs. (7.53) and (7.58). Solving these equations for λ, we get the relationship that the fraction of the fee income each co-underwriter obtains as

$$\frac{c_H - c_L}{\eta^2} N^2 (N-1) \leq \lambda \leq \frac{1}{N-1} - \frac{c_H - c_L}{\eta^2} N^2. \tag{7.60}$$

The first inequality arises from the need of co-underwriters to obtain income sufficiently high to cover their costs and induce effort, while the second inequality represents the need for this fee income of co-underwriters to not be too high such that lead underwriters can maintain profitability and exert effort. This inequality has a possible solution for λ if both inequalities are fulfilled and thus if $N^3(N-1) \leq \frac{\eta^2}{c_H - c_L}$. Hence, we have established a maximum size of the syndicate.

If the lead underwriter were to extract all surplus from the co-underwriters such that $\Pi_B^H = 0$, then Eq. (7.54) holds with equality, and using Eq. (7.49), we get that $\lambda = \frac{N^2 c_H}{\eta(N-\eta)}$. The first inequality in Eq. (7.60) will be fulfilled as this can easily demonstrated by recovering condition (7.55) with equality as required. Let us furthermore assume that the lead underwriter only gives as much of the fee income to their co-underwriters as necessary such that they exert effort, hence $\Pi_B^H = \Pi_B^L$. In this case, Eqs. (7.53) and (7.54) have to be fulfilled with equality, and then Eq. (7.55) also has to hold with equality, ensuring that the syndicate size is given by N^* in Eq. (7.56).

Inserting $\lambda = \frac{N^2 c_H}{\eta(N-\eta)}$ into the second inequality of Eq. (7.60), we obtain a condition on the maximum size of the syndicate as

$$N^2(N-1)\left(\eta c_H + (N-\eta)(c_H - c_L)\right) \leq \eta^2 (N-\eta), \tag{7.61}$$

which needs to be fulfilled for $N = N^*$.

Let us now assume for a moment that no lead underwriter exists and all underwriters are equal such that $\lambda = \frac{1}{N}$. In this case, lead underwriters and co-underwriters are identical, and the second inequality in Eq. (7.60) will be fulfilled with equality. This then implies that we require $N^3 c_H = \eta (N - \eta)$ from setting both inequalities equal. This relationship has to be fulfilled for $N = N^*$. It is only then that the syndicate is optimal for issuers and underwriters make profits and exert efforts. These conditions are unlikely to be fulfilled, and it is the use of lead underwriters that allows optimal syndicate sizes to be viable for a much wider range of parameter constellations.

We can derive the following properties of the optimal syndicate size:

$$\frac{\partial N^*}{\partial \eta} = \frac{1}{2} + \frac{\frac{1}{2}(1+\eta) + \frac{c_L}{c_H - c_L}}{2\sqrt{\frac{1}{4}(1+\eta)^2 + \frac{\eta c_L}{c_H - c_L}}} > 0, \tag{7.62}$$

$$\frac{\partial N^*}{\partial c_L} = \frac{\eta}{2(c_H - c_L)\sqrt{\frac{1}{4}(1+\eta)^2 + \frac{\eta c_L}{c_H - c_L}}} > 0,$$

$$\frac{\partial N^*}{\partial (c_H - c_L)} = -\frac{\eta c_L}{2(c_H - c_L)\sqrt{\frac{1}{4}(1+\eta)^2 + \frac{\eta c_L}{c_H - c_L}}} < 0,$$

where in the second line we assume that $c_H - c_L$ remains constant; thus, we shift the level of costs through c_L. In the final line, we assume that c_L remains fixed, i.e., we only change the difference in the costs between exerting effort and not exerting effort while keeping the level of costs constant at c_L. We easily see that a less efficient identification of potential investors, η, increases the syndicate size; this allows for more syndicate members to exert effort and thereby increase the proceeds of the issue. Higher costs c_L also increase the syndicate size, which we can explain with the need for higher proceeds to cover these increased costs, which can only be achieved by more search from more underwriters. Finally, if the differences in costs between exerting effort and not exerting effort increase, it will be more difficult to induce co-underwriters to exert this effort, and they need to obtain a larger fraction of the fee income. This is, however only possible if either there are less syndicate members or the lead underwriter obtains a smaller fee income, where the latter will then induce him to not exert effort, ruling this possibility out.

With $0 < \eta < 1$, the optimal syndicate size N^* will generally be small, unless the costs differences between exerting effort and not doing so, $c_H - c_L$, is very small. This fits well with the observation that syndicates are a standard feature in security underwriting, but the number of actively participating syndicate members is usually small. The reason for this result is the need to induce effort for all underwriters, which will require that any moral hazard is limited.

Summary While issuers would in principle prefer to appoint the largest number of underwriters in a syndicate that is feasible, this number will be limited to ensure all underwriters take active part in identifying potential investors rather than free-riding on the efforts of other underwriters. The syndicate size balances the fact that proceeds are increasing in the number of underwriters as more potential investors can be identified and the requirements to induce all underwriters to actually exert effort. It is the appointment of a lead underwriter that provides flexibility in the allocation of fee income within the syndicate that makes the syndicate size optimal for issuers while ensuring participating in the syndicate for investment banks is both profitable and provides incentives to exert effort in identifying potential investors.

While it seems that for the viability of optimal syndicates many constraints need to be fulfilled, and generally a lead underwriter will extract any surplus from co-underwriters, the widespread use of syndicates suggests that these conditions are met in most cases. The resulting syndicates are commonly found to be small, which is driven by the need to exclude free-riding of syndicate members.

Reading Pichler and Wilhelm (2001).

Resumé

A key concern for issuers of investment banks is that they make the best use of their contacts with investors to create a high demand for their securities and thus enable a high offer price. With such investors commonly associated with a specific investment bank and investment banks rewarding their investors with allocations of the securities for providing them with information, there is limited scope for investors to participate in issues underwritten by other investment banks. The use of their network of investors is not free for investment banks, and costs might include the requirement to compensate investors they contacted through future allocations of securities or other benefits that require resources cannot be used for alternative purposes. Therefore, investment banks will not contact more potential investors than necessary. It is for this reason that it is usually optimal for issuers to appoint underwriters directly rather than through a tendering process, even if the chosen investment bank does not raise the highest possible proceeds for the issuer. The uncertainty of obtaining the underwriting business in a tender will reduce the efforts of investment banks to seek out potential investors, and thus they will not be able to guarantee an offer price as high as if they were appointed directly.

The disadvantage of directly appointing underwriters can be compensated for by appointing multiple underwriters in an underwriting syndicate. While the larger number of investment banks involved should increase the investor base that can be explored and should therefore lead to higher prices, there will be overlaps in the network of investment banks, making the gains limited, while the costs of each investment bank will not reduce significantly in such a situation, which will naturally limit the size of the syndicate. In addition, the syndicate will suffer a free-rider problem in that an investment bank can fail to use their network of investors and thus contribute nothing to increasing the proceeds while receiving their fee income. Therefore, incentives need to be included that prevent such behaviour, limiting the size of the syndicate further. A lead underwriter is appointed in such a syndicate, who would not only take the most prominent role on the administration of the issue, but it also provides flexibility in the sharing of the fee income between underwriters by distinguishing the lead underwriters' part from that of the co-underwriters. Such a structure allows for syndicates of sizes that are optimal for issuers and at the same time provide incentives for all syndicate members to exert effort in promoting the issue.

7.3 Underpricing

Investment banks contact potential investors to gauge the interest in a specific security, and based on the responses received, they will determine the offer price, among other aspects of the underwriting process. Using their network of contacts to such potential investors, it is not possible for investment banks to explore the assessment of all possible investors in the market, and as such the offer price determined based on the information available might be set too low; while this ensures the issue is sold fully within the network of investors as maintained by the underwriter, or the syndicate of underwriters, there can well be unidentified demand for the security that would have allowed a higher offer price. Once the security is traded in the market, this hidden demand will emerge, and the price subsequently will rise.

If the trading price of a security just after trading commences is higher than the offer price, this is referred to as underpricing. The abovementioned incomplete survey of potential investors will lead to underpricing. However, there are other causes of underpricing that are a deliberate act of the investment bank; thus, they advise on the offer price in full knowledge that underpricing will occur. The motivation for such behaviour is manifold and includes the ability to sell securities that are less well received by the market (see Sects. 7.3.1 and 7.3.2). While this seems to benefit the issuer in the first place, as it allows all securities to sell, we firstly will see that issuers with highly desirable securities are facing underpricing, and it is these issuers that would have been able to sell their securities at full value. Secondly, with the widespread firm commitment contract, the issuer is guaranteed to sell their securities, and it is the underwriter benefitting from the ability to sell all securities, rather than having to hold on to them. Underpricing also allows the investment bank to offset the costs of any litigation launched by disgruntled investors as Sect. 7.3.5 shows, and it can also be an additional income from the subsequent trading of the securities as outlined in Sect. 7.3.4. Finally, as argued in Sect. 7.3.5, they benefit professional investors, who often provide the information on which the investment bank determines the offer price, by allocating them a larger proportion of the security than would be optimal for the issuer. The underpricing required to ensure the allocation to such professional investors will allow them to make excess profits, and this can be interpreted as a way by the investment bank to reward them for sharing any information they might have. The following models will discuss these aspects in more detail.

7.3.1 Preventing Adverse Selection

The value of securities is often not known by the investment bank until the information obtained from potential investors have been collected through their network. While such investors will have good information about the value of the security to be issued, other investors will not necessarily have this information until the price of the security is revealed; this will be after they have submitted their bids for the security. They will know that if the security is of high value, informed investors will submit bids, leaving only a small allocation for uninformed investors. On the other hand, if the security has a low value, the demand by informed investors will be low, allowing uninformed investors to obtain a high allocation. Uninformed investors are thus faced with a situation in which they receive a small allocation of a desirable security and a high allocation of an undesirable security. Thus, they face adverse selection and, if the losses from undesirable securities are sufficiently high, would not participate in the market, leaving the investment bank unable to sell the entire issue. Employing underpricing can alleviate this situation.

Let us assume that there are informed and uninformed investors. Informed investors know the value of the security; it will be either V_H or $V_L < V_H$, while uninformed investors only know that V_H occurs with probability π and V_L with probability $1 - \pi$. We assume that informed investors cannot buy the entire issue but that uninformed investors can. If informed investors buy securities, they buy at most $\overline{Q} < Q$, where Q is the issue size. This leaves $\overline{Q} - Q$ securities for uninformed investors.

Informed investors are willing to pay at most V_i, while uninformed investors are willing to pay the expected value of the security, $\hat{S} = \pi V_H + (1 - \pi) V_L$. This implies that if the low value V_L is realised, uninformed investors submit higher bids than informed investors and hence take up the entire issue. In this case, their profits are given by

$$\Pi_C^L = \left(V_L - \hat{S}\right) Q = -\pi (V_H - V_L) Q, \tag{7.63}$$

where we have inserted for the price that uninformed investors are buying, $\hat{S}$, in the assumption that this is the offer price as all bids will be at this level and investment banks seek to maximise the proceeds for their client.

If the high value V_H is realised, uninformed investors obtain an allocation of $Q - \overline{Q}$ securities as informed investors are participating at any offer price $S \leq V_H$. The profits of uninformed investors are then given by

$$\Pi_C^H = (V_H - S) \left(Q - \overline{Q}\right). \tag{7.64}$$

In order to induce uninformed investors to participate in the market and take up the issue if V_L is realised, they need to at least break even. Thus, we require

$$\Pi_C = \pi \Pi_C^H + (1 - \pi) \Pi_C^L \geq 0. \tag{7.65}$$

This solves for

$$S \leq S^* = V_H - (1-\pi)(V_H - V_L)\frac{Q}{Q-\overline{Q}}. \tag{7.66}$$

We easily see that $S^* \leq V_H$; hence, informed investors make a profit and also $S^* < \hat{S}$, giving profits also to uninformed investors to compensate them for the losses arising from the overpricing of the issue if V_L is realised.

In order to maximise the proceeds to the issuer, we set the offer price such that $S = S^*$ if the value of the security is V_H and $S = \hat{S}$ if the value of the security is V_L. The expected offer price and hence expected proceeds to the company are then given by

$$\begin{aligned} E[S] &= \pi S^* + (1-\pi)\hat{S} \qquad (7.67) \\ &= \pi V_H \left(1 - (1-\pi)\frac{\overline{Q}}{Q-\overline{Q}}\right) \\ &\quad + (1-\pi) V_L \left(1 + \pi \frac{\overline{Q}}{Q-\overline{Q}}\right) \\ &\leq \hat{S}. \end{aligned}$$

In the second equation, the first term in brackets is less than 1, and the second term in brackets is larger than 1, implying that the average offer price is below the expected value, $\hat{S}$; hence, on average the issue is underpriced. The average underpricing arises from the fact that if the value of the security is low and uninformed investors make losses, they receive a large allocation of securities, while for securities with high value, where they make profits, they only receive a small allocation. It is easy to see that the higher the underpricing, the higher the allocation to informed investors, $\overline{Q}$. This arises because the allocation of profitable securities of high value to uninformed investors reduces, necessitating a higher underpricing to compensate for this effect.

Hence, underpricing ensures the issue is sold regardless of the quality of securities by compensating uninformed investors for the losses they make if they obtain a security which has low value.

Summary Underpricing emerges as a mechanism to compensate uninformed investors for making losses from undesirable securities by ensuring their participation in highly desirable securities is profitable. As the allocation in such securities is less than in undesirable securities, we obtain underpricing on average, even though undesirable securities are overpriced. This incentive for uninformed investors to participate in the issue and, if necessary, take losses from an undesirable security and ensuring the success of the issue the investment bank has underwritten, is not paid for by the investment bank. Instead, the issuer receives lower proceeds than they would have if the issue was priced fairly.

It is also worth pointing out that the losses issuers make from the underpricing of highly desirable securities and profits from overpricing of less desirable securities are not accruing to the same issuer. A security is either not desirable or highly desirable, and issuers are not commonly issuing a large number of securities that have mixed properties. Hence, we can interpret the underpricing of highly desirable securities as a cross-subsidisation of these issuers to those issuers selling less desirable securities.

Reading Rock (1986).

7.3.2 Relationship Building

Investment banks make use of the information investors have about issuers and their securities, including market perceptions. This allows them to provide better guidance and advice on the appropriate offer price for the securities they underwrite. Of course, some securities will be highly valued and hence easy to sell to such sophisticated investors, while others will not be valued highly and would prove to be much more difficult to sell. It is often only once investment banks contact investors in their network that this information emerges, and at that point, the investment bank is often committed to the underwriting of the securities. With investors in their network reluctant to buy the securities, they will generally have to rely on less sophisticated investors to sell the issue. Of course, such investors would know that they will receive a larger allocation of securities if they are deemed to be unattractive, which might lead to a situation in which they are not willing to purchase them or require a much lower offer price. Such adverse selection can make the sale of such securities difficult. We will see here how investment banks can use the building of relationships with such less sophisticated investors to induce them to participate in issues that are not valued highly by sophisticated investors in their network.

Let us assume that the true value of an issue is either V_H with probability π or $V_L < V_H$ otherwise, and some investors can learn this value at some cost C. If the investor reveals the value that it assesses an issue to be of value V_H (V_L), the offer price will be set at S_H (S_L) and the quantity allocated to this investor Q_H (Q_L). An investor having acquired information does not have to reveal it truthfully; instead, if he has obtained information H (L), he can decide to reveal information L (H) as information is not verifiable.

Informed Investors For an informed investor, the profits made are the difference between its assessed value V_i and the offer price for the information j that has been revealed, S_j, for each of the Q_j allocated securities. Facing information costs C, the profits are thus $\left(V_i - S_j\right) Q_j - C$.

To induce truth-telling, we require that revealing the true value of the security gives the informed investor higher profits than revealing the wrong information. Thus, we need

$$\Pi_C^{HH} = (V_H - S_H)\, Q_H - C \geq (V_H - S_L)\, Q_L - C = \Pi_D^{HL}, \qquad (7.68)$$
$$\Pi_C^{LL} = (V_L - S_L)\, Q_L - C \geq (V_L - S_H)\, Q_H - C = \Pi_D^{LH},$$

where the first expressions denote the truthful revelation of the information and the right-hand side the wrong information being provided. We see that the first condition is least restrictive if $Q_L = 0$ as of course $S_L \leq V_H$ and $Q_L \geq 0$, which then allows the price of the highly valued security, S_H, to be highest. Inserting this into the second equation, we require that

$$S_H \geq V_L \qquad (7.69)$$

to ensure that identifying the low-value security as such is preferred. The expected profits of an informed investor are then given by

$$\Pi_C = \pi \Pi_C^{HH} + (1 - \pi)\, \Pi_C^{LL} = \pi \Pi_C^{HH} - (1 - \pi)\, C \qquad (7.70)$$

as $\Pi_C^{LL} = -C$ due to $Q_L = 0$.

Uninformed Investors An uninformed investor obtains an allocation of $\hat{Q}_i$ securities, depending on its value. Hence, his expected profits are given by

$$\hat{\Pi}_C = \pi\, (V_H - S_H)\, \hat{Q}_H + (1 - \pi)\, (V_L - S_L)\, \hat{Q}_L. \qquad (7.71)$$

To provide incentives for investors to become informed if they can, we require $\Pi_C \geq \hat{\Pi}_C$, which easily solves for

$$\pi\, (V_H - S_H) \left(Q_H - \hat{Q}_H \right) \geq (1 - \pi)\, (V_L - S_L)\, \hat{Q}_L + C. \qquad (7.72)$$

Let us now assume that uninformed investors, in the case that the security is valued lowly, get additional benefits B to induce them to participate in the issue. They would require in this case that their profits are positive; hence,

$$(V_L - S_L)\, \hat{Q}_L + B \geq 0 \qquad (7.73)$$

or

$$S_L \leq V_L + \frac{B}{\hat{Q}_L}. \qquad (7.74)$$

If we assume that $V_H - V_L \geq \frac{B}{Q}$, then $S_L \leq V_H$ as required in the incentives for informed investors to reveal their information truthfully.

In this case, the issue would be overpriced as we set the price as high as feasible to maximise the revenue to the issuer and thereby the fee income of the investment bank. The benefits B of uninformed investors that could not obtain information might consist of guaranteeing their future involvement in issues which might be more profitable. These uninformed investors have to participate in the offer as due to $Q_L = 0$, the issue could otherwise not be sold or only be sold at a lower price.

As $Q_L = 0$, we know that uninformed investors obtain the full allocation for low-valued securities and informed investors do not purchase any such securities. This implies that as the issuer is not willing to sell below V_L, which is the lowest possible value, uninformed investors will not make a profit but with any costs of participating in the issue would make a loss while having to purchase the entire issue. As the information on the value of the security is revealed truthfully, they know the securities to be of low value; therefore, there is no incentive for uninformed investors to buy any of these securities. The consequence is that low-valued securities could not be sold, and the underwriting of the investment bank might lead to losses for them. Providing uninformed investors with additional benefits B in this case induces them to purchase the security, and in addition, it raises more funds for the issuer. If the investment bank were not able to sell the securities at least at value V_L, we would have a situation akin to the market breakdown in adverse selection. The investment bank would not be willing to underwrite securities where the probability of them being of low value is too high. Providing benefits to uninformed investors eliminates this potential market breakdown. We will see that in equilibrium, these benefits are provided by highly valued securities.

Equilibrium Offer Prices If Q securities are sold in the issue, we require that the demand of informed and uninformed investors equals this amount, regardless of whether the issue has a high or low value. Thus

$$Q = Q_i + \hat{Q}_i \tag{7.75}$$

and as from above that $Q_L = 0$, we get $\hat{Q}_L = Q$. Requiring that uninformed investors are not making a loss, thus $\hat{\Pi}_C \geq 0$, we get from using Eq. (7.71) after inserting for the offer price of the low-valued security from Eq. (7.74) as an equality, due to the highest possible prices being chosen to benefit the issuer and investment bank alike, and noting that $\hat{Q}_L = Q$, that

$$S_H \leq V_H - \frac{1-\pi}{\pi} \frac{B}{\hat{Q}_H}, \tag{7.76}$$

Inserting Eqs. (7.74) and (7.76) as an equality to maximise the proceeds for issuers, as well as $\hat{Q}_L = Q$ into the constraint that investors want to become informed if possible, Eq. (7.72), we obtain that

$$\hat{Q}_H = \frac{(1-\pi)B}{C} Q_H. \tag{7.77}$$

We here assumed that $\Pi_C = \hat{\Pi}_C$ and incentives to become informed are minimal. This maximises the demand by informed investors and hence the overall proceeds from the issue. From Eq. (7.75), we have $Q = Q_H + \hat{Q}_H$, which now solves for

$$Q_H = \frac{C}{C + (1-\pi)B} Q, \tag{7.78}$$
$$\hat{Q}_H = \frac{(1-\pi)B}{C + (1-\pi)B} Q.$$

Using this result in Eq. (7.76), we then find

$$S_H = V_H - \frac{C + (1-\pi)B}{\pi Q}. \tag{7.79}$$

We thus see that all uninformed investors buy the issue at a loss if the value is low as $S_L > V_L$, but if the value is assessed as being high, all investors benefit from the underpricing of the issue as $S_H \leq V_H$. The expected offer price is

$$E[S] = \pi S_H + (1-\pi) S_L = \pi V_H + (1-\pi) V_L - \frac{C}{Q}, \tag{7.80}$$

where the first two terms denote the expected value of the issue and $\frac{C}{Q}$ the expected underpricing, compensating for the information costs of investors. Here the information costs that are incurred by investors are not covered by the investment bank but are borne by the issuer through underpricing.

The benefits B that are paid to investors if the issue has a low value are giving rise to a higher offer price in this scenario, while the offer price is reduced if the valuation of the securities is high. On average, these two effects cancel each other out, and the expected offer price is not affected by the benefits provided. However, it results in higher underpricing of highly valued securities and an overpricing of securities with low value. We can thus interpret the existence of benefits as a subsidy that is provided by issuers with highly valued securities to issuers with securities of low value.

We can interpret such an arrangement with uninformed investors as relationship building. In order to buy an overpriced issue that informed investors would not be willing to purchase and thus help the investment bank to sell an issue that is of low value, they are rewarded in the future with profits from more highly priced issues. These rewards are provided through the allocation of shares, $\hat{Q}_H$, in these cases, which is at the discretion of the investment bank.

Summary In order to induce investors to become informed, investment banks underprice issues on average to compensate them for the associated costs. It is noteworthy that such costs, which benefit the investment bank through the information these investors provide them with to determine the appropriate offer price, are not covered by the investment bank, but the issuer pays for them by receiving a lower offer price. This is a costs to the issuer in addition to the underwriting spread and other fees charged by the investment bank. In order to ensure the investment bank can also sell less well-received securities, they increase the underpricing of successful issues to allow some investors to make additional gains as compensation. Again, these costs are borne by the issuer of highly valued securities through a higher-than-average underpricing. On the other hand, securities of low value are overpriced, and issuers benefit from these future rewards for uninformed investors. While the expected value is unaffected by these future benefits, they nevertheless imply a cross-subsidisation of issuers with securities of low value by those with securities of high value.

Reading Sherman (2015).

7.3.3 Litigation Risk

A duty of investment banks is not to misrepresent information or omit relevant information that is made available to the potential buyers of the security they are underwriting either on purpose by neglecting to collect it. While it is often difficult to assess whether all relevant information has been disclosed properly, litigation against investment banks acting as underwriters is often launched by investors who acquired securities at the offer price and subsequently made losses as the trading price fell below the offer price. The fact they made losses from purchasing the security at the offer price is then used as evidence that the information disclosed was not comprehensive enough or misleading. The resulting litigation imposes additional costs on the investment bank who have to defend such claims or settle out of court. Even if no legal liability arises in such a scenario, the reputational damage to the investment bank arising from its lower standing with companies seeking their advice as well as investors might also cause them losses from attracting less, or less profitable, future business.

Assume that if the price of a stock P falls below its offer price S as trading commences, the investment bank has to pay a compensation c of this difference, $S - P$. These costs c include any damages that might have to be paid but also the likelihood of such damages to be paid. It might include a partial compensation but also legal costs, reputational damage, and possible punitive damages, and as such we find that $c > 1$.

Let us furthermore assume that the price of the security after trading commences is uniformly distributed in $\left[\underline{P}; \overline{P}\right]$, such that the density is $g(P) = \frac{1}{\overline{P}-\underline{P}}$. If banks receive a fee f for the underwriting of the issue, then its profits are given by

$$\Pi_B = fS - \int_{\underline{P}}^{S} c\left(P - S\right) dG\left(P\right), \tag{7.81}$$

with the first term denoting the revenue of the bank from the underwriting fee and the second term the costs arising from any litigation if the issue turns out to be overpriced, that is, the compensation is only to be paid and any reputational damage only occurs if the price falls below the offer price. $G\left(\cdot\right)$ denotes the distribution function of the price after trading has commenced.

The optimal offer price S is then given by maximising the investment bank's profits, leading to the first-order condition that

$$\frac{\partial \Pi_B}{\partial S} = f - c\int_{\underline{P}}^{S} dG\left(P\right) = f - c\frac{S - \underline{P}}{\overline{P} - \underline{P}} = 0, \tag{7.82}$$

where we applied the Leibniz integral rule. This easily solves for the optimal offer price to be given by

$$S = \underline{P} + \frac{f}{c}\left(\overline{P} - \underline{P}\right). \tag{7.83}$$

With the expected value of the issue being $\frac{1}{2}\left(\overline{P} + \underline{P}\right)$, we easily see that the issue price S will be below this value as long as $2f < c$, i.e., the costs of litigation are sufficiently high. Hence, the investment bank issues the security at a lower price and thereby achieves two effects. On the one hand, the costs of any litigation become smaller as the losses to investors will be smaller, and the lower the offer price is. On the other hand, the probability of such a loss occurring in the first place is reduced as the likelihood of a price falling below the offer price is reduced. This is balanced against the reduced fee income from underwriting the issue.

Summary Investment banks seek to underprice securities they underwrite to reduce their risk of costly litigation from investors purchasing a security at the offer price and subsequently making losses if the market price falls below the offer price. They optimally trade off the benefits of a higher fee income from higher-priced issues against the increased losses from investors seeking compensation if the issue was overpriced. This insurance against litigation costs will be paid for by the issuers of securities in the form of underpricing, which reduces the proceeds they obtain from the issue.

Reading Hughes and Thakor (2015).

7.3.4 Security Flipping

Underwriting fees are only part of the revenue an underwriter can generate from underwriting an issue, the other part arises from investors trading the issue afterward, the so-called flipping activity. If an issue is underpriced, we assume that once trading the issue commences, the issue will be traded at its equilibrium price. Underpriced issues will have allocated some securities to investors who value the security below the equilibrium price, but above the offer price. If, once trading commences, the security can be sold for its equilibrium price, and these investors will want to sell their securities. On the other hand, the issue will have been rationed in that not all investors willing to pay the equilibrium price or more will have been able to obtain the security. Therefore, there will be investors who value the security above the equilibrium price and who would be willing to buy. This allows trade to happen. It is reasonable to suggest that those investors who have been allocated the security have a sufficiently close relationship with the investment bank such that they are likely to use their brokerage division to conduct their sale of the security. This allows the investment bank to gain more revenue from such trading activity. This gives them incentives to increase the trading volume, leading to higher underpricing.

Let us assume at the offer price S the demand for the security was Q, exceeding the issue of $\hat{Q}$ securities. Hence, the issue needs to be rationed with only a fraction $\gamma = \frac{\hat{Q}}{Q}$ of this demand being met. The unmet demand is therefore $(1-\gamma)\,\hat{Q}$ and will be traded. In equilibrium, the offer price S^* would be such that $Q = \hat{Q}$.

The profits of the investment bank consist of the underwriting fee f, applied to $\hat{Q}$ securities sold at the offer price S, and the broker fee $\hat{f}$, applied to the trading demand $(1-\gamma)\,\hat{Q}$ traded at S^*. Thus we have

$$\Pi_B = fS\hat{Q} + \hat{f}\,(1-\gamma)\,\hat{Q}S^*. \tag{7.84}$$

We define the elasticity of demand for the issue as $\eta = \frac{\partial Q}{\partial S}\frac{S}{Q} < 0$, the sign arising from the fact that as the offer price increases, the demand will decrease, $\frac{\partial Q}{\partial S} < 0$. With $\gamma = \frac{\hat{Q}}{Q}$ as the unmet demand, we get the optimal price from the first-order condition of maximising investment banking profits as

$$\frac{\partial \Pi_B}{\partial S} = f\hat{Q} + \hat{f}S^*\hat{Q}\frac{\hat{Q}}{Q^2}\frac{\partial Q}{\partial S} = \hat{Q}\left(f + \hat{f}\frac{S^*}{S}\frac{\hat{Q}}{Q}\eta\right) = 0, \tag{7.85}$$

which easily solves for

$$S = -\frac{\gamma\hat{f}\eta}{f}S^*. \tag{7.86}$$

This expression can only be implicitly solved for the optimal offer price S as γ includes Q, which in turn is a function of S.

For underpricing to occur, the offer price needs to be below the equilibrium price, $S < S^*$, and we need that $-\frac{\gamma\lambda\eta}{f} < 1$, or

$$\eta > -\frac{f}{\gamma \hat{f}}. \tag{7.87}$$

If the elasticity of demand for the security is not be too large (in absolute terms), underpricing will occur. With a low elasticity, the demand is not reduced too much as the price rises from the offer price to its equilibrium price, causing sufficient trading demand to offset the losses from the lower underwriting fee with the increased income from brokerage.

Summary Underpricing creates an additional source of revenue for investment banks in that trading will be higher after the issue, generating additional revenue from brokerage. This trading demand arises from some investors who value the security highly, not having been allocated securities, while others valuing the security not highly had them allocated; this allows them to trade and the investment bank to earn brokerage fee. The higher the underpricing, the higher the fee income from brokerage, but it will also reduce the fee income from underwriting. Hence, investment banks will balance these two aspects in the optimal level of underpricing. The additional revenue obtained by the investment causes a loss to the issuer as they obtain lower proceeds than they otherwise would have had been able to.

Reading Boehmer and Fishe (2000).

7.3.5 Monitoring of Issuing Company

Professional investors have the ability to enhance the value of a security. They might do so by monitoring the activities of the issuer and thereby reducing the moral hazard of management decisions, or they might be providing advice and support directly to the issuer. The incentives of professional investors to provide such value-enhancing activities will depend on the level of benefits they can obtain, which are accruing to all security holders. Thus, holding a larger fraction of the security will induce a higher level of effort by the investor, but they will also face increasing costs as providing more advice will be more costly, in addition to having more resources bound by the investment into these securities. If such investors are available, investment banks might want to consider the impact allocating them securities has on their intrinsic value and thus the proceeds raised for their client.

Let us assume that some investors, labelled professional investors, have the ability through exercising efforts e to increase the value V of the security to $V + e$. Such efforts might enhance the value of a security by providing advice to the issuer, and any profligacy is limited through the pressure of monitoring. These professional investors face marginal costs c of their effort, and we assume they control a fraction γ of the security.

In addition to professional investors, there are a retail investors, who do not enhance the value of the security; they control a fraction $\hat{\gamma}$ of the issue. We will first consider the incentives of professional investors before analysing retail investors and then the optimal decision to maximise the proceeds to the issuer.

Professional Investors Having paid a price of S when the security was issued, we have the profits of professional investors given by

$$\Pi_I = \gamma\left((V+e)-S\right) - \frac{1}{2}z\gamma^2\sigma_V^2 - \frac{1}{2}ce^2, \tag{7.88}$$

where the value of the securities is given by $V+e$ and the offer price S, such that for each security, the immediate profits are $(V+e)-S$, and they obtain a fraction γ of these securities. They face costs of $\frac{1}{2}ce^2$ to provide the effort of enhancing the security value and due to their risk aversion z lose utility from the variance of the security value, σ_V^2.

The optimal effort level is then given if $\frac{\partial \Pi_I}{\partial e} = 0$, which solves for

$$e = \frac{\gamma}{c}, \tag{7.89}$$

and gives us the profits of professional investors as

$$\Pi_I = \gamma\left(V-S\right) + \frac{\gamma^2}{2}\left(\frac{1}{c} - z\sigma_V^2\right). \tag{7.90}$$

Let us now assume that the offer price is a linear function of the fraction allocated to professional investors, such that

$$S = \beta_0 + \beta_1\gamma, \tag{7.91}$$

where $\beta_0 \geq 0$ and $\beta_1 \geq 0$. This relationship between professional investors holding the security and the offer price can arise from the information they hold on the prospects of the issuer.

The allocation of securities to retail investors is assumed to have no influence on the offer price. This transforms Eq. (7.90) into

$$\Pi_I = \gamma\left(V-\beta_0\right) - \frac{\gamma^2}{2}\left(2\beta_1 - \frac{1}{c} + z\sigma_V^2\right) \tag{7.92}$$

and the optimal allocation of securities to professional investors is then given from the solution to

$$\frac{\partial \Pi_I}{\partial \gamma} = V - \beta_0 - 2\gamma\beta_1 + \frac{\gamma}{c} - z\gamma\sigma_V^2 \tag{7.93}$$
$$= V - S - \gamma\beta_1 + \gamma\left(\frac{1}{c} - z\sigma_V^2\right) = 0,$$

where we have included Eq. (7.91) in the second equality. This expression solves for

$$S = V - \gamma\left(\beta_1 + \frac{1}{c} - z\sigma_V^2\right) \tag{7.94}$$

and shows the negative relationship between the fraction of securities allocated to professional investors, γ, and the offer price.

Retail Investors Retail investors, being allocated a fraction $\hat{\gamma}$ of the security, do not enhance the value of the security but nevertheless benefit from the monitoring of professional investors as the value of the security increases. Their profits are, in analogy to professional investors and acknowledging that they face no costs of providing effort, given by

$$\hat{\Pi}_I = \hat{\gamma}\left((V + e) - S\right) - \frac{1}{2}z\hat{\gamma}^2\sigma_V^2 \tag{7.95}$$
$$= \hat{\gamma}\gamma\left(\beta_1 + \frac{1}{c} + z\sigma_V^2\right) - \frac{1}{2}z\hat{\gamma}^2\sigma_V^2,$$

having inserted for the offer price S from Eq. (7.94) to obtain the second equality. Their optimal allocation of the security is given from the first-order condition that

$$\frac{\partial \hat{\Pi}_I}{\partial \hat{\gamma}} = V - S + \frac{\gamma}{c} - z\sigma_V^2\hat{\gamma} = 0 \tag{7.96}$$

using the first equality in Eq. (7.95). Inserting from Eq. (7.94) for the offer price, this solves for

$$\hat{\gamma} = \frac{\gamma}{z\sigma_V^2}\left(\beta_1 + z\sigma_V^2\right). \tag{7.97}$$

Retail investors would seek an allocation of $\hat{\gamma}$ from the investment bank, whose decision we consider next.

Optimal Offer Price for Issuers The issuer would like the investment bank to maximise the offer price S. Let us assume they seek to extract all surplus from retail investors, such that $\hat{\Pi}_I = 0$, and the equilibrium condition that all securities are allocated exactly to either professional or retail investors, $\gamma + \hat{\gamma} = 1$. As retail investors do not contribute to the value of the security, their surplus is reduced to the minimum possible to ensure their participation. We thus get the Lagrangian function of this maximisation problem as

$$\mathcal{L} = S + \zeta \hat{\Pi}_I, \tag{7.98}$$

with ζ being the Lagrange multiplier. The optimisation concerns the allocation to professional investors as well as the pricing schedule from Eq. (7.91), restricted here to the sensitivity of the offer price to the allocation of securities to professional investors, β_1. We get the first-order conditions as

$$\begin{aligned} \frac{\partial \mathcal{L}}{\partial \beta_1} &= -\gamma + \zeta\gamma(1-\gamma) = 0, \\ \frac{\partial \mathcal{L}}{\partial \gamma} &= -\beta_1 + \frac{1}{c} - z\sigma_V^2 \\ &\quad + \zeta\left((1-2\gamma)\left(\beta_1 + z\sigma_V^2\right) + z(1-\gamma)\sigma_V^2\right) = 0, \end{aligned} \tag{7.99}$$

the first condition solves for $\zeta = \frac{1}{1-\gamma}$, and inserting this into the second condition gives us

$$\gamma\left(\beta_1 + z\sigma_V^2\right) = (1-\gamma)\left(\frac{1}{c} + z\sigma_V^2\right). \tag{7.100}$$

Inserting this relationship into Eq. (7.97) such that the allocation is also optimal for retail investors, we get

$$\hat{\gamma} = (1-\gamma)\left(1 + \frac{1}{cz\sigma_V^2}\right) > 1 - \gamma. \tag{7.101}$$

We thus see that the optimal allocation to retail investors is too high for it to be consistent with an optimal allocation to professional investors. To maintain optimality for both professional and retail investors, the investment bank can adjust the offer price towards S^*

We can solve Eq. (7.96), using Eqs. (7.94) and (7.100), and transform this relationship such that

$$\begin{aligned} 1-\gamma &= \frac{1}{z\sigma_V^2}\left(V - S^* + \frac{\gamma}{c}\right) \\ &= \frac{1}{z\sigma_V^2}\left(V - S + \frac{\gamma}{c}\right) + \left(S - S^*\right)\frac{1}{z\sigma_V^2} \end{aligned} \tag{7.102}$$

$$= \frac{1}{z\sigma_V^2}\gamma\left(\beta_1 + z\sigma_V^2\right) + \left(S - S^*\right)\frac{1}{z\sigma_V^2}$$

$$= \frac{1}{z\sigma_V^2}\frac{1-\gamma}{c} + (1-\gamma) + \left(S - S^*\right)\frac{1}{z\sigma_V^2},$$

which solves for

$$S^* = S + \frac{1-\gamma}{c}. \tag{7.103}$$

We thus clearly see that the offer price S^*, maximising the proceeds for the issuer, is higher than the optimal offer price for professional investors, S. If the investment bank caters to the interest of professional investors rather than their clients, they will choose the offer price that is optimal for them, S, and thus underprice the issue.

Summary Investment banks rely on informed investors to provide them with information that leads to the adequate valuation of securities. Such investors are often also those that have the skills and knowledge to enhance the value of these securities, either through monitoring or advising the issuer. A way to reward such investors for their information is to allocate them securities at this lower price, allowing them to make instant gains. While they add value to the security and thus the offer price, the overall impact on the issuer is negative in that the level of underpricing exceeds the value added to the security; thus, the issuer is worse off. It is the issuer who has indirectly provided professional investors with a reward for sharing their information with investment banks.

Reading Stoughton and Zechner (1998).

Resumé

Underpricing is used by investment banks to generate additional benefits to themselves or investors affiliated with the underwriters. It allows to overcome an adverse selection problem in that uninformed investors know that they will receive a larger allocation of securities that have less good prospects and lower allocations of securities with good prospects. Hence, uninformed investors might generally be reluctant to provide bids for issues as they expect to make losses due to informed investors taking the best securities. Such that all securities can be sold, underpricing allows uninformed investors to make a profit on their small allocation of the desirable securities, compensating them for the losses they make from subscribing to less-desirable securities. Such compensation might be postponed to the participation in future security offerings by other issuers. The underpricing and associated allocation of securities to investors with a positive assessment of a security can also provide incentives for informed investors to disclose their information truthfully.

These aspects benefit mainly investment banks who do not have to compensate investors for providing their assessment of the security, and it allows them to sell all securities. The latter is particularly beneficial in firm commitment underwriting contracts as it prevents the underwriters from having to retain the security on their own account after buying it from the issuer.

There are, in addition, direct benefits to investment banks from underpricing. Given the wide-ranging duties of investment banks in the underwriting process, in particular with respect to providing information to the public, litigation by investors is common and is mostly found in cases where investors suffered losses relative to the offer price. Having a lower offer price reduces the chances of any such litigation being commenced as prices need to fall substantially from the equilibrium price to cause losses to investors. Having underpriced the security, the demand at the offer price exceeds the securities issued, and hence, we will have a situation where some investors have been allocated the security that value it above its offer price but below its equilibrium price; once the equilibrium price is reached as trading commences, they would sell the security. Similarly, there will be investors who value the security above the equilibrium price but have not received an allocation and therefore would purchase the security even at the equilibrium price. These two groups would trade the security, opening up the possibility of brokerage income for the investment bank from such trades. As those having received an allocation and wanting to sell the security are mostly affiliated with the underwriter, it is likely they will use the brokerage division of that investment bank.

Professional investors might be able to enhance the value of a security, either through monitoring the issuer or advising them; they are also the type of investors who are most likely informed and thus sought out by investment banks to provide their assessment of the security value. Investment banks will want to reward them for their information and can do so by allocating them more securities than is optimal when maximising the offer price for their clients. Using underpricing rewards these investors for providing the information, but as they also benefit the issuer and hence the security value, the underpricing is partly offset by this increased security value.

Overall, we see that investment bank use underpricing to reward investors for participating in an offer or providing information, as well as gaining additional benefits from trading in the issue and reducing litigation costs. Issuers are not charged for these costs that investment banks face directly but pay indirectly through receiving less for their securities than they could achieve in equilibrium, the underpricing. However, there is a benefit from using underpricing rather than charging clients directly for these costs or including it into the underwriting fee or underwriting spread. This benefit is that while all the costs are incurred by banks, when using underpricing, they are not cumulative. An underpriced issue reduces the litigation risk, generates additional brokerage commission, induces informed investors to reveal information, and allows uninformed investors to participate in offers that would otherwise be unsuccessful. Hence, underpricing can be seen as an efficient tool to reduce the costs to clients.

7.4 Greenshoe Option

If given a Greenshoe option, the investment bank can sell additional securities at the offer price to meet any excess demand that is not met, for example, arising from the underpricing of the issue. This sale takes the form of a short sale that requires the investment bank to purchase back these securities at the prevailing market price, usually the equilibrium price as trading commences. This option is available to all investment banks, subject to short-selling rules in the market. With the Greenshoe option, however, the issuer of the security agrees to sell to the investment bank additional securities to cover their short position, up to a maximum amount. The investment bank pays for these securities the same amount as for the original offer and thus receives a discount in the form of the underwriting spread.

We now assume that the securities are issued at the offer price S that generated demand Q for securities, of which $\hat{Q} < Q$ could be satisfied from the original issue. Thus, as we have excess demand, the issue must be underpriced. The equilibrium price in trading, S^*, is such that the demand equals the amount of securities issued, $\hat{Q}$. Obviously, we have $\frac{\partial Q}{\partial S} < 0$ as demand will be decreasing in the offer price. Investment banks may sell up to a fraction β of the issue size $\hat{Q}$ as a Greenshoe.

The profits of the investment bank consist of its fee f on the securities $\hat{Q}$ sold through the offer to the public at the offer price S and the securities sold to meet the excess demand, $Q - \hat{Q}$, which are sold at the offer price S and re-bought in the market at the equilibrium price S^*. To cover this position, the investment bank can buy from the issuer, at a net price $(1 - f)\, S$, additional securities up to $\beta\hat{Q}$, making profits $S^* - (1 - f)\, S$ as they obtain the security worth S^* at the price of $(1 - f)\, S$. Thus, investment bank profits are given by

$$\begin{aligned} \Pi_B = {} & fS\hat{Q} + (S - S^*)\left(Q - \hat{Q}\right) \\ & + \left(S^* - (1 - f)\, S\right) \min\left\{Q - \hat{Q}; \beta\hat{Q}\right\}. \end{aligned} \tag{7.104}$$

Low Demand Scenario If the excess demand at the offer price is not too high, i.e., underpricing not too severe, such that this excess demand can be covered fully by the Greenshoe, $Q - \hat{Q} < \beta\hat{Q}$, and hence $\min\left\{Q - \hat{Q}; \hat{Q}\right\} = Q - \hat{Q}$, we have the first-order condition for the optimal offer price S that maximises the investment bank's profits given by

$$\begin{aligned} \frac{\partial \Pi_B}{\partial S} = {} & f\hat{Q} + \left(Q - \hat{Q}\right) + (S - S^*)\frac{\partial Q}{\partial S} \\ & - (1 - f)\left(Q - \hat{Q}\right) + \left(S^* - (1 - f)\, S\right)\frac{\partial Q}{\partial S} = 0. \end{aligned} \tag{7.105}$$

If no Greenshoe option were available, thus $\beta = 0$, the final term in Eq. (7.104) is absent, and we have the optimal offer price determined by

$$\frac{\partial \Pi_B}{\partial S} = f\hat{Q} + \left(Q - \hat{Q}\right) + \left(S - S^*\right) \frac{\partial Q}{\partial S} = 0. \tag{7.106}$$

Inserting Eq. (7.106) into Eq. (7.105) and noting that $\frac{\partial Q}{\partial S} < 0$, we see that at the price as determined by Eq. (7.106) without a Greenshoe option causes Eq. (7.105) to be negative. Having the first derivative negative suggests that the offer price is too high. Hence, with the Greenshoe option, the offer price must be lower, and underpricing is increased.

Using that for low excess demand, we have $\min\left\{Q - \hat{Q}; \hat{Q}\right\} = Q - \hat{Q}$; from Eq. (7.104), we have $\Pi_B = fS\hat{Q} + fS\left(Q - \hat{Q}\right)$. Without using the Greenshoe option, the profits would only be the revenue from underwriting the original offer of $\hat{Q}$ securities, giving profits of $fS\hat{Q}$. Thus, it is profitable to exercise the Greenshoe in all circumstances.

High-Demand Scenario With excess demand higher due to larger underpricing such that the Greenshoe cannot cover the full excess demand, $Q - \hat{Q} > \beta\hat{Q}$, we have $\min\left\{Q - \hat{Q}, \beta\hat{Q}\right\} = \beta\hat{Q}$, and the optimal offer price maximising the investment bank's profits is given by the first-order condition

$$\frac{\partial \Pi_B}{\partial S} = f\hat{Q} + \left(Q - \hat{Q}\right) + \left(S - S^*\right) \frac{\partial Q}{\partial P} - (1 - f)\beta\hat{Q} = 0. \tag{7.107}$$

Again, the price is lower than without the Greenshoe option as inserting Eq. (7.106) would make Eq. (7.107) negative again as only the final term is left. Thus, with both low and high excess demand for the security, the Greenshoe option increases underpricing. The larger the Greenshoe option is (β), the more pronounced this underpricing becomes.

To exercise the Greenshoe, we require that the profits from doing so are higher than only underwriting the existing offer. Using that $\min\left\{Q - \hat{Q}, \beta\hat{Q}\right\} = \beta\hat{Q}$, we see that using Eq. (7.104), this requires $fS\hat{Q} + (S - S^*)\left(Q - \hat{Q}\right) + (S^* - (1 - f)S)\beta\hat{Q} > fS\hat{Q}$. From this, we obtain that

$$\beta \geq \frac{S^* - S}{S^* - (1 - f)S} \frac{Q - \hat{Q}}{Q}, \tag{7.108}$$

implying the Greenshoe has to be large enough to be profitable with excess demand exceeding the Greenshoe. This is because if the excess demand the investment bank meets is too high, the losses from having to cover their short position at the market price are too high to be covered by the profits they make from being able to purchase these at a discount from the issuer, given that the purchase amount will be limited by the Greenshoe size.

Summary A Greenshoe allows the underwriter to sell additional securities at the offer price to meet any excess demand at that price. They can obtain additional securities from the issuer for this purpose, but the amount will be limited. As long as the amount available as a Greenshoe covers the excess demand, it is always profitable for investment banks to exercise the Greenshoe option. It is only if the excess demand exceeds the Greenshoe that this might no longer be the case and the Greenshoe option might be too small to be profitable. In both cases, if the Greenshoe option is exercised, it increases the underpricing of the security. This is detrimental to the issuer if we assume that the underpricing was determined optimally without the need for a Greenshoe. While they can issue more securities due to the Greenshoe, the underpricing increases such that the overall revenue would fall; this is because it is no longer optimal. On the other hand, the investment bank benefits from the increased revenue, suggesting that it is in their interest to agree a Greenshoe option and exercise it as long as excess demand, relative to the Greenshoe, is not too high.

Reading Fishe (2002).

7.5 Choice of Underwritten Securities

Investment banks may select which securities they underwrite, with many of the highly reputable investment banks only focusing on highly valued securities. In doing so, they are, however, giving up revenue from underwriting securities of lower value, neglecting any effect underwriting such securities would have on their reputation and thus long-term ability to generate income. This selection process often involves an initial screening in which they seek to determine whether a security is actually of high or low value. Contacting a very select number of potential investors for this purpose, often informally, they might get an initial assessment on the value of the security and based on this assessment decide whether to pursue the underwriting.

Let us assume that a security can be of high or low quality, which is reflected in their value of V_H for high-value securities and $V_L < V_H$ for low-value securities. The probability of a high-value security is given by π, and therefore that of a low-value security is $1-\pi$. Investment banks have costs c to obtain a signal on the value of the security, and it has precision

$$Prob\,(H|V_H) = Prob\,(L|V_L) = \rho \geq \frac{1}{2}. \tag{7.109}$$

Based on the initial assessment of V_i from contacting selected investors, we assume that the information provided through the initial valuation is correct with probability ρ. The signal only has value if $\rho > \frac{1}{2}$ as only then does the probability of having the correct valuation increase. We now know that with this information, the probability of the security having high value is given by

$$Prob\,(V_H) = \rho\pi + (1-\rho)\,(1-\pi)\,, \tag{7.110}$$

where the first term denotes the actual value to be V_H (π) and this being correctly identified (ρ) and the second term that the actual value is V_L $(1-\pi)$, but it is observed with a wrong signal $(1-\rho)$. This gives us the expected value of the security as

$$\begin{aligned} E\,[V] &= Prob\,(V_H)\,V_H + Prob\,(V_L)\,V_L \\ &= V_H - (\pi - \rho\,(2\pi - 1))\,(V_H - V_L)\,, \end{aligned} \tag{7.111}$$

using that $Prob\,(V_L) = 1 - Prob\,(V_H)$. We assume the issue price reflects the expected value of the issue, ignoring any underpricing.

Investment banks have now to decide whether to underwrite only securities they consider being of high quality or underwrite both types of securities.

Underwriting All Securities We assume that the costs associated with obtaining the signal are increasing the more its precision ρ exceeds $\frac{1}{2}$; this might be due to contacting more investors in their network or more knowledgeable investors that are more difficult to approach. The expected profits of investments are determined by the income from the underwriting fee f on the expected proceeds $E\,[V]$, less the costs of obtaining the signal with precision ρ. This gives us

$$\Pi_B = fE\,[V] - \frac{1}{2}c\left(\rho - \frac{1}{2}\right)^2. \tag{7.112}$$

After inserting from Eq. (7.111) for the expected proceeds and using the first-order condition $\frac{\partial \Pi_B}{\partial \rho} = 0$, the optimal signal precision is given by

$$\rho^* = \frac{1}{2} + \frac{f}{c}\,(2\pi - 1)\,(V_H - V_L)\,. \tag{7.113}$$

Inserting this solution back into Eq. (7.112), we get the expected profits of the investment bank as

$$\Pi_B^* = \frac{1}{2}f\,(V_H + V_L) + \frac{1}{2}\frac{f^2}{c}\,(2\pi - 1)^2\,(V_H - V_L)^2\,. \tag{7.114}$$

These expected profits of investment banks underwriting high-value as well as low-value securities can now be compared to the profits if only high-quality securities are underwritten by the investment bank.

Underwriting Only High-Value Securities The investment bank could decide to only bring to the market securities, which have been assessed as having a high value, V_H. This case is equivalent to setting $V_L = 0$ as the bank does not obtain any revenue from the issuer of a low-value security. Inserting this specification into Eq. (7.113), we obtain the optimal precision of the signal as

$$\hat{\rho}^* = \frac{1}{2} + \frac{f}{c}(2\pi - 1)\, V_H. \tag{7.115}$$

We see immediately that $\hat{\rho}^* > \rho^*$ and investment banks increase their effort to obtain a more precise signal as the expected revenue from only underwriting high-quality securities is higher. The expected revenue increases from a higher expected value as the likelihood of having identified correctly the high-value security increases. Using again that $V_L = 0$, the expected profits of the investment bank in this case are given by

$$\hat{\Pi}_B^* = \frac{1}{2} f V_H + \frac{1}{2}\frac{f^2}{c}(2\pi - 1)^2\, V_H^2. \tag{7.116}$$

The strategy of underwriting only securities of high value is preferred by an investment bank if $\hat{\Pi}_B^* \geq \Pi_B^*$, and it is more profitable than underwriting all securities. Using Eqs. (7.114) and (7.116), this solves for

$$\frac{f}{c}(2\pi - 1)(2V_H - V_L) > 1. \tag{7.117}$$

For a possible solution, we clearly need $\pi > \frac{1}{2}$ as $V_H > V_L$; thus, securities of high value must be more common than those of low value, and the more high-value securities are in the market, the less revenue is lost from not underwriting low-value securities. The higher revenue from the higher values of the actually underwritten securities compensates for this loss more easily. Higher underwriting fees allow to generate sufficient income with high-value securities, and lower costs of increasing the precision of the signals enable the investment bank to increase their precision and thus the expected value of the security as it is more likely to actually be of high value.

We see that as all components on the right-hand side are positive, the expression for low underwriting fees f is never fulfilled, while for larger fees, this expression can be fulfilled. Thus with underwriting fees sufficiently high, only securities that can achieve a high value are underwritten by investment banks and those of lower value are not underwritten. The reason is that the higher precision signal, arising from the higher expected revenue, allows banks to identify these high-value securities better, which compensates them for not underwriting low-value securities. A higher difference between high-value and low-value securities will of course favour the underwriting of high-value securities only.

Summary Investment banks may forego the revenue from underwriting low-value securities in favour of focusing on high-value securities only. The higher efforts they exert to identify such high-value securities at an early stage in the underwriting process will increase the expected proceeds as they are more likely to identify them correctly. This increased revenue from underwriting higher-valued securities compensates the investment bank for the higher costs of identifying such securities and foregoing the revenue from other securities. It is especially investment banks that can charge high underwriting fees or face low costs of identifying the type of security that have an advantage over other investment banks without these abilities. With investment banks known for underwriting securities of high value being able to charge higher fees, this might amplify the separation of the underwriting market into top-tier investment banks, focusing on and attracting high-value securities exerting high efforts to identify such securities, and a lower tier who will inevitably obtain more low-value securities and exert much less effort at such an early stage. This gives also rise to differences in the quality of investment banking services that may well be reflected in a lower underwriting fee, which makes focusing on high-value securities even less attractive, further separating investment banking markets.

Reading Chemmanur and Fulghieri (1994).

7.6 Underwriting by Universal Banks

Universal banks are active in commercial banking, comprising mainly lending and deposit taking, as well as investment banking. Underwriting a security for a client they also provided a loan to can change their financial position and thus affect the value of the loan. For example, underwriting shares will increase the equity of a company and should therefore reduce the risks on the loans that have been provided, giving additional benefits to the universal bank, beyond receiving the underwriting income.

Let us assume that a security can be of high or low quality, which is reflected in their value of V_H for high-value securities and $V_L < V_H$ for low-value securities. The probability of a high-value security is given by π, and therefore that of a low-value security is $1-\pi$. Investment banks have costs c to obtain a signal on the value of the security, and it has precision

$$Prob\,(H|V_H) = Prob\,(L|V_L) = \rho \geq \frac{1}{2}. \tag{7.118}$$

Based on the initial assessment of V_i from contacting selected investors, we assume that the information provided through the initial valuation is correct with probability ρ. The signal only has value if $\rho > \frac{1}{2}$ as only then does the probability of having the correct valuation increase. We now know that with this information, the probability of the security having high value is given by

$$Prob\,(V_H) = \rho\pi + (1-\rho)\,(1-\pi)\,, \tag{7.119}$$

where the first term denotes the actual value to be V_H (π) and this being correctly identified (ρ) and the second term that the actual value is V_L $(1-\pi)$, but it is observed with a wrong signal $(1-\rho)$. This gives us the expected value of the security as

$$\begin{aligned} E\,[V] &= Prob\,(V_H)\,V_H + Prob\,(V_L)\,V_L \\ &= V_H - (\pi - \rho\,(2\pi-1))\,(V_H - V_L)\,, \end{aligned} \tag{7.120}$$

using that $Prob\,(V_L) = 1 - Prob\,(V_H)$. We assume the issue price reflects the expected value of the issue, ignoring any underpricing.

We can now assess the different impact investment and universal banks have on the precision of the signal they seek.

Investment Banks For the investment bank, the expected profits consist of the underwriting fee f_I applied to the expected proceeds of the issue $E_I\,[V]$ less the costs of obtaining a signal of quality ρ_I larger than $\frac{1}{2}$. This gives us

$$\Pi_B^I = f_I E_I\,[V] - \frac{1}{2}c_I\left(\rho_I - \frac{1}{2}\right)^2 \tag{7.121}$$

and after inserting from Eq. (7.120) for the expected proceeds, we get from the first-order condition $\frac{\partial \Pi_B^I}{\partial \rho_I} = 0$ the optimal precision of the signal as

$$\rho_I^* = \frac{1}{2} + \frac{f_I}{c_I}\,(2\pi - 1)\,(V_H - V_L)\,. \tag{7.122}$$

Using the signal quality, we can then determine the expected proceeds to the issuer, $E_I\,[V]$, on which he has to pay an underwriting fee of f_I, leading to net proceeds for the client of $(1-f_I)\,E_I\,[V]$. We can now compare these net proceeds with those obtained when instructing a universal bank to underwrite the security.

Universal Banks We assume that a universal bank has given their client a loan of L at interest rate r_L and that raising equity to the amount of $E_U\,[V]$ changes the default rate from $\hat{\pi}$ to $\frac{E_U[V]}{E_U[V]+L}\hat{\pi}$; thus, the increased equity reduces the risk to the universal bank due to the additional resources put into the company. Hence, the profits of the commercial bank from underwriting are now given by

$$\Pi_B^C = f_U E_U[V] + \left(1 - \frac{E_U[V]}{E_U[V]+L}\right)\hat{\pi}(1+r_L)L - \frac{1}{2}c_U\left(\rho_U - \frac{1}{2}\right)^2. \tag{7.123}$$

The first term denotes the revenue from underwriting the issue, and the second term denotes the benefits from the reduction on the default rate of the company, with the final terms covering the cost of obtaining the signal. The first-order condition $\frac{\partial \Pi_B^C}{\partial \rho_U} = 0$ can be solved for

$$\rho_U^* = \frac{1}{2} + \frac{f_U}{c_U}(2\pi - 1)(V_H - V_L) + \frac{2\pi - 1}{c_U}(V_H - V_L)\frac{\hat{\pi}(1+r_L)L^2}{(E_U[V]+L)^2}. \tag{7.124}$$

Suppose now that $f_U = f_I$ and $c_U = c_I$; then, we see that the first line in Eq. (7.124) is identical to ρ_I^* in Eq. (7.122), and as the second line is positive, we easily get that $\rho_U^* > \rho_I^*$. With identical costs and underwriting fees, universal banks exert more effort to obtain a precise valuation of the security. The reason for this result is that the additional benefits from the reduction in the default rate of their client provide incentives to this effect. Thus, with the expected proceeds positively related to the precision of the signal, assuming $\pi > \frac{1}{2}$, universal banks would be able to raise more funds from the issue than investment banks. Of course, such a situation could not persist as investment banks would not attract any underwriting business. Competition between these two types of banks would ensure that the net proceeds are identical, $(1 - f_I) E_I[V] = (1 - f_U) E_U[V]$. Inserting for $E_i[V]$ and ρ_i, this condition easily solves for

$$f_U = \frac{f_I E_I[V] + (2\pi - 1)^2 (V_H - V_L)^2 \frac{\hat{\pi}(1+r_L)L^2}{c_U(E_U[V]+L)^2}}{E_I[V] + (2\pi - 1)^2 (V_H - V_L)^2 \frac{\hat{\pi}(1+r_L)L^2}{c_U(E_U[V]+L)^2}} > f_I. \tag{7.125}$$

Having stronger incentives to exert more effort to obtain a signal of higher precision, universal banks can charge their clients a higher underwriting fee than investment banks. The proceeds clients receive from universal banks will be higher, but this advantage is eroded by being charged higher underwriting fees.

We might also note differences in the costs these two types of banks are facing. On the one hand, universal banks might face lower costs of obtaining a precise signal because of the relationship they already have established with their client and thus require less effort to gain this additional information. On the other hand, investment banks have the specialist knowledge and an extensive network of potential investors from which to gain additional information, offsetting some of the advantages universal banks might have. Strict rules on sharing information between different departments might make the use of information gained in the course of lending less available, in addition to different information being required when underwriting securities, especially the perception by investors. Thus, cost differences might well be small between the two bank types.

Summary The additional benefits universal banks derive from underwriting for their commercial banking clients, such as a reduction in the risks of loans, provide incentives to increase their effort to increase the value of the securities in the underwriting process as this increases not only the proceeds from the underwriting fee but also value to their commercial banking activities. Obtaining higher proceeds for their clients allows universal banks to charge higher fees than investment banks while still maintaining the same net proceeds to their clients and thus staying competitive with investment banks.

Universal banks have the advantage in recruiting new clients to their underwriting business as a relationship has already been established through the provision of loans and associated services. This makes it easier for universal banks to gain underwriting business through cross-selling.

Reading Puri (1999).

Conclusions

If we accept that investment banks have comparative advantages in assessing the value of a security compared to the issuer, engaging them as underwriters has the advantage of reducing the overall risk involved in the issuance of shares, improving welfare. Unless the underwriting fee is too high, the welfare is maximised if the investment bank purchases the securities from the investment bank at a fixed price and then sells it on to investors. This way, the risk to issuers is completely eliminated, while the lower risks faced by investment banks increase the overall welfare. The underwriting fee is then used to compensate investment banks for the risk they are taking. With information a critical element for investment banks, their costs of obtaining such information are not compensated for by the underwriting fee. Instead, they reward investors providing them with such information through underpricing. This way, they can reward those investors that are helpful by providing information truthfully through an abnormal return when subscribing to the security offer; other investors can also be rewarded for their previous involvement in less successful issues that they ensured could sell in full. Contractual arrangements are in place to facilitate the provision of information and provide incentives for investors to reveal their information truthfully, most notably book-building. Similarly, the formation of syndicates and their direct appointment without a tendering process provides incentives for investment bank to make use of their access to investors as much as possible.

Underpricing, though, does not only reward investors for participating in the issue of the security, but it can also be used to cover costs of investment banks, such as those of potential litigation from investors, and to generate additional profits from trading the security among investors. The advantage of using underpricing is that the benefits in the form of investor participation and information provision, as well as the coverage of litigation costs and generation of additional benefits to the investment bank, can all be achieved simultaneously. It is not required to accumulate the costs underpricing seeks to cover, but instead a single level of underpricing can address all of these aspects at once. In this sense, underpricing is an effective tool to generate profits for the investment bank while limiting the costs to issuers, allowing the underwriting fee to be small.

Therefore, the costs to the issuer of securities will consist of the underwriting fee and the underpricing of the security. The analysis provided above suggests that the arrangements made are effective in that they provide the investment bank with a range of benefits in form of covering their costs and generating income while ensuring that the costs imposed on issuers are kept low. Conflicts of interest between investment banks and issuers persist; for example, the Greenshoe option increases the profits to the investment bank while increasing underpricing to the detriment of the issuer. The extent of these conflicts of interest are, however, mitigated by underpricing at the same time covering other costs of the investment bank that otherwise would be charged through an increased underwriting fee, such as litigation costs.

Review of Part II

Providing advice to their clients is a complex task for investment banks. Not only do they need to balance their own interests of making profits from their activities with the interests of their clients, but they also need to ensure they have access to information on which any such advice will be based. To this effect, they require contact with knowledgeable market participants, usually investors, who are willing to share their assessment. This is especially prominent in securities underwriting but for gauging market perceptions also in the advice given in M&A. Investors will not be willing to provide information to investment banks for free, unless it is in their own interest to do so, and therefore, investment banks need to establish a way to reward them for providing truthful information. With information not directly observable and subject to interpretation, it is often best to rely on incentives to solicit the actual information, rather than direct payments. Adding thus another layer of conflicts of interest between the investment bank and their information sources, beyond that of the investment bank and their client, will inevitably lead to an increase in the complexity of the contractual arrangements necessary.

Investment banks, and their clients, have over time established a number of contractual arrangements that have withstood the test of time and are commonly used across investment banks in different cultural settings as well as regulatory frameworks. This suggests that the key elements of such contracts, most notably the contingent fee contract in M&A, and the combination of firm-commitment contracts with book-building and the direct appointment of syndicates in underwriting, are efficient. They do not resolve all conflicts of interest between investment banks and clients as well as information providers, and it is well possible that different contractual arrangements might be preferred by all participants. However, if these arrangements are even more complex than those currently used, it might well be that the transaction costs of negotiating such contracts and implementing them outweigh the benefits that can be gained. Competition between investment banks would lead to a quick dissemination if another contractual form was more beneficial overall.

Part III

Research

Investment banks regularly publish their assessments on individual securities, most commonly stocks. This work is conducted by so-called buy-side analysts, who previously were often also involved in the assessment of securities as part of mergers and acquisition advisory or securities underwriting, often referred to as sell-side analysts. Such an arrangement was seen as leading to conflicts of interests between these dual roles of analysts. On the one hand in their role as buy-side analysts, they are supposed to provide unbiased advice to potential investors, while on the other hand, they take the role of sell-side analysts working in the interests of the companies that seek advice. It was surmised that combining these two roles was detrimental to the quality of advice given to investors. Consequently, these two roles were separated, and the involvement of buy-side analysts in other areas of investment banking is very much limited, including that no remuneration should be given to buy-side analysts that induce them to take anything but the quality of their advice into account. Despite these changes, it is still that analysts are overall excessively positive about the securities they cover and adverse developments are not reported or only very late once they are more widely known.

While buy-side financial analysts are supposed to work in the interests of their customers, they still operate in a situation in which they need access to information provided by companies. Hence, they need to balance the ability to gain access with the demands companies might make on them for this privilege, usually the provision of positive coverage. Similarly, with revenue from selling information, buy-side analysts are barely able to cover the costs of providing analyst cover from selling their reports; hence financial analysts will still be incentivised to consider the impact their research will have on the ability of the other parts of the investment bank to attract business. As clients usually appoint investment banks that are positively inclined towards them, this provides an incentive for investment banks to bias their reports towards these demands. Chapter 8 assesses the impact of these incentives on the bias in the recommendation of financial analysts.

Furthermore, financial analysts will also consider the impact their reports have on their standing in the profession. An analyst providing recommendations that are going against the majority of other opinions might find their position significantly weakened if they are found to be inaccurate. Of course, on the other hand, them being found to be accurate might improve their standing. These aspects need to be balanced against the safety of providing an analysis that stays close to the consensus of other analysts. The consequences for the truthful reporting of the information analysts have obtained are discussed in Chap. 9.

The separation of buy-side and sell-side analysts has been hailed as one element to improve the quality of recommendations provided by buy-side analysts, together with more information on their remuneration packages. We will see in Chap. 10 how these efforts affected the incentives of analysts and the consequences it has for the quality of their published work.

8 Biased Analyst Recommendations

The primary role of financial analysts should be to provide investors with information about the future prospects of securities, in most cases shares in companies. Such information is often provided in the form of forecasts on the future price of the shares or, equivalently, of returns, commonly with reference to a benchmark such as a market index. When providing this forecast, financial analysts have to rely on information they have obtained from a wide range of sources. While financial analysts will make use of publicly available information, such as annual and quarterly reports, along with filings made with regulatory authority to disclose information, they will also use their knowledge of the industry and competitor companies. In addition, financial analysts maintain contacts with senior management in the company they cover. While regulation commonly requires information to be disclosed publicly, such personal contacts can and are used to ascertain the impact any disclosed information might have on the company or its competitors, likely reactions of the management to mitigate any adverse effects or exploitation of new opportunities. Such, often informal, contacts can add to the precision of information that financial analysts hold.

Companies are interested in obtaining positive coverage from financial analysts. This is because providing a positive assessment of a company's future will commonly increase its share price, which can provide a deterrent for any hostile takeover, provide the company with attractive shares to use in negotiated mergers or acquisitions, and reduce the cost of capital. Companies might therefore be more inclined to provide additional information to financial analysts who assess them more positively. In Sect. 8.1, we will see that in such a case, it is optimal for the financial analyst to provide a forecast that is excessively optimistic in return for access to additional information.

Financial analysts do not only work in the interest of investors using their information to improve their decisions, but they can also be used to obtain additional contracts for the investment bank. Given that contact to senior managers are commonly established, financial analysts can be used as a point of contact to gain

A. Krause, *Theoretical Foundations of Investment Banking*, Springer Texts in Business and Economics, https://doi.org/10.1007/978-3-031-58060-4_8

any such business. If companies are awarding additional contracts on the basis of how positive financial analyst reports are, there is an incentive for investment banks to publish analyst reports that are overly positive as we will discuss in Sect. 8.2. Such analyst reports will not be purely based on the information obtained but take into account the additional benefits more positive reports can generate for the investment bank.

8.1 Financial Analyst Access to Company Information

The aim of financial analysts is to provide investors with guidance on the future development of the company they cover, most notably the value of their securities, mostly shares. As such, financial analysts publish forecasts on the future price of the shares or, equivalently, information on their expected returns. They base this forecast on information they have analysed. It is essential that financial analysts have access to internal information provided by the company itself to set them apart from the information available to the general public. While disclosure rules apply limits on the ability of companies to provide information selectively to only financial analysts or even individual financial analysts, personal contacts can be used to provide much sought-after clarifications or classification of information that is otherwise widely available. Companies are aware that financial analysts rely on access to information directly from companies to improve their forecasts. Of course, companies prefer a positive report on their future prospects and can use access to additional information as a tool to induce more positive coverage than they would otherwise obtain.

Let us now assume that financial analysts obtain a signal s that provides them with imperfect information on the true future price or current value P of the security such that $s = P + \varepsilon$. The uncertainty of the signal s with respect to the true value of the shares, P, is expressed through the term ε and the level of this uncertainty is measured by its variance $Var\left[\varepsilon\right] = \sigma_\varepsilon^2$. The variance of the true value, absent any signal s, is given by $Var\left[P\right] = \sigma_P^2$. The financial analyst will issue a forecast $\hat{P}$, and we can compare this forecast to the actual value P by means of the forecasting error, which, having received signal s, is defined by

$$\begin{aligned}\Pi_B &= E\left[\left(\hat{P} - P\right)^2 \middle| s\right] \\ &= E\left[\left(\left(\hat{P} - E\left[P|s\right]\right) - \left(P - E\left[P|s\right]\right)\right)^2 \middle| s\right] \\ &= E\left[\left(\hat{P} - E\left[P|s\right]\right)^2 \middle| s\right] + E\left[\left(P - E\left[P|s\right]\right)^2 \middle| s\right] \\ &= E\left[\left(\hat{P} - E\left[P|s\right]\right)^2\right] + Var\left[P|s\right].\end{aligned} \tag{8.1}$$

Defining the bias in the forecast of the financial analyst as the difference between the forecast, $\hat{P}$, and an objective forecast based on the signal received, $E[P|s]$, we define $b = \hat{P} - E[P|s]$ as the bias and note that Bayesian learning results in $Var[P|s] = \frac{1}{\frac{1}{\sigma_P^2}+\frac{1}{\sigma_\varepsilon^2}}$ if we assume all variables to be normally distributed. Using this definition of the bias and the result on the conditional variance, we can rewrite Eq. (8.5) as

$$\Pi_B = b^2 + \frac{1}{\frac{1}{\sigma_P^2} + \frac{1}{\sigma_\varepsilon^2}}. \tag{8.2}$$

Using our above assertion that companies will reward financial analysts providing a more positive coverage with access to more or more precise information, we see that $\frac{\partial \sigma_\varepsilon^2}{\partial b} < 0$. The more precise the information, the lower the variance σ_ε^2 and a more positive coverage we identify here as a positive bias b. Thus, companies seek to induce financial analysts to provide a forecast that is more positive than it would be objectively. Please note that the information provided to the financial analyst remains unbiased such that positive and negative information are disclosed equally.

We can now determine the optimal bias by minimising the forecast error, Π_B, giving us the first-order condition from Eq. (8.2) as

$$\frac{\partial \Pi_B}{\partial b} = 2b + \frac{\partial \sigma_\varepsilon^2}{\partial b}\left(\frac{\sigma_P^2}{\sigma_P^2 + \sigma_\varepsilon^2}\right)^2 = 0, \tag{8.3}$$

which easily solves for

$$b = -\frac{1}{2}\frac{\partial \sigma_\varepsilon^2}{\partial b}\left(\frac{\sigma_P^2}{\sigma_P^2 + \sigma_\varepsilon^2}\right)^2 > 0. \tag{8.4}$$

Thus, analysts would optimally publish positively biased recommendations. This positive bias is the result of a trade-off between accuracy of the forecast and gaining access to information that allows financial analysts to improve the accuracy of their signal. We clearly see that if companies do not provide additional information in return for a more positive coverage, $\frac{\partial \sigma_\varepsilon^2}{\partial b} = 0$, then financial analysts would publish their forecast unbiased. The more access the company provides to information in return for a positive coverage, the higher (in absolute terms) $\frac{\partial \sigma_\varepsilon^2}{\partial b}$ will be and thus the higher the bias will be. In this case the additional information provided allows the financial analyst to reduce the forecast error more easily and thus could increase the bias to gain access to this information without negatively affecting the forecast error.

If the uncertainty in the market about the value of the shares, σ_P^2, increases, the lower the bias will be. The reason for this finding is that with high uncertainty, the financial analyst can reduce the forecast error significantly, and introducing a bias will reduce these benefits. Furthermore, the more precise the signal obtained is, a lower ε, the larger the bias will be. If the signal is already small, the forecast error will be small, and an increase to introduce a bias would nevertheless cause the forecast error to remain low.

Summary Financial analysts have to trade off the accuracy of their forecast with their ability to access information to provide such a forecast. If companies will give preferential access to information if an analyst provides a more positive forecast than the available information suggests, this will induce a positive bias into the forecast of financial analysts. Despite this positive bias in the forecast financial analysts publish, given the constraints on access to information, the forecast error will be reduced. Thus the biased forecast will be more precise than an unbiased forecast based on less information. This will benefit investors relying on analyst forecasts for their decision-making as they get the most precise forecast that is available.

Reading Lim (2001).

8.2 Obtaining Future Investment Banking Business

Financial analysts provide investors with forecasts on the future performance of securities, most notably shares of companies. Making precise forecasts increases the reputation of an investment bank and would increase the number of investors seeking their advice and using their brokerage services, thus increasing profits to the investment bank. Companies covered by financial analysts generally have an interest in obtaining positive coverage. As many companies will, at some point in the future, seek advice from investment banks, either for mergers and acquisitions or other services, they can use this future revenue as a tool to induce financial analysts to bias their forecasts in the companies' favour.

Let us assume that financial analysts of N investment banks are covering a company, which also has future investment banking business that provides benefits V_B to the investment bank. Each investment bank obtains a noisy signal s_i of the true value of the security, P, such that $s_i = P + \varepsilon_i$ with the variance of the true value given by $Var[P] = \sigma_P^2$ and the variance of the uncertainty in the signal ε_i being $Var[\varepsilon_i] = \sigma_i^2$.

An analyst publishing a forecast $\hat{P}_i$ for the value of the security has, based on the value of its signal s_i, a bias $b_i = E\left[\hat{P}_i - E[P|s_i]\right]$, where $E[P|s_i]$ represents the expected value of the security, given the signal the analyst has received; thus, it is the unbiased forecast. The forecast error is then given by

$$\begin{aligned} & E\left[\left(\hat{P}_i - P\right)^2 \middle| s_i\right] \\ &= E\left[\left(\left(\hat{P}_i - E\left[P|s_i\right]\right) - \left(P - E\left[P|s_i\right]\right)\right)^2 \middle| s_i\right] \\ &= E\left[\left(\hat{P}_i - E\left[P|s_i\right]\right)^2 \middle| s_i\right] + E\left[\left(P - E\left[P|s_i\right]\right)^2 \middle| s_i\right] \\ &= E\left[\left(\hat{P}_i - E\left[P|s_i\right]\right)^2\right] + Var\left[P|s_i\right] \\ &= b_i^2 + Var\left[P|s_i\right] \\ &= b_i^2 + \frac{1}{\frac{1}{\sigma_P^2} + \frac{1}{\sigma_i^2}}, \end{aligned} \tag{8.5}$$

where the last line uses the result from Bayesian learning that $Var\left[P|s_i\right] = \frac{1}{\frac{1}{\sigma_P^2}+\frac{1}{\sigma_i^2}}$ if we assume all variables to be normally distributed.

Investment banks will now balance the forecast error with the ability to obtain additional revenue from the company they cover.

Competitive Investment Banks The company has the choice who to give their future investment banking business to, and we assume they assign a probability p_i to give this business to bank i. Banks thus chosen by the company obtain benefits V_B. However, we assume that they also face a reputational loss if they are getting their forecast wrong. We thus assume that the profits of bank i are given by

$$\begin{aligned} \Pi_B^i &= p_i V_B - \alpha_B E\left[\left(\hat{P}_i - P\right)^2 |s_i\right] \\ &= p_i V_B - \alpha_B \left(b_i^2 + \frac{1}{\frac{1}{\sigma_P^2} + \frac{1}{\sigma_i^2}}\right), \end{aligned} \tag{8.6}$$

with α_B denoting the relative importance of the forecasting error and having inserted for the forecasting error from Eq. (8.5). If an analyst provides a forecast with high errors, its recommendations are less valuable to investors, and they might seek to trade less or use another broker to trade, causing the investment bank to have lower profits. In addition, by publishing recommendations that are proven to be wrong, they might damage their reputation and thus long-term profits in all business areas. The extent of this loss of profits is given by α_B.

If banks are competitive such that $\Pi_B^{\prime i} = 0$, we easily obtain that the bias must fulfill

$$b_i = \sqrt{\frac{p_i V_B}{\alpha_B} - \frac{1}{\frac{1}{\sigma_P^2} + \frac{1}{\sigma_i^2}}}. \tag{8.7}$$

We clearly see that higher future revenue V_B increases the bias, the same effect as an increase in the likelihood of obtaining this revenue p_i. Hence, investment banks are competing for additional revenue by seeking a high probability p_i, which we easily see is associated with a high bias. Thus, in order to attract additional investment banking business, investment banks will forego some revenue from investors and damage their reputation by providing biased forecast. That such a bias induces the company to provide an investment bank with the additional business will be analysed below.

Optimising Companies We assume that companies prefer positive coverage by analysts and thus benefit from a positive bias in their recommendations. The profits of the company are then derived from the average bias of all N banks, less the costs of supplying information to investment banks, which forms their signal s_i. These costs to provide the signal to bank i are denoted by C_i, and the precision of the signal is $\frac{1}{\sigma_i}$. We assume that $\frac{\partial C_i}{\partial \frac{1}{\sigma_i^2}} > 0$ such that a more precise signal increases the costs to the company. The benefits to the company might be that a positive analyst coverage allows them to conduct mergers at more favourable conditions if payment is made by shares, that it becomes less attractive to hostile takeover, or that due to a higher share price its cost of capital are reduced.

Hence, the profits of companies are given by

$$\Pi_C = \alpha_C \frac{1}{N} \sum_{i=1}^{N} b_i + \sum_{i=1}^{N} C_i, \tag{8.8}$$

where α_C denotes the relative importance of the bias for the company. Companies allocate the investment banking business to bank i with probability p_i; hence, $\sum_{i=1}^{N} p_i = 1$. Inserting for b_i from Eq. (8.7) into Eq. (8.8), we can obtain the Lagrangian function $\mathcal{L} = \Pi_C - \zeta \left(\sum_{i=1}^{N} p_i - 1 \right)$, and the first-order conditions for choosing the optimal precision of information $\frac{1}{\sigma_i^2}$ and allocation to investment banking business, p_i, using the Lagrange multiplier ζ become

$$\frac{\partial \mathcal{L}}{\partial p_i} = \frac{\alpha_C V_B}{2N b_i} - \zeta = 0, \tag{8.9}$$

$$\frac{\partial \mathcal{L}}{\partial \frac{1}{\sigma_i^2}} = \frac{\alpha_C}{2Nb_i}\left(\frac{1}{\frac{1}{\sigma_P^2}+\frac{1}{\sigma_i^2}}\right)^2 - \frac{\partial C_i}{\partial \frac{1}{\sigma_i^2}} = 0.$$

From the second equation, we easily obtain that

$$b_i = \frac{\alpha_C}{2N}\frac{1}{\frac{\partial C_i}{\partial \frac{1}{\sigma_i^2}}\left(\frac{1}{\sigma_P^2}+\frac{1}{\sigma_i^2}\right)^2} > 0 \tag{8.10}$$

setting this expression equal to the bias of competing investment banks from Eq. (8.7), we can obtain the expression for the signal precision $\frac{1}{\sigma_i^2}$. Using this result then can be used to obtain the optimal probability p_i of awarding the investment banking business to investment bank i. As all banks are identical, they will have equal probabilities of being selected; thus, $p_i = \frac{1}{N}$.

In order to secure future business, investment banks provide biased analyst coverage as we can see from Eqs. (8.7) and (8.10). We see that this bias is increasing in the importance of this bias to companies (α_C) and decreasing if the retention of investors is important to investment banks (α_B). The number of analysts covering a company will reduce the bias. This is because the impact of each analyst on the average bias is becoming smaller, and thus the costs to banks of providing a biased forecast, its loss of business from investors and damage to reputation, become more important, and hence they reduce the bias. If the costs of supplying the bank with information, $\frac{\partial C_i}{\partial \frac{1}{\sigma_i^2}}$, are increasing, e.g., due to disclosure requirements that make it more difficult to provide information only to selected analysts, the bias should also decrease as the net benefits to companies are reduced.

We thus see that investment banks compete with each other for additional revenue from companies by providing a biased forecast of their future prospects. As there is a positive relationship between the probability of obtaining this additional revenue and the bias, investment banks will balance the additional revenue from attracting this business against the loss of business from investors and their loss of reputation. Companies encourage such competition because it allows them to obtain the more positive analyst coverage they seek and will provide this additional business more often to the investment bank exhibiting the highest bias.

Summary Companies seek positive analyst coverage, and by selecting investment banks according to the extent they provide such positive forecasts, they induce investment banks to bias their forecasts positively. While this implies that analyst reports are less useful for investors and investment bank will lose business due to publishing such biased reports, the additional business they can obtain from the companies they cover are outweighing these losses.

Any regulatory measures to severe the link between gaining investment banking business and the positivity of analyst coverage, equivalent to increasing α_B, will reduce the bias. However, at the same time, it will also make the investment bank revenue from investors more sensitive to any remaining bias, which may imply that analyst coverage is no longer profitable and thus investment banks provide less coverage. That would reduce the number of financial analysts covering a company, increasing the bias as the impact on the company of each financial analyst is increased. Thus, the overall effect of such a policy to severe the ties of analyst coverage and investment banking business is diminished or, depending on parameter constellations, might even lead to an increased bias of the few remaining financial analysts.

Reading Teo (2000).

Conclusions

The recommendations and forecasts of financial analysts are commonly positively biased in the sense that the projected return or future stock price is higher than what it would have been when based solely on information available at the time. We have seen that there might be two reasons for such an observation, with one being driven by the desire to access information from the company and reduce the forecast error and the other with the aim of attracting additional investment banking business from the company. If gaining access to additional information from the company is only possible if the report is positively biased, the financial analyst has to weigh up the overly positive forecast against the reduction in forecast errors due to having better information. The optimal outcomes, in terms of minimising the forecast error, are to publish reports with a positive bias. While the report will be positively biased, any investor, even if not recognising the existence of such a bias, will benefit as the forecast error is minimised. Therefore, biased analyst reports are in the interest of investors too.

In contrast to that, it is detrimental to investors to attempt to attract additional investment banking revenue. The positive bias is introduced so that the investment bank can increase its profits by attracting more business from the company they cover, and it does not lead to a reduction in the forecast error. In many cases, however, these two reasons for providing positively bias analyst reports will be combined, and the financial analyst will obtain additional information in return for the positive coverage and be rewarded with additional investment banking business. Therefore, the biased recommendation of financial analysts benefits the company due to a more positive coverage, the investment bank by obtaining additional business, and investors by being giving information with a lower forecast error. Of course, the bias arising to gain additional investment banking business from the company might be larger than is optimal to minimise the forecast error, in which case investors are not benefitting optimally.

Analyst Reputation

9

Financial analysts are concerned about the reputation they obtain about the quality of their recommendations. Their abilities are not directly observable, but only the recommendations they make public. The assessment of their ability can be conducted comparing their recommendations with the realised value of the security. The financial analyst will not be concerned with the quality of its forecasts directly, but only to the extent that they affect the assessment of their ability. Achieving a reputation for high ability will allow financial analysts to obtain higher remuneration and allow them to be employed by more reputable investment banks. It is for this reason that they will seek to maximise their reputation by issuing recommendations strategically.

Let us assume that an analyst i receives a signal $s_i = H$ or $s_i = L$ about the value of a security, most commonly a share, which can be either P_H with probability π or P_L with probability $1-\pi$. This signal received is correct with probability ρ_i; thus, $Prob_i\left(H|P_H\right) = Prob_i\left(L|P_L\right) = \rho_i \geq \frac{1}{2}$. We have two types of analysts, strong and weak analysts, where the precision of the signal for strong analysts, ρ_S, exceeds that of weak analysts ρ_W, such that $\rho_S > \rho_W$. We assume that there is a fraction γ of strong analysts covering a stock.

Forecasts and Inference of Analyst Quality Bayes' theorem gives us the probability that the value of the security is high (low) if the signal received is high (low) as

$$Prob_i\left(P_H|H\right) = \frac{\rho_i\pi}{\rho_i\pi + \left(1-\rho_i\right)\left(1-\pi\right)}, \tag{9.1}$$

$$Prob_i\left(P_L|L\right) = \frac{\rho_i\left(1-\pi\right)}{\rho_i\left(1-\pi\right) + \left(1-\rho_i\right)\pi},$$

A. Krause, *Theoretical Foundations of Investment Banking*, Springer Texts in Business and Economics, https://doi.org/10.1007/978-3-031-58060-4_9

respectively. The best possible forecast of the value of the security is then determined as the expected value of the stock, given the signal received. For an analyst of type i receiving signal s_i, this becomes

$$\begin{aligned} \hat{P}_i^{s_i} &= E_i\left[P|s_i\right] \\ &= P_H Prob_i\left(P_H|s_i\right) + P_L Prob\left(P_L|s_i\right) \\ &= P_L + \left(P_H - P_L\right) Prob_i\left(P_H|s_i\right) \end{aligned} \tag{9.2}$$

and it is easy the see using Eq. (9.1) that we have

$$P_H > \hat{P}_S^H > \hat{P}_W^H > \pi P_H + (1-\pi) P_L > \hat{P}_W^L > \hat{P}_S^L > P_L, \tag{9.3}$$

if we assume that $P_H > P_L$. The term $\pi P_H + (1-\pi) P_L$ represents the expected value of the stock in the absence of any signal and can be interpreted as the current consensus forecast of the analysts and the market. We see that if receiving a positive signal (H), the higher accuracy of that signal for the strong analyst makes his forecast move more from this consensus than the same signal received by a weak analyst. Similarly for low signals L, the same signal causes the forecast of the strong analyst to deviate more than for the weak analyst.

Signals received by analysts cannot be verified, nor does the public reading their forecast know their type; thus, analysts could publish any forecast, $\hat{P}_W^H$, $\hat{P}_W^L$, $\hat{P}_S^H$, or $\hat{P}_S^L$. We will argue below that a financial analyst will only choose to publish recommendations consistent with those of strong analysts, thus $\hat{P}_S^H$ or $\hat{P}_S^L$, and consequently focus our attention on these two possible forecasts.

We need to compare the forecasts of financial analysts with the outcome observed to assess their strength. Ex post, the forecast of the analyst, $\hat{P}_S^{s_i}$, can be compared to the realised outcome, P_i. Financial analysts can provide a forecast consistent with their signal; this $\hat{P}_S^H$ is $s_i = H$ or $\hat{P}_S^L$ if $s_i = L$; or they change their forecast to $\hat{P}_S^H$ if $s_i = L$ and $\hat{P}_S^L$ if $s_i = H$. We assume that they change their forecast with probability λ. Let $\Upsilon_i^j = Prob\left(S|\hat{P}_S^i, P_j\right)$ be the probability of an analyst seen as strong if he has made forecast $\hat{P}_S^i$, and the actual price realised is P_j. We can use Bayesian learning to determine this probability and obtain

$$\begin{aligned} \Upsilon_L^L &= \frac{\rho_S \gamma}{\rho_S \gamma + \rho_W (1-\gamma) + \lambda (1-\rho_W)(1-\gamma)}, \\ \Upsilon_L^H &= \frac{(1-\rho_S)\gamma}{(1-\rho_S)\gamma + (1-\rho_W)(1-\gamma) + \lambda \rho_W (1-\gamma)}, \\ \Upsilon_H^L &= \frac{(1-\rho_S)\gamma}{(1-\rho_S)\gamma + (1-\rho_W)(1-\gamma)(1-\lambda)}, \\ \Upsilon_H^H &= \frac{\rho_S \gamma}{\rho_S \gamma + \rho_W (1-\gamma)(1-\lambda)}. \end{aligned} \tag{9.4}$$

Here we look at the probability of an analyst being strong, given the forecast it published and the realisation of the value. In the first expression, the numerator assesses the likelihood of the strong analyst (γ) having made the forecast and got the forecast correct (ρ_S). The denominator accounts for all ways this forecast and value could have been achieved. It could arise from the strong analyst and the weak analyst (γ and $1-\gamma$) getting the forecast right (ρ_S and ρ_W), as well as the weak analyst ($1-\gamma$) getting the forecast wrong ($1-\rho_W$) but reporting a different forecast (λ). Similarly, the second expression shows in the numerator the strong analyst getting the forecast wrong and the denominator having expressions for the strong and weak analysts getting the forecast wrong, plus the weak analysts getting the forecast right but changing their forecast. The third expression again shows in the numerator the strong analyst getting the forecast wrong, while the denominator shows the weak analysts that do not change forecasts. Similarly, the final expression shows all those getting the forecast right and not changing it.

We can now analyse the optimal forecasts of analysts that maximise their probability of being recognised as being strong. We will first consider the decisions of weak analysts receiving high and low signals, respectively, before commencing with the analysis of strong analysts.

Weak Analysts with High Signals Weak analysts, knowing their signal s_i, will seek to maximise the expected probability that they are seen as a strong analyst through the best forecast to publish, $\hat{P}$. This expected probability will be given for their assessment of the probability of realising the high and low values, respectively. We thus have

$$E_i\left[Prob\left(S|\hat{P},P\right)\middle|s_i\right] = Prob_i\left(P_H|s_i\right)Prob\left(S|\hat{P},P_H\right) + Prob_i\left(P_L|s_i\right)Prob\left(S|\hat{P},P_L\right). \tag{9.5}$$

We first analyse the weak analyst observing the high signal H. Define

$$\Psi_W^H = E_W\left[Prob\left(S|\hat{P}_S^L,P\right)\middle|H\right] - E_W\left[Prob\left(S|\hat{P}_S^H,P\right)\middle|H\right] \tag{9.6}$$

as the difference between publishing a report using the low forecast $\hat{P}_S^L$ and the high forecast $\hat{P}_S^H$ if the high signal is received. Inserting Eqs. (9.1) and (9.4) into Eq. (9.5) and this into Eq. (9.6), we can easily show that

$$\frac{\partial \Psi_W^H}{\partial \lambda} < 0. \tag{9.7}$$

Thus, the higher the probability that weak analysts alter their forecast, the smaller this difference between weak analysts being assessed as strong if they publish low forecasts over high forecasts.

Let us now evaluate Ψ_W^H at $\lambda = 0$, the situation where weak analysts report their signal truthfully. We then get by inserting all terms as before into Eq. (9.6) that

$$\Psi_W^H = \frac{(Prob_W(P_H|H) - Prob_W(P_L|H))\,\gamma\,(1-\gamma)\,(\rho_W - \rho_S)}{(\rho_S\gamma + \rho_W(1-\gamma))\,((1-\rho_S) + (1-\rho_W)(1-\gamma))} \tag{9.8}$$

and as $\rho_W < \rho_S$, the final term of the numerator is negative. From Eq. (9.1), we get that the first term is positive if $\pi > 1 - \rho_W$. In this case, $\Psi_W^H < 0$, and hence, it is more profitable to report the signal truthfully.

In the case that $\pi < 1 - \rho_W$, we have $\Psi_W^H > 0$, and hence analysts would prefer to change their forecast to the low forecast, despite receiving the high signal. This is inconsistent with $\lambda = 0$, and hence $\lambda = 0$ is not an equilibrium. We can further show that for $\lambda = 1$, we have

$$\begin{aligned}\Psi_W^H = {} & Prob_W(P_H|H)\,\frac{(1-\rho_S)\,\gamma}{(1-\rho_S)\,\gamma + (1-\gamma)} \\ & + Prob_W(P_H|L)\,\frac{\rho_S\gamma}{\rho_S\gamma + (1-\gamma)} - 1 < 0\end{aligned} \tag{9.9}$$

and hence rather than changing their forecast ($\lambda = 1$), weak analysts prefer to report truthfully; therefore, always changing the forecast cannot be an equilibrium. Thus, as $\frac{\partial\Psi_W^H}{\partial\lambda} < 0$, there exists an λ^* such that $\Psi_W^H = 0$, and this $1 > \lambda^* > 0$ gives us the equilibrium probability of changing to the low forecast.

We thus see that if $\pi > 1 - \rho_W$, the weak analyst will report the high forecast truthfully and if $\pi < 1 - \rho_W$, he changes to the low forecast with probability λ^*. The reasoning for this result is that with a sufficiently high value of π, the signals received by strong analysts are quite commonly high as well. Thus, the forecasts of strong analysts, as we will see when discussing them below, will be high, and weak analysts will not be distinguishable from them in those cases. Once the probability of having a high stock value falls sufficiently, the likelihood of strong analysts receiving high signals reduces; hence, the weak analyst will stand out more as such and therefore switch to submitting low forecasts to blend into the forecasts submitted by strong analysts.

Weak Analysts with a Low Signal If the weak analyst receives the low signal L, we can, similarly to Eq. (9.6), define

$$\Psi_W^L = E_W\left[Prob\left(S|\hat{P}_S^L, P\right)|L\right] - E_W\left[Prob\left(S|\hat{P}_S^H, P\right)|L\right], \tag{9.10}$$

as the difference in the likelihood of being perceived as strong if submitting the low and high forecast. The only difference to Ψ_W^H in Eq. (9.6) are $Prob_W(P_H|L)$ and $Prob_W(P_L|L)$, and we find that $\frac{\partial\Psi_W^L}{\partial\lambda} > 0$.

At $\lambda = 0$, we have

$$\Psi_W^L = \frac{(Prob_W(P_H|L) - Prob_W(P_L|L))\,\gamma\,(1-\gamma)\,(\rho_W - \rho_S)}{(\rho_S\gamma + \rho_W(1-\gamma))\,((1-\rho_S)\,\gamma + (1-\rho_W)(1-\gamma))}, \tag{9.11}$$

and the first term of the numerator is negative if $\pi < \rho_W$. Thus $\Psi_W^L > 0$ and the weak analysts would truthfully report the low signal L.

If $\pi > \rho_W$, then it would be optimal to change to the high forecast, which is inconsistent with $\lambda = 0$, which implies that the forecast reveals the signal truthfully. Hence this would not be an equilibrium. Similarly to the case of a high signal, we find that for $\lambda = 1$, we have $\Psi_W^L < 0$, implying that changing the forecast is also not an equilibrium and the solution of λ^{**} at $\Psi_W^L = 0$ denotes the probability of a weak analyst changing to the high forecast.

We thus see that if $\pi < \rho_W$, the weak analyst will report the low forecast truthfully and if $\pi > \rho_W$, he changes to the high forecast with probability λ^{**} The reasoning for this result is that with a sufficiently low value of π, the signals received by strong analysts are quite commonly low as well. Thus, the forecasts of strong analysts, as we will see when discussing them below, will be low, and the weak analysts will not be distinguishable from them in those cases. Once the probability of having a high stock value increases sufficiently, the likelihood of strong analysts receiving low signals reduces; hence, the weak analyst will stand out more as such and therefore switch to submitting high forecasts to blend into the forecasts submitted by strong analysts.

As in equilibrium $\Psi_W^L = \Psi_W^H = 0$, we can use the implicit function theorem to get

$$\begin{aligned} \frac{\partial \lambda^*}{\partial \pi} &< 0, \\ \frac{\partial \lambda^{**}}{\partial \pi} &> 0, \\ \frac{\partial \lambda^*}{\partial \gamma} &> 0, \\ \frac{\partial \lambda^{**}}{\partial \gamma} &> 0. \end{aligned} \tag{9.12}$$

as we can show that $\frac{\partial \Psi_W^i}{\partial \pi} < 0$, $\frac{\partial \Psi_W^i}{\partial \gamma} < 0$, $\frac{\partial \Psi_W^H}{\partial \lambda} < 0$, and $\frac{\partial \Psi_W^L}{\partial \lambda} > 0$.

We see that if there are more strong financial analysts covering a stock, γ, the probability of weak analysts changing their forecasts is increased. The reason for this result is that with more strong analysts, the potential for submitting a forecast that is different to other financial analysts is increased, making them easier to be identified as weak. Hence, if weak financial analysts observe a signal that deviates from the consensus forecast sufficiently, they are more likely to change it towards the consensus forecast such that they cannot be differentiated from other, strong, financial analysts.

If the likelihood of high stock values P_H, π, becomes more extreme, either higher or lower, then the likelihood of weak financial analysts changing their forecasts reduces. This arises because more and more strong financial analysts will have obtained the same signal and thus provide the same forecast as the signal received by the weak analyst, making a change of the forecast unnecessary.

Strong Analyst Looking at the strong analyst, we can, similar to Eq. (9.6), define Ψ_S^j. It is easy to show that show that if $\Psi_W^j = 0$, we have $\Psi_S^H < 0$ and $\Psi_S^L > 0$, and hence strong analysts report their signals correctly if $\pi < 1 - \rho_W$ and $\pi > \rho_W$, respectively. In the case that $1 - \rho_W < \pi < \rho_W$, the incentives are unchanged from weak analysts, and they provide a truthful forecast. Thus, strong analysts always provide forecasts that are consistent with their signal.

The strong analyst seeks to make the weak analyst copying him as costly as possible by choosing $\hat{P}_S^H$ and $\hat{P}_S^L$. If the weak analyst changes its forecast, having to change it to that of the forecast of the strong analysts implies the biggest change and hence is most costly to him. Thereby, he protects his status as being identified as strong. Of course the weak analyst will not publish a forecast of $\hat{P}_W^j$ as that would distinguish him instantly from the strong analysts, who use $\hat{P}_H^j$, and in his attempt to copy their behaviour, he will provide the same forecast.

Summary We find that financial analysts who receive signals of lower quality submit forecasts that are consistent with having received signals of higher quality. This is done to avoid being identified as being a weak financial analyst. Furthermore, if weak financial analysts are receiving a signal that is opposite to the perceived consensus, e.g., they receive a low signal when the ex ante probability of obtaining such a low signal is low, they will change their forecast to be in line with the perceived consensus. As signals the financial analysts receive cannot be observed by the public, financial analysts will be assessed on the quality of their forecasts. A financial analyst knowing that he himself is weak will not want to deviate from the consensus he expects the stronger analysts to reach and will thus provide a forecast consistent with what he expects the signal of the strong financial analysts to be.

This result shows how financial analysts are avoiding to make forecasts that are different from that of other financial analysts. If the likelihood of having received the correct signal is sufficiently low, then the likelihood of making a correct forecast is also low. If they are the only financial analyst making such a forecast or part of a small group of financial analysts, their reputation will be damaged. On the other hand, if they are successful, their reputation will be enhanced. However, the likelihood of being successful is small, and the overall impact on their reputation will be negative. If instead submitting a forecast at the consensus, they can expect to find many other similar forecasts, and their forecast being wrong will therefore not damage their reputation significantly, nor will it enhance much if the forecast is correct. Thus, financial analysts provide the forecast that they see as safer for their reputation by using the consensus forecast.

Therefore, by being more concerned for their reputation as providing high-quality forecasts, weaker investors will neglect their information in many cases and provide forecasts consistent with the market consensus, and we see an excess of such forecasts and financial analysts will underperform compared to a situation in which they follow their signals.

Reading Trueman (1994).

Regulation of Financial Analysts

10

It is often observed that the quality of financial analyst coverage is low. The observation is that the recommendations made by financial analysts are overly positive and the predictive power low. Regulatory attempts have been made to improve the quality of coverage, most notably by addressing a conflict of interest in that financial analysts are providing assistance in gaining additional investment banking business for their employer and are rewarded accordingly. Requiring the remuneration of financial analysts to be solely based on the quality of their coverage, not including any additional revenue they might have brought to the investment bank, was intended to increase the standard in this area. Such Chinese Walls have failed to improve the analyst coverage significantly.

Let us assume that the value of a stock is P_H with probability π and $P_L < P_H$ with probability $1 - \pi$. We have strong analysts whose signal is correct with probability ρ_S and weak analysts whose signals are correct with probability $\rho_W < \rho_S$ such that

$$Prob_i \left(H | P_H \right) = Prob_i \left(L | P_L \right) = \rho_i. \tag{10.1}$$

The probability of being a strong analyst is γ, and through effort an analyst can increase his abilities at total costs of $\frac{1}{2} c_I \gamma^2$. Analysts, and the banks employing them, know which type an analyst is, but this is not observable outside of the bank. Analysts suffer a reputation loss if their prediction $\hat{P}$ is wrong, causing a loss of $c_P E\left[\left(\hat{P} - P_j\right)^2\right]$. Such reputation loss might affect their chances of future promotions or the ability to obtain different, better-paying positions with investment banks or other companies. With wages w_i for an analyst of type i, we have the expected utility of analysts as

$$\Pi_A = \gamma w_S + (1 - \gamma) w_W - \frac{1}{2} c_I \gamma^2 - c_P E\left[\left(\hat{P} - P_j\right)^2\right]. \tag{10.2}$$

A. Krause, *Theoretical Foundations of Investment Banking*, Springer Texts in Business and Economics, https://doi.org/10.1007/978-3-031-58060-4_10

We note that with probability γ, the analyst is strong and receives the appropriate remuneration w_S, while with probability $1-\gamma$, he is a weak analyst and obtains remuneration w_W.

For the forecasting error, we now have that $(\hat{P}-P_j)^2=(P_H-P_L)^2$ if the prediction is wrong, which happens with probability $1-\rho_i$ and $(\hat{P}-P_j)^2=0$ if the prediction is correct. Hence, the expected forecast error is

$$E\left[\left(\hat{P}-P_j\right)^2\right]=\gamma\left(1-\rho_S\right)\left(P_H-P_L\right)^2 \qquad (10.3)$$
$$+\left(1-\gamma\right)\left(1-\rho_W\right)\left(P_H-P_L\right)^2$$
$$=\left(\left(1-\rho_W\right)-\gamma\left(\rho_S-\rho_W\right)\right)\left(P_H-P_L\right)^2,$$

where we took into account that analysts are either strong, γ, or weak, $1-\gamma$.

Investment banks gain business from their clients if they publish positive reports about them, which in the context of this model implies that the forecasted future value of the company is high, $\hat{P}=P_H$. Hence with benefits V from obtaining additional investment banking business, we get the profits of investment banks as

$$\Pi_B=Prob\left(P_H\right)V-\left(\gamma w_S+\left(1-\gamma\right)w_W\right), \qquad (10.4)$$

where the final term denotes the remuneration the investment bank pays financial analysts. A positive coverage is provided if the true value is high (π) and the signal received reflects this (ρ_i) or the actual value is low ($1-\pi$) but the signal does not reflect this state ($1-\rho_i$). Thus, we here assume that financial analysts publish their assessment truthfully. As the analyst publishing the forecast is either strong (γ) or weak ($1-\gamma$), we have the probability of providing a positive coverage given by

$$Prob\left(P_H\right)=\gamma\left(\rho_S\pi+\left(1-\rho_S\right)\left(1-\pi\right)\right) \qquad (10.5)$$
$$+\left(1-\gamma\right)\left(\rho_W\pi+\left(1-\rho_W\right)\left(1-\pi\right)\right)$$
$$=1-\pi+\rho_W\left(2\pi-1\right)+\gamma\left(\rho_S-\rho_W\right)\left(2\pi-1\right).$$

Throughout, we will assume that analysts are competitive, thus $\Pi_A=0$, such that

$$\gamma w_S+\left(1-\gamma\right)w_W=\frac{1}{2}c_I\gamma^2+c_PE\left[\left(\hat{P}-P_j\right)^2\right], \qquad (10.6)$$

and the expected wages are determined such that they cover the costs of the financial analysts, the costs of becoming a strong analyst, and the possible reputation loss from making wrong predictions.

We will first consider the case of no regulation affecting the decisions of financial analysts and banks, before then continuing with the impact of regulatory constraints on their decisions.

Unregulated Analysts Analysts will seek to maximise their expected profits in Eq. (10.2) over their optimal probability of obtaining a precise signal γ and thus being a strong analyst. After inserting Eq. (10.3) into Eq. (10.2) and using $\frac{\partial \Pi_A}{\partial \gamma} = 0$, the first-order condition solves for

$$\gamma = \frac{w_S - w_W}{c_I} + \frac{c_P}{c_I} (\rho_S - \rho_W) (P_H - P_L)^2 . \tag{10.7}$$

The bank will set optimal wages w_S and w_W by maximising their profits from Eq. (10.4), which, after inserting Eqs. (10.5) and (10.6), gives us from the first-order condition $\frac{\partial \Pi_B}{\partial w_i} = 0$ that

$$\gamma = \frac{2\pi - 1}{c_I} (\rho_S - \rho_W) V + \frac{c_P}{c_I} (\rho_S - \rho_W) (P_H - P_L)^2 . \tag{10.8}$$

Comparing this result with the optimal solution of financial analysts in Eq. (10.7) allows us to determine that

$$w_S - w_W = (2\pi - 1) (\rho_S - \rho_W) V > 0, \tag{10.9}$$

where the final inequality holds if $\pi > \frac{1}{2}$. Inserting this result into Eq. (10.6) allows us to solve for the wages explicitly. The differences between the wages of strong and weak analysts are larger if the value of the investment banking business they attract, V, is higher, as in this case the bank makes more profits from a positive coverage and therefore seeks to induce them to increase their quality as this increases the likelihood of a positive report, as long as $\pi > \frac{1}{2}$, and thus values on average are high. Similarly, a higher differential between strong and weak analysts $\rho_S - \rho_W$ will make it more attractive for the bank to have strong analysts as this again increases the likelihood of a positive report. A higher wage differential increases the quality γ of analysts as it provides incentives to increase the costs and become a strong analyst. That this is the case is obvious from Eq. (10.7), where γ is shown to increase in $w_S - w_W$.

Inserting Eq. (10.9) into Eq. (10.7), we obtain that without any regulation, the quality of analysts is given by

$$\gamma^* = \frac{\rho_S - \rho_W}{c_I} \left((2\pi - 1) V + c_P (P_H - P_L)^2 \right) . \tag{10.10}$$

Not surprisingly, the quality of analysts is increasing in the uncertainty about the value of the company, $P_H - P_L$, which will manifest itself in higher forecast errors. These forecast errors reduce the profits of the analyst due to reputation loss, and he seeks to compensate for this by making such errors less likely. Higher reputation losses if forecasts are wrong, c_P, will increase efforts too, while increased costs of increasing the quality, c_I, will obviously reduce the overall quality. Finally, if strong analysts make much more precise forecasts than weak analysts, $\rho_S - \rho_W$, the benefits in terms of a lower forecast error are larger, as well as the wages obtained by strong analysts, giving incentives to increase their quality.

Using this result as a benchmark, we can now investigate the impact regulatory efforts have on the quality of analysts.

Chinese Walls With Chinese Walls, banks cannot reward analysts through the revenues from other investment banking activities. Thus, they cannot be rewarded for attracting other business from clients to the investment bank. Therefore, let us assume that their wages are determined only by their forecast precision, such that a higher forecast error reduces their wages. We specifically propose that

$$w_i = \frac{w_0}{E_i\left[\left(\hat{P} - P_j\right)^2\right]} = \frac{w_0}{(1-\rho_i)(P_H - P_L)^2}, \tag{10.11}$$

where w_0 can be interpreted as a benchmark salary for a given forecasting error. The forecast error is $P_H - P_L$ if the signal is wrong, $1 - \rho_i$, and zero otherwise.

The incentives for the analyst remain unchanged by this specification of wages as financial analysts took wages as given. Thus the optimal quality of the analyst, γ, is still given by Eq. (10.7). Similarly, the incentives for the bank are unchanged, and Eq. (10.9) still applies. We obtain using Eq. (10.11) that

$$w_S - w_W = \frac{w_0}{(P_H - P_L)^2}\left(\frac{1}{1-\rho_S} - \frac{1}{1-\rho_W}\right) \tag{10.12}$$

and now have to set w_0 such that it meets the requirements in Eq. (10.9). Through this effect, the investment bank can now set $w_0 = (2\pi - 1)(1-\rho_S)(1-\rho_W) V(P_H - P_L)$ and obtains again that $w_S - w_W = (2\pi - 1)(\rho_S - \rho_W) V$ and hence

$$\gamma^{**} = \frac{\rho_S - \rho_W}{c_I}\left((2\pi - 1) V + c_P (P_H - P_L)^2\right) = \gamma^*. \tag{10.13}$$

Hence, the quality of the financial analysts remains unchanged with Chinese Walls. Limiting the remuneration to be based on the quality of analyst coverage alone will not achieve an increase in the quality of financial analysts because the incentives for investment banks and analysts are unchanged; it is only that the wages cannot be directly related to the amount of investment banking business analysts attract through their recommendations. Investment banks are finding a way around this constraint by setting w_0, the benchmark salary, such that the pay differential between strong and weak analysts is identical to the case of no regulation, given the best solution for analysts and banks as before.

Disclosure of Wages Assume now that banks have to disclose the remuneration of their analysts, which reflects whether the analyst is strong or weak, as known to the bank and analyst, but not the clients they seek to attract additional investment banking business from. Using the information from this disclosure, the client knows the quality of the analyst as that can be inferred from their remuneration. Let us assume that only the strong analyst's positive assessment of the client will result in investment banking business, and the analyst is only rewarded if he is strong as we set $w_W = 0$, given he makes no contribution to the investment bank's profits, as he is not gaining any investment banking business. Hence, the analyst profits are given by

$$\Pi_A = \gamma w_S - \frac{1}{2} c_I \gamma^2 - c_P E\left[\left(\hat{P} - P_j\right)^2\right], \tag{10.14}$$

reflecting that remuneration is only paid to strong analysts. The first-order condition $\frac{\partial \Pi_A}{\partial \gamma} = 0$ solves for

$$\gamma = \frac{w_S}{c_I} + \frac{c_P}{c_I} (\rho_S - \rho_W) (P_H - P_L)^2 . \tag{10.15}$$

The bank only obtains additional revenue if the analyst is strong; hence, its profits are

$$\Pi_B = \gamma \left((\rho_S (2\pi - 1) + (1 - \pi)) V - w_S \right) \tag{10.16}$$

as $Prob(V_H) = \pi \rho_S + (1 - \rho_S)(1 - \pi) = (1 - \pi) + \rho_S (2\pi - 1)$, because the strong analyst forecasts P_H if he receives this signal and it is correct ($\pi \rho_S$) or he receives the alternative signal and this signal is wrong, $(1 - \rho_S)(1 - \pi)$. From $\frac{\partial \Pi_B}{\partial w_S} = 0$ as the first-order condition, we get, after using $\Pi_A = 0$ in Eq. (10.14) to replace γw_S, that

$$\gamma^{***} = \frac{\rho_S (2\pi - 1) + (1 - \pi)}{c_I} V + \frac{c_P}{c_I} (\rho_S - \rho_W) (P_H - P_L)^2 > \gamma^* \tag{10.17}$$

and from comparison with γ^* in Eq. (10.7), we see immediately that $\gamma^{***} > \gamma^* = \gamma^{**}$; thus, the probability of analysts being strong has increased with the disclosure of their wages and therefore indirectly the quality of their coverage.

Comparison of Eq. (10.17) with Eq. (10.15) gives us then that

$$w_S = w_S - w_W = (\rho_S (2\pi - 1) + (1 - \pi)) V, \tag{10.18}$$

noting that $w_W = 0$. We now see that compared with Eq. (10.9), the wage differential between strong and weak analysts, $w_S - w_W$, is larger with wage disclosure as long as $\pi > \frac{1}{2}$. The reason for the improved analyst quality is that with analysts being identified to clients as weak or strong, clients can refuse to give additional investment banking business to an investment bank if a weak analyst covers the company. This reduces the value of such weak analysts to the investment bank and allows them to reduce their remuneration, while strong analysts are more valuable as positive reports are more likely to be published and thus being of more value to the investment bank. This is reflected in higher remuneration for strong analysts; therefore, the differential between their remuneration increases. An increased differential in remuneration will in turn provide an incentive for analysts to invest into becoming strong, increasing their likelihood of being strong; thus, the quality of analyst coverage increases.

Hence, we see that disclosing the remuneration of financial analysts and thereby revealing their quality will help improve the quality of analyst coverage.

Summary Analysts can contribute to investment banking profits by attracting additional revenue from clients they are covering. Such business is more likely to be obtained if positive coverage is provided, and for individual analysts, an incentive to provide positive coverage would arise if their remuneration is linked to the amount of revenue they are able to attract. Investing into their own abilities can increase the amount of revenue they bring in, and they will balance the costs of doing so against the higher remuneration. Severing that link between attracting additional investment banking business and analyst remuneration through Chinese Walls, allowing remuneration to be based only on the ability of analysts in covering companies, can be circumvented by investment banks through setting benchmark salaries accordingly. It is the disclosure of information on the actual quality of analysts that allows clients to distinguish analyst quality and provide additional business only if strong analysts are appointed. This increases the incentives of analysts to invest into their own quality and thus raises the overall quality of analyst coverage.

Reading Chen and Marquez (2009).

Review of Part III

Empirically, we observe that financial analyst reports are overly positive and tend to convey very similar information. While the aim of financial analysts is to provide information to investors on the prospects of the company they cover, they are subject to a number of pressures that will affect their published assessment. They might have to bias their reports in order to gain access to information provided by the company, attract additional business from companies to cover their own costs, and also be affected by a desire to enhance their reputation for providing accurate reports. Having these multiple objectives to be balanced against the main objective of providing the best possible advice to investors leads to biased reports that lack the diversity of information that informed them.

The lack of revenue arising from the limited market for analyst reports makes a focus on their quality difficult. Other objectives, such as the need to use analyst reports as a tool to attract additional revenue in other areas of the investment bank, such as mergers and acquisitions advisory, will induce a bias into the reports that will make their use less valuable to investors. Taken together with the incentives to access information and for financial analysts themselves to establish their position in the market, these conflicts of interest leave clear signs in the quality of the reports published. Professional investors that use analyst reports are, of course, aware of these conflicts of interest and will take any biases into account, especially discounting positive assessments of companies to some extent.

Regulation has been introduced that seeks to severe the link between financial analysts and other parts of the investment bank by enforcing that financial analysts are rewarded only for the quality of their analyst reports rather than the revenue they attract otherwise. While this might reduce one source of the bias observed in analyst reports, the access to information and analysts concerns about their standing in the industry remain as a source of conflicts of interest. In addition, investment banks can develop mechanisms that comply with the rules imposed but have the effect to not changing the incentives of financial analysts. Consequently, the imposed regulation of Chinese Walls had very limited impact on the quality of analyst reports.

One effect of limiting the use of financial analyst reports to attract additional revenue to the investment bank is that as this business is less profitable, the investment bank is not providing the necessary investment to enable quality analyst reports. In addition, the number of analysts employed to cover companies might well be reduced, giving rise to less analyst reports for investors to choose from. Such adverse developments have been observed in the aftermath of the introduction of such rules. This shows how well-meant regulatory initiatives can have unwelcome side effects, even without impacting positively the area of concern the regulation sought to address.

Part IV

Trading and Sales

Corporate finance with its advice to clients on mergers and acquisitions as well as the underwriting of securities is often seen as the core business of investment banks. In addition, the provision of research reports into individual companies and markets to inform investors about investment opportunities, often linked to companies that have been advised previously, while reduced in importance, is still seen as another core part of the business as well. Many investment banks, however, offer additional services beyond such core business. For example, they will react to client demands for solutions to manage risk exposures or tax liabilities by providing financial innovations. After underwriting securities, investors will want to trade these, and investment banks facilitate such trading through the provision of brokerage services as well as market making. The former routes any trading demands towards an exchange, and the latter allows investors to trade the security at any time without the need to find an offsetting demand. For investors lacking the time or knowledge to manage their investments directly, investment banks offer asset management services where investment banks conduct these activities within agreed guidelines. Finally, investment banks use their knowledge and access to information in order to trade on their own account in what is commonly referred to as proprietary trading. All these services, often summarised as trading and sales, will be discussed in more detail in the coming chapters.

Investment banks offer these services in addition to their core business of corporate finance and research for reasons of revenue generation and building relationships with clients. Corporate finance is overall a very profitable business line for most investment banks, but it is also very cyclical in that activities in merger and acquisitions advice as well as securities underwriting are high in time of securities markets performing well and activity reduces significantly during downturns. Revenue from trading and sales business lines can not only be used to increase revenue but also diversify. Revenue from brokerage and proprietary trading might be counter-cyclical in that trading increases and hence does fee income from brokerage, if security markets are not performing well. Using their information advantage, investment banks may also be able to extract larger profits from trading. In areas like asset management, the revenue will remain stable as investors will rely even more on investment banks to provide their expertise in managing investments. The revenue from financial innovations can be unpredictable as much will depend not only on being able to provide an innovation that meets the demands of clients but also the emergence of regulatory constraints or changes to taxation that make such innovations desirable for clients.

In addition to supplementing and diversifying revenue, trading and sales activities can also support further the core business of corporate finance. They enable investment banks to build a relationship with their clients, offering services meeting a wide range of their needs and thereby gaining a better understanding of their business. Personal contacts to senior management of corporate clients, for example, from asset management, can also be used to propose services in mergers and acquisitions or securities underwriting. On the other hand, access to such senior managers through corporate finance activities can be used to seek additional business in asset management or brokerage, but also financial innovations. Hence cross-selling of services to corporate clients or to managers of such clients can support the core business of corporate finance, but also provide additional revenue to complement corporate finance.

Trading and sales do not only provide additional revenue and can be used to support the acquisition of clients for the corporate finance division; it can also be essential to maintain such contacts in direct support for corporate finance activities. In corporate finance, investment banks rely on information being provided by well-informed investors. Such investors will have to use brokers to access securities markets, and hence providing brokerage services allows investment banks to build up a network of such investors, on which they can rely to provide the best advice to their clients. Similarly, asset management can provide access to wealthy individuals and institutional investors that might be willing to subscribe to new security offerings or support a merger. Thus trading and sales will also directly support the advice given to clients in corporate finance.

Of course, providing such additional services to clients can give rise to further conflicts of interest. Investment bank might seek to sell services that are either not needed or not sufficiently beneficial to their client to justify the fee charged. They might develop financial innovations that are of limited value to their clients, develop trading ideas to increase their brokerage income, or include recently underwritten securities into the portfolio of clients in order to support the sale of these, rather than meet the interests of their clients. Such conflicts are arising in many instances where different products and services are offered to clients and access to them can be used to sell additional products and services to those additionally sought. However, even if a service is desired by their clients, we will see in the coming chapters that conflicts of interest remain.

11 Financial Innovation

Financial innovations can take many forms. They encompass new instruments for the use of investors and issuers alike. This might include alternative forms of investments, for example, exchange traded funds, money market funds, or index funds but also new derivatives such as credit derivatives, catastrophe bonds, and similar. New technologies like cash machines, online banking, or the use of big data and artificial intelligence provide another avenue for such innovations. New institutions are the final and, often most influential, innovation. It will include new forms of banking, such as Islamic banks, electronic exchanges, or shadow banks. Investment banks are mostly involved in developing new instruments but might provide support in any of the other areas of innovation. The benefits to clients of such innovation might be in efficient access to markets that were previously difficult to enter, for example, the market for investing in an index, but also in access to instruments that allow for effective diversification or the hedging of risks.

Most innovations have the property that they can be copied by competitors quite easily as all information has to be disclosed and protections as intellectual property or through patents are difficult to obtain and enforce. In addition, many innovations seek to exploit regulatory loopholes or circumvent tax regulation, with the reaction of regulators or tax authorities to either prohibit the use of these innovations or make them ineffective. Additional regulatory constraints might also increase the costs and thereby limit the benefits to clients or the investment bank. With such reactions following quickly after the introduction of innovations, investment banks have limited time to recover any costs they have faced when developing these.

With these properties, the development of financial innovations becomes risky in that through regulatory intervention or copying by competitors, the revenue arising from their introduction is difficult to predict. This has implications for the development of such innovations in the first place, as Sect. 11.1 will show, but also how any innovation is brought to the market, as detailed in Sect. 11.2. Innovations might be introduced immediately, be phased in, or be sold to another investment bank with a larger client base. The benefits of using financial innovations are often

A. Krause, *Theoretical Foundations of Investment Banking*, Springer Texts in Business and Economics, https://doi.org/10.1007/978-3-031-58060-4_11

not immediately known but can only be learned over time as investment banks introduce them and gain experience. Section 11.3 will look into the process of adopting financial innovations in such a realistic case.

11.1 Incentives to Innovate

While financial innovations may be beneficial to their clients or reduce costs to the investment bank, it must be profitable to provide such innovations in the first place. Financial innovations are often easily copied by competitors as the innovation needs to be made public in order to sell it to a wider client base and it cannot easily be protected by patents. This poses the risk of any benefits from developing the innovation being eroded quickly by competition, with the investment bank having to bear the costs of developing the innovation nevertheless.

Assume that the value of an innovation to the investment bank is V, which is the cost reduction or the revenue, net of any costs, that can be charged to clients for using the financial innovation. The costs to the investment bank of providing this innovation are $C < V$, such that a profitable price can be agreed between the investment bank and its clients. If only a single investment bank offers the innovation, the investment bank can extract all benefits and obtain these benefits V. In the case that two or more investment banks offer this innovation, competition will reduce these benefits to zero. This might arise if the cost reduction will have to be reflected in lower prices being charged to their clients or the price that can be charged for the innovation is just covering the current costs. The costs C of developing the innovation are assumed to be fixed costs that are incurred whenever an innovation is developed and as such are sunk costs.

We will now see how likely investment banks are to offer an innovation if other investment banks could also offer the same innovation or very quickly copy the developed innovation. We will at first focus on a situation in which investment banks offer the innovation as a service to any client and seek to generate profits from this offer (transaction banking) and then look at the implications of losing a client and its revenue to another investment bank (relationship banking).

Transaction Banking An investment bank derives its revenue solely from the sale of their innovation. If none of the other investment banks were offering the innovation, then an investment bank could offer the innovation and, being the only supplier, make a profit of $V - C$. Hence, not to develop the innovation is not an equilibrium. If all investment banks develop the innovation, then competition erodes the revenue to zero, causing losses of C to each investment bank, while not developing the innovation would result in no revenue or costs, giving zero profits. Hence, all investment banks developing the innovation is also not an equilibrium. Instead, investment banks will develop the innovation with probability p. An investment bank only obtains revenue if no other investment bank develops the same innovation. Hence, with N investment banks in the market, the investment bank profits are

$$\Pi_B = p\left((1-p)^{N-1} V - C\right). \tag{11.1}$$

Here we require all $N - 1$ other investment banks to not offer the innovation to obtain revenue V, which happens with probability $1 - p$, while the investment bank concerned needs to offer this innovation and only in this case faces costs of C. As in competitive markets we would have $\Pi_B = 0$, we can solve for the equilibrium probability of developing the innovation. From Eq. (11.1), we easily obtain that

$$p^* = 1 - \sqrt[N-1]{\frac{C}{V}}. \tag{11.2}$$

Not surprisingly, we see that if the cost-benefit ratio $\frac{C}{V}$ is lower, financial innovations are more likely. This is because the lower the costs or the higher the revenue to an investment bank is, the easier it is to cover the costs from the expected revenue, if no other investment bank introduces the innovation. More investment banks possibly introducing the financial innovation reduces the likelihood of introducing it as it is less likely to be only one investment bank offering it.

We can now compare the probability of investment banks providing an innovation if they only focus on the transaction itself with that of investment banks establishing relationships with their clients and generating additional revenue from existing services they provide.

Relationship Banking If no innovation is offered, an investment bank would be able to retain their client and thus preserve the profits V_B from this existing business. Only if the investment bank fails to provide the innovation would a client switch their business to an innovating investment bank. If they innovate themselves, other clients will switch to the innovation, and the investment bank will obtain revenue V as before if they are the only investment bank offering this innovation, or competition will erode any benefits to the investment bank if competitors also introduce the innovation. In this case, the investment bank profits are then

$$\hat{\Pi}_B = (1-p)^N V_B + p\left((1-p)^{N-1} V - C\right) = (1-p)^N V_B + \Pi_B. \tag{11.3}$$

The first term denotes the retention of the existing revenue if no investment bank innovates and the second term the revenue if the innovation is introduced.

In competitive markets, we again find that $\hat{\Pi}_B = 0$. As the second term in Eq. (11.3) corresponds to the profits in transaction banking, Π_B, given in Eq. (11.1). The first term is positive, and the second term must then be negative in competition. If the likelihood of innovation were the same here as in transaction banking, $p^{**} = p^*$, then the second term would be zero; hence, to ensure it is negative, we need $p^{**} > p^*$. We thus find that investment banks are more likely to innovate. We can easily obtain that

$$\frac{\partial \hat{\Pi}_B}{\partial p} = -(1-p)^{N-2}(N(1-p)V_B + V(N-2+p)) - C < 0, \quad (11.4)$$

$$\frac{\partial \hat{\Pi}_B}{\partial V} = p(1-p)^{N-1} > 0,$$

$$\frac{\partial \hat{\Pi}_B}{\partial C} = -p < 0,$$

$$\frac{\partial \hat{\Pi}_B}{\partial N} = (1-p)^N((1-p)V_B + pV)\ln(1-p) < 0,$$

$$\frac{\partial \hat{\Pi}_B}{\partial V_B} = (1-p)^N > 0,$$

where the first inequality holds for any $N \geq 2$. Using the implicit function theorem, we find the same relationships of p^{**} with V, C, and N as in the case of transaction banking, using the same rationale. In addition, we find that $\frac{\partial p^{**}}{\partial V_B} > 0$ and a more profitable relationship bank is more innovative. These investment banks can use their higher profits from other investment bank revenue to recover any losses if facing competition when providing innovations. It is thus that investment banks can subsidise financial innovation with profits from existing relationships with clients. They do so to remain competitive with their clients as they might otherwise switch their business to other investment banks where they could benefit more frequently from the introduction of financial innovations.

Summary Investment banks engaging in relationship banking are more innovative than those relying on transaction banking. With relationship banking, investment banks also compete for clients through their provision of financial innovations. They can use the profits generated from existing arrangements with their clients to cross-subsidise the introduction of financial innovations and thus cover the costs of developing them, even if competitors are likely to introduce them at the same time and erode any revenue the innovation might generate. Of course, losing the client to a competitor that introduces a financial innovation is an additional incentive to provide the financial innovation.

Reading Boot and Thakor (1997).

11.2 Introduction to Innovations

Financial innovations are often copied by competitors with only a short delay to understand the innovation, develop appropriate pricing mechanisms, and develop the requisite legal framework to offer the innovation to their clients. Hence, investment banks developing such innovations have to recover any costs quickly before competition from other investment banks erodes their advantage. Furthermore, as many financial innovations are designed to circumvent tax rules or other regulatory restrictions, their use might be banned quickly or the benefits curtailed as tax authorities, and regulators become aware of the impact such innovations have.

Let us therefore assume that any innovation might be used for only one time period before it can easily be copied by competitors or is being abolished by regulation. The total value of the innovation to the client is V. The client can delay the adoption of the innovation by one time period, in which case, they lose benefits worth C_D but would be able to obtain the innovation for free due to the arising competition, provided it has not been banned. If there are multiple investment banks operating, clients might also switch their investment banks at cost C_S to take advantage of the innovation offered by a competitor.

Using this framework, we will now investigate how likely an innovation is introduced and in what way, either as a single large innovation, a phased introduction over many time periods with smaller innovations at every step, or by being sold to another investment bank.

Controversial Innovations Let us assume that a financial innovation will be rendered ineffective by tax authorities or regulators with probability p after one time period. A client waiting with the adoption of the innovation will only be able to obtain its benefits if it is not rendered worthless by its use being prohibited, getting expected value of $(1 - p)\,V - C_D$, taking into account the delayed adoption, if this is positive. Competition between investment banks at that point makes the innovation free to adopt. Adopting this innovation immediately will get the client the full benefits of V, less the price P they are charged. We thus can determine the price such that the client is indifferent between adopting the innovation instantly and waiting for it to become freely available through other investment banks copying the financial innovation and competition leading to a reduction in price to zero. Hence, the price is determined such that

$$V - P = \max\left\{(1 - p)\,V - C_D, 0\right\}, \tag{11.5}$$

from which we get

$$P = \begin{cases} V & \text{if } C_D \geq (1 - p)\,V \\ pV + C_D & \text{if } C_D < (1 - p)\,V \end{cases}. \tag{11.6}$$

The price, and hence the revenue of the investment bank, is increasing in p for low delay costs C_D. Hence with fixed costs to investment banks for developing the innovation, they have an incentive to develop innovations that might be controversial and will most likely be banned. The highest profits are made from innovations with the highest risk of being abolished. The reason is that, in this case, the costs to clients of delaying their adoption do not only consist of costs C_D but also the risk of not being able to use the innovations later for free. This gives incentives for clients to adopt the innovation, and the investment bank can charge a high price for its development.

Phasing of Innovations Investment banks having developed an innovation can split up the innovation into a number of small innovations, each with benefits V_t, where $V = \sum_{t=1}^{T} V_t$, with T being the number of steps in which the innovation is introduced. Delaying the adoption of the innovation costs C_D for each of the small innovations and setting T such that $V = TC_D$, thus waiting until the innovation has been fully revealed, leaves clients with no net benefits due to the costs of delaying the adoption of the innovation. The delay costs C_D are identical, regardless of the size of the innovation, and if the full innovation is introduced immediately in a single step, the delay costs to clients would still be C_D.

The benefits to a client from adopting such an innovation is V_t, and delaying adoption would cost C_D; thus, the price the investment bank can charge to one of their own clients is $\min\{V_t, C_D\}$. They might also attract new clients switching to them to take advantage of the innovation. The benefits of these new clients are reduced by the switching costs, and hence the price that can be charged to them is $\max\{\min\{V_t, C_D\} - C_S, 0\}$. If investment bank i has market share α_i and there are N potential clients, we have, neglecting the costs of developing the innovation, the revenue of investment bank i at time t as

$$\Pi_B^{i,t} = \alpha_i N \min\{V_t, C_D\} + (1-\alpha_i) N \max\{\min\{V_t, C_D\} - C_S, 0\}. \tag{11.7}$$

The first term denotes the revenue arising from their existing customers, and the second term represents the revenue from attracting the clients of other investment banks, charging a lower price to these.

Let us focus on the case that $V_t \geq C_D$ and the early adoption of each step is beneficial to their own clients. In this case, Eq. (11.7) simplifies to become

$$\Pi_B^{i,t} = \alpha_i N C_D + (1-\alpha_i) N \max\{C_D - C_S, 0\}. \tag{11.8}$$

The size of each innovation, V_t, can be freely set by the investment bank with the constraint that $V_t > C_D$ and $V = \sum_{t=1}^{T} V_t$. As $V_t > C_D$, we can write $V_t = C_D + \Delta$, and in Eq. (11.7), we get the relationship as shown in Eq. (11.8), which we would also get for $V_t = C_D$. If $V_t = C_D + \Delta$, then we need at least one t' in which

$V_{t'}$ is smaller; thus, $V_{t'} = C_D - \Delta'$. This arises because $V = \sum_{t=1}^{T} V_t = TC_D$. In this case, Eq. (11.7) becomes

$$\Pi_B^{i,t'} = \alpha_i N \left(C_D - \Delta'\right) + (1 - \alpha_i) N \max\left\{C_D - C_S - \Delta', 0\right\}, \tag{11.9}$$

which is clearly less than the expression in Eq. (11.8). Hence, it is optimal to phase the innovation into T equal steps with $V_t = C_D$. An implication is that if delay costs are smaller, then we will see more steps given that T will have to increase to match $V = TC_D$.

Investment banks may face regulatory constraints or action by tax authorities that prevent the further use of this particular innovation after one time period. Alternatively, an innovation may be copied by competing investment banks, and competition erodes any revenue that may be generated. If the innovation is copied or prohibited with probability p in every time period, the total expected revenue of the investment bank from an innovation, when using Eq. (11.8), is given by

$$\begin{aligned} \Pi_B^i &= \sum_{t=0}^{T} (1-p)^t \, \Pi_B^{i,t} = \frac{1-(1-p)^T}{p} \Pi_B^{i,t} \\ &= \frac{1-(1-p)^T}{p} \left(\alpha_i N C_D + (1-\alpha_i) N \max\left\{C_D - C_S, 0\right\}\right), \end{aligned} \tag{11.10}$$

noting that after every innovative step, further steps can only be introduced if the innovation is not copied or prohibited.

A investment bank could alternatively decide to introduce the innovation in one big step instead. As the delay costs are still only C_D but the value V is now exceeding this, the investment bank would gain the full market as long as $V > C_D + C_S$ as we obtain from inserting for $V_t = V$ in Eq. (11.7) that

$$\hat{\Pi}_B^i = NC_D. \tag{11.11}$$

If $\hat{\Pi}_B^i \leq \Pi_B^i$, the investment bank would prefer to phase the innovation in. Using Eqs. (11.10) and (11.11), we get

$$\alpha_i \geq \alpha^* = \frac{pC_D - \left(1-(1-p)^T\right) \max\left\{C_D - C_S, 0\right\}}{\left(1-(1-p)^T\right) \min\left\{C_D, C_S\right\}} < 1. \tag{11.12}$$

Thus, investment banks with a large market share of potential clients for their innovation would introduce innovations in phases, while smaller investment banks would prefer to use a single large innovation step. The switching of many clients to small investment banks outweighs the risks of the innovation being proscribed.

Selling Innovations Rather than introducing an innovation itself, an investment bank could also sell its innovation to another investment bank. The price charged to the other investment bank cannot be higher than C_D, as otherwise the buying investment bank cannot make a profit given that their clients would delay the adoption if they in turn charge their clients a higher price. It can also not be larger than C_S because if the buyer has to charge more, the clients could switch to the original innovator instead and obtain higher benefits, net of costs. Hence, the price an investment bank j with market share α_j is willing to pay for an innovation is

$$P = \alpha_j N \min\{C_D, C_S\}, \tag{11.13}$$

where we assume that they are limited to offering the innovation only to their own clients and are not able to attract clients from other investment banks. This might be a constraint in the conditions of sale. Of course, the originally innovating investment bank would sell its innovation to the largest competitor as this gives them the highest price.

If $C_S > C_D$, then no client will switch investment banks as the costs are higher than delaying the adoption. In this case, the revenue of the innovating investment bank when not selling the innovation is $\alpha_i N C_D$ from Eq. (11.8). Comparing this with the revenue of selling the innovation in Eq. (11.13), we see that as long as $\alpha_j > \alpha_i$, selling is always preferable. Thus, all but the largest investment bank would sell their innovation to the largest investment bank.

If $C_S \leq C_D$, the revenue of not selling the innovation is given from Eq. (11.8) as $\alpha_i N C_D + (1 - \alpha_i) N (C_D - C_S)$. Comparing this to $\alpha_j N C_S$ in Eq. (11.13) when selling the innovation, we see that selling is preferable if

$$\alpha_i \leq \alpha^{**} = 1 - \left(1 - \alpha_j\right) \frac{C_D}{C_S} < 1. \tag{11.14}$$

Hence, if the innovating investment bank is sufficiently small, then it will sell its innovation to a larger investment bank. The larger the buying investment bank is, the larger the innovator itself can be. Also, higher switching costs C_S increase this threshold as do lower delay costs C_D.

While the sale can be instigated for a single innovation step in a phased introduction as well as the immediate introduction of the innovation, we have to notice that with an immediate introduction, the innovating investment bank is able to attract the entire market and hence effectively $\alpha_i = 1$. The condition in Eq. (11.14) can never be fulfilled. Hence, if the immediate introduction of an innovation is preferable to a phased introduction, a sale of the innovation is not sought.

Optimal Strategy for Small Investment Banks If $\alpha_i > \alpha^*$, then the innovation is either phased in or sold to a larger competitor, and if $\alpha_i < \alpha^{**}$, the innovation is sold to a larger investment bank, provided it is phased in. Thus, in the case that

Fig. 11.1 Format of introducing financial innovations

	$C_S > C_D$, $\alpha_j \leq \overline{\alpha}$	$C_S > C_D$, $\alpha_j > \overline{\alpha}$	$C_S \leq C_D$
$\alpha_i \leq \alpha^*$	immediate introduction	immediate introduction	immediate introduction
$\alpha^* < \alpha_i \leq \alpha^{**}$	phased introduction	sale	sale
$\alpha_i > \alpha^{**}$	phased introduction	phased introduction	sale

$\alpha^* \leq \alpha_i \leq \alpha^{**}$, it would lead to the selling of the innovation. We need $\alpha^* \leq \alpha^{**}$ for a feasible solution, which requires

$$\alpha_j \geq \overline{\alpha} = \frac{p}{1-(1-p)^T}. \tag{11.15}$$

Thus, for innovations to be sold, the buyer of the innovation must be sufficiently large. If the switching costs are below the cost of delaying the adoption of the innovation, the investment bank would always sell the innovation rather than phasing it in. Figure 11.1 summarises the results we have obtained on the introduction of financial innovations.

Summary Financial innovations are most profitable if they are controversial in that any benefits might quickly be reduced due to regulatory changes. The possibility of any benefits being withdrawn in the future reduces any future benefits from delaying the adoption, thus avoiding paying a high price for the innovation. This will in turn induce clients to adopt the innovation immediately, allowing the investment bank to charge a higher price. It might also be possible to introduce innovations piece by piece and thereby extract surplus at any stage, while competitors and regulator seek to catch up on these small innovation steps. If the investment bank is small, such a step is not optimal as they could introduce the innovation immediately and gain a substantial market share by inducing clients of all banks to switch investment banks. Midsized investment banks might phase in innovations in order to maximise their revenue that way, or they sell the innovation to a larger investment bank, and large investment banks would generally not sell their innovations as the price they can obtain is not sufficient given their already large size. Only if switching costs for clients are low would they sell the innovation to a larger investment bank, unless they are the largest investment bank.

We thus observe that small investment banks may be seen as most innovative as they introduce innovations in a single step, while large investment banks will only provide small innovations frequently. Midsized investment banks would seek alliances with larger investment banks to introduce their innovations.

Reading Bhattacharyya and Nanda (2000).

11.3 Adoption of Innovations

While the development of financial innovations is costly and they can easily be copied by other investment banks, their adoption can nevertheless be costly to investment banks, and the benefits might not be perfectly known. This situation arises if an investment bank introduces a new product or a new technology, but it is not clear how widely it will be taken up by their clients, how much they are willing to pay for this innovation, or how high the cost savings to the investment bank are. Costs might arise from the marketing of any products, the training of staff, the development of tools to price a product, or the implementation of the technology needed for the innovation.

Therefore, let us assume that investment banks differ in the costs they face when implementing a financial innovation. The costs to investment banks are known and such that $0 \leq \underline{C} \leq C_i \leq \overline{C}$, and there is a continuum of investment banks within this interval. For simplicity, we order investment banks by their costs, such that $C_i \leq C_{i+1}$. The benefits V arising to investment banks are not known to them, but they have an initial expected value of V_0 with variance σ_0^2. We assume that $\underline{C} < V < \overline{C}$, implying that the adoption of the innovation is profitable for some investment banks but not all. Investment banks will learn from the experience of other investment banks adopting the financial innovation and update their beliefs on the benefits the innovation provides to them, giving them expected benefits of V_t and a variance of σ_t^2. Such beliefs are updated using Bayesian learning.

Implementing Innovations An investment bank, finding the innovation to be profitable, hence $V_t > C_i$, can either adopt the innovation or delay the adoption until a future date. They will compare the current profits, $V_t - C_i$ with the profits of adopting the innovation at a future date $T > t$, $E\left[\max\left\{V_T - C_i, 0\right\}\right]$. In the future, with expected benefits V_T, the investment bank can either adopt the innovation, giving it profits $V_T - C_i$, or not adopt the innovation and make zero profits. The investment bank will delay the adoption of the innovation if $E\left[\max\left\{V_T - C_i, 0\right\}\right] > V_t - C_i$.

Waiting with the adoption of the innovation can be interpreted as an option. If the option is exercised, the innovation is adopted, and if the option is not exercised, the innovation is not adopted. Such an option to wait is more valuable if the uncertainty about the benefits is high, hence for higher variances σ_t^2. As we will show below, through learning, this uncertainty will reduce, and hence the option to wait with the adoption of the innovation will become less valuable, making it more likely that is exercised and hence the innovation adopted, provided this is profitable and $V_t \geq C_i$.

Let us assume there is, in addition to investment bank i, another investment bank with higher costs $C_j > C_i$ and investment bank i delays the adoption of the innovation. We then have

$$\begin{aligned} E\left[\max\left\{V_T - C_j, 0\right\}\right] &= E\left[\max\left\{V_T - C_i, C_j - C_i\right\}\right] - \left(C_j - C_i\right) \\ &\geq E\left[\max\left\{V_T - C_i, 0\right\}\right] - \left(C_j - C_i\right) \\ &> V_t - C_i - \left(C_j - C_i\right) \\ &= V_t - C_j \end{aligned} \tag{11.16}$$

and hence investment bank j with higher costs will also delay adopting the financial innovation. The first inequality uses that $C_j > C_i$ and the second inequality our assumption that the investment bank with costs C_i does not adopt the innovation. Similarly, assume an investment bank with costs C_i adopts the innovation; hence, $E\left[\max\left\{V_T - C_i, 0\right\}\right] < V_t - C_i$, and we consider another investment bank j with costs lower costs $C_j < C_i$. In this case, we get

$$\begin{aligned} E\left[\max\left\{V_T - C_j, 0\right\}\right] &= E\left[\max\left\{V_T - C_i, C_j - C_i\right\}\right] - \left(C_j - C_i\right) \\ &\leq E\left[\max\left\{V_T - C_i, 0\right\}\right] - \left(C_j - C_i\right) \\ &< V_t - C_i - \left(C_j - C_i\right) \\ &= V_t - C_j, \end{aligned} \tag{11.17}$$

implying that the investment bank with lower costs than investment bank i will also adopt the innovation. We can therefore focus our considerations on the adoption of the financial innovation onto the investment bank with the lowest costs that adopts. Any investment bank with lower costs will also adopt, and those with higher costs will delay adoption of the innovation. As we know that at if at time t investment bank C_i adopts the innovation, but investment bank C_{i+1} does not do so, we can identify the last investment bank adopting the innovation at time t by C_t. The number of investment banks adopting in a time period we can then define as $N_t = C_t - C_{t-1}$.

Let us finally assume that the profits made by investment banks are not only given by the difference of the true, but unknown, benefits V and the investment bank costs C_i but that there is a random element $\hat{\varepsilon}$ to these profits for each investment banks adopting the innovation, which might reflect fluctuations in market conditions or the composition of clients a specific investment bank might have. The expected value of this random fluctuation in profits is zero and its variance is $\hat{\sigma}^2$. If we have N_t investment banks adopting the financial innovation, then the average random element will be $\varepsilon_t = \frac{1}{N_t}\int_{C_t}^{C_{t+1}} \hat{\varepsilon} dC_i$ and $Var\left[\varepsilon_t\right] = \sigma_{\varepsilon,t}^2 = \frac{\hat{\sigma}^2}{N_t}$.

We can now obtain the average profits of investment banks adopting the innovation in time period $t+1$ as

$$\Pi_B^t = \frac{1}{N_t}\int_{C_{t-1}}^{C_t} \left(V - C_i\right) dC_i + \varepsilon_t. \tag{11.18}$$

The profits of each investment bank are given by $V - C_i$, where we consider all those banks with costs $C_{t-1} \leq C_i \leq C_t$, of which there are N_t, and the random fluctuation is aggregated into ε_t. The expected benefits of the innovation are given by V_t, and hence the expected average profits are given by $E_t\left[\Pi_B^t\right] = \frac{1}{N_t}\int_{C_{t-1}}^{C_t}(V_t - C_i)\,dC_i$.

Investment banks not yet adopting the innovation observe the actual profits of those investment banks having recently adopted it. Based on this information, they use Bayesian updating to obtain their new beliefs about the expected value and variance of the benefits of the innovation. Assuming all variables to be normally distributed, we get

$$\begin{aligned} V_{t+1} &= V_t + \frac{\frac{1}{\sigma_{\varepsilon,t}^2}}{\frac{1}{\sigma_t^2} + \frac{1}{\sigma_{\varepsilon,t}^2}}\left(\Pi_B^t - E_t\left[\Pi_B^t\right]\right) \\ &= \frac{\frac{1}{\sigma_t^2}}{\frac{1}{\sigma_t^2} + \frac{N_t}{\hat{\sigma}^2}}V_t + \frac{\frac{N_t}{\hat{\sigma}^2}}{\frac{1}{\sigma_t^2} + \frac{N_t}{\hat{\sigma}^2}}(V + \varepsilon_t), \\ \frac{1}{\sigma_{t+1}^2} &= \frac{1}{\sigma_t^2} + \frac{1}{\sigma_\varepsilon^2} = \frac{1}{\sigma_t^2} + \frac{N_t}{\hat{\sigma}^2}. \end{aligned} \tag{11.19}$$

The variance of beliefs, σ_t^2, is decreasing as more information becomes available, and this will reduce the value of the option to wait with the adoption of the financial innovation. This in turn will provide an incentive for investment banks to adopt the innovation rather than wait as $E\left[\max\left\{V_T - C_i, 0\right\}\right] > V_t - C_i$ is less likely to be fulfilled if the value of the left-hand side is reduced. However, as the uncertainty on the benefits is never vanishing, the option will always remain valuable.

We can now see that if no new investment banks were to adopt the innovation, thus $N_t = 0$, we have $V_{t+1} = V_t$ and $\sigma_{t+1}^2 = \sigma_t^2$, and thus no information will be updated by investment banks, implying that there are no further adoptions of the innovation. The incentive to wait for investment banks not yet adopting will remain the preferred strategy. Adoptions of the innovation will cease if $V_{t+1} \leq C_t$; in this case, there are no more investment banks who can make a profit from adopting the innovation, given the information available. As we must have $V_t \geq C_t$ in order for the final investment bank to adopt the innovation in the previous time period, we find that for the final investment banks adopting the innovation, we observe that $V_{t+1} \leq V_t$. Using Eq. (11.19), this implies that $\Pi_B^t \leq E_t\left[\Pi_B^t\right]$, and thus the final group of investment banks adopting the innovation will realise smaller-than-expected profits. However, it has to be noted that not every reduction in the expected benefits V_t leads to the adoption process stopping. As long as $V_{t+1} > C_t$, there will be investment banks with costs just above C_t that continue to adopt the innovation as $V_{t+1} - C_t > 0$. Knowing that without adopting the innovation there is no new information emerging, they are aware that to not adopt will result in them never adopting and foregoing a profitable strategy; hence they will adopt the innovation.

Based on these considerations, we can now investigate the speed with which an innovation is spreading across investment banks.

Diffusion of Innovations All those investment banks making profits are adopting the innovation. Having updated their beliefs on the expected benefits to V_{t+1}, the next time period will see all those investment banks adopting the financial innovation that have costs below V_{t+1}; thus, the marginal investment bank to adopt the innovation will have costs $C_{t+1} = V_{t+1}$. We can now write this as $V_{t+1} - C_t = C_{t+1} - C_t = N_{t+1}$. Inserting from Eq. (11.19), we obtain that

$$N_{t+1} = \frac{\frac{1}{\sigma_t^2}}{\frac{1}{\sigma_t^2} + \eta N_t} V_t + \frac{\eta N_t}{\frac{1}{\sigma_t^2} + \eta N_t} (V + \varepsilon_t) - C_t. \tag{11.20}$$

The adoption of the innovation is increasing if $N_{t+1} > N_t$. Suppose now that $C_t = 0$, implying that no investment bank has adopted the innovation and hence $N_t = 0$, from which we obtain that $N_{t+1} = V_t > 0 = N_t$. This can be interpreted as the adoption of the financial innovation accelerating if sufficiently low numbers of investment banks have already adopted the innovation. If the adoption rate were to continue to increase, then we would obtain that C_t is becoming larger ever faster. The value of N_t can remain finite but will increase, which implies that the first term in Eq. (11.20) reduces and the second term increases towards $V + \varepsilon$, both terms remaining finite. With C_t increasing at ever higher rates, it will become arbitrarily large, causing the whole expression to become negative. As the growth rate must be positive, this expression cannot be bigger than N_t, given that $N_t \geq 0$ as it represents the increase in the number of investment banks adopting the innovation. Hence, the adoption rate of the innovation cannot continue to increase permanently. There will exist a value C^* for C_t at which point $N_{t+1} < N_t$, and the adoption rate reduces. Therefore, for $C_t < C^*$, the adoption rate is increasing, while for $C_t > C^*$, it would be decreasing. We have established that the adoption rate of financial innovations is S-shaped. A slow initial uptake of the innovation is followed to a quick and widespread adoption phase, before the adoption rate slows down again.

Summary The benefits of financial innovations are not always apparent and often difficult assess, leading to uncertainty about the profitability of adopting such innovations. Investment banks facing the lowest costs of adoption will be pioneering the adoption as their profits are sufficiently high to overcome the uncertainty of the benefits and thereby provide valuable information to other investment banks on the likely benefits. This uncertainty in benefits may arise from the level of market demand for the innovation or the willingness of clients to pay. Updating their belief on the benefits will lead to an adoption process where the level of adoption is represented by an S-shape, a slow initial uptake of the innovation, followed by a fast spread of the innovation after the initial phase, before then the innovation is slowly adopted by a few investment banks seeing higher adoption costs. Once the beliefs formed by investment banks are such that no additional investment banks are willing to adopt the innovation, as is the case if the adoption costs exceed the expected benefits, no further adoptions will be made in the future. As no further adoptions have happened, no further information is available to investment banks to update their beliefs. The adoption process comes to a halt.

Financial innovations, even though they often can be copied easily from other investment banks, are not necessarily adopted instantly, but we see a gradual diffusion of the innovation as investment banks learn of the benefits they provide them or their clients with. Having such a gradual process of adoption will allow the innovating investment bank a longer time to recover their initial costs of developing the innovation. Therefore, facing uncertainty about the benefits of financial innovation can be advantageous for the development of such innovations as it gives developing investment banks more opportunities to recover their development costs.

Reading Persons and Warther (1997).

Conclusions

Financial innovations can provide significant benefits to their clients, but the profits to investment banks can be severely limited. This might be due to the innovations being adopted by other investment banks quickly, thus eroding any competitive advantage a bank might have and competition reducing profits. Alternatively, financial innovations might be proscribed by regulators. Operating in a market with such properties will limit the development of financial innovations in the first place and also have implications for the introduction of financial innovations that have been developed. It is an opportunity for investment banks to show their innovative strength and attract new customers by making bold innovations that provide large benefits for their clients. This is in particular attractive to smaller investment banks, while larger investment banks will rely on revenue from their existing client base and seek to maximise the surplus to be extracted from them by introducing small innovations frequently, or they cooperate with each other by selling the innovation. Considering that the benefits of financial innovations can only be learned from the experience of investment banks adopting the innovation early, the innovation will spread rapidly once it has been established with sufficient certainty that their adoption is profitable to investment banks. This delay in the adoption of financial innovations gives the initial innovator additional time to recover their development costs and might therefore provide sufficient incentives to develop financial innovations.

The benefits of financial innovations are not only directly in the revenue they provide investment banks with but also the ability to provide clients with innovations that are beneficial to them, thereby retaining their custom. Providing solutions to client problems will induce them to return not only for more financial innovations but more importantly for other business that is more profitable to investment banks, such as the underwriting of securities or seeking advice in mergers and acquisitions. Thus, providing financial innovations can be seen as an important element in relationship banking.

12 Asset Management

Rather than merely providing advice on investing to their clients, investment banks also offer to manage the funds of clients on their behalf such that investment decisions are taken by the investment bank directly. Clients will seek to delegate their portfolio management partly for convenience but also to make use of the superior information investment banks have about the market and their skills in managing portfolios. Asset management is an important service investment banks offer to wealthy clients and institutional investors. Apart from generating stable fee income for investment banks, it also serves as a tool to maintain personal contacts to investors, who are often in leading positions of companies that would be potential clients in other business lines, such as securities underwriting and mergers and acquisitions advisory. They might also be using financial innovations to optimise their tax position or hedge-specific risks. However, investment banks also face competition in this line of business from many private banks and investment consultancies.

Let us assume that the investment bank charges a fee for this service of asset management that consists of a management fee f_0 levied on the total amount invested and a performance fee f_1 that is levied on the return R of the risky asset exceeding a benchmark return, here assumed to be the risk-free rate r. The investment bank will invest a fraction ω of the initial client wealth W_0 into the risky asset and the remainder into the risk-free asset. The total fee income F of the bank is given by

$$F = f_0 W_0 + f_1 \omega (R - r) W_0. \tag{12.1}$$

We can now evaluate how a client would optimally invest their funds and compare this to the investment into the risky asset that the investment bank would conduct.

A. Krause, *Theoretical Foundations of Investment Banking*, Springer Texts in Business and Economics, https://doi.org/10.1007/978-3-031-58060-4_12

Clients Investing Directly Clients in general will have information on the risky assets, and we assume that they assess them to have mean returns of μ_C and a variance σ_C^2. Their final wealth W_1 will be given by the return on the investment into the risk-free asset and the return R on the investment into the risky asset. We thus have

$$\begin{aligned} W_1 &= (1-\omega)(1+r)W_0 + \omega(1+R)W_0 \\ &= (1+r)W_0 + \omega(R-r)W_0. \end{aligned} \tag{12.2}$$

Using this expression, the expected utility of the client with risk aversion z is then given by

$$\begin{aligned} U_C &= E[W_1] - \frac{1}{2}zVar[W_1] \\ &= (1+r)W_0 + \omega(\mu_C - r)W_0 - \frac{1}{2}z\omega^2\sigma_C^2W_0^2. \end{aligned} \tag{12.3}$$

The optimal portfolio of the client not using the investment bank to manage their portfolio is then given from solving the first-order condition $\frac{\partial U_C}{\partial \omega} = 0$, which gives us

$$\omega^* = \frac{\mu_C - r}{z\sigma_C^2W_0}, \tag{12.4}$$

such that the expected utility of the client is given by

$$U_C = (1+r)W_0 + \frac{(\mu_C - r)^2}{2z\sigma_C^2}. \tag{12.5}$$

We can use this utility level to compare with the utility obtained when delegating the management of the portfolio to the investment bank.

Delegated Investment Let us now assume that the investment bank has information regarding the expected return of the risky asset, μ_B, and its variance σ_B^2. In general, we will assume that the information of the investment bank is more precise, such that $\sigma_B^2 < \sigma_C^2$. With the same risk aversion z as their clients, the utility of the investment bank is given by

$$\begin{aligned} U_B &= E[F] - \frac{1}{2}zVar[F] \\ &= f_0W_0 + f_1\omega(\mu_B - r)W_0 - \frac{1}{2}zf_1^2\omega^2\sigma_B^2W_0^2, \end{aligned} \tag{12.6}$$

using Eq. (12.1) to replace the fee income F. Investment banks would not seek to maximise the wealth of their clients but their own income, here the fee income they can derive from managing the portfolio for their client. The optimal investment into the risky asset is given by maximising equation (12.6) through setting $\frac{\partial U_B}{\partial \omega} = 0$, from which we easily obtain that

$$\omega^{**} = \frac{\mu_B - r}{z f_1 \sigma_B^2 W_0}. \tag{12.7}$$

Inserting this expression back into Eq. (12.6), we get the utility level of the investment bank as

$$U_B = f_0 W_0 + \frac{(\mu_B - r)^2}{2z\sigma_B^2}. \tag{12.8}$$

If investment banks are competitive, they will not increase their utility from managing the portfolio, such that $U_B = 0$. In this case, the management fee f_0 can easily be determined as

$$f_0 = -\frac{(\mu_B - r)^2}{2z\sigma_B^2 W_0} < 0. \tag{12.9}$$

Hence, investment banks will subsidise the portfolio they manage through a negative fee and obtain all their income from the performance fee. The negative management fee is required to offset the revenue generated from the performance fee in perfect competition. A negative management fee might take many form in practice, other than a monetary refund. For example, investment banks might not charge the full costs of providing brokerage services to asset management clients through providing them with a discount on the fees charged to other clients.

The final wealth of the client is then given by

$$\begin{aligned} W_1 &= (1 + r) W_0 + \omega^{**} (R - r) W_0 - F \\ &= (1 + r - f_0) W_0 + (1 - f_1) \omega^{**} (R - r) W_0, \end{aligned} \tag{12.10}$$

where we use Eq. (12.1) to replace the total fees F the client pays. The expected utility becomes, after inserting from Eqs. (12.7) for the portfolio chosen by the investment bank and (12.9) for the management fee while recognising that he learns the information of the investment bank regarding the expected return and variance of asset, μ_B and σ_B^2:

$$\begin{aligned}\hat{U}_C &= (1 + r - f_0)\, W_0 + (1 - f_1)\, \omega^{**}\, (\mu_B - r)\, W_0 \\ &\quad - \frac{1}{2}\,(1 - f_1)^2\, \omega^{**2} \sigma_B^2 W_0^2 \\ &= (1 + r)\, W_0 + 2\frac{(\mu_B - r)^2}{2z\sigma_B^2} - \frac{(\mu_B - r)^2}{2z\sigma_B^2} \left(\frac{1 - 2f_1}{f_1}\right)^2 .\end{aligned} \tag{12.11}$$

Banks seek to extract any surplus from clients choosing to have their assets managed by them and hence select the performance fee such that $U_C = \hat{U}_C$, which solves for

$$f_1 = \frac{1}{2 + \sqrt{2 - \frac{\sigma_B^2}{\sigma_C^2}\left(\frac{\mu_C - r}{\mu_B - r}\right)^2}} < \frac{1}{2}. \tag{12.12}$$

Of course we can now compare the optimal portfolio of the client, ω^*, and that chosen by the investment bank, ω^{**}. If we assume that the expected returns on the risky asset of the client, μ_C, and the investment bank, μ_B, are roughly identical, it is obvious when comparing equations (12.4) and (12.7) that $\omega^{**} > \omega^*$. This arises firstly as we reasonably assumed that investment banks can assess the risks of the asset more precisely and $\sigma_B^2 < \sigma_C^2$ and the observation that $f_1 < \frac{1}{2}$. Thus, investment banks invest more into the risky asset than the client would have done. The reason for the investment bank allocating more wealth into the risky asset than the client would is, apart from having more precise information, that they only generate income from the performance fee and this fee is only generated by the risky asset; hence, they allocate more funds to increase their fee income. As this also increases the risk of the investment bank, given the uncertainty of the return of the risky asset and hence the fee income, the amount invested into the risky asset will be limited of course.

This comparison is, however, not using decisions based on the same information. We need to consider what the client would have chosen as portfolio if he had the same information, thus $\mu_C = \mu_B$ and $\sigma_C^2 = \sigma_B^2$, as well as having to pay the fee F to the investment bank. We will address such an analysis next.

Clients with Equal Information Let us now assume that clients have the same information as investment banks; thus, $\mu_C = \mu_B$ and $\sigma_C^2 = \sigma_B^2$. Taking into account the fee clients have to pay, they would have to maximise the first line in Eq. (12.11). Requiring the first-order condition $\frac{\partial \hat{U}_C}{\partial \omega} = 0$, we easily obtain

$$\omega^{***} = \frac{\mu_B - r}{z\,(1 - f_1)\, \sigma_B^2 W_0}. \tag{12.13}$$

From Eq. (12.12), we see that for $\mu_C = \mu_B$ and $\sigma_C^2 = \sigma_B^2$, we obtain $f_1 = \frac{1}{3}$, and inserting this into Eqs. (12.7) and (12.13), we easily obtain that $\omega^{**} = 2\omega^{***}$ and the investment bank allocates twice as much into the risky asset than the client would find optimal. Thus, investment banking portfolios are more risky than those clients would choose. As pointed out earlier, this arises from the distortion the fee F induces into the incentives of the investment bank, which remains even if the information asymmetry between investment banks and clients is eliminated.

Summary Allowing investment banks to determine the investment of assets will result in an allocation that is biased towards risky assets, even if taking into account the different information investment banks and clients might have. The fees investment banks charge distort incentives towards higher risk investment as this allows investment banks to earn a higher performance fee due to the higher expected returns of such assets. While this reduces the utility of clients, the superior information of investment banks might well make the arrangement worthwhile for them and increase their utility.

Given the distortion of the asset allocation towards the risky asset, portfolios managed by investment banks would be found more biased towards investments into stock markets and other more risky investment classes. As such an allocation exposes the portfolio more towards the risks of these asset classes than is optimal, the performance of the portfolio as a whole will depend more on the performance of the risky assets, and thus, the assessment of these assets by the investment bank becomes ever more important for the performance of the portfolio. Therefore, the skills of the investment bank becomes more apparent to the client, and in order to retain the client, it needs to maintain and enhance these skills constantly.

Reading Bhattacharya and Pfleiderer (1985).

Brokerage Services 13

Clients are required to use brokers to trade in security markets. Brokers are ensuring that any trades are settled, thus for buy orders the money transferred to the seller and the bought security allocated to their client. For sell orders the broker ensures that the security is transferred and the money obtained is allocated to the seller. In accepting to route an order to the security market, the broker accepts responsibility to ensure the order, once executed, is settled. For this service the broker would charge a fee. A broker that only provides such a service is commonly referred to as a *discount broker* or *execution-only broker*. Investment banks, however, are *full-service brokers* and as such will provide investment advice to their clients, normally free of charge, who then, based on this advice, decide to buy or sell securities. We will investigate the fees of such full-service brokers and how the provision of information is optimally rewarded.

Let us assume that the broker has obtained a signal s about the return R of an asset such that $R = s + \varepsilon$, where $E[R] = \mu$ and $E[\varepsilon] = 0$ such that ε is an error term that captures the remaining uncertainty about the return of an asset. This information is provided to the client. We further define for notational simplicity $Var[s] = \sigma_s^2$ and $Var[\varepsilon] = \sigma_\varepsilon^2$ such that $Var[R] = \sigma_R^2 = \sigma_s^2 + \sigma_\varepsilon^2$. Of the total wealth of the client, W_0, a fraction $1 - \omega$ is invested into a risk-free asset with return r and a fraction ω into the risky asset.

As a benchmark, we will first consider the decision a client would be making if the investment bank would not reveal their information, then compare this to the case where the information is revealed, and based on the difference in decisions determine the broker fee.

A. Krause, *Theoretical Foundations of Investment Banking*, Springer Texts in Business and Economics, https://doi.org/10.1007/978-3-031-58060-4_13

Uninformed Clients If the client has obtained no additional information from the investment bank, we then have after one time period that the wealth of the client is given by

$$\begin{aligned} W_1 &= (1-\omega)(1+r)W_0 + \omega(1+R)W_0 \\ &= (1+r)W_0 + \omega(R-r)W_0. \end{aligned} \tag{13.1}$$

The investment of ω into the risky asset will yield a return of R and the remainder invested into the risk-free asset will yield r. We then have

$$\begin{aligned} E[W_1] &= (1+r)W_0 + \omega(\mu-r)W_0, \\ Var[W_1] &= \omega^2\sigma_R^2W_0^2. \end{aligned} \tag{13.2}$$

With risk aversion z, the expected utility is given by $U_U = E[W_1] - \frac{1}{2}zVar[W_1]$ and hence

$$U_U = (1+r)W_0 + (\mu-r)W_0 - \frac{1}{2}z\omega^2\sigma_R^2W_0^2.$$

The first-order condition of maximising the utility over the optimal allocation of wealth into the risky asset, $\frac{\partial U_U}{\partial \omega} = 0$, then solves for

$$\omega_U^* = \frac{\mu-r}{z\sigma_R^2W_0}.$$

This allocation into the risky asset by an uninformed client can now be compared to the allocation obtained if information is provided by the broker.

Informed Clients Let us now assume that the investment bank provides the information they have obtained to their client and charge them indirectly through a trading fee of F for the entire amount traded. A client having learned the signal s infers that

$$\begin{aligned} E[W_1|s] &= (1+r)W_0 + \omega(s-r)W_0, \\ Var[W_1|s] &= \omega^2\sigma_\varepsilon^2W_0^2. \end{aligned} \tag{13.3}$$

The utility of such a trader, $U_I = E[W_1|s] - \frac{1}{2}zVar[W_1|s]$, is then given by

$$\hat{U}_I = (1+r)W_0 + \omega(s-r)W_0 - \frac{1}{2}z\omega^2\sigma_\varepsilon^2W_0^2 - F, \tag{13.4}$$

from which we get after solving the first-order condition $\frac{\partial U_I}{\partial \omega} = 0$ that

$$\omega_I^* = \frac{s - r - f}{z\sigma_\varepsilon^2 W_0}, \tag{13.5}$$

where $f = \frac{\partial F}{\partial \omega}$ denotes the brokerage fee expressed as a fraction of the amount traded.

If the broker were to charge a fee of $f = 0$, the optimal allocation to the risky asset would be

$$\omega_I^{**} = \frac{s - r}{z\sigma_\varepsilon^2 W_0}, \tag{13.6}$$

and the additional trading a client does due to the information obtained, neglecting the brokerage fee f, is then given by $\left|\omega_I^{**} - \omega_U^*\right| W_0$. Thus, we focus our investigation not on the total amount traded, but the amount traded in addition to what the client would have traded without any information provided by the investment bank. If $\omega_I^* > \omega_U^*$, the client would buy additional amounts of the risky asset and otherwise buy less of the risky asset ("sell"). The condition that $\omega_I^* > \omega_U^*$ solves for

$$s > s^* = r + f + (\mu - r)\frac{\sigma_\varepsilon^2}{\sigma_R^2}. \tag{13.7}$$

Thus, if $s > s^*$ the client buys additional amounts of the risky asset compared to being uninformed and if $s \leq s^*$ the client will buy less of the risky asset ("sell").

If we let $G(\cdot)$ be the distribution of the signal s, then additional amounts are bought with probability $1 - G(s^*)$ and sold with probability $G(s^*)$. We can easily define the density function of the signal s at $s = s^*$ as

$$g\left(s^*\right) = \frac{\partial G\left(s^*\right)}{\partial s^*} = \frac{\partial G\left(s^*\right)}{\partial s^*}\frac{\partial s^*}{\partial f} = \frac{\partial G\left(s^*\right)}{\partial f}, \tag{13.8}$$

having used Eq. (13.7) to obtain that $\frac{\partial s^*}{\partial f} = 1$.

As the investment bank knows the signal s, we have the expected profits of the broker given by

$$\Pi_B = \begin{cases} \left(1 - G\left(s^*\right)\right) f\left(\omega_I^{**} - \omega_U^*\right) W_0 & \text{if } s > s^* \\ G\left(s^*\right) f\left(\omega_U^* - \omega_I^{**}\right) W_0 & \text{if } s \leq s^* \end{cases}, \tag{13.9}$$

where a buy order is submitted with probability $1 - G(s^*)$ if the actual signal s is larger than the threshold for a buy order, s^*, and the fee f is charged on the actual amount traded in excess of what would be traded in the absence of information, $\omega_I^{**} - \omega_U^*$. Similarly for a sell order, being submitted with probability $G(s^*)$ if the signal s is below the threshold s^*, the fee f is charged on the excess trading $\omega_U^* - \omega_I^{**}$.

Thus, the first-order condition for the optimal fee f of the broker, $\frac{\partial \Pi_B}{\partial f} = 0$, solves for

$$f = \begin{cases} \frac{1-G(s^*)}{g(s^*)} & \text{if } s > s^* \\ -\frac{G(s^*)}{g(s^*)} & \text{if } s \leq s^* \end{cases}, \tag{13.10}$$

where we used Eq. (13.8).

Let us now define the hazard function as $h(x) = \frac{g(x)}{1-G(x)}$ with the assumption that $\frac{\partial h(x)}{\partial x} > 0$, where x is a normalised variable. Define further

$$\begin{aligned} \phi^* &= \frac{s^* - \mu}{\sigma_s} = \frac{f + z\omega_I^* \sigma_\varepsilon^2 W_0 - (\mu - r)}{\sigma_s} \\ &= \frac{f + z\left(\sigma_\varepsilon^2 \omega_I^{**} - \sigma_V^2 \omega_U^*\right) W_0}{\sigma_s} \end{aligned} \tag{13.11}$$

as the standardised threshold signal s^*, such that Eq. (13.10) can be rewritten as

$$f = \begin{cases} \frac{1}{h(\phi^*)} & \text{if } s > s^* \\ -\frac{1}{h(-\phi^*)} & \text{if } s \leq s^* \end{cases}, \tag{13.12}$$

assuming that $g(\phi^*)$ is symmetric such that $1 - G(\phi^*) = G(-\phi^*)$.

The broker fee is decreasing in the amount traded (the larger ω_I^* is for a given ω_U^*). Hence, traders are charged more overall for information that causes large trades and is thus valuable, but the marginal costs are reducing. This is because charging a higher fee will reduce the trading amount ω_I^* as we see from Eq. (13.5), and thus, the revenue to the investment bank is reduced, which has to be balanced against the higher revenue from a higher fee.

We easily obtain that

$$\begin{aligned} \frac{\partial f}{\partial s} &= -\frac{1}{h(\phi^*)^2} \frac{\partial \phi^*}{\partial \omega_I^*} \frac{\partial \omega_I^*}{\partial s} \frac{\partial h(\phi^*)}{\partial \phi^*} < 0, \\ \frac{\partial f}{\partial \sigma_\varepsilon^2} &= -\frac{1}{h(\phi^*)^2} \frac{\partial \phi^*}{\partial \sigma_\varepsilon^2} \frac{\partial h(\phi^*)}{\partial \phi^*} < 0, \\ \frac{\partial f}{\partial \sigma_R^2} &= -\frac{1}{h(\phi^*)^2} \frac{\partial \phi^*}{\partial \sigma_R^2} \frac{\partial h(\phi^*)}{\partial \phi^*} > 0. \end{aligned} \tag{13.13}$$

As a more extreme signal provided by the investment bank will lead to more trading, the investment bank could charge a higher broker fee, but this would limit the amount of trading and hence fee income. It is optimal to reduce the fee as trading increases, thus providing a discount for large trading amounts, to induce more trading and increase revenue through this increased trading volume. If the information is less precise, it is worth less, and hence for a larger σ_ε^2, representing the precision of the information, the investment bank can only charge a lower fee. Similarly, if the uncertainty about the value of the security is high, a high σ_R^2, the value of the information the investment bank provides will be high and the client will benefit more from this information, allowing the investment bank to charge a higher fee.

Providing full-service brokerage is only feasible if $U_I \geq U_U$, and the utility clients obtain from the information, net of the broker fee the investment bank charges, has to exceed that of remaining uninformed, the equivalence of using execution-only brokers.

Summary Investment banks provide full-service brokerage and the broker fee is used to compensate investment banks for providing this added value. As it is impossible to charge for signals directly, investment banks charge for the consequence of clients using the information they provide, which results in a change in trading. Thus, the broker fee will be proportional to the amount of trading and be increasing in the value this information has to clients. While it might not be easy to determine how much a client would be trading if not informed, it is not unreasonable to propose that without any information, no trade at all would happen; thus, the current holdings are viewed as optimal. Only additional information would change that optimum and induce trade. Of course such additional information might also be obtained independently by the client, for example, through the financial press, and some trades might well be induced by other motifs, such as the availability of additional funds or the need to withdraw funds from investment. Neglecting these final aspects, we see that if a client is better informed, a smaller fee should be charged in those cases. Negotiating the broker fee by larger and well-informed clients should thus result in smaller broker fees.

Reading Brennan and Chordia (1993).

14 Market Making

Investment banks also facilitate trading in security markets by acting as counterparty to a trader who seeks to buy or sell the security. A buyer (seller) would buy (sell) the security from the investment bank at prices they state publicly prior to the trade. Therefore, the buyer (seller) is not reliant on the presence of another trader who wishes to sell (buy) the security. The investment bank will sell (buy) the security, with the aim of buying back (selling) the security to another trader at a later point. The aim of the investment bank is not to hold the security, but only to offset the position as soon as possible. This activity is referred to as market making or acting as a dealer. It facilitates trading for the benefit not only of the clients of an investment bank, but all market participants as the orders are submitted anonymously and the market maker is neither able nor allowed to discriminate between traders.

A market maker faces two challenges in providing this service. On the one hand, he needs to set prices such that the buy and sell orders he receives are approximately balanced and he will not build up large positions of the security or run out of it, being unable to facilitate any more buying. With the amount of shares held in deviation of his optimal holdings, called his inventory, an investment bank would seek to maintain an inventory of zero. On the other hand, market makers need to be aware that some traders will have superior information to them and every trade will cause them losses as they are selling (buying) the security below (above) the actual value assessed by such informed investors. Such adverse selection will also affect how prices are set by market makers as they seek to avoid making losses from their activity.

We will thus in Sect. 14.1 first look at the optimal behaviour of market makers concerned about managing their inventory of securities before in Sect. 14.2 we investigate the impact of adverse selection on the prices market makers will quote to traders.

A. Krause, *Theoretical Foundations of Investment Banking*, Springer Texts in Business and Economics, https://doi.org/10.1007/978-3-031-58060-4_14

14.1 Inventory Control

Market makers will have to hold a portfolio consisting of the security and cash. The security is used to satisfy the demand arising from buy orders by investors and the cash to meet the requirements arising from sell orders. There will exist an optimal portfolio and any deviation from this portfolio will reduce the utility of the market maker, requiring the market maker to be compensated if accepting a transaction that takes him away from this optimal portfolio. As market makers cannot charge fees for their services, they adjust the prices at which they are willing to buy and sell from investors and their compensation is derived from the differences in the prices at which they are willing to conduct trades.

The prices market makers quote are referred to as bid prices, at which they are accepting sell orders from investors, and ask prices, at which they are accepting buy orders from investors. The difference between bid and ask prices is called the bid-ask spread; there are two such bid-ask spreads, the bid-ask spread a single market maker quotes and the market spread, which is the difference between the lowest ask price and the highest bid price quoted by any market maker.

We will determine the costs of a market maker for deviating from their optimal portfolio and then consider how this affects their price setting behaviour as well as the market spread we find.

Optimal Portfolio Assume that a market maker has provided a total amount W_0 for market making activities in a specific security. This amount needs to be optimally split between holding cash with which to pay any trader seeking to sell their security and the security itself, from which it is supplied to any buyer in exchange for cash. The market maker invests a fraction ω into the security and we assume that the holding of cash does not yield any return. The initial amount W_0 after one time period of such investments is then given by

$$W_1 = \omega (1 + R) W_0 + (1 - \omega) W_0 = (1 + \omega R) W_0, \tag{14.1}$$

where R denotes the return of the security. Defining the expected return of the security as $E[R] = \mu$ and its variance as $Var[R] = \sigma^2$, we easily obtain

$$\begin{aligned} E[W_1] &= (1 + \omega\mu) W_0, \\ Var[W_1] &= \omega^2 \sigma^2 W_0^2, \end{aligned} \tag{14.2}$$

such that the expected utility of the market maker is given by $U = E[W_1] - \frac{1}{2} z Var[W_1]$, where z denotes the risk aversion of the market maker. Maximising the expected utility over the optimal holding of the security, ω, the first-order condition $\frac{\partial U}{\partial \omega} = 0$ easily solves for

$$\omega^* = \frac{\mu}{z\sigma^2 W_0^2}. \tag{14.3}$$

Any deviations from this portfolio would reduce the utility of the market maker and he would require compensation for accepting any such trade.

Accepting Trades Deviating from this optimal allocation would reduce the utility of the market maker. Assume now that the market maker deviates from this allocation by an amount of I, which we call the inventory of the market maker. The market maker will now be forced to accept a trade of size Q, where $Q > 0$ for a sell order as this increases the holding of the security for the market maker and $Q < 0$ for a buy order. We further denote by F the fee of the market maker to conduct a trade of this size Q, which is to be included into the quoted prices. The wealth after one time period is then given by

$$\begin{aligned} W_1^* &= \left(1-\omega^*\right) W_0 + \left(\omega^* W_0 + I\right)(1+R) \\ &\quad + (1+R)\,Q - I - Q + F \\ &= \left(1 + \left(\omega^* + \frac{I}{W_0}\right) R\right) W_0 + RQ + F. \end{aligned} \tag{14.4}$$

The first term denotes the value from holding cash and the second term that of the security, which is held in the optimal portfolio and the inventory, and the third term the value of the trade just accepted. The cash holding, compared to the optimal portfolio, is reduced by the inventory that has been built up and the trade just accepted. To this we add the fee F that has been charged for this recent trade.

We then easily obtain that

$$\begin{aligned} E\left[W_1^*\right] &= \left(1 + \left(\omega^* + \frac{I}{W_0}\right)\mu\right) W_0 + \mu Q + F, \\ Var\left[W_1^*\right] &= \sigma^2 \left(W_0\left(\omega^* + \frac{I}{W_0}\right) + Q\right)^2, \end{aligned} \tag{14.5}$$

from which the expected utility $U^* = E\left[W_1^*\right] - \frac{1}{2} z Var\left[W_1^*\right]$ can be obtained.

In order for a market maker to accept a trade of size Q, he needs to be at least as well off as if he does not accept this trade. Not accepting a trade is equivalent to accepting a trade of size $Q = 0$ and gaining no fee F, such that using Eq. (14.5), we easily obtain

$$\begin{aligned} E\left[W_1^{**}\right] &= \left(1 + \left(\omega^* + \frac{I}{W_0}\right)\mu\right) W_0, \\ Var\left[W_1^{**}\right] &= \sigma^2 W_0^2 \left(\omega^* + \frac{I}{W_0}\right)^2, \end{aligned} \tag{14.6}$$

with expected utility $U^{**} = E\left[W_1^{**}\right] - \frac{1}{2} z Var\left[W_1^{**}\right]$.

Thus, we can now determine the minimum fee F such that $U^* \geq U^{**}$ and accepting the trade is preferred. If we insert from Eqs. (14.5), (14.6) and insert for ω^* from Eq. (14.3), this easily solves for

$$F \geq F^* = z\left(\frac{1}{2}Q^2 + QI\right)\sigma^2. \tag{14.7}$$

Thus, charging a fee of at least F^* would make the market maker accept a trade of size Q. This minimum fee depends on a characteristic of the security; the variance of the fundamental value σ^2; a characteristic of the trade, namely, the trade size Q; and two characteristics of the market maker, his risk aversion z and his inventory position I.

It is more natural to assume the trade size to be always positive. Define $\hat{Q} = |Q|$ as the trade size and we get the costs for accepting a buy order with $Q > 0$, F_a, and for accepting a sell order with $Q < 0$, F_b, by

$$F_a = z\sigma^2\left(\frac{1}{2}Q^2 - \hat{Q}I\right), \tag{14.8}$$

$$F_b = z\sigma^2\left(\frac{1}{2}Q^2 + \hat{Q}I\right). \tag{14.9}$$

The relative costs a market maker faces are then given by

$$f_a = \frac{F_a}{\hat{Q}} = z\sigma^2\left(\frac{1}{2}\hat{Q} - I\right), \tag{14.10}$$
$$f_b = \frac{F_b}{\hat{Q}} = z\sigma^2\left(\frac{1}{2}\hat{Q} + I\right).$$

When buying the security, the market maker reduces the price at which he is willing to buy compared to the fundamental value P^* of the security and increases it when selling the security. Therefore, the reservation prices of a market maker for the entire trade of size $\hat{Q}$ are given by

$$\hat{Q}P_a = \hat{Q}P^* + F_a, \tag{14.11}$$
$$\hat{Q}P_b = \hat{Q}P^* - F_b,$$

or

$$P_a = P^* + f_a, \tag{14.12}$$
$$P_b = P^* - f_b.$$

The difference between the bid price (at which the market maker is willing to buy) and the ask price (at which it is willing to sell) is known as the bid-ask spread, s. From Eqs. (14.10) and (14.12) we get

$$s = P_a - P_b = f_a + f_b = z\sigma^2 \hat{Q} \geq 0 \tag{14.13}$$

and see that the spread does not depend on the inventory of the market maker, but only on his risk aversion, the trade size, and the variance of the fundamental value of the security.

The inventory does not influence the spread, but only the level of prices. If a market maker accepts a sell order, that is, buys the security, its inventory will increase, and therefore, the costs f_a will reduce and f_b will increase as we see from Eq. (14.10), reducing both P_a and P_b as implied by Eq. (14.12). Thus, after a sell order is submitted to the market, the prices will fall. Similarly, after a buy order the prices will rise. Market makers balancing their inventories drive this result. They seek to discourage buy orders if their inventory is low to prevent a further reduction and discourage sell orders if the inventory is high to prevent a further increase. The price adjustments encourage the submission of orders in the opposite direction to revert the inventory to its optimal level of zero.

We can rewrite equation (14.12) when inserting from Eq. (14.10) and using Eq. (14.13) as

$$\begin{aligned} P_a &= \left(P^* - z\sigma^2 I\right) + \frac{1}{2}s, \\ P_b &= \left(P^* - z\sigma^2 I\right) - \frac{1}{2}s. \end{aligned} \tag{14.14}$$

If the inventory is sufficiently small, the bid price might be above that of the fundamental value and for high inventories the ask price might be below the fundamental value.

The bid and ask prices as determined above represent the reservation prices of market makers, but in order to be profitable would quote lower bid and higher ask prices, if possible. We therefore have to investigate the impact competition has on the prices actually quoted in markets.

Price Competition If there are multiple market makers, they will compete with each other to obtain orders. As the inventory will change after every such trade, market makers will have different reservation prices P_a^i and P_b^i. It cannot be that $P_a^i < P_b^j$ as in this case market maker i could trade with market maker j, as market maker i is willing to sell at P_a^i and market maker j willing to buy at P_b^j; hence, there is a trade surplus for these two market makers to trade. Thus, we find that $P_a^i \geq P_b^j$.

Market makers will not quote their reservation prices as they would not make any profits. If they increase (decrease) the ask (bid) price above (below) P_a^i (P_b^i),

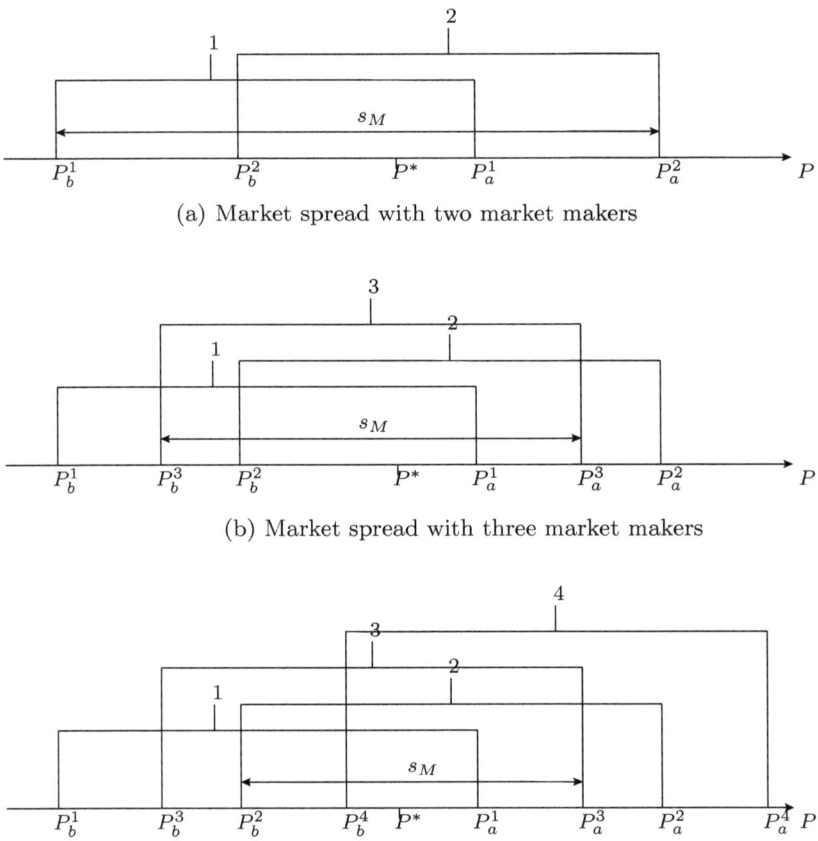

(a) Market spread with two market makers

(b) Market spread with three market makers

(c) Market spread with more than three market makers

Fig. 14.1 Competitive price setting by market makers

no market maker could compete with their price until this price reaches that of the market maker with the second lowest reservation price. Thus, the best available prices in the market are the reservation prices of the market maker with the second lowest reservation price. Of course, with the reservation spread being equal for all market makers, the second lowest reservation prices are not from the same market maker, but in general different market makers.

In Fig. 14.1 we illustrate the resulting market spread s_M, which is the difference between the best bid and ask prices available to traders. We see that for two market makers, the lowest spread that could be observed is the reservation spread s; this is the case if both market makers have the same inventory and hence the same reservation prices. The largest difference between reservation prices is if $P_a^1 = P_b^2$ as for larger differences the requirement that $P_a^i < P_b^j$ induces trades between the market makers. In this case the market spread would be $2s$. We thus find that if two market makers are present, the market spread will be in the interval $s \leq s_M \leq 2s$.

If there are three market makers, the second best market maker is the same on both sides of the trade; it will be the market maker with the intermediate inventory. In this case the market spread will always be $s_M = s$. With more than three market makers, we see from Fig. 14.1c that the spread will reduce, as now the additional market makers will have reservation prices between this intermediate market maker and the others such that $0 \leq s_M \leq s$. We would expect that with an increasing number of market makers, the market spread reduces.

We see that with only two market makers competing, the observed market spread is larger than implied by the reservation prices of individual market makers, but for four or more competing market makers, the observed spread will be below the spread implied by the reservation prices. The reason for this result is that market makers face different costs due to having taken a different number of trades previously, and hence, the costs for buying and selling are not identical across market makers. This latter result allows different market makers to post the best available price to traders, causing the market spread to vary as indicated.

Summary Market makers accepting trades from investors are facing costs that arise from their optimal holdings of the security being disturbed. They are compensated for these costs by quoting prices for accepting trades that are higher (for buy orders) and lower (for sell orders) than the fundamental value and take into account any existing deviations from their optimal holdings as well. As such inventories adjust, the prices quoted will move with the order flow and thus increase as more buy orders are received and decrease as more sell orders are received. With market makers having different costs as orders are executed sequentially and hence only a single market maker at a time being selected to accept a trade, the quoted price can be more competitive than a single market maker could offer, even if charging its reservation price.

These inventory costs of market makers impose costs on the trading of securities as buyers have to pay a higher price and seller receives less, the total turn-around costs being equivalent to the market spread. The advantage investors have is that they can trade immediately without having to rely on the existence of an offsetting order, and as prices are quoted, they know the transaction price as well, eliminating any uncertainties.

Reading Stoll (1978) and Ho and Stoll (1980).

14.2 Adverse Selection

Some traders will have better information about the value of a security than other traders or the market maker. Such traders will only trade if it is profitable for them to do so, thus accepting a price below its value to buy the security and a price above its value to sell. With an informed trader making profits, it is the market maker that incurs losses from such a transaction; thus if accepting such trades, they need to ensure they make additional profits from other trades. Such profits can be derived from uninformed traders and the market maker will ensure to set prices such that he is not making any losses. As market makers cannot charge any other fees for their services, they can only hope to recover these losses from setting prices adequately.

Let us assume the fraction of informed investors is γ and uninformed investors buy the security with probability p and sell them with probability $1 - p$. Thus, only informed investors will react to the prices quoted by market makers and buy the security if its assessment of the value, P^*, is above the ask price, P_a. If the bid price P_b is above the assessed value, the informed trader would sell. The probability of observing a buy order B is given if an informed trader submits the order and it is $P^* \geq P_a$, or an uninformed trader submits such an order. Similarly, a sell order is observed if submitted by an informed trader, provided $P^* \leq P_b$ or an uninformed trader submits this order. Hence

$$\begin{aligned} Prob\,(B) &= \gamma \text{Prob}(P^* \geq P_a) + (1-\gamma)p, \\ Prob\,(S) &= \gamma \text{Prob}(P^* < P_b) + (1-\gamma)(1-p). \end{aligned} \tag{14.15}$$

The expected profits of the market maker for a trade of size Q are then given by

$$\Pi_B = \left(P_a - E\left[P^*|B\right]\right) Prob\,(B)\,Q + \left(E\left[P^*|S\right] - P_b\right) Prob\,(S)\,Q. \tag{14.16}$$

The first term denotes the profits from serving a buy order and the second term that of a sell order. The profits made are the difference of the price the trade happens at and the value the market maker infers from the type of order that has been submitted.

In competition, profits of market makers would be zero; hence, $\Pi_B = 0$. Market makers cannot trade off a loss on a buy order against profits on a sell order, or vice versa. The reason is that a loss on a buy order occurs if the market maker quotes a low price; thus, any buyer would accept their offer. A profit on a sell order implies that the market maker bought at a too low price, which could easily be undercut by other market makers offering a higher price. Thus, a profit on the sell order is not possible and the market maker would only incur a loss on the buy order. Therefore, market makers need also to break even on the buy order. Using Eq. (14.16), we thus require

$$\begin{aligned} P_a &= E\left[P^*|B\right], \\ P_b &= E\left[P^*|S\right]. \end{aligned} \tag{14.17}$$

The bid and ask prices reflect the values the market maker can infer from the order, sell or buy, they have received.

Using Bayes' theorem, we get that

$$\begin{aligned} Prob\left(P^* > P_a|B\right) &= \frac{Prob\left(B|P^* > P_a\right) Prob\left(P^* > P_a\right)}{Prob\left(B\right)} \\ &= \frac{\left(\gamma + (1-\gamma)\, p\right) Prob\left(P^* > P_a\right)}{Prob\left(B\right)} \\ &= \frac{\left(\gamma + (1-\gamma)\, p\right) Prob\left(P^* P_a\right)}{\gamma Prob\left(P^* > P_a\right) + (1-\gamma)\, p} \\ &\geq Prob\left(P^* > P_a\right), \\ Prob\left(P^* < P_b|S\right) &= \frac{Prob\left(S|P^* < P_b\right) Prob\left(P^* < P_b\right)}{Prob\left(S\right)} \\ &= \frac{\left(\gamma + (1-\gamma)(1-p)\right) Prob\left(P^* < P_b\right)}{Prob\left(S\right)} \\ &= \frac{\left(\gamma + (1-\gamma)(1-p)\right) Prob\left(P^* < P_b\right)}{\gamma Prob\left(P^* < P_b\right) + (1-\gamma)(1-p)} \\ &\geq Prob\left(P^* < P_b\right). \end{aligned} \tag{14.18}$$

If $\gamma > 0$, i.e., informed traders are present, the inequality is strict. We can furthermore show that $\frac{\partial Prob\left(P^*>P_a|B\right)}{\partial\gamma} > 0$ and $\frac{\partial Prob\left(P^*<P_b|S\right)}{\partial\gamma} > 0$; thus, the more informed traders there are, the more these probabilities increase. In deriving the second lines of Eq. (14.18) we used that a buy (sell) order, provided $P^* > P_a$ ($P^* < P_b$), is observed from an informed trader or the unformed trader.

Given the probability that the true value P^* exceeds (is below) the ask (bid) price P_a (P_b) has increased after observing a buy (sell) order, we can therefore conjecture that $E\left[P^*|B\right] \geq E\left[P^*\right]$ and $E\left[P^*|S\right] \leq E\left[P^*\right]$, such that with Eq. (14.17) we have $P_a \geq E\left[P^*\right] \geq P_b$, with the equalities being strict in the presence of informed traders, $\gamma > 0$, and the differences increasing in the fraction of informed traders, γ. The bid-ask spread emerges as a mechanism to ensure the market maker is covering any losses from trading with the informed trader when trading with uninformed traders. It thus compensates the market maker for the adverse selection they face due to the presence of informed traders.

If a market maker observes a buy (sell) order, then Eq. (14.17) implies that his best guess of the true value moves to P_a (P_b). In the coming time period this becomes his $E\left[P^*\right]$, and thus, after receiving a buy order, the market maker increases the price, while for a sell order, he will decrease the price. Hence, the price moves in the direction of the order flow, increasing for buy orders and decreasing for sell orders.

Summary Informed traders can take advantage of their information and make profits at the expense of the market maker, who has to sell to them at the stated prices. To offset these losses, market makers will quite prices with a bid-ask spread that allow them to make profits when trading with uniformed investors. Such adverse selection costs to market makers result in the bid-ask spread that impose costs on uninformed traders. More informed investors will increase the bid-ask spread and make trading more costly for uniformed traders, but also prices adjust more quickly to the information contained in orders submitted and thus facilitates all uninformed market participants to learn the information concerned.

Reading Glosten and Milgrom (1985).

Conclusions

Market makers impose costs on traders by quoting bid and ask prices separated by a spread. This spread compensates the market maker for the requirement to accept trades and therefore built up an inventory of the security, in deviation from his optimal portfolio. Furthermore, the spread also compensates the market maker for adverse selection costs arising from the presence of informed traders. While both costs to market makers are present, the spread can accommodate them both simultaneously and are not additive, providing an efficient way to address these costs. Competition between market makers cannot reduce the adverse selection costs that have to be included into the spread, while inventory costs differ across market makers and the resulting market spread will reduce.

Facing the bid-ask spread increases the trading costs of uninformed traders and reduces the profits of informed traders. These additional costs have to be balanced against the benefits of such trading arrangements, namely, the ability of trading instantly without having to wait for an offsetting order by another trader. While for frequently traded securities such waiting times would be minimal, it is especially for securities that are infrequently traded that these benefits can be substantial. Furthermore, the price at which an order is executed will be known due to the prices posted by the market maker, rather than complying with the condition imposed by the order with which the trader is matched. This reduces the uncertainty about the transaction and thereby increases the utility of traders.

Of course, alternative methods are available to address some of the uncertainties in trading. The use of limit orders can ensure that trades are not executed at unfavourable prices, but it can delay the execution of the order until the limit price can be complied with. This might increase the costs to traders. Market makers and the submission of limit orders commonly coexist, suggesting that with different preferences by traders, such as an emphasis on the speed of execution favouring the use of market makers and existing limit orders, while an emphasis on the price might favour the submission of limit orders.

Investment banks provide market making not primarily for the profitability of market making, but it allows them to maintain a presence in the market and, for less frequently traded securities, serves to support the issuer or purchasers of these securities by maintaining a market. Hence, in these cases market making can be interpreted as an additional service provided to issuers whose securities have been underwritten as well as those purchasing such securities, but also for purchasers of financial innovations that might have a limited market and allows investors to reduce or increase their holdings. Having a market that allows investors to buy and sell securities will enhance its value.

Proprietary Trading 15

Most investment banks employ a trading desk, where employees trade securities with the aim of generating profits for the bank. Such proprietary trading is generally very profitable to investment banks, but has also been the subject of substantial losses, especially if traders have been successful in concealing their losses for a longer period of time and accumulating them into amounts that have caused severe losses for the investment bank overall.

Traders at investment banks are able to generate substantial profits by having superior skills compared to the average trader in the market, but will also face competition from trading desks at other investment banks. Facing competition from other similarly sophisticated traders will lead to an arms race in terms of knowledge and sophistication as discussed in Sect. 15.1. The need to employ only highly skilled traders will not only require the investment bank to attract them to work at their trading desk but also distinguish between those that are highly skilled and those that have lower skills and would not generate profits. In Sect. 15.2 we will see how banks use salaries based on their trading performance to ensure they are only employing highly skilled traders. However, relying on salaries that are based on their trading performance gives rise to incentives to overstate the profits they generate and Sect. 15.3 will assess how effective investment banks are in ensuring such behaviour is not widespread.

While proprietary trading of investment banks, as the trading of other professional investors, makes their profits at the expense of less sophisticated investors, in particular retail investors, giving investment banks access to additional information can increase competition between such traders to the benefit of small retail investors. Section 15.4 will explore the impact of dual capacity on retail investors. Giving some traders access to information on the type of investors that are submitting orders can reduce the profits sophisticated investors can make at the expense of retail investors due to the increased competition. This would then benefit less sophisticated traders by reducing adverse selection and hence the losses they are making from trading.

A. Krause, *Theoretical Foundations of Investment Banking*, Springer Texts in Business and Economics, https://doi.org/10.1007/978-3-031-58060-4_15

15.1 Investment in Expertise

A trade is efficient if the buyer of a security values it more highly than the seller; in this case a price between these two valuations can be agreed that improves the welfare of both traders. These differences in value do not only arise from different information, but can also arise from diversification effects in portfolios of assets or the impact of a security on the risk profile of a trader, such as in hedging, amongst others. Let us denote this improvement of the utility of traders from completing a trade by ΔV.

The trading process itself will rely on the information and skills of a trader, which we term here expertise. We assume that expertise can only be used if a trader holds the security and thus acts as a seller. A buyer will not be able to acquire expertise to improve their profits from trading. Trading itself generates only a surplus if ΔV amongst traders, which then is distributed between them. Thus, a seller with higher expertise, such as information about the security, should be able to obtain a higher profit at the expense of the uninformed seller.

The security has value V_H with probability π and $V_L < V_H$ with probability $1 - \pi$. A trader may want to invest an amount C_i to receive a signal s_i, which is either H or L, that predicts the value of the asset in case he is a seller of the security. We assume that the signal of trader i is correct with probability ρ_i such that

$$Prob\,(V_H|H) = Prob\,(V_L|L) = \rho_i \geq \pi. \tag{15.1}$$

We can interpret $e_i = \rho_i - \pi$ as the level of expertise of trader i and assume that $\frac{\partial C_i}{\partial e_i} > 0$ and $\frac{\partial^2 C_i}{\partial e_i^2} > 0$.

Buyer Setting Low Price If buyer i offers a price $P^* = E\,[V|L]$ for the security, a seller j will only sell if the signal is low. As $E\,[V|H] \geq E\,[V|L]$, offering this price P^* will not induce the seller to sell if he receives the high signal as he would have to sell the security below its value; hence, no trade occurs and no surplus is generated to either trader. As the low signal is observed if the value is high (π) and the signal of the seller is wrong ($1 - \rho_j$) or the value is low ($1 - \pi$) and the signal correct (ρ_j), this probability of the seller observing a low signal is given by $\pi\left(1 - \rho_j\right) + (1 - \pi)\left(1 - \rho_j\right)$. Hence, the surplus of the buyer is

$$\begin{aligned} \Pi_B^i &= \left(\pi\left(1 - \rho_j\right) + (1 - \pi)\left(1 - \rho_j\right)\right)\left(E\,[V|L] + \Delta V - P^*\right) \\ &= \left(\pi\left(1 - \rho_j\right) + (1 - \pi)\left(1 - \rho_j\right)\right)\Delta V. \end{aligned} \tag{15.2}$$

The buyer will assess the value of the security to be low, because he infers that this must be the signal the seller has received, given that he is willing to sell. He thus obtains this value of the security, in addition to the benefits of the trade, ΔV, and he pays the price P^* for the security. Of course, as indicated above, the trade only happens if the low signal is received by the seller.

This trading profit when offering the low price P^* can now be compared to the trading profits when offering a higher price.

Buyer Setting High Price If buyer i were to offer $P^{**} = E[V|H]$, seller j would always sell as he would never value the security higher; hence, the expected profits are given by

$$\begin{aligned}\hat{\Pi}_B^i &= E[V] + \Delta V - P^{**} \\ &= \pi V_H + (1-\pi) V_L + \Delta V - \left(\rho_j V_H + \left(1-\rho_j\right) V_L\right) \\ &= \left(\pi - \rho_j\right)(V_H - V_L) + \Delta V \\ &= \Delta V - (V_H - V_L)\, e_j.\end{aligned} \tag{15.3}$$

As sellers always sell the security, the buyer cannot extract any information as to the value of the security from this willingness to sell; hence, the value of the security is given by $E[V] = \pi V_H + (1-\pi) V_L$, which increases by ΔV for the trading benefits and he pays P^{**} for the security. We furthermore have that $P^{**} = Prob(V_H|H)\, V_H + (1 - Prob(V_H|H))\, V_L = \rho_j V_H + \left(1-\rho_j\right) V_L$ and note that we defined the expertise as $e_j = \rho_j - \pi$.

If $\hat{\Pi}_B^i > \Pi_B^i$, the buyer would offer P^{**} and the trade would always occur. Inserting equations (15.2) and (15.3) we easily get that this is the case if

$$\rho_j \leq \rho^* = \frac{\pi + (1-\pi)\frac{\Delta V}{V_H - V_L}}{1 + (1-2\pi)\frac{\Delta V}{V_H - V_L}}. \tag{15.4}$$

The level of expertise of the seller must not be too high; otherwise, the buyer will not be willing to offer a high purchase price. The reason is that a high level of expertise by the seller requires a high price to be paid, which implies high losses to the buyer if the signal the seller receives was negative. While the trade will commence, such adverse selection costs will reduce the profitability of the trade and make a lower offer price, which may not be accepted but prevents any losses, more attractive. We will now assume that the level of expertise is such that trade will always occur.

Optimal Expertise Rather than taking the expertise level as given, traders will make optimal investments into their expertise. We know that the total surplus of trading is ΔV; hence, the surplus of the seller and the buyer have to equal this surplus such that $\hat{\Pi}_S^j + \Pi_B^i = \Delta V$. In this case, using Eq. (15.3), the profits of the seller are given by

$$\hat{\Pi}_S^j = (V_H - V_L)\, e_j \tag{15.5}$$

Assuming that ex ante being a buyer or seller is equally likely, we get the total expected profits of trader i as

$$\begin{aligned}\hat{\Pi}^i &= \frac{1}{2}\hat{\Pi}^i_B + \frac{1}{2}\hat{\Pi}^i_S - C_i \\ &= \frac{1}{2}\left(\Delta V - (V_H - V_L)\, e_j\right) + \frac{1}{2}(V_H - V_L)\, e_i - C_i \\ &= \frac{1}{2}\Delta V + \frac{1}{2}(V_H - V_L)\left(e_i - e_j\right) - C_i,\end{aligned} \tag{15.6}$$

having inserted from Eqs. (15.3) and (15.5). The optimal expertise level is then given from the first-order condition

$$\frac{\partial \hat{\Pi}^i}{\partial e_i} = \frac{1}{2}(V_H - V_L) - \frac{\partial C_i}{\partial e_i} = 0, \tag{15.7}$$

or

$$\frac{\partial C_i}{\partial e_i} = \frac{1}{2}(V_H - V_L) > 0. \tag{15.8}$$

From this we get that the optimal level of expertise is positive, $e_i > 0$, and hence, costs are incurred, $C_i > 0$. If these costs are identical for traders, then $e_i = e_j$, and hence, Eq. (15.6) simplifies to

$$\hat{\Pi}^i = \frac{1}{2}\Delta V - C_i. \tag{15.9}$$

We assume here that $\hat{\Pi}^i \geq 0$ and participating in this market is profitable, as well as $\rho_i < \rho^*$.

If both traders were to refrain from investing into expertise such that $e_i = e_j = 0$ and hence $C_i = 0$, profits would be $\frac{1}{2}\Delta V$ and higher than the optimal profits in Eq. (15.9) as no costs of obtaining expertise are incurred. We can thus conclude that traders' investment into expertise is individually rational, but socially not optimal as all traders would be better off refraining from making any such investments. However, if a trader were to choose $e_i = 0$, then another trader has an incentive to choose $e_j > 0$ and that way increases their profits while reducing those of the other trader. Hence, the other trader will have to invest into expertise to counter this investment, leading to an arms race that does not increase their trading profits, but only increases the costs of acquiring such expertise.

Summary Investing into expertise is an inefficient way to seek profits from trading. With any profits taken from other traders, it results in an arms race between traders, which does not improve the profits from trading, but only increases the costs. It is rational for investment banks to participate in such an arms race, even though it is socially inferior to no investment bank investing into expertise. This results in overqualified traders and investment banks allocating funds inefficiently. However, the investment into expertise can have benefits if other market participants cannot respond to the expertise shown by traders in investment banks, and thus, investment banks obtain additional profits from such traders.

Reading Glode et al. (2012).

15.2 Remuneration of Traders

Investment banks cannot perfectly identify whether a trader they employ is informed or uninformed. Assume that a trader employed by the investment bank is informed with probability γ and uninformed with probability $1 - \gamma$. Apart from being employed by an investment bank, traders can also remain independent and trade on their own account; in this case they face transaction costs of f, which are not present when employed by an investment bank. These transaction costs might include broker fees that are charged to independent traders, but also the increased costs of accessing information and setting up an appropriate infrastructure for trading.

We further assume that, in the absence of any additional information, the current price reflects the value of the stock. Information is then obtained on the change of this value, ΔV, resulting in a price change ΔP. With efficient markets, we assume that the price is set such that given the information the market has from observing trading, the total demand D, the price is set such that $\Delta P = E[\Delta V|D]$. Hence, the price change reflects the change in the value of the security as inferred from observing the total trading demand. This relationship we assume to be linear such that

$$\Delta P = \lambda D. \tag{15.10}$$

We can interpret λ as the liquidity of the market; a high value implies that the price reacts significantly with trading demand and a low value means that prices barely move.

Traders who have no information on the change in the security value anticipate no change, thus $E[\Delta V] = 0$, but are uncertain about this change and the variance of changes is denoted by $Var[\Delta V] = \sigma_V^2$. Informed traders will know the value of ΔV perfectly. In addition to informed and uninformed traders, there are also noise traders, who trade randomly for exogenous reasons, with their total demand being U, where $E[U] = 0$ such that on average their trading demand is nil. We also define the variance of the trading demand by noise traders as $Var[U] = \sigma_U^2$.

With the demand D being stochastic due to the randomness of noise trader demand and the information informed traders have, the liquidity λ can be determined as a regression coefficient of Eq. (15.10) and as such it becomes

$$\lambda = \frac{Cov\left[\Delta V, D\right]}{Var\left[D\right]}. \tag{15.11}$$

In such a market, we can now investigate the behaviour of informed and uninformed traders if acting independently. This will form a benchmark against which the employment of traders needs to be assessed.

Independent Traders An informed trader is assumed to know the change in the value of the security, ΔV, and given this information will seek to maximise its expected trading profits, which are given by

$$\Pi_T = E\left[\left(\Delta V - (1+f)\,\Delta P\right) Q_I | \Delta V\right], \tag{15.12}$$

where Q_I denotes its demand and f the transaction costs if the trader acts independently. If working at the trading desk of an investment bank, we set $f = 0$ and assume that the trader will still seek to maximise its individual trading profits. The profits of the traders are then given by how much the value of the security changes, relative to the price change, adjusted for the fees incurred.

Uninformed traders will not be able to make profits as they will lose to informed traders due to the superior information these have, such that if acting independently their trading demand is $Q_U = 0$. If uninformed traders were trading, they will either trade with an informed trader or a noise trader. As a noise trader is also uninformed, any profits or losses they make from trading would be purely random and its expected value is zero. An informed trader will only trade if it is profitable to do so, with the profits coming from either the uninformed traders or the noise traders. With noise traders not concerned about profits or losses from trading, they will continue to demand U, but uninformed traders will make a loss and hence not trade.

Thus, total demand for securities will be $D = Q_I + U$. Inserting equation (15.10) into Eq. (15.12) and noting that $E\left[U\right] = 0$, we easily get

$$\Pi_T = \left(\Delta V - (1+f)\,\lambda Q_I\right) Q_I. \tag{15.13}$$

The first-order condition $\frac{\partial \Pi_I}{\partial Q_I} = 0$ for the optimal trading amount of informed traders easily solves for

$$Q_I = \frac{\Delta V}{2\,(1+f)\,\lambda}. \tag{15.14}$$

Inserting equation (15.14) into Eq. (15.13), taking expectations to consider the situation prior to obtaining the information on ΔV, as well as noting that

$E\left[\Delta V^2\right] = \sigma_V^2$ due to $E\left[\Delta V\right] = 0$, we get

$$E\left[\Pi_T\right] = \frac{\sigma_V^2}{4\left(1+f\right)\lambda}. \tag{15.15}$$

These are the profits an informed trader deciding to stay independent would expect to make. Thus, to induce informed traders to join an investment bank, the remuneration they have to be paid has to equal at least this amount. The remuneration can be paid as a fixed wage that does not depend on the profits generated. Alternatively, the remuneration could consist of performance-related pay, where traders obtain a fraction of the profits they generate to the investment bank; such arrangements are commonly found in the form of performance-related bonuses.

Fixed Wages To induce informed traders to join the trading desk of an investment bank, the wage offered must be least the amount they can expect to obtain when remaining independent. As the investment bank will not pay more than is required to attract such traders, they will set $w = E\left[\Pi_T\right]$ and the fixed wage w will be equal to the expected trading profits they make. We assume that the investment bank cannot distinguish between informed and uninformed traders, while traders themselves know their type. Hence, offering a wage below this value would leave the investment bank with only uninformed traders, who would not generate any profits. It is therefore that the wage is set at the level of profits that informed traders could generate independently.

While uninformed traders would not make profits from trading, they would nevertheless trade when employed by investment banks as otherwise it would be known that they are uninformed. They would seek to imitate informed traders and assume a change in security value of $\Delta\hat{V}$, on which they base their own demand Q_U. This assumed change in security value is chosen randomly and not based on any information, implying that $Var\left[\Delta V\right] = Var\left[\Delta\hat{V}\right]$ and $Cov\left[\Delta V, \Delta\hat{V}\right] = 0$. An informed trader not hired by the investment bank would trade on his own account, generating demand $\hat{Q}_I$. An uninformed trader not hired would not trade as he would make losses.

A trader hired by the investment bank is informed with probability γ and will trade $Q_I = \frac{\Delta V}{2\lambda}$ based on Eq. (15.14) where we set $f = 0$. As the informed trader has been hired, he will not trade independently such that $\hat{Q}_I = 0$ and the uniformed trader is not trading independently, making $\hat{Q}_U = 0$. If the investment bank hires the uninformed trader, which happens with probability $1-\gamma$, then there is no trading at the investment bank by informed traders; hence, $Q_I = 0$. The uninformed trader will seek to copy the informed trader, and we have $Q_U = \frac{\Delta\hat{V}}{2\lambda}$ with its assumption of

$\Delta\hat{V}$. The informed traders would trade independently with demand $\hat{Q}_I = \frac{\Delta V}{2(1+f)\lambda}$. Thus, total expected demand, including the noise traders, is

$$D = \gamma Q_I + (1-\gamma)\left(Q_U + \hat{Q}_I\right) + U \tag{15.16}$$
$$= \gamma\frac{\Delta V}{2\lambda} + (1-\gamma)\left(\frac{\Delta\hat{V}}{2\lambda} + \frac{\Delta V}{2(1+f)\lambda}\right) + U$$
$$= \frac{\Delta V}{2\lambda}\frac{1+\gamma f}{1+f} + (1-\gamma)\frac{\Delta\hat{V}}{2\lambda} + U.$$

Hence, we obtain

$$Cov[\Delta V, D] = \frac{\sigma_V^2(1+\gamma f)}{2(1+f)\lambda}, \tag{15.17}$$
$$Var[D] = \frac{\sigma_V^2(1+\gamma f)^2}{4(1+f)^2\lambda^2} + \frac{(1-\gamma)^2}{4\lambda^2} + \sigma_U^2,$$

where we used the assumption that $Cov\left[\Delta V, \Delta\hat{V}\right] = 0$ and $Var[\Delta V] = Var\left[\Delta\hat{V}\right]$. Inserting equation (15.17) into Eq. (15.11) gives us after solving for λ that

$$\lambda = \frac{1}{2}\frac{\sigma_V}{\sigma_U}\sqrt{2\frac{1+\gamma f}{1+f} - \left(\frac{1+\gamma f}{1+f}\right)^2 - (1-\gamma)^2}. \tag{15.18}$$

Using Eq. (15.15) for the informed trader not employed at the trading desk of the investment bank, we get the fixed wage to be

$$w = E[\Pi_T] = \frac{\sigma_V^2}{4(1+f)\lambda} \tag{15.19}$$
$$= \frac{1}{2}\frac{\sigma_U\sigma_V}{1+f}\frac{1}{\sqrt{2\frac{1+\gamma f}{1+f} - \left(\frac{1+\gamma f}{1+f}\right)^2 - (1-\gamma)^2}}.$$

The trading profits of the investment bank depend on the type of trader the bank hired. If the informed trader is hired, we have total demand of $D_I = Q_I + U$, and if the uninformed trader is hired, it is $D_U = Q_U + \hat{Q}_I + U$. Using Eq. (15.10), the trading profits for the investment bank are given by

$$\Pi = \gamma E[(\Delta V - \Delta P)Q_I|\Delta V] + (1-\gamma)E[(\Delta V - \Delta P)Q_U] \tag{15.20}$$
$$= \gamma(\Delta V - \lambda D_I)Q_I + (1-\gamma)(\Delta V - \lambda D_U)Q_U.$$

Inserting all variables and noting that $Cov\left[\Delta V, \Delta \hat{V}\right] = 0$, we get

$$E\left[\Pi\right] = \frac{2\gamma - 1}{2} \frac{1}{\sqrt{2\frac{1+\gamma f}{1+f} - \left(\frac{1+\gamma f}{1+f}\right)^2 - (1-\gamma)^2}}. \tag{15.21}$$

Then the investment bank profits from combining (15.19) and (15.21) are given by the trading profits less the fixed wages paid. This gives us

$$\begin{aligned} \Pi_B &= E\left[\Pi\right] - w \\ &= \left(\gamma - \frac{1}{2}\frac{2+f}{1+f}\right) \frac{\sigma_U \sigma_V}{\sqrt{2\frac{1+\gamma f}{1+f} - \left(\frac{1+\gamma f}{1+f}\right)^2 - (1-\gamma)^2}}. \end{aligned} \tag{15.22}$$

Investment banks will only hire a trader and thus operate a trading desk if $\Pi_B \geq 0$. Therefore, we require that

$$\gamma \geq \frac{1}{2}\frac{2+f}{1+f}. \tag{15.23}$$

Only if the fraction of informed traders is sufficiently high will an investment bank hire traders and pay them a fixed wage. If too many uninformed traders are hired, the profits generated by the few informed traders are too low to be able to cover the wages they need to pay in order to attract them; they would be better off staying independent. Given that trading costs for independent traders will in general be quite low, the fraction of informed traders hired by the investment bank must be close to one, thus requiring investment banks to be able to select traders well by ability.

Performance Wages Alternatively to a fixed wage, investment banks may offer a performance contract where traders receive some fraction of the profit they generate. In this case the uninformed trader would not trade as they generate losses only and thus not receive a positive remuneration. Thus, the total demand is then given by the informed traders, either employed by the investment bank or independent, in addition to the noise traders. We thereby obtain

$$D = \gamma Q_I + (1-\gamma)\hat{Q}_I + U = \frac{\Delta V}{2\lambda}\frac{1+\gamma f}{1+f} + U, \tag{15.24}$$

using Eq. (15.14) with $f = 0$ for traders employed by the investment bank. We then have

$$Cov\left[\Delta V, D\right] = \sigma_V^2 \frac{1+\gamma f}{2\left(1+f\right)\lambda}, \tag{15.25}$$

$$Var\left[D\right] = \sigma_V^2 \frac{\left(1+\gamma f\right)^2}{4\left(1+f\right)^2\lambda^2} + \sigma_U^2,$$

which gives us after inserting into Eq. (15.11) and solving for λ that

$$\lambda = \frac{1}{2}\frac{\sigma_V}{\sigma_U}\frac{\sqrt{\left(1+\gamma f\right)\left(2\left(1+f\right)-\left(1+\gamma f\right)\right)}}{1+f}. \tag{15.26}$$

Then using this result in Eq. (15.15), the expected remuneration for informed traders is given by

$$\begin{aligned} w = E\left[\Pi_T\right] &= \frac{\sigma_V^2}{4\left(1+f\right)\lambda} \\ &= \frac{1}{2}\frac{\sigma_U\sigma_V}{\sqrt{\left(1+\gamma f\right)\left(2\left(1+f\right)-\left(1+\gamma f\right)\right)}}. \end{aligned} \tag{15.27}$$

As uninformed traders do not trade, such that $Q_U = 0$, the trading profits of the investment bank are given solely from the profits generated by the informed traders. With Eq. (15.10) we obtain that

$$\Pi = \gamma\left(\Delta V - \Delta P\right)Q_I = \gamma\left(\Delta V - \lambda\left(Q_I + U\right)\right)Q_I. \tag{15.28}$$

After inserting for all variables we easily obtain

$$E\left[\Pi\right] = \gamma\frac{\sigma_V^2}{4\lambda} = \frac{\gamma\left(1+f\right)}{2}\frac{\sigma_U\sigma_V}{\sqrt{\left(1+\gamma f\right)\left(2\left(1+f\right)-\left(1+\gamma f\right)\right)}}. \tag{15.29}$$

As traders are receiving a fraction of the trading profits $E\left[\Pi\right]$, they generate as remuneration, and we will set this fraction such that it matches the expression of w in Eq. (15.27). This way the trader employed by the investment bank would be willing to join the trading desk rather than work independently.

If we now assume that such a performance contract needs monitoring at costs C to ensure that traders report their trading profits accurately and noting that these wages are only paid to informed traders, the bank profits are

$$\hat{\Pi}_B = E\left[\Pi\right] - \gamma w - C = \frac{\gamma f}{2}\frac{\sigma_U\sigma_V}{\sqrt{\left(1+\gamma f\right)\left(2\left(1+f\right)-\left(1+\gamma f\right)\right)}} - C. \tag{15.30}$$

Uninformed traders are not trading, knowing they will make no profits, and are thus not receiving any remuneration. Thus, performance wages allow investment banks to indirectly discriminate between informed and uninformed traders as their different behaviour identifies their status.

In order for investment banks to employ a trading desk, we need $\hat{\Pi}_B \geq 0$, or

$$\sigma_U \sigma_V \geq \frac{2C}{\gamma f} \sqrt{(1+\gamma f)\left(2(1+f) - (1+\gamma f)\right)}. \tag{15.31}$$

Thus, if the joint uncertainty of the change in the security value, σ_V, and the demand by noise traders, σ_U, is sufficiently large, banks will operate a trading desk paying traders performance-related wages. There needs to be sufficient uncertainty in the value of the security for informed traders to be able to generate profits at the expense of other traders in the market, most notably noise traders due to the absence of uniformed traders. These profits will then be able to cover the costs of monitoring traders. In addition, there need to be sufficiently active noise traders in which informed market makers can hide their trades and not move prices too much as to reveal all of their information through the adjustment of the price, which would deteriorate profits too much. If it is more likely that informed traders are hired, the profits these traders to the investment bank generate will increase and thus allow to cover the monitoring costs for a lower uncertainty.

Optimal Trader Remuneration If both fixed and performance wages are sustainable, thus $\Pi_B \geq 0$ and $\hat{\Pi}_B \geq 0$, the bank will prefer a performance-related wage to a fixed wage if it is more profitable, thus $\hat{\Pi}_B \geq \Pi_B$, or

$$\sigma_U \sigma_V \geq \frac{C}{\frac{\gamma f}{2} \frac{1}{\sqrt{(1+\gamma f)(2(1+f)-(1+\gamma f))}} - \frac{\gamma - \frac{1}{2}\frac{2+f}{1+f}}{\sqrt{2\frac{1+\gamma f}{1+f} - \left(\frac{1+\gamma f}{1+f}\right)^2 - (1-\gamma)^2}}}. \tag{15.32}$$

Investment banks will prefer performance-related contracts if the overall uncertainty, $\sigma_U \sigma_V$, is sufficiently high. In this case the ability by informed traders to generate profits at the expense of other traders, as well as being required to remunerate only informed traders, will outweigh the additional monitoring costs that performance wages require. As the likelihood of hiring informed traders increases, the benefits of not having to pay uninformed traders and these traders not making trading losses become less important and the monitoring costs dominate the considerations, such that ever higher uncertainties are required to generate the requisite additional profits to the investment bank to make performance wages preferable.

Figure 15.1 illustrates our results. We see that if investment banks are not able to hire a sufficiently high fraction of informed traders, γ, no trading desk will be operated. In this case the profits generated by informed traders are not sufficient to offset the losses incurred by uninformed traders or cover the monitoring

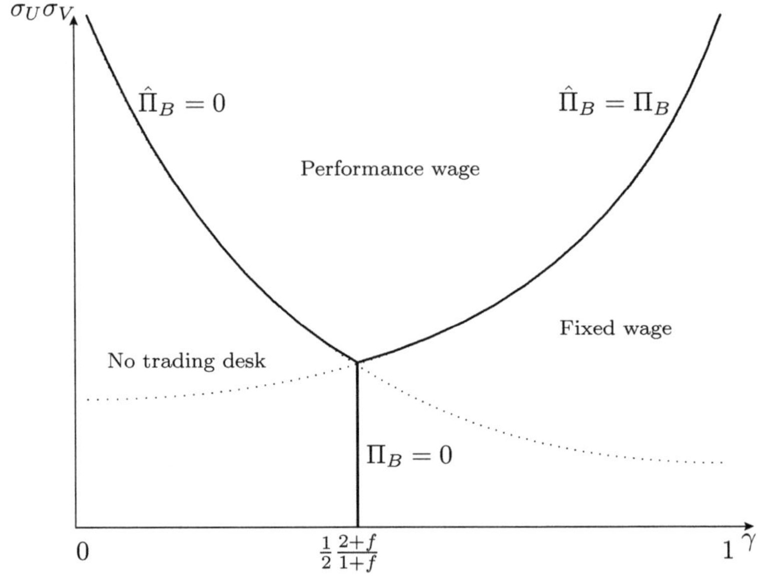

Fig. 15.1 Equilibrium remuneration contracts for traders

costs. The latter can be covered better the higher the uncertainty in the market, $\sigma_U\sigma_V$, is, as this allows informed traders to generate higher profits from their informational advantage. With low market uncertainty, the additional monitoring costs of traders in the case of performance-related wages cannot be covered from the exclusion of loss-making uninformed traders. Once market uncertainty increases, these benefits increase as uninformed traders make ever higher losses if they trade within the regime of fixed wages and the monitoring costs C can be covered, making performance wages more attractive. If only very few uninformed traders remain, the benefits from excluding them from trading and remuneration become smaller, making covering these monitoring costs more difficult, and hence, fixed wages will become more beneficial to investment banks.

Summary Performance wages are preferred by investment banks if market uncertainty is sufficiently high and the fraction of informed traders they are able to employ is not too high. The threshold on the fraction of informed traders an investment bank employs is very high, as long as we assume that trading costs of independent traders are not prohibitively high, and hence, observing fixed wages at trading desks are not commonly found. If either the market uncertainty is low or investment banks are unable to select informed traders with sufficient precision, no trading desk will be operated.

The implications of these findings are that in markets that are generally well understood, investment banks will not operate trading desks. The uncertainty in such markets is too small for traders to be able to generate sufficient profits that allow the investment bank to be profitable. The same applies in markets that are not well understood, but where employing traders with the requisite expertise is difficult. In this case the uncertainty whether the employed traders will be able to generate profits might hold the investment bank off from opening a trading desk for such markets. They are most likely to be active in market that are not well understood and thus have a high degree of uncertainty, but where the investment bank has the ability to identify or train traders of high ability.

Reading Instefjord and Sasaki (2007).

15.3 Misrepresentation of Trading Outcomes

Traders are commonly remunerated based on their performance and as such have an incentive to present their performance as positively as possible. They might be able to resort to underreporting the risks they took in generating their profits, but can also influence the profits themselves, for example, by recognising unrealised gains or delaying the recognition of losses. In some instances, traders may also resort to outright fraud by hiding loss-making trades from their accounts. Such misrepresentation of trading outcomes have the potential to increase the remuneration of traders and they have therefore an incentive to engage in such behaviour.

Let us assume that traders generate value V_H with probability π and value $V_L < V_H$ with probability $1-\pi$. Despite these realised outcomes, which are known to the trader, he might claim to have achieved V_H, even though he only has achieved V_L. There is no incentive for a trader to claim to have achieved V_L if V_H has been realised; thus, traders will only ever overrepresent their outcomes, but never underrepresent them if their remuneration is linked to these values. Let us assume that this misrepresentation of the outcome by a trader happens with probability p. Without additional efforts, such as monitoring by a manager or an auditing process, the true value generated cannot be verified by the investment bank.

We will now consider the incentives of traders to misrepresent the value they generated in the presence of monitoring and auditing, before then considering the incentives of managers to conduct such monitoring.

Incentives for Traders The trader receives a remuneration that is linked to the value generated as he reports it; he obtains a fraction w_T of this value, giving him total remuneration $w_T V_i$. We focus on the situation where the low value is realised, as in this case the trader might misrepresent the outcome. If the trader misrepresents the outcome, this is detected with probability λ_M through monitoring by the manager and a fine F_T is imposed on the trader and he foregoes his remuneration. Such a fine might represent future costs, such as dismissal from their position or the cancellation of future bonuses. In addition, with probability λ_A, the trader's behaviour is audited, and if found to be having acted fraudulently, the same fine F_T is imposed. If neither the monitoring or the audit detects his misrepresentation, he will be able to retain his remuneration of $w_T V_H$. We assume that if monitoring or auditing occurs, any misrepresentation will be identified.

Hence, if reporting the outcome truthfully, the trader obtains $\Pi_T = w_T V_L$, and if he misrepresents the outcome, his expected remuneration is

$$\hat{\Pi}_T = -\lambda_M F_T + (1 - \lambda_M)(-\lambda_A F_T + (1 - \lambda_A) w_T V_H). \tag{15.33}$$

These profits consist of the fine that is imposed if the manager monitors the trader or if an audit occurs. An audit occurring if the trader is monitored has no impact on the outcome as the monitoring will already have detected the misrepresentation. If the trader is not monitored and no audit takes place, he will be able to retain his remuneration.

The trader will report the outcomes truthfully if the expected remuneration of doing so outweighs those of misrepresenting the outcome. Thus, we require that $\Pi_T \geq \hat{\Pi}_T$, or

$$\lambda_M \geq \lambda_M^* = \frac{w_T ((1 - \lambda_A) V_H - V_L) - \lambda_A F_T}{(1 - \lambda_A)(F_T + w_T V_H)}. \tag{15.34}$$

Hence, if monitoring is sufficiently likely to happen, then traders will report their results truthfully. It is straightforward to show that $\lambda_M^* < 1$, and monitoring does not have to be perfect to avoid traders misrepresenting returns. We also see that $\frac{\partial \lambda_M^*}{\partial \lambda_A} < 0$ and auditing can substitute for monitoring. The reason is that a higher likelihood of auditing increases the chances of misrepresentations being detected, allowing for lower monitoring, which has the same effect.

Having established the conditions under which traders misrepresent outcomes, we can now look into the incentives of managers to monitor their traders.

Incentives for Managers We assume that managers participate in the value the traders generate under their supervision. They receive a fraction w_M of the value their trader declares, thus $w_M V_i$ and monitoring a trader imposes costs C on the manager. A successful trader would always disclose the true value V_H, while an unsuccessful trader would misrepresent the value V_L of the value generated as V_H with probability p. Hence, when monitoring the traders, the manager's remuneration is given by

$$\Pi_M = \pi (w_M V_H - C) + (1 - \pi)(w_M V_L - C). \tag{15.35}$$

With monitoring the trader will not be able to misrepresent the value they generated and have to report truthfully. Therefore, the manager will receive his remuneration dependent on the outcome of the trader, less its monitoring costs.

If the manager fails in his duties to monitor the trader and an audit reveals that the trader has misrepresented the outcome, the manager will be fined the amount of F_M. If he has monitored the trader on the other hand and thus detected the misrepresentation, he faces no sanctions. Thus, his expected profits are given by

$$\hat{\Pi}_M = \pi w_M V_H + (1-\pi)\left(p\left(-\lambda_A F_M + (1-\lambda_A) w_M V_H\right) + (1-p) w_M V_L\right).$$

If the trader generates high value, no misrepresentation can occur, and if the low value is realised, the trader misrepresents the outcome with probability p, where an audit will detect this misrepresentation with probability λ_A and the fine be imposed on the manager, or the audit does not detect the misrepresentation and the manager obtains his remuneration. If the trader does not misrepresent the outcome, the manager will obtain the remuneration for the low value.

Monitoring will occur if the expected remuneration from doing so is higher. Thus, we require that $\Pi_M \geq \hat{\Pi}_M$, which solves for

$$p \geq p^* = \frac{C}{\lambda_A (1-\pi)(F_M + w_M V_H)}. \tag{15.36}$$

If traders are sufficiently likely to misrepresent the value they generate, managers will monitor them. As long as monitoring costs are not too high, we find that $p^* < 1$ and traders do not always have to behave fraudulently to induce monitoring by managers.

Given these incentives of traders and managers, we can now proceed to determine the overall equilibrium of misrepresenting outcomes by traders and monitoring by their managers.

Equilibrium Outcome Let us assume that $\lambda_M > \lambda_M^*$; then traders would always report outcomes truthfully, implying $p = 0$, and hence, $\Pi_M < \hat{\Pi}_M$, such that monitoring is not instigated. If no monitoring is instigated, however, then for $\lambda_M = 0$ we have that $\hat{\Pi}_T > \Pi_T$, and hence, all traders would misrepresent their outcome, $p = 1$, making monitoring preferred. Similar arguments can be used for $\lambda_M < \lambda_M^*$ as well as $p < p^*$ and $p > p^*$. Thus, the equilibrium requires that $\lambda_M = \lambda_M^*$ and $p = p^*$.

We can use Eq. (15.34) to solve for λ_A and obtain

$$\lambda_A = \frac{w_T (V_H - V_L) - \lambda_M^* (F_T + w_T V_H)}{\left(1-\lambda_M^*\right)(F_T + w_T V_H)}. \tag{15.37}$$

Similarly, we can solve equation (15.36) for λ_A to get

$$\lambda_A = \frac{C}{p^* (1-\pi)(F_M + w_M V_H)}. \tag{15.38}$$

Setting Eqs. (15.37) and (15.38) equal and solving for p^*, we obtain the trade-off between the monitoring λ_M^* and misrepresentation p^* as

$$p^* = \frac{\left(1 - \lambda_M^*\right)\left(F_T + w_T V_H\right) C}{\left(1 - \pi\right)\left(F_M + w_M V_H\right)\left(w_T\left(V_H - V_L\right) - \lambda_M^*\left(F_T + w_T V_H\right)\right)}. \tag{15.39}$$

It is straightforward to show that $\frac{\partial p^*}{\partial \lambda_M^*} < 0$, and hence, less monitoring results in more misrepresentation of outcomes. We furthermore find from Eq. (15.36) that $p^* > 0$, and thus, in equilibrium traders have a positive probability of misrepresenting the outcome. This result is easily explained by the incentives of traders, who will trade off the fine F_T if their misrepresentation is detected against the additional remuneration from misrepresenting the outcome. Similarly, the manager will make the same consideration, leading to imperfect monitoring and enabling traders to misrepresent their outcomes.

Summary Traders have an incentive to misrepresent the outcome of trading if low values have been realised to increase their remuneration. They do so despite the possibility of such misrepresentation being detected, either by their managers monitoring their actions or an audit process. As managers are benefitting from such misrepresentations as well if their remuneration is based on the performance of the traders they supervise, they have limited incentives to monitor them and eliminate such misrepresentations. The only incentive to do so are repercussions if they have not monitored traders and an audit finds traders have misrepresented their outcomes. Such auditing also affects the behaviour of traders directly as it affects the likelihood misrepresentations are detected and thus reduces the effort of managers in monitoring traders.

Misrepresentation of trading success by traders cannot be eliminated completely as long as there is the potential of traders and their managers, who could monitor such behaviour, might benefit from such behaviour. Increasing the auditing of traders does not fully address this problem as it lowers the incentives of managers to monitor. Given the potentially large value traders can generate on the one hand and the large losses that might accumulate in other instances; there will be strong incentives to act fraudulently and for managers to not question positive results.

Reading Instefjord et al. (2014).

15.4 Dual Capacity

Trading in organised security markets, such as exchanges, is conducted anonymously. The identity of the trader submitting an order is not known and it is therefore also not known whether the trader holds information or is uninformed. Investment banks, acting as brokers, though, will commonly have knowledge about the motivations of their clients when submitting an order; in particular whether it is based on information or other reasons for trading are dominant. If this information is shared with the trading desk of the investment bank, their traders can take advantage of such information. Traders at a trading desk will then know some of the order flow being driven by informed or uninformed traders, reducing the overall uncertainty about the causes of any demand in the security. Having thus an informational advantage, they could use this information to trade profitably.

An arrangement where the broker division of an investment bank can convey information to their trading desk is referred to as dual trading or dual capacity. This is distinct from front-running, where traders at the trading desk obtain information on orders that have not yet been submitted and can take advantage of this information to place their own orders ahead to the orders of the investment banks' clients. Here the information is given after the order has been submitted and will identify the order flow from uninformed traders.

Let us assume that an investment bank is able to identify some, but not all noise traders, that is, traders that are uninformed and trade for exogenous reasons. There are N investment banks, each identifying their own noise traders placing orders U_i, which in the absence of that information has a mean of zero and a variance of σ_U^2. However, not all noise traders are identified as such; an amount of U_0, with expected value of zero and variance σ_0^2, remains unknown across all investment banks. This might be due to incomplete information by investment banks on the motivation of traders. The change in the value of the security, ΔV, is known to an informed trader; to those not informed it has a mean of zero and variance of σ_V^2. The informed trader demands securities Q_I and each investment bank will trade Q_B^i units of this security, but is here assumed to be otherwise uninformed about the security.

The total demand for trading is then given by the unidentified noise trading, the noise traders identified by each investment bank, the trading demand of the investment banks, and the trading demand of the informed investor. Hence,

$$D = U_0 + \sum_{i=1}^{N} U_i + \sum_{i=1}^{N} Q_i^B + Q_I. \tag{15.40}$$

Prices are set efficiently in that the price change ΔP reflects the change in the value of the security, ΔV, given the information available to all market participants, the total demand D. We assume this price change to be linear in total demand, such that

$$\Delta P = E\left[\Delta V | D\right] = \lambda D, \tag{15.41}$$

where λ represents the liquidity of the market as it measures how much the price will change with demand. The informed trader has a demand that is assumed to be linear in the change of the difference between the value and the price; hence,

$$Q_I = \beta_1 \left(\Delta V - \Delta P\right), \tag{15.42}$$

where β_1 denotes the strength of the informed traders reaction to this change. Hence, if the informed trader sees the value increase more than the price, he will buy the security; in the reverse case he would sell the security. The investment bank reacts to the identified noise trader demand as well as the price change by having demand

$$Q_B^i = -\beta_2 U_i - \beta_3 \Delta P \tag{15.43}$$

and β_i representing the strengths of this reaction.

Inserting equations (15.40), (15.42), and (15.43) into Eq. (15.41), we get

$$\Delta P = \lambda \left(U_0 + (1 - \beta_2) \sum_{i=1}^{N} U_i - N\beta_3 \Delta P + Q_I \right), \tag{15.44}$$

and hence, rearranging for ΔP we obtain

$$\Delta P = \frac{\lambda}{1 + N\beta_3\lambda} \left(U_0 + (1 - \beta_2) \sum_{i=1}^{N} U_i + Q_I \right). \tag{15.45}$$

Using these assumptions, we can derive the properties of the resulting equilibrium by determining the demands for informed traders as well as investment banks and from there obtain the properties of the price changes that emerge. In order to do so, we have to identify the parameters β_i and λ.

Demand of Informed Traders The expected profits of the informed trader's given by the gains made from comparing the changes in the security value with the price change for each security purchased. He will use his information on the change in the value of the security in determining his optimal demand. We thus have the profits given by

$$\Pi_T = E\left[(\Delta V - \Delta P)\, Q_I | \Delta V \right], \tag{15.46}$$

from which we get when replacing ΔP with Eq. (15.45) that the first-order condition for maximum profits are given by

$$\begin{aligned} \frac{\partial \Pi_T}{\partial Q_I} &= -\frac{\partial \Delta P}{\partial Q_I} Q_I + (\Delta V - \Delta P) \\ &= -\frac{\lambda}{1 + N\beta_3\lambda} Q_I + (\Delta V - \Delta P) \\ &= 0, \end{aligned} \tag{15.47}$$

and hence,

$$Q_I = \frac{1 + N\beta_3\lambda}{\lambda} (\Delta V - \Delta P) . \tag{15.48}$$

Comparing coefficients with the assumption on the linearity of trading demand in Eq. (15.42), we easily see that

$$\beta_1 = \frac{1 + N\beta_3\lambda}{\lambda} . \tag{15.49}$$

We observe that the demand by informed traders will not only depend on the liquidity of the market, λ, thus how strongly the price will react to the total demand, but also the reaction of investment banks to price changes, β_3. If investment banks react stronger to price changes, the informed trader will submit larger orders.

Demand of Investment Banks The total demand by traders, informed traders, investment banks, and noise traders, is given from Eq. (15.40), and using the expressions for Q_I and Q^i_B, we can rewrite this as

$$D = U_0 + (1 - \beta_2) \sum_{j=1}^{N} U_j - N\beta_3\Delta P + \beta_1 (\Delta V - \Delta P) . \tag{15.50}$$

Investment banks know the noise trading of their customers, U_i, their own trading demand Q^i_B, and inferences about the trading of other investment banks as they behave similar to themselves, and they can observing the price change ΔP. If we eliminate all these variables from the total demand, we can define

$$\Psi^i_B = U_0 + (1 - \beta_2) \sum_{j=1, j\neq i}^{N} U_i + \beta_1 \Delta V \tag{15.51}$$

as representing the elements not readily identified by the investment bank. However, the investment bank can observe total demand, as can all market participants and hence can deduce Ψ^i_B and use this expression as information for their trading decision. The expected profits of investment banks are then given similarly to that of informed investors by

$$\Pi^i_B = E\left[(\Delta V - \Delta P) Q^i_B | \Psi^i_B \right] , \tag{15.52}$$

where the information investment banks have is Ψ^i_B rather than ΔV as in the case of informed investors.

Using Eq. (15.41) and inserting for the total demand D from Eq. (15.50), we get

$$\Delta P = \lambda \left(U_0 + U_i + Q_B^i + (1-\beta_2) \sum_{j=1,j\neq i}^{N} U_i \right. \\ \left. -\beta_3 \sum_{j=1,j\neq i}^{N} \Delta P + \beta_1 (\Delta V - \Delta P) \right), \tag{15.53}$$

where we explicitly separated the demand of investment bank i. This expression can now be transformed into

$$\Delta P = \frac{\lambda}{1 + \lambda\beta_1 + (N-1)\lambda\beta_3} \\ \times \left(U_0 + U_i + Q_B^i + (1-\beta_2) \sum_{j=1,j\neq i}^{N} U_i + \beta_1 \Delta V \right), \tag{15.54}$$

such that the first-order condition for investment banks maximising their profits becomes

$$\frac{\partial \Pi_B^i}{\partial Q_B^i} = E\left[-\frac{\partial \Delta P}{\partial Q_B^i} Q_B^i + (\Delta V - \Delta P) \middle| \Psi_B^i \right] \\ = E\left[-\frac{\lambda}{1 + \lambda\beta_1 + (N-1)\lambda\beta_3} Q_B^i + (\Delta V - \Delta P) \middle| \Psi_B^i \right] \\ = 0 \tag{15.55}$$

and hence,

$$Q_B^i = \frac{1 + \lambda\beta_1 + (N-1)\lambda\beta_3}{\lambda} E\left[\Delta V - \Delta P | \Psi_B^i \right]. \tag{15.56}$$

We can now easily get that

$$Var\left[\Psi_B^i\right] = \sigma_0^2 + (N-1)(1-\beta_2)^2 \sigma_U^2 + \beta_1^2 \sigma_V^2, \\ Cov\left[\Psi_B^i, \Delta V\right] = \beta_1 \sigma_V^2, \tag{15.57}$$

where all identified noise trading across different investment banks is assumed to be independent of each other as well as independent of any unidentified noise trading.

We then have with conditional expectations that

$$E\left[\Delta V|\Psi_B^i\right]=\frac{Cov\left[\Psi_B^i,\Delta V\right]}{Var\left[\Psi_B^i\right]}\Psi_B^i, \tag{15.58}$$

using that $E\left[\Delta V\right]=0$.

We get from Eqs. (15.41) and (15.50), using the definition of Ψ_B^i from Eq. (15.51), that

$$D=\frac{\Delta P}{\lambda}=\Psi_B^i+U_i+Q_B^i-(N-1)\,\beta_3\Delta P+\beta_1\Delta P, \tag{15.59}$$

and hence,

$$\Psi_B^i=-U_I-Q_B^i+\frac{1+\lambda\beta_1+(N-1)\,\lambda\beta_3}{\lambda}\Delta P. \tag{15.60}$$

We now insert equations (15.57) and (15.60) into Eq. (15.58) and this then into Eq. (15.56), such that we obtain

$$\begin{aligned}Q_B^i=&-\frac{1-\frac{1+\lambda\beta_1+(N-1)\lambda\beta_3}{\lambda}\frac{\beta_1\sigma_V^2}{\beta_1^2\sigma_V^2+(N-1)(1-\beta_2)^2\sigma_U^2+\sigma_0^2}}{1+\frac{1+\lambda\beta_1+(N-1)\lambda\beta_3}{\lambda}\frac{\beta_1\sigma_V^2}{\beta_1^2\sigma_V^2+(N-1)(1-\beta_2)^2\sigma_U^2+\sigma_0^2}}\\&\times\frac{1+\lambda\beta_1+(N-1)\,\lambda\beta_3}{\lambda}\Delta P\\&-\frac{\frac{1+\lambda\beta_1+(N-1)\lambda\beta_3}{\lambda}\frac{\beta_1\sigma_V^2}{\beta_1^2\sigma_V^2+(N-1)(1-\beta_2)^2\sigma_U^2+\sigma_0^2}}{1+\frac{1+\lambda\beta_1+(N-1)\lambda\beta_3}{\lambda}\frac{\beta_1\sigma_V^2}{\beta_1^2\sigma_V^2+(N-1)(1-\beta_2)^2\sigma_U^2+\sigma_0^2}}U_i\end{aligned} \tag{15.61}$$

and comparing coefficients with the linear structure of the demand by investment banks from Eq. (15.43) gives us easily that

$$\begin{aligned}\beta_3=&-\frac{1-\frac{1+\lambda\beta_1+(N-1)\lambda\beta_3}{\lambda}\frac{\beta_1\sigma_V^2}{\beta_1^2\sigma_V^2+(N-1)(1-\beta_2)^2\sigma_U^2+\sigma_0^2}}{1+\frac{1+\lambda\beta_1+(N-1)\lambda\beta_3}{\lambda}\frac{\beta_1\sigma_V^2}{\beta_1^2\sigma_V^2+(N-1)(1-\beta_2)^2\sigma_U^2+\sigma_0^2}}\\&\times\frac{1+\lambda\beta_1+(N-1)\,\lambda\beta_3}{\lambda},\\\beta_2=&\frac{\frac{1+\lambda\beta_1+(N-1)\lambda\beta_3}{\lambda}\frac{\beta_1\sigma_V^2}{\beta_1^2\sigma_V^2+(N-1)(1-\beta_2)^2\sigma_U^2+\sigma_0^2}}{1+\frac{1+\lambda\beta_1+(N-1)\lambda\beta_3}{\lambda}\frac{\beta_1\sigma_V^2}{\beta_1^2\sigma_V^2+(N-1)(1-\beta_2)^2\sigma_U^2+\sigma_0^2}}.\end{aligned} \tag{15.62}$$

Using the expression for the total demand from Eq. (15.50),

$$D = U_0 + (1 - \beta_2) \sum_{i=1}^{N} U_i + \beta_1 \Delta V - (N\beta_3 + \beta_1) \Delta P, \tag{15.63}$$

we get for a given price change ΔP that

$$\begin{aligned} Cov\left[D, \Delta V\right] &= \beta_1 \sigma_V^2, \\ Var\left[D\right] &= \sigma_0^2 + N\left(1 - \beta_2\right)^2 \sigma_U^2 + \beta_1^2 \sigma_V^2. \end{aligned} \tag{15.64}$$

These expressions can now be used to determine the price change as we easily get using conditional expectations that

$$\Delta P = E\left[\Delta V | D\right] = \frac{Cov\left[\Delta V, D\right]}{Var\left[D\right]} \left(D + (N\beta_3 + \beta_1) \Delta P\right). \tag{15.65}$$

Solving for ΔP and inserting from Eq. (15.64), we obtain

$$\Delta P = \frac{\beta_1 \sigma_V^2}{\sigma_0^2 + N\left(1 - \beta_2\right)^2 \sigma_U^2 - N\beta_1\beta_3\sigma_V^2} D, \tag{15.66}$$

and using that we assumed the price change to be linear in the total demand from (15.41), we thus have

$$\lambda = \frac{\beta_1 \sigma_V^2}{\sigma_0^2 + N\left(1 - \beta_2\right)^2 \sigma_U^2 - N\beta_1\beta_3\sigma_V^2}. \tag{15.67}$$

Inserting this expression into Eq. (15.49), we can obtain the expression for β_1 as

$$\beta_1 = \frac{\sqrt{\sigma_0^2 + N\left(1 - \beta_2\right)^2 \sigma_U^2}}{\sigma_V}. \tag{15.68}$$

For convenience define the expressions

$$\begin{aligned} \Phi_1 &= \frac{1 + \lambda\beta_1 + (N - 1)\,\lambda\beta_3}{\lambda}, \\ \Phi_2 &= \frac{\beta_1 \sigma_V^2}{\beta_1^2 \sigma_V^2 + (N - 1)\left(1 - \beta_2\right)^2 \sigma_U^2 + \sigma_0^2}, \end{aligned} \tag{15.69}$$

and inserting from Eq. (15.49) for β_1, we obtain that

$$\Phi_1 = 2\beta_1 - \beta_3 \tag{15.70}$$

and we can express β_2 as

$$\beta_2 = \frac{\Phi_1\Phi_2}{1+\Phi_1\Phi_2}. \tag{15.71}$$

This expression then can be manipulated such that

$$\begin{aligned}
1-\Phi_1\Phi_2 &= 1-\beta_2\left(1+\Phi_1\Phi_2\right)\\
\left(1-\beta_2\right)\left(1+\Phi_1\Phi_2\right) &= 1\\
1+\Phi_1\Phi_2 &= \frac{1}{1-\beta_2} &(15.72)\\
1-\Phi_1\Phi_2 &= 1-\beta_2\left(1+\Phi_1\Phi_2\right) = \frac{1-2\beta_2}{1-\beta_2}. &(15.73)
\end{aligned}$$

As we also can show that

$$\beta_3 = \Phi_1\frac{1-\Phi_1\Phi_2}{1+\Phi_1\Phi_2}, \tag{15.74}$$

we insert from Eqs. (15.72) and (15.73) such that with Eq. (15.70) we obtain

$$\beta_3 = \beta_1\frac{1-2\beta_2}{1-\beta_2}. \tag{15.75}$$

Using that $1-\beta_2 = \frac{1}{1+\Phi_1\Phi_2}$, we can write this expression as

$$\begin{aligned}
0 = {} & \left(1-\beta_2\right)^3\left(2N-1\right)\sigma_U^2 - \left(1-\beta_2\right)^2\left(N-1\right)\sigma_U^2 &(15.76)\\
& +2\left(1-\beta_2\right)\sigma_0^2 - \sigma_0^2.
\end{aligned}$$

The sign of the first two terms must be different from the sign of the final two terms to make the entire expression equal to zero. Letting the first two terms being positive we get

$$\beta_2 \le \frac{N}{2N-1}$$

and from the last two terms being negative that

$$\beta_2 \ge \frac{1}{2},$$

hence, we need

$$\frac{1}{2} \leq \beta_2 \leq \frac{N}{2N-1}$$

and for not too small N it is $\beta_2 \approx \frac{1}{2}$. Hence, investment banks buy up approximately half of the identified noise traders' demand. The opposite signs of the two terms in Eq. (15.76) are not viable as that would imply $\frac{1}{2} \geq \beta_2 \geq \frac{N}{2N-1}$, which cannot be fulfilled. Of course, using numerical methods, an explicit value for β_2 could be determined. Having solved for β_2, we can now proceed to obtain β_1 from Eq. (15.68) and then subsequently β_3 from Eq. (15.75), which then allows us to obtain the liquidity λ from Eq. (15.67).

With all parameters thus determined, we can now get

$$\begin{aligned} \Delta P &= \lambda D \\ &= \lambda \left(U_0 + (1-\beta_2) \sum_{i=1}^{N} U_i + \beta_1 (\Delta V - \Delta P) - N\beta_3 \Delta P \right), \end{aligned} \tag{15.77}$$

which solves for

$$\begin{aligned} \Delta P &= \frac{\lambda}{1+\lambda\beta_1 + N\beta_3\lambda} \left(U_0 + (1-\beta_2) \sum_{i=1}^{N} U_i + \beta_1 \Delta V \right) \\ &= \frac{1}{2\beta_1} \left(U_0 + (1-\beta_2) \sum_{i=1}^{N} U_i \right) + \frac{1}{2} \Delta V, \end{aligned} \tag{15.78}$$

using Eq. (15.49) to replace β_3. From this we then easily get

$$\Delta V - \Delta P = \frac{1}{2} \Delta V - \frac{1}{2\beta_1} \left(U_0 + (1-\beta_2) \sum_{i=1}^{N} U_i \right), \tag{15.79}$$

and hence, with Eq. (15.68) this can be rewritten as

$$E\left[(\Delta V - \Delta P)^2 \right] = \frac{1}{4}\sigma_V^2 + \frac{1}{4\beta_1^2} \left(\sigma_0 + (1-\beta_2)^2 N\sigma_U^2 \right) = \frac{1}{2}\sigma_V^2. \tag{15.80}$$

The profits of the informed trader are ex ante, i.e., before having obtained the information on ΔV, given by

$$\Pi_T = E\left[(\Delta V - \Delta P) Q_I \right] = \beta_1 E\left[(\Delta V - \Delta P)^2 \right] = \frac{1}{2}\beta_1 \sigma_V^2. \tag{15.81}$$

Using the results on ΔP, we obtain that

$$\begin{aligned} E\left[\Delta V U_i\right] &= 0, \\ E\left[\Delta V \Delta P\right] &= \frac{1}{2}\sigma_V^2, \\ E\left[\Delta P U_i\right] &= \frac{1-\beta_2}{2\beta_1}\sigma_U^2, \\ E\left[\Delta P^2\right] &= \frac{1}{2}\sigma_V^2. \end{aligned} \tag{15.82}$$

We then have the ex ante expected profits of the investment bank given by

$$\begin{aligned} \Pi_B^i &= E\left[(\Delta V - \Delta P)\, Q_B^i\right] \\ &= -E\left[(\Delta V - \Delta P)\left(\beta_2 U_i + \beta_3 \Delta P\right)\right] \\ &= \frac{\beta_2\left(1-\beta_2\right)}{2\beta_1}\sigma_U^2. \end{aligned} \tag{15.83}$$

The losses for noise traders are the same as the profits of the informed trader and the investment bank combined, given that the trading process generates zero surplus in aggregate. Thus, using Eq. (15.68) we get

$$\begin{aligned} \Pi_N &= -\left(\Pi_T + N\Pi_B^i\right) \\ &= -\left(\frac{1}{2}\beta_1\sigma_V^2 + N\frac{\beta_2\left(1-\beta_2\right)}{2\beta_1}\sigma_U^2\right) \\ &= -\frac{1}{2\beta_1}\left(\sigma_0^2 + \left(1-\beta_2\right)N\sigma_U^2\right), \end{aligned} \tag{15.84}$$

where we made the assumption that all investment banks are identical.

Having obtained the profits of all market participants as well as the implications for the price change of the security, we can now compare these results with those obtained if there was no dual capacity. Such a situation might arise if either strict regulation prevents the passing of information from the brokerage division to trading desks or investment banks engaged in brokerage are not allowed to conduct proprietary trading.

Absence of Dual Capacity Without dual capacity, investment banks would not trade as they have no information and hence would incur a loss trading against informed traders and would be unable to offset these losses against trades with noise traders, who are equally uninformed. Hence, we have $\beta_3 = \beta_2 = 0$. Using

Eq. (15.68), we then get that informed traders will have a higher trading demand as

$$\hat{\beta}_1 = \frac{\sqrt{\sigma_0^2 + N\sigma_U^2}}{\sigma_V} > \beta_1 \tag{15.85}$$

and Eq. (15.78) becomes

$$\Delta\hat{P} = \frac{1}{2\hat{\beta}_1}\left(U_0 + \sum_{i=1}^{N} U_i\right) + \frac{1}{2}\Delta V \tag{15.86}$$

such that with Eq. (15.68) we find

$$E\left[\left(\Delta V - \Delta\hat{P}\right)^2\right] = \frac{1}{4\hat{\beta}_1}\left(\sigma_0^2 + N\sigma_U^2\right) + \frac{1}{4}\sigma_V^2 = \frac{1}{2\hat{\beta}_1}\left(\sigma_0^2 + N\sigma_U^2\right). \tag{15.87}$$

The informed traders' profits are now given by

$$\hat{\Pi}_T = \hat{\beta}_1 E\left[\left(\Delta V - \Delta\hat{P}\right)^2\right] = \frac{\sigma_0^2 + N\sigma_U^2}{2\hat{\beta}_1} \tag{15.88}$$

and due to $\beta_3 = \beta_2 = 0$ we have $Q_B^i = 0$ such that obviously $\hat{\Pi}_B = 0$, and noise traders lose

$$\hat{\Pi}_N = -\hat{\Pi}_T = -\frac{\sigma_0^2 + N\sigma_U^2}{2\hat{\beta}_1}. \tag{15.89}$$

Informed traders will trade more as they do not face competition from investment banks extracting some information from knowing some of the noise trading demand as evidenced by our finding that $\hat{\beta}_1 > \beta_1$, which in turn increases their profits. As informed investors maximise their profits, they will fully take into account the impact their trading has on the total demand and hence on the price change, while with dual capacity investment banks were also affecting total demand. This competition between informed traders and investment banks will reduce the profits to informed traders. In the absence of investment banks, informed traders will make higher profits, but not as much as to capture the whole profits made by investment banks. This arises from the fact that investment banks had a different source of information, the identification of noise traders, that is not available to informed traders.

The ratio of the losses of noise traders with and without dual capacity is given by

$$\frac{\Pi_N}{\hat{\Pi}_N} = \frac{\sigma_0^2 + (1-\beta_2)\, N\sigma_U^2}{\sigma_0^2 + N\sigma_U^2} \frac{\hat{\beta}_1}{\beta_1} \tag{15.90}$$

$$= \sqrt{\frac{\left(\sigma_0^2 + (1-\beta_2)\, N\sigma_U^2\right)^2}{\left(\sigma_0^2 + (1-\beta_2)^2 N\sigma_U^2\right)\left(\sigma_0^2 + N\sigma_U^2\right)}} < 1,$$

implying that noise traders are better off with dual capacity.

We can now determine the largest improvement to noise traders from dual capacity by selecting the optimal amount of noise trading that remains unidentified. We obtain the minimum losses to noise traders from the first-order condition

$$\frac{\partial \frac{\Pi_N}{\hat{\Pi}_N}}{\partial \sigma_0} = \frac{N\beta_2^2\sigma_U^2\left(\sigma_0^2 + (1-\beta_2)\, N\sigma_U^2\right)\left(\sigma_0^2 - (1-\beta_2)\, N\sigma_U^2\right)}{2\eta\left(\sigma_0^2 + (1-\beta_2)^2 N\sigma_U^2\right)^2\left(\sigma_0^2 + N\sigma_U^2\right)^2} = 0 \tag{15.91}$$

and easily obtain that we require

$$\sigma_0^2 = (1-\beta_2)\, N\sigma_U^2. \tag{15.92}$$

As $\beta_2 \approx \frac{1}{2}$, each of the N investment banks would need to identify approximately half the noise trading that originates with them.

Thus, noise traders benefit from dual capacity by making less losses, while informed traders would prefer the absence of dual capacity such that they are the only informed traders.

Impact of Dual Capacity on Prices Dual capacity does not only affect the profits of informed traders and noise traders, but also the price adjustments and thereby indirectly the efficiency of the market. Prices should adjust to new information, represented by trading demand of informed investors, but not to the demand of noise traders. A market with low liquidity would react sensitively to the trading demand of noise traders and reduce the efficiency of the price.

We can determine the impact of noise traders on price changes with dual capacity from Eq. (15.78) by determining its sensitivity to trading demand by unidentified noise traders U_0 and identified noise traders, U_i. Taking the respective derivatives, we obtain

$$\frac{\partial \Delta P}{\partial U_0} = \frac{1}{2\beta_1} > \frac{1-\beta_2}{2\beta_1} = \frac{\partial \Delta P}{\partial U_i} \tag{15.93}$$

and observe that known noise traders have only about half the impact on prices compared to unidentified noise traders as $\beta_2 \approx \frac{1}{2}$. Those traders that have been identified by their investment bank as being noise traders and therefore not providing any information on the change in the security value will be ignored by their investment bank, and hence, their impact on the price change will be smaller.

Furthermore, from Eqs. (15.78) and (15.86) we see that

$$\frac{\partial \Delta \hat{P}}{\partial U_0} = \frac{\partial \Delta \hat{P}}{\partial U_i} = \frac{1}{2\hat{\beta}_1} < \frac{1}{2\beta_1} = \frac{\partial \Delta P}{\partial U_0}, \tag{15.94}$$

and hence, the impact of unidentified noise traders with dual capacity is higher than without dual capacity. The reason for this observation is that with investment banks identifying some traders as noise traders, the amount of unknown noise trading is reduced; this gives the trading demand of informed investors a higher weight in the overall unknown trading demand, and hence, prices will react more strongly to this demand.

For identified noise traders in the market, the impact is reduced as

$$\frac{\partial \Delta P}{\partial U_i} = \frac{1 - \beta_2}{2\beta_1} < \frac{1}{2\hat{\beta}_1} = \frac{\partial \Delta \hat{P}}{\partial U_i}. \tag{15.95}$$

With dual capacity identifying some noise traders to the investment bank and ignoring their trading demands, the impact such traders will have is smaller than if dual capacity is absent and no such information is available.

We thus see that dual capacity reduces the price impact of those noise traders that investment banks have identified, increasing the liquidity of the market and thereby increasing market efficiency as price adjustments to uninformed trading demand are reduced. Only the unidentified noise traders will reduce market liquidity and thereby market efficiency, as informed traders will find it more difficult to disguise their trading demand in the smaller amount of unidentified noise traders.

Summary With dual capacity, the profits of informed traders are lower than without dual capacity and the losses to noise traders lower. Thus, dual capacity benefits noise traders, and optimally, investment banks should identify about half the noise trading in the market to achieve the highest benefits to noise traders. With many retail investors lacking information about securities, we can readily identify them as noise traders and see that dual capacity is to their benefit. Investment banks' trading desks act as competitors to informed traders, and this competition reduces the overall profits informed traders and investment banks combined can make, thus allowing noise traders to reduce their losses.

On the other hand, informed traders, which will commonly come in the form of professional and institutional investors, as well as proprietary trading originating in investment banks, are making smaller profits with dual trading. The competition with investment banks, who have information on the amount of noise trading, will reduce their profits and they would benefit from dual capacity being abolished. Thus, the presence of dual capacity benefits small retail investors and harms the profits of large professional investors, with investment banks benefiting from dual capacity as well, if we neglect the impact on their proprietary trading.

Reading Röell (1990).

Conclusions

Trading desks at investment banks are highly active and to a large extent producing significant profits. As trading is either a zero-sum game, in which the profits of one trader is the loss of another trader, or a small surplus can be obtained as a result of obtaining a superior allocation of securities, investment banks seeking to make profits from trading are locked in a game of increasing sophistication of their traders and trading systems, often at significant expense.

With trading dominated by investment banks and other institutional investors employing professional traders, investment banks are locked into a game seeking to extract profits from each other. This leads to an arms race of employing and training more knowledgeable traders and developing ever more sophisticated electronic trading systems, often at significant expense. While investment into trading activities makes sense for each individual investment bank, there are no social benefits from doing so. Facing fierce competition and requiring traders to exert all possible effort to generate profits for their investment bank, they are commonly awarded salaries that are to a large degree based on their trading performance. While this allows investment banks to induce effort in knowledgeable traders, it would dissuade traders of lower quality from taking up trading positions as they would not be able to generate any profits against more sophisticated traders. Thereby, investment banks would address an adverse selection problem in that it is often difficult for them to assess the ability of traders when employing them. With salaries depending on trading performance, those traders with low abilities would be dissuaded to apply.

The downside of relying on performance-related pay is that it gives strong incentives for traders to increase their performance artificially, either through the use of creative ways of recognising profits and losses, attempting to reduce the risks reported from their trading activities, or even fraud. The ability of traders to influence how their trading results are reported requires them to be monitored to ensure common principles are followed. However, the supervisors of traders themselves, such as those operating a trading desk with a group of traders, will be receiving a salary that is based on the trading performance of their traders. This makes the supervisor, who is best placed to monitor their activities, interested in traders reporting high profits rather than reporting results objectively. Such arrangements will limit the effectiveness of supervision and monitoring, opening the door to widespread malpractice.

Rather than relying only on the sophistication of their traders, investment bank can also use sources of information that are not open to other types of traders. Collecting information from their brokerage division on the composition of traders, informed and uninformed, they can make use of such information without having access to information about the value of securities. While this allows investment banks to generate additional profits, the ensuing competition with informed traders will benefit uninformed traders, such as small retail investors. Hence, the involvement of investment banks can also benefit these types of investors.

Proprietary trading has investment banks in an arms race against each other and other professional investors, imposing significant losses on small retail investors that lack the sophistication in investment banks. Relying on attracting the best traders and exerting maximum effort from them exposes investment banks to the risk of trading outcomes being reported overly positive and having subsequently to be revised. These costs of proprietary trading has to be weighed against the profits the trading itself is able to generate at the expense of retail investors.

Review of Part IV

The core business of investment banks, corporate finance and research, is in most cases supplemented by additional services, summarised as trading and sales. As with other services offered, the advice given by investment banks will be biased towards maximising their own profits, rather than the benefits to their clients. Financial innovations might be phased in with the aim to extract the maximum surplus from any clients adopting their newly developed product, and wealth managed by investment banks is invested too readily in risky assets that allow investment banks to obtain higher fee income. When engaging in proprietary trading, investment banks are directly competing with informed traders, who will often be their clients using the brokerage services they offer. Having superior information to clients relying on the provision of specific services would allow investment banks to exploit their dominant role. However, they need to maintain their reputation for competence, which is central for their ability to attract business to the highly profitable business of corporate finance. With bad advice often becoming apparent retrospectively, they will be constrained in exploiting any such conflicts of interest.

Furthermore, investment banks also rely on many of their clients to gain access to information on which to base their advice in corporate finance. These clients are often investors seeking other services, such as brokerage, and they will be reluctant to provide poor advice as this might jeopardise their access to information in the long run. Furthermore, trading and sales, to a large degree, is not very profitable. The profit margins in brokerage and market making are in most cases very low, and sometimes these areas are even seen as loss leaders to investment banks. Financial innovations can be very costly to develop and the revenue they might generate is highly uncertain, making this business line highly risky. They are often seen as an addition to their core business of corporate finance with the aim of providing clients with all services they might need and thus preclude the need for contacts with other investment banks who might seek the opportunity to attract their corporate finance business. It is mainly only proprietary trading that is highly profitable to investment banks.

Larger investment banks have the resources to offer all such services and be a "full-service" investment bank, while smaller investment banks will only be able to offer some of these additional services and are called "boutique" investment banks. In many cases they will cooperate with other investment banks to offer the full range of services to their clients. Through such cooperations the risk of clients switching investment banks is reduced, especially as boutique investment banks built up substantial expertise in their core business, often specialised to specific industries or geographical regions, that most full-service investment banks cannot match.

Part V

Conducting Investment Banking Business

Investment banks are offering a wide range of services to clients, who are to a large extent supplied independently of each other by different departments. While there are connections between these different services, these are mostly arising from client use, for example, a client might read an analyst report and then decide to buy or sell shares in that company through the brokerage division. Having such independently run, but still interconnected, services will lead to each department having its own employment and business practices. There are, however, some common features in investment banks that are widespread across departments, but also across investment banks.

One common observation is that investment bankers are particularly well paid, even taking into account the often long working hours, and given a high level of responsibility at a younger age than in commercial banks or many other industries. Chapter 16 will investigate the reasons for the high pay observed and how giving responsibilities to staff at an early stage in their career provides incentives to exert maximum effort.

Until the 1990s, it had been common for investment banks to be organised as partnerships, where a small number of senior employees would own the business and existing staff would be invited to join as partners if they were deemed to deserve this step, for example, by having shown exceptional performance in their roles over a prolonged period of time. The conditions under which such partnerships are feasible are considered in Chap. 17, alongside the implications that being organised as partnerships have for the quality services offered. The large extent of autonomy that investment banks give their employees and the minimal level of senior management in a flat organisational structure, even as investment banks outgrew the traditional partnerships, is analysed in Chap. 18.

As investment banks provide services that in many instances rely on detailed knowledge of the company, it would be beneficial to investment banks if they can rely on information previously obtained and merely add any changes to their information or add aspects that have so far not been relevant. Such relationship banking may well come at a cost to investment banks, who have to ensure they at all times have the capacity to advise such clients, which may increase staffing costs.

Chapter 19 will explore the implications of such relationship banking for investment banks and the fees they are able to charge.

It is not only for investment banks to offer services, but these services also have to meet the needs of their clients. In Chap. 20, we will therefore look at the degree of specialisation and expertise an investment bank should have. Banks and their clients will not always find the same level of specialisation to be optimal, depending on how their contracts are structured. Even if investment banks have a structure that allows them to provide quality services to their clients, the quality of these services will necessarily vary, and the surplus they can provide to their clients will not be identical, as much as the profits investment banks make from each client will differ. These differences will in part also be dependent on characteristics of the clients, such as the level of demand for services or their complexity. With limited capacity at the best investment banks, we will also look at ways to match investment banks with clients.

16 Employment Policies

A distinct element of investment banks is the high pay employees receive and a significant level of responsibility given to employees with often limited experience. On the other hand, investment banks expect employees to work long hours and complete many tasks in short periods of time under often severe pressure, and employees that are not performing well enough in this environment are often facing redundancy.

Comparing these practices with those of commercial banks, we observe that employees in investment banks are higher paid, even taking into account the higher workload and greater responsibilities they are taking on. They also face lower employment security than employees in other industries, including commercial banking, even when taking into account the more cyclical nature of investment banking business. These characteristics of investment bank employment are therefore quite different from most other industries, except those that operate similar businesses to that of investment banks, such as fund management or investment consultancy. The only other industry with comparable employment practices is management consultancy.

Investment banking is very much dependent on the use of information and thus depends to a large extent on the willingness of employees to source information and to invest into their expertise to interpret the information they have obtained. Both require substantial levels of effort, which is difficult to assess objectively. This chapter will show how investment banks seek to provide incentives to employees to exert this effort. Section 16.1 will investigate why investment bankers, and traders in particular, are much better remunerated than their commercial banking colleagues. We will then in Sect. 16.2 look at the reasons why employees in investment banks are given significant responsibilities at an early stage in their career, rather than having to earn such positions by proving their ability.

A. Krause, *Theoretical Foundations of Investment Banking*, Springer Texts in Business and Economics, https://doi.org/10.1007/978-3-031-58060-4_16

16.1 Optimal Remuneration

Investment banks employ two types of employees with distinct roles. The "bankers" originate loans and, through their assessment of borrowers prior to granting loans and monitoring throughout its lifetime, add value by increasing the probability of loans being repaid. Such bankers would normally be employed not in the investment banking division but the commercial banking arm of a universal bank. In an investment banking context they might be financial analysts that through their assessment of the issuer of securities ensures their value remains high. Firmly located within the investment banking business are "traders". They assess the loans given by other banks and decide the price at which it is profitable to buy these loans, if they are offered. Thus, traders do not add value to the security, as the provision of loans to borrowers and the subsequent monitoring by bankers does to finance investments, they merely redistribute wealth between banks by seeking to maximise the profits for the bank they are working for at the expense of reducing profits by the same amount to the bank they are buying the loans from.

Let us assume we have N banks that each has given loans L at a loan rate r_L. The loan of each bank i is either repaid with probability π_H^i or $\pi_L^i = \delta\pi_H^i < \pi_H^i$, where $\delta < 1$ and state H occurs with probability p and state L with probability $1 - p$. This state is exogenously determined but loan specific in that different loans may have different states. Investment banks obtain a signal on the state of a specific loan issued by other banks at no costs beyond those of paying wages to employees seeking out this information. The originating bank knows the probability of default of their own loans.

We can now determine the value of such a loan that a different bank has originated.

Loan Values Bank i does not know the probability with which the loans of other banks are repaid, π_s^j, but will have to rely on forming expectations, $E_i\left[\pi_s^j\right]$. However, it obtains a signal s about the state of the loan originated by other banks. The probability that the signal received is correct is given by $\rho_i > \frac{1}{2}$. The price bank i is willing to pay for another bank j's loan is then, for signals L and H, respectively, given by

$$\begin{aligned}
P_L^{ij} &= \rho_i E_i\left[\pi_L^j\right](1 + r_L) L \\
&\quad + (1 - \rho_i) E_i\left[\pi_H^j\right](1 + r_L) L \\
&= E_i\left[\pi_H^j\right](\rho_i\delta + (1 - \rho_i))(1 + r_L) L \\
&= E_i\left[\pi_H^j\right]((p + (1 - p)\delta) \\
&\quad + (1 - \delta)(1 - \rho_i - p))(1 + r_L) L
\end{aligned} \tag{16.1}$$

$$
\begin{aligned}
&= E_i\left[\pi_H^j\right](V + (1-\delta)(1-\rho_i - p)(1+r_L)L), \\
P_H^{ij} &= \rho_i E_i\left[\pi_H^j\right](1+r_L)L \\
&\quad + (1-\rho_i)E_i\left[\pi_L^j\right](1+r_L)L \\
&= E_i\left[\pi_H^h\right](\rho_i + (1-\rho_i)\delta)(1+r_L)L,
\end{aligned}
$$

where we define $V = (p + (1-p)\delta)(1+r_L)L$ for convenience. The value of the loan, and hence the price the bank is willing to pay, consists of the inference by bank i of the probability the loan of bank j being repaid in states H and L, $E_i\left[\pi_s^j\right]$, and the accuracy of the signal they received, ρ_i. If the signal L is correct, which happens with probability ρ_i, then the expected repayment obtained when buying the loan is $E_i\left[\pi_L^j\right](1+r_L)L$, while with probability $1-\rho_i$ the signal L is wrong and state H occurs with the expected repayment being $E_i\left[\pi_H^j\right](1+r_L)L$. The same rationale applies when receiving signal H. Using $\pi_L^i = \delta\pi_H^i$ gives us the second line for both signals in Eq. (16.1) and the third line for P_L^{ij} is obtained by expanding the expression in brackets, before then inserting for V as defined above in the final line for state L.

We assume that $\rho_i > \frac{1}{2}$, such that the information of the signal is valuable in that it is more likely than not to provide the correct information. We then can easily see that when receiving a low signal the value attributed to the loan is lower than when receiving a high signal, we have $P_L^{ij} < P_H^{ij}$. Bank i could always offer P_L^{ij}, but would only be able to offer P_H^{ij} if it receives the signal H, which ex ante has probability p. Hence, a seller should accept an offer P_L^{ij} if $P_L^{ij} > pP_H^{ij}$ as then the certainty of selling the loan provides them with higher proceeds than the expected revenue they would obtain waiting to be offered the higher price P_H^{ij}, which will only happen if the high signal is received, which has probability p. Knowing that the selling bank would accept P_L^{ij} if this condition is fulfilled, no bank would pay more than this amount, even if they obtain signal H. Thus, the price at which the loan is sold is always P_L^{ij}. Inserting from Eq. (16.1), this requires

$$
\rho_i \leq \frac{1 - p\delta}{(1-\delta)(1-p)}, \tag{16.2}
$$

implying that the signal must not be too precise for an offer of P_L^{ij} to be accepted. In this case the adverse selection to the seller is not too high to overcome the uncertainty from holding out for a higher price. We assume in the following that this condition on ρ_i is fulfilled and the loan is always sold at P_L^{ij}. Therefore, the seller of a loan will obtain its full value if the probability of repayment is low and make a loss if it is high.

Using this price at which loans are bought and sold, we can now determine the profits of banks if they are forced by liquidity shocks to sell loans that are bought up by banks not facing such a liquidity shock.

Bank Profits Banks face a liquidity shortage with probability λ that forces them to sell their loans in order to raise cash. If they face no liquidity shortage, they would buy up such loans from other banks facing a liquidity shock to make use of their excess liquidity. They also engage N_T^i traders at a wage of w_T who evaluate these loan purchases through the precision of their signal, ρ_i, and N_B^i bankers at a wage of w_B to manage loans by affecting the probability of these being repaid, π_H^i.

If bank i faces a liquidity shock, it sells their loans at a price P_L^{ji} to bank j, the price bank j is willing to pay for bank i's loans. If not facing a liquidity shock, bank i retains its loans that are repaid with probabilities π_H^i or π_L^i, respectively, depending on the state occurring. The bank knows the probability with which their own loans are repaid and the probability of each state occurring for their own loans. In addition, without a liquidity shock, the bank will purchase loans from bank j at a price P_L^{ij} and obtain the revenue from these purchased loans. With deposits D, deposit rate r_D, and the salaries for bankers, we then have the bank profits given by

$$\begin{aligned}
\Pi_B^i = {} & \lambda P_L^{ji} + (1-\lambda)\left(p\pi_H^i (1+r_L) L + (1-p)\pi_L^i (1+r_L) L\right. \\
& + \left(pE_i\left[\pi_H^j\right](1+r_L) L\right. \\
& \left.\left. + (1-p) E_i\left[\pi_L^j\right](1+r_L) L - P_L^{ij}\right)\right) \\
& - (1+r_D) D - w_T N_T^i - w_B N_B^i \\
= {} & \pi_H^i V - (1+r_d) D - w_T N_T^i - w_B N_B^i \\
& + (1-\delta) E_i\left[\lambda\pi_H^i (1-\rho_j - p)\right. \\
& \left. - (1-\lambda)\pi_H^j (1-\rho_i - p)\right](1+r_L) L,
\end{aligned} \tag{16.3}$$

where

$$\begin{aligned}
P_L^{ji} &= E_i\left[\rho_j\right]\pi_L^i (1+r_L) L + \left(1 - E_i\left[\rho_j\right]\right)\pi_H^i (1+r_L) L \\
&= \pi_H^i V + \pi_H^i (1-\delta)\left(1 - E_i\left[\rho_j\right] - p\right)(1+r_L) L
\end{aligned} \tag{16.4}$$

as the expected price obtained from other bank for the loan based on Eq. (16.1). As we do not know the precision of the signal received by the other bank, ρ_j, we have to make inferences. We do know, however, the probability of our own loans being repaid, π_s^i. Using $\pi_L^i = \delta\pi_H^i$ and the definition of V gives us the second expression of this equation.

Rather than taking the probability of loans being repaid, π_s^i, and the precision of signals on the state of loans, ρ_i, as given, we can now evaluate how bankers and traders can affect these.

The Effect of Bankers and Traders We now assume that hiring more bankers increases the success probability π_H^i in state H; therefore, $\frac{\partial \pi_H^i}{\partial N_B^i} > 0$. As $\pi_L^i = \delta \pi_H^i$, the success probability in state L is likewise affected. However, as π_L^i is a fraction of π_H^i, the absolute differences between these two probabilities will increase as the probabilities themselves increase. Similarly, more traders increase the precision of the signal ρ_i, such that $\frac{\partial \rho_i}{\partial N_T^i} > 0$.

The total number of bankers and traders is limited to N_B and N_T, respectively, such that after bank i hires N_K^i employees, for each of the remaining $N-1$ banks, the number of traders ($k = T$) or bankers ($k = B$) is given by

$$N_k^j = \frac{N_k - N_k^i}{N-1}. \tag{16.5}$$

We can then evaluate how bank i employing more bankers or traders affects the probability of loans being repaid and the precision of signals at another bank j. We obtain using Eq. (16.5) that

$$\begin{aligned} \frac{\partial \pi_H^j}{\partial N_B^i} &= \frac{\partial \pi_H^j}{\partial N_B^j}\frac{\partial N_B^j}{\partial N_B^i} = -\frac{1}{N-1}\frac{\partial \pi_H^j}{\partial N_B^j} < 0, \\ \frac{\partial \rho_j}{\partial N_T^i} &= \frac{\partial \rho_j}{\partial N_T^j}\frac{\partial N_T^j}{\partial N_T^i} = -\frac{1}{N-1}\frac{\partial \rho_j}{\partial N_T^j} < 0. \end{aligned} \tag{16.6}$$

We see that hiring bankers or traders does not only increase a bank's own probability that the loans are repaid or the precision of its own signals increased, but it is detrimental to their competitors by reducing their probability of loans they originated being repaid and the precision of their signals. This is because a bank employing more staff will deprive other banks of staff, reducing their ability to increase their probabilities of loans being repaid and the precision of signals.

We can now determine the optimal number of bankers and traders each bank seeks to employ. We will firstly consider the case where banks do not consider the impact their hiring of employees has on competitors. This will serve as a benchmark case for evaluating the wages paid to bankers and traders, before then considering the case where banks take into account the competition for a limited number of bankers and traders.

Efficient Wages Let us now look at the optimal allocation of employees in a bank. To this effect we ignore the effects that hiring additional bankers and traders have on competitors. We thus do not consider Eq. (16.6) and instead assume the derivatives to equal zero. From Eq. (16.3) we easily obtain the marginal products of employing traders and bankers, respectively, by taking the first derivatives such that

$$\frac{\partial \Pi_B^i}{\partial N_T^i} = (1-\delta)(1-\lambda)(1+r_L)\,E_i\left[\pi_H^j\right]\frac{\partial \rho_i}{\partial N_T^i} - w_T = 0, \tag{16.7}$$

$$\frac{\partial \Pi_B^i}{\partial N_B^i} = \frac{\partial \pi_i}{\partial N_B^i}\left(V + (1-\delta)\lambda\left(1 - E_i\left[\rho_j\right] - p\right)(1+r_L)\,L\right) - w_B$$
$$= 0.$$

This expression can now easily be solved for the wages w_T and w_B. As our model implicitly assumed that all banks are equal, in equilibrium we would infer that all banks behave alike, and hence, bank i would expect bank j to employ the same resources as itself such that $E_i\left[\pi_H^j\right] = \pi_H^i$ and $E_i\left[\rho_j\right] = \rho_i$. This gives us

$$w_T^* = (1-\lambda)(1-\delta)\,\pi_H^i\,(1+r_L)\,L\frac{\partial \rho_i}{\partial N_T^i} \tag{16.8}$$

$$w_B^* = (V + (1-\delta)\lambda(1-\rho_i - p)(1+r_L)\,L)\,\frac{\partial \pi_H^i}{\partial N_B^i}.$$

If banks employ resources efficiently, the marginal products for both bankers and traders will be identical and equal to their respective wages. Hence, we would obtain that $w_T^* = w_B^* = w^*$. To fulfill this requirement of the wages for bankers and traders, they would be adjusted through the terms $\frac{\partial \rho_i}{\partial N_T^i}$ and $\frac{\partial \pi_H^i}{\partial N_B^i}$, thus the number of bankers and traders hired.

This wage serves as a benchmark and we will now complete our analysis by taking into account the effect hiring an employee has on competitors.

Competitive Effects Taking into account the competitive effects hiring a trader or banker has on other banks as detailed in Eq. (16.6), the first-order conditions, when using Eq. (16.3), for maximal profits become

$$\frac{\partial \Pi_B^i}{\partial N_T^i} = (1-\delta)\,E_i\left[\frac{\lambda \pi_H^i}{N-1}\frac{\partial \rho_j}{\partial N_T^j} + (1-\lambda)\,\pi_H^j\frac{\partial \rho_i}{\partial N_T^i}\right](1+r_L)\,L - w_T = 0, \tag{16.9}$$

$$\frac{\partial \Pi_B^i}{\partial N_B^i} = \frac{\partial \pi_H^i}{\partial N_B^i} V + E_i \left[\lambda \frac{\partial \pi_H^i}{\partial N_B^i} (1 - \rho_j - p) + \frac{\partial \pi_H^j}{\partial N_B^i} \frac{1-\lambda}{N-1} (1 - \rho_i - p) \right] - w_B = 0.$$

Again using our implicit assumption that banks are all equal and hence in equilibrium will behave alike, we obtain $E_i \left[\pi_H^j \right] = \pi_H^i$ and $E_i \left[\rho_j \right] = \rho_i$. Using Eq. (16.8) we then easily get that

$$\begin{aligned} w_T^{**} &= (1-\delta) \left((1-\lambda) + \frac{\lambda}{N-1} \right) (1 + r_L) L \frac{\partial \rho_i}{\partial N_T^i} \\ &= \frac{\lambda + (1-\lambda)(N-1)}{(N-1)(1-\lambda)(p + \rho_i - 1)} w^* > w^*, \\ w_B^{**} &= \frac{\partial \pi_H^i}{\partial N_B^i} \left(V + \left(\lambda + \frac{1-\lambda}{N-1} \right) (1-\delta)(1 - \rho_i - p)(1 + r_L) L \right) \\ &= w^* - \frac{\partial \pi_H^i}{\partial N_B^i} \frac{1-\lambda}{N-1} (\rho_i + p - 1)(1-\delta)(1 + r_L) L < w^*. \end{aligned} \tag{16.10}$$

For the final relationship, we assume that $\rho_i + p > 1$. Given that $\rho_i > \frac{1}{2}$ and banks would not lend if they infer state H to be too unlikely to occur, this assumption does not impose a significant constraint on the outcome.

We thus find that

$$w_T^{**} > w^* > w_B^{**} \tag{16.11}$$

and traders are remunerated above their marginal product, while bankers are rewarded below their marginal product. Compared to their productivity within the bank, as represented by their marginal product w^*, traders are overpaid and bankers are underpaid. Traders obtain higher wages because they do not only directly contribute to bank profits through the evaluation of the loans bought, but employing them also limits the ability of other banks to evaluate the loans they acquire, thus giving the bank a higher sales price for their loans while lowering the purchase price for loans they acquire as we can easily show that $\frac{\partial P_L^{ij}}{\partial \rho_i} < 0$. Less traders in other banks will reduce ρ_j and therefore increase the price for their own loans, P_L^{ij}, while increasing the number of traders in this bank i will increase ρ_i and thus lower the prices for loans of the other bank, P_L^{ji}. This gives banks benefits on two fronts, making traders more valuable than the value they add directly to the bank, increasing their wages above their marginal product.

Bankers, on the other hand, provide a positive externality. Through improving the probability of repayment of loans, they increase the value to the bank employing them, but they also hand over more valuable loans to purchasers, causing employing them to have positive effects for other banks, who do not have to pay the full value of these loans as banks only obtain P_L^{ji} when selling a loan, even though the loan is worth P_H^{ji} if the state occurring is H. Hence, bank i will make a larger loss, partially offsetting the benefits of employing more bankers and reducing their wages below their marginal product.

Summary If we define bankers as those originating and monitoring loans, while traders are those buying such loans from other banks, then bankers are paid less than traders. Bankers improve the quality of loans a bank provides, but this also benefits the buyer of the loans. Due to the forced nature of sales arising from liquidity shortages, loans are not sold at full value, causing a positive externality for the benefit of other banks, and hence, banks do not pay bankers the full benefits they create to the bank directly. On the other hand, traders do not only create value by evaluating loans the bank buys more accurately and thereby allowing the bank to buy them more cheaply, but due to the limited number of traders in the market, this also limits the quality of evaluations by other banks and these banks will buy loans at higher prices. Thus, banks benefit directly from being able to buy loans cheaper from other banks and indirectly if they sell their own loans at higher prices. These combined benefits lead to higher wages for traders. These results depend crucially on the market for bankers and traders to be of fixed size and thus both types of employees to be in short supply. Without this assumption, both banks could employ as many traders and bankers as was optimal, equalising the pay to the marginal product. It is, however, a shortage in both, bankers and traders, that gives rise to these results, not merely the shortage in one of these groups.

From a welfare perspective, bankers add value as they are reducing the default rate of loans, while traders only redistribute profits between banks without adding value. It is thus that activities that are socially desirable, the employment of bankers, are remunerated less well than activities that fail to do so, the employment of traders. The private benefit to banks of employing traders drives the discrepancy in wages.

Reading Glode and Lowery (2016).

16.2 Promotion Practices

Investment bankers are given significant responsibilities at early stages in their careers, but find themselves sidelined from promotions quickly if they do not perform sufficiently well, are assigned less prestigious roles, or even face dismissal. On the other hand, investment bankers that perform well are promoted quickly.

Let us assume that an investment bank has available two tasks on which to recruit employees. Task L is low-risk in that if the task is not fulfilled successfully, the investment bank does not suffer any losses. These tasks might be with the back office and subject to many checks such that losses are unlikely to occur, for example, in market making or brokerage. In high-risk tasks, the investment bank will suffer a loss E if the task fails. Such a task might be proprietary trading, but also middle office tasks such as risk management, or the losses arising from losing clients in deals that have not been completed or completed badly when working in corporate finance. The profits to the investment bank from each task, if completed successfully, are V_H for high-risk tasks and V_L for low-risk tasks, where $V_H > V_L$, and we can interpret high-risk tasks as high risk-high return and low-risk tasks as low risk-low return. There are two time periods t in which these tasks are performed and employees can be moved between low-risk and high-risk tasks freely. Employees will exert effort at some cost C_t in each period that affects their probability of success, π_t, such that these costs are increasing in the success rate, $\frac{\partial C_t}{\partial \pi_t} > 0$. We also assume that $\frac{\partial^2 C_t}{\partial \pi_t^2} > 0$, such that marginal costs are increasing in the success rate.

Employees are paid for both time periods according to their success or failure in the task allocated, independent of the task itself. We thus abstract from the commonly observed higher pay in high-risk tasks; this can be justified from the employee's perspective due to the higher level of commitment high-risk tasks usually require and we can interpret their pay as the net benefits they receive after taking into account the level of commitment they have to show to their task. The wages paid are w_{SS} for success in both time periods, w_{FS} if failing in period 1 and succeeding in period 2, w_{SF} for the reverse situation, and w_{FF} if the employee fails in both time periods. We furthermore assume that wages are only paid after the outcomes of both time periods are known; this might be achieved with clawback clauses in contracts, delayed bonuses, or the payment in the form of shares or options on shares in the investment bank that link the wage to the performance of the investment bank, applying a suitable lock-in period in which these securities cannot be sold or exercised.

We can now explore the allocation of tasks in time period 2, given that he has been failing in time period 1. Subsequently, we will investigate the case that he is successful in time period 1 and finally will consider the allocation of tasks in the first time period.

Task Allocation After Failure Let us now assume the employee has failed in the first time period. For the second time period his expected revenue consists of the wage w_{FS} if he is successful in the allocated task and w_{FF} if he also fails in the second time period; from this we have to deduct the costs of exerting effort in time period 2, such that his profits are given by

$$\Pi_M^2 = \pi_2 w_{FS} + (1 - \pi_2)\, w_{FF} - C_2. \tag{16.12}$$

The optimal effort level, represented by the probability of success, is given from the first-order condition

$$\frac{\partial \Pi_M^2}{\partial \pi_2} = w_{FS} - w_{FF} - \frac{\partial C_2}{\partial \pi_2} = 0, \tag{16.13}$$

from which we easily obtain that

$$\frac{\partial C_2}{\partial \pi_2} = w_{FS} - w_{FF}. \tag{16.14}$$

As $\frac{\partial^2 C_2}{\partial \pi_2^2} > 0$, the effort exerted is highest if the difference $w_{FS} - w_{FF}$ is biggest, i.e., w_{FS} is maximal and $w_{FF} = 0$. Setting $w_{FF} = 0$ minimises the costs to investment banks without affecting the incentives of employees.

The expected profits of the investment bank in the second time period is given by

$$\begin{aligned} \Pi_B^{2L} &= \pi_2 V_L - \left(\pi_2 w_{FS} + (1-\pi_2)\, w_{FF}\right), \\ \Pi_B^{2H} &= \pi_2 V_H - \left(\pi_2 w_{FS} + (1-\pi_2)\, w_{FF}\right) - (1-\pi_2)\, E, \end{aligned} \tag{16.15}$$

for low-risk tasks L and high-risk-tasks H, respectively. The revenue V_i is obtained if the task is completed successfully and the investment bank has to pay the wages of the employee, the size of which depends on whether the task was completed successfully or not. In case of the high-risk task, the investment bank also faces losses E if the task is not completed successfully.

We now see that

$$\begin{aligned} \frac{\partial \Pi_B^{2L}}{\partial \pi_2} &= V_L - \left(w_{FS} - w_{FF}\right), \\ \frac{\partial \Pi_B^{2H}}{\partial \pi_2} &= V_H - \left(w_{FS} - w_{FF}\right) + E. \end{aligned} \tag{16.16}$$

For the low-risk task this is positive if $V_L > w_{FS} - w_{FF}$. Using $w_{FF} = 0$, we get from Eq. (16.15) that requiring $\Pi_B^{2L} \geq 0$, we need $w_{FS} \leq V_L$ and hence (16.16) is positive for low-risk tasks and we set the largest possible wage giving nonnegative profits, thus $w_{FS} = V_L$. Inserting this result into the second equation for the high-risk task, we get $\Pi_B^{2H} = \pi_2 (V_H - V_L) - (1-\pi_2)\, E$. We now find that the profits for high-risk tasks are negative, $\Pi_B^{2H} < 0$, if

$$E > \frac{\pi_2}{1-\pi_2} \left(V_H - V_L\right). \tag{16.17}$$

If we thus assume that losses from unsuccessfully completed high-risk tasks are sufficiently high, high-risk tasks will not be allocated to employees that have previously failed. As the profits from low-risk tasks are $\Pi_B^{2L} = 0$, the investment bank will allocate low-risk tasks after an employee fails in the first time period.

Having established that after failing in time period 1, the employee is allocated a low-risk task, we now proceed to the allocation if he succeeded in the first time period.

Task Allocation After Success If an employee is allocated a high-risk task in period 1 and he succeeds, let us assume that he will still be allocated a low-risk task in the second time period. Thus, regardless of the outcome of period 1, he will be allocated a low-risk task, making the second time period irrelevant for his choice of effort in the first time period. Therefore, the same scenario emerges that we have analysed above. As the task allocation in the second time period is independent of the outcome in the first time period, we are reduced to a single time period consideration as above, and thus, allocating the high-risk task H becomes unsustainable in the first time period. Therefore, having been allocated a high-risk task in the first time period, the employee remains in a high-risk task, provided he has been successful in the first time period.

If the low-risk task has been allocated to the employee in the first time period, the considerations in the second time period are identical to that of an employee having been allocated a high-risk task. If the employee fails, then he will again be allocated a low-risk task, and if he succeeds, the investment bank will change his task to the high-risk task H. Using the same arguments as above, we would find that $w_{SF} = 0$ and $w_{SS} = V_L$.

Having established that an employee failing at a task in the first time period will result in being allocated the low-risk task in the second time period, while success implies that the employee is allocated the high-risk task, we now turn to the allocation of tasks in the first time period.

Initial Allocation of a Low-Risk Task Let us assume that after an employee fails in the first time period when being allocated the low-risk task, his expected remuneration is zero in the second time period, i.e., from Eq. (16.12) we obtain that his profits are $\Pi_M^2 = \pi_2 w_{FS} + (1 - \pi_2)\, w_{FF} - C_2 = \pi_2 V_L - C_2 = 0$, which solves for $C_2 = \pi_2 V_L$, after inserting our result that $w_{FS} = V_L$ and $w_{FF} = 0$. Assuming zero remuneration if the employee fails in time period 1 allows the investment bank to provide incentives for employees to exert maximal efforts in the first time period at minimal cost to the investment bank, the same rationale as setting $w_{FF} = 0$ in time period 2. The fact that the employee has been allocated the low-risk task, which we can reasonably assume to be less demanding, makes the prospect of the employee being dismissed for his poor performance and hence not receiving any remuneration realistic.

If we now assume the task initially allocated was the low-risk task, we then have the total profits of the employee across both time periods given by

$$\begin{aligned}\Pi_M^L &= \pi_1 \left(\pi_2 w_{SS} + (1-\pi_2)\, w_{SF} - C_2\right) - C_1 \\ &= -C_1 < 0,\end{aligned} \tag{16.18}$$

where the employee only obtains a positive profit if he succeeds in time period 1 (π_1) and then obtains the wages depending on the success in time period 2. If he fails his task, we have assumed that no remuneration is paid. He also has to bear the costs of exerting effort in both time periods, where, if he knows that he will not receive any remuneration in time period 2, he will not exert any effort. If we then insert our previous results that, if having been allocated low-risk task, we have $w_{SS} = V_L$ and $w_{SF} = 0$, together with our assumption that $C_2 = \pi_2 V_L$, we obtain the result in the second line. With negative profits to the employee, he would not enter employment and the initial allocation to low-risk tasks is not possible.

We thus turn now to the case that employees are allocated high-risk tasks when starting with the investment bank.

Initial Allocation of a High-Risk Task If the employee is allocated the high-risk task, we obtain similar to Eq. (16.18) that the profits of employees are given by

$$\Pi_M^H = \pi_1 \left(\pi_2 w_{SS} + (1-\pi_2)\, w_{SF} - C_2\right) - C_1. \tag{16.19}$$

Again after failure in the first time period, the employee would not receive any remuneration. The employee would now determine his optimal effort levels in each of the two time periods if allocated the high-risk task in the first time period. The first-order conditions are given by

$$\begin{aligned}\frac{\partial \Pi_M}{\partial \pi_1} &= w_{SF} + \pi_2 \left(w_{SS} - w_{SF}\right) - C_2 - \frac{\partial C_1}{\partial \pi_1} = 0, \\ \frac{\partial \Pi_M}{\partial \pi_2} &= \pi_1 \left(w_{SS} - w_{SF} - \frac{\partial C_2}{\partial \pi_2}\right) = 0.\end{aligned} \tag{16.20}$$

Let us define $\Delta w = w_{SS} - w_{SF}$ as the difference in wages between success and failure in the second time period; given success in the first time period, we can rewrite the first-order conditions as

$$\begin{aligned}\frac{\partial C_1}{\partial \pi_1} &= w_{SF} + \pi_2 \Delta w - C_2, \\ \frac{\partial C_2}{\partial \pi_2} &= \Delta w.\end{aligned} \tag{16.21}$$

Investment bank profits are then given by

$$\begin{aligned}\Pi_B &= \pi_1 V_H - (1-\pi_1)\,E \\ &\quad +\pi_1\left(\pi_2 V_H - (1-\pi_2)\,E - \pi_2 w_{SS} - (1-\pi_2)\,w_{SF}\right) \\ &\quad +(1-\pi_1)\left(\pi_2 V_L - \pi_2 w_{FS} - (1-\pi_2)\,w_{FF}\right) \\ &= \pi_1\left(V_H - w_{SF} + \pi_2\left(V_H - \Delta w\right) - (1-\pi_2)\,E\right) \\ &\quad -(1-\pi_1)\,E. \end{aligned} \tag{16.22}$$

Starting with an allocation to the high-risk task, the investment bank obtains V_H if the task is completed successfully and makes losses E if the task is not successfully completed. In the case of success, the high-risk task is allocated again in the second time period and the requisite wages paid, and in the case of failure, in the second time period the low-risk task is allocated and again wages are paid. Due to $w_{FS} = V_L$ and $w_{FF} = 0$, the last term vanishes and we can simplify the investment bank profits.

The optimal remuneration is now given by maximising the investment bank profits in Eq. (16.22), which gives us when recognising that π_i will depend on the remuneration of employees, the first-order conditions as

$$\begin{aligned}\frac{\partial \Pi_B}{\partial \Delta w} &= \frac{\partial \pi_1}{\partial \Delta w}\left(V_H - w_{SF} + \pi_2\left(V_H - \Delta w + E\right)\right) \\ &\quad +\pi_1 \frac{\partial \pi_2}{\partial \Delta w}\left(V_H - \Delta w + E\right) - \pi_1\pi_2 = 0, \\ \frac{\partial \Pi_B}{\partial w_{SF}} &= \frac{\partial \pi_1}{\partial w_{SF}}\left(V_H - w_{SF} + \pi_2\left(V_H - \Delta w + E\right)\right) \\ &\quad +\pi_1 \frac{\partial \pi_2}{\partial w_{SF}}\left(V_H - \Delta w + E\right) - \pi_1 = 0, \end{aligned} \tag{16.23}$$

which we can solve for

$$\begin{aligned}\frac{\Pi_B + E}{\pi_1} &= \pi_1\left(\pi_2 - \frac{\partial \pi_2}{\partial \Delta w}\left(V_H - \Delta w + E\right)\right)\frac{\partial \Delta w}{\partial \pi_1}, \\ &= \pi_1\left(1 - \frac{\partial \pi_2}{\partial w_{SF}}\left(V_H - \Delta w + E\right)\right)\frac{\partial w_{SF}}{\partial \pi_1}. \end{aligned} \tag{16.24}$$

Solving this equation, we then obtain

$$\left(V_H - \Delta w + E\right)\left(\frac{\partial \pi_2}{\partial w_{SF}}\frac{\partial w_{SF}}{\partial \pi_1} - \frac{\partial \pi_2}{\partial \Delta w}\frac{\partial \Delta w}{\partial \pi_1}\right) = \frac{\partial w_{SF}}{\partial \pi_1} - \pi_2 \frac{\partial \Delta w}{\partial \pi_1}. \tag{16.25}$$

From the first line of Eq. (16.21), we obtain that $\frac{\partial^2 C_1}{\partial \pi_1 \partial w_{SF}} = 1$ and $\frac{\partial^2 C_1}{\partial \pi_1 \partial \Delta w} = \pi_2$ and hence

$$\frac{\frac{\partial^2 C_1}{\partial \pi_1 \partial \Delta w}}{\frac{\partial^2 C_1}{\partial \pi_1 \partial w_{SF}}} = \frac{\frac{\partial w_{SF}}{\partial \pi_1}}{\frac{\partial \Delta w}{\partial \pi_1}} = \pi_2, \tag{16.26}$$

such that $\frac{\partial w_{SF}}{\partial \pi_1} - \pi_2 \frac{\partial \Delta w}{\partial \pi_1} = 0$ and the right-hand side of Eq. (16.25) is zero, which then requires

$$\Delta w = V_H + E. \tag{16.27}$$

Inserting this relationship into Eq. (16.23) provides us with the revised first-order conditions

$$\begin{aligned} \frac{\partial \Pi_B}{\partial \Delta w} &= \frac{\partial \pi_1}{\partial \Delta w} (V_H - w_{SF}) - \pi_1 \pi_2 = 0, \\ \frac{\partial \Pi_B}{\partial w_{SF}} &= \frac{\partial \pi_1}{\partial w_{SF}} (V_H - w_{SF}) - \pi_1 = 0. \end{aligned} \tag{16.28}$$

As $\frac{\partial w_{SF}}{\partial \pi_1} = \pi_2 \frac{\partial \Delta w}{\partial \pi_1}$, these two conditions are identical and we can determine the value of w_{SF} from the second equation, then subsequently using Eq. (16.27) to obtain w_{SS}.

Let us now assume that $\pi_1 > \pi_2$, implying that due to increasing marginal costs, $\frac{\partial C_1}{\partial \pi_1} > \frac{\partial C_2}{\partial \pi_2}$, and hence from Eq. (16.21) we get that $\frac{\partial C_1}{\partial \pi_1} > \frac{\partial C_2}{\partial \pi_1} = \frac{C_2 - w_{SF}}{\pi_1}$, and as $\frac{\partial C_2}{\partial \pi_2} = \Delta w$, this solves for $w_{SF} > (1 - \pi_2) \Delta w + C_2$. Using that $\Delta w = V_H + E$, the investment bank profits from Eq. (16.22) can be rewritten as

$$\Pi_B < \pi_1 (\pi_2 V_H - C_2) - (1 + \pi_1 - \pi_1 \pi_2) E. \tag{16.29}$$

Suppose that $C_2 = \pi_2 V_H$, then $\frac{\partial C_2}{\partial \pi_2} = V_H$, but as Eq. (16.21) implies that $\frac{\partial C_2}{\partial \pi_2} = \Delta w = V_H + E > V_H$, we require a higher C_2. This makes the first term in Eq. (16.29) negative, and with the second term being clearly positive, the entire expression is negative. Hence, if $\pi_1 > \pi_2$, the investment bank would not be profitable and we need that $\pi_1 < \pi_2$. Thus, after initial success, older employees are more likely to succeed than younger employees.

Summary We have seen that investment banks would hire employees to work on high risk-high return tasks and only if they are not successful will they be demoted to low risk-low return tasks. This threat of demotion to such tasks, together with the associated pay cut, motivates employees to exert high effort that increases their chances of being successful and retaining their position with the more prestigious and financially more rewarding high risk-high return tasks. If employees were to start with low risk-low return tasks, there would not be a threat of demotion to motivate employees exerting sufficient effort. It is thus only older and initially not successful employees that can be found conducting low-risk low-return tasks.

In addition, the threat of losing pay accumulated from success in the first time period motivates employees to increase their efforts in the next time period and avoid failure. This implies that older employees, once they have been successful, are increasing their efforts and thereby are more likely to be successful than younger employees. It is not the experience that increases the success rate of older employees, but the desire to retain the accumulated benefits from previous success. This emerges as we have assumed that pay is delayed until the success or failure across multiple times periods is revealed and only consistent success will trigger payment of wages; this is akin to delayed bonuses or being remunerated with shares or options whose value can only be realised after a lengthy lock-up period.

Reading Axelson and Bond (2015).

Conclusions

Investment banks pay their employees well, in particular their traders. The number of potential employees that have the skills to be successful in a bank, be it in commercial or investment banking, will be limited like in most highly skilled professions. The common result of this situation is that companies compete for employees and will pay them according to their marginal productivity. If an employee decides to join another company, the production of this company will increase while that of his former company will reduce, and this marginal product the employee will obtain as a wage. In investment banking, especially trading, there is an additional effect; the former employer will not only lack an employee generating profits for them, the employee is now generating profits for another investment bank. As overall trading does not generate any surplus, this implies that by losing an employee to a competitor they are not only losing the profits he made, but will lose additional profits as he now uses his expertise against his former employer. Thus, an investment bank is willing to increase pay beyond the marginal product of the employee.

On the other hand, commercial bank employees add value to companies seeking loans by monitoring their behaviour. This will, on the one hand, increase the profits of their employer as the default risk reduces, but, on the other hand, it will also reduce their profits as they are unlikely to recover these benefits if they have to dispose of loans in case of a liquidity shortage. Hence, their net contribution is below their marginal product and they are paid less well. Given that productivity in the banking industry overall is high compared to many other industries, bankers are still well paid.

As the generation of profits relies on efforts to obtain information and investment into expertise to interpret this information, both of which cannot be measured well, investment banks have to rely on incentives rather than monitoring and supervision to ensure that employees are performing well. Giving employees significant responsibilities at an early stage provides them with incentives to exert a high level of effort. The policy of demoting or making redundant employees that are not performing well provides an incentive to this effect; this incentive is stronger than seeking promotion as not gaining such promotion and retaining lower pay is less strict than losing pay. This is then compounded by deferred remuneration, which is only paid if the employee retains its high performance. Having to show consistent performance over a long time to ensure that already earned remuneration is retained provides additional incentives to retain a high performance, and as more remuneration is accumulated, the stronger this incentive becomes. Investment banks have therefore addressed the problem of motivating employees to perform well through the threat of demotion or dismissal as well as deferred remuneration. Combined with the high remuneration of traders, we have obtained the common feature of employment policies found in investment banks.

17 Partnerships

Traditionally, investment banks have been organised as partnerships and remained as such in most cases until the early 1990s, while commercial banks gave up their partnerships in the majority of cases well before the Second World War. Partnerships operate such that there are no traditional shareholders, but the owners, called "partners" are active in the business themselves. Each partner will hold a specified stake in the company and any profits generated are distributed to the partners. This is different from shareholder-owned investment banks, whose owners are not actively engaged in thc investment bank's business. Another main difference is that partners are typically chosen from existing employees, often referred to as "associates". On becoming partner, they buy a stake of the investment bank, and when they leave the investment bank, on resigning or retirement, they sell this stake again. These stakes might be sold to newly appointed partners or be returned to the investment bank. Similarly, buying a stake can be from an exiting partner leaving the investment bank or a newly issued stake created by the investment bank. Thus, for employees in partnerships there is the prospect of being promoted to a partner and becoming a co-owner of the investment bank. While many senior employees in shareholder-owned investment banks are given remuneration packages that include shares or share options in the investment bank, the employee does not directly invest his own funds into the business and the stake held is usually very small. In contrast, the stake of a partner is substantial.

In Sect. 17.1 we will explore under which conditions partnerships are viable such that employees want to join as associates and then accept becoming a partner. Assuming partnerships exist, we will then in Sect. 17.2 compare partnerships and shareholder-owned investment banks to see under which conditions partnerships are the preferred setup of doing business and what this implies for the quality of the service they offer.

A. Krause, *Theoretical Foundations of Investment Banking*, Springer Texts in Business and Economics, https://doi.org/10.1007/978-3-031-58060-4_17

17.1 Viability of Partnerships

Partnerships commonly recruit future partners from their pool of employees, called associates. It is the partners who will develop these associates' skills and also identify whether they are suitable to be promoted to become partners. Such mentoring of associates will impose costs on partners in the form of time required for mentoring that cannot be used working on client projects.

We assume that there are two types of employees: highly skilled employees produce a surplus of V_H to the investment bank and low-skilled employees a surplus of $V_L < V_H$. Partners cannot distinguish between these types of employees and even the employees themselves do not know initially what type they are. The investment bank is organised as a partnership consisting of M partners, who each look after N associates. Each partner faces costs C for mentoring the associates allocated to them and learning their type. After one time period, the partner retires and selects one of the associates he has been mentoring, as his successor.

The profits accruing to a partner in the first time period, assumed to be highly skilled, are given by its own surplus, V_H, and that generated by his N associates, less the wages w_A they are each paid. We assume that associates are not fully trained yet and even if they are highly skilled, they will only produce a surplus V_L. Hence, we obtain that

$$\Pi_P = V_H + N(V_L - w_A) \tag{17.1}$$

We will now investigate under which conditions such a partnership can be sustained. We will initially look at conditions for associates to join a partnership, before then looking at whether the offer to become a partner is accepted. We will also consider conditions to ensure that only highly skilled associates are offered partnerships and that partners are willing to mentor associates.

Associates Joining the Partnership As associates do not know their own type, they assign a probability of $\frac{1}{N}$ of being highly skilled and consequently appointed partner in the second time period, thus giving themselves an equal chance amongst all the associate's that a partner manages. When joining the investment bank as an associate, the associate's profits consist of his salary w_A in period 1, and the future profits as a partner, less the mentoring costs he has to spend for mentoring associates himself in the second time period, C, discounted to its present value with discount factor $\rho > 1$. If not appointed partner, we assume that he can obtain a wage of V_L, which is the same salary he could earn when not joining the partnership, where future income is discounted to obtain the present value. Implicitly we assume here that outside of the investment bank, associates could earn the surplus they are generating. Thus, an associate will join the investment bank if the profits from doing so exceed those of being employed outside the investment bank. This requires that

$$\frac{1}{N}\left(w_A + \frac{\Pi_P - C}{\rho}\right) + \left(1 - \frac{1}{N}\right)\left(w_A + \frac{V_L}{\rho}\right) \geq V_L + \frac{V_L}{\rho} \tag{17.2}$$

This expression now solves for

$$w_A \geq w_A^* = V_L - \frac{(V_H - V_L) - C}{N(\rho - 1)} \tag{17.3}$$

Let us now assume that

$$C \leq C^* = V_H - V_L(1 + (\rho - 1) N) \tag{17.4}$$

implying that w_A^* is negative and we can set $w_A = 0$ to maximise the partner's profits in Eq. (17.1). A viable solution requires that $C^* > 0$, or $\frac{V_H}{V_L} \geq 1+(\rho - 1) N$, and the surplus generated by highly skilled partners must be sufficiently high relative to low-skilled employees.

Having thus established conditions for which associates would be joining the partnership, we now have to investigate whether they would be taking up the offer of becoming partners.

Taking Up Partnership Offers With partners being paid wages w_P, the dividend the partnership can pay is $\hat{\Pi}_B = \Pi_B - w_P = V_H + NV_L - w_P$, using $w_A = 0$ to obtain the second equality. As this profit is obtained in every time period, this dividend can be paid perpetually, giving the present value of the partnership as

$$P^* = \frac{V_H + NV_L - w_P}{\rho - 1} s \tag{17.5}$$

If an associate refuses to take up a partnership despite being offered it, the market knows that of the total $M(N - 1) + 1$ released associates, one is highly skilled while the remaining $M(N - 1)$ associates are low-skilled. The salary in the market for released associates will reflect that there is one highly skilled associate who generates surplus V_H, and hence, the salary they obtain will be $\frac{M(N-1)V_L+V_H}{M(N-1)+1}$, the average surplus they are expected to generate. Thus, an associate accepts a partnership if the surplus from being a partner, Π_P, less the mentoring costs exceeds this salary; hence, we require that

$$\Pi_P - C = V_H + NV_L - C \geq \frac{M(N - 1) V_L + V_H}{M(N - 1) + 1} \tag{17.6}$$

which easily solves for

$$C \leq C^{**} = \frac{M(N - 1) V_H + \left(M(N - 1)^2 + 1\right) V_L}{M(N - 1) + 1} \tag{17.7}$$

Hence, if mentoring costs are not too high, accepting a partnership is optimal. Compared to the constraint on mentoring costs in Eq. (17.4), this expression may be more or less constraining, depending on specific parameter values.

While we showed that under these conditions highly skilled associates would become partners, we also have to make sure that no associates with lower skills are offered partnerships. This would allow us to signal that the partnership will consist only of highly skilled individuals generating high surplus for the investment bank, but also their clients.

Not Appointing Unskilled Partners We so far assumed that only highly skilled associates become partners. Assume now that if unskilled partners are appointed, the investment bank loses reputation and cannot be resold, its value becoming zero. Low-skilled associates will accept a partnership if

$$V_L + NV_L - \rho P \geq V_L \tag{17.8}$$

In a partnership, the low-skilled partner obtains the benefits from contributing V_L by himself, and the contributions of his N associates, and then loses the previous purchase price P of the partnership as it cannot be resold. This has to exceed the wage he could earn outside of the partnership, V_L. Hence, we require that

$$P \leq P^{**} = \frac{NV_L}{\rho} \tag{17.9}$$

to avoid appointing unskilled partners from accepting such offers, as P^{**} is the highest price the unskilled partner would be paying.

If only $M - 1$ partners were appointed, to exclude the unskilled associate from joining the partnership, we require that the value the remaining $M - 1$ partners generate in the partnership consisting of only skilled partners, exceeds the value if the unskilled partner is included. Therefore, we need

$$(M - 1) P^* \geq MP^{**} \tag{17.10}$$

This achieves that the joint value of the partnership is higher with only skilled partners and therefore provides an incentive to not appoint unskilled partners.

Inserting Eqs. (17.5) and (17.9) into Eq. (17.10), we obtain the requirement that

$$w_P \leq w_P^* = V_H + \left(1 - \frac{\rho - 1}{\rho} \frac{M}{M - 1}\right) NV_L \tag{17.11}$$

The salary drawn by partners must not be too high as otherwise the importance of the drop in the value of the partnership due to unskilled partners being appointed is not sufficiently high to incentivise these to be kept out of the partnership. A sufficiently high fraction of the total remuneration of partners should be derived from the profits of the partnership rather than fixed salaries.

For a viable solution, we need that $w_P^* \geq 0$, and hence,

$$\frac{V_H}{V_L} \geq N\left(\frac{\rho - 1}{\rho}\frac{M}{M-1} - 1\right) \tag{17.12}$$

which means that the difference between skilled and unskilled partners must be sufficiently large.

The last step in maintaining a partnership is to ensure that associates are trained and those with high skills identified. Partners need to have the incentives to conduct this costly mentoring.

Mentoring of Associates Finally, we need to ensure that monitoring, and hence, identifying of highly skilled associates occurs. If all partners mentor associates, the partnership value is given by Eq. (17.5). If a partner does not mentor and then does not appoint a new partner, leaving $M - 1$ partners, the value of the partnership reduces to $\frac{M-1}{M}P^*$ due to the size of the partnership having been reduced. Hence, we require that the value of the partnership, P^*, less the mentoring costs, C, has to exceed the value of the partnership without mentoring associates and not appointing a new partner. Thus, we require that $P^* - C \geq \frac{M-1}{M}P^*$, which after inserting for P^* from Eq. (17.9) becomes

$$C \leq C^{***} = \frac{V_H + NV_L - w_P}{M(\rho - 1)} \tag{17.13}$$

which is least restrictive for $w_P = 0$, and partners derive their entire income from the profits of the partnership.

If Eqs. (17.4), (17.7), (17.12), and (17.13) are fulfilled, then a partnership is sustainable. These constraints are rewritten here for convenience.

$$C \leq C^* = V_H - V_L(1 + (\rho - 1)N)$$

$$C \leq C^{**} = \frac{M(N-1)V_H + \left(M(N-1)^2 + 1\right)V_L}{M(N-1) + 1}$$

$$C \leq C^{***} = \frac{V_H + NV_L}{M(\rho - 1)}$$

$$\frac{V_H}{V_L} \geq 1 + (\rho - 1)N$$

$$\frac{V_H}{V_L} \geq N\left(\frac{\rho - 1}{\rho}\frac{M}{M-1} - 1\right)$$

We see that the costs of mentoring and identifying highly skilled associates must not be too high, while the benefits of being highly skilled, relative to being lower skilled, have to be sufficiently large to meet all these restrictions. A partnership is viable if $C \leq \min\{C^*; C^{**}; C^{***}\}$ and $\frac{V_H}{V_L} \geq \max\left\{1 + (\rho - 1) N; N\left(\frac{\rho-1}{\rho}\frac{M}{M-1} - 1\right)\right\}$.

Summary Partnerships are sustainable if the costs of mentoring and identifying highly skilled associates is not too costly and the surplus generated by them sufficiently higher than those of unskilled associates. Associates accept low salaries, but are compensated by the prospects of higher profits from the partnership once they become partners. While partners' salaries are also kept low to incentivise them mentoring associates, they benefit from the profits of the partnership, giving rise to large differences in the income between associates and partners.

If the demands on partners in terms of the time they have to work with clients are increasing, the costs of mentoring indirectly increase. The opportunity costs of engaging in mentoring and neglecting client work will increase the costs and make partnership less viable. With expanding investment banking business, partnerships have to increase the number of partners, which increases the need for highly skilled associates to be identified as potential partners, making training more important if natural talent is limited, also increasing the costs of mentoring. Additionally, as alternative employment opportunities emerge, the low pay as associate makes joining partnerships less attractive and partnerships may struggle to attract the requisite number of highly skilled associates. These developments can lead to the decline of partnerships in investment banking.

Reading Morrison and Wilhelm Jr (2008).

17.2 The Impact on Service Quality

Investment banks hire employees of differing abilities, having a minimum standard of recruitment. The abilities of their employees will affect the surplus they can generate to their clients and thus the price that can be charged for the services rendered. Incorporated investment banks have employees in the traditional sense and pay them wages for their efforts. The remaining surplus is then distributed among the owners of the investment bank. Partnerships, in contrast, do not have employees, but the partners are also the owners of the investment bank. They do not obtain a salary, but instead share the profits the investment bank makes. We will investigate how incorporated investment banks and partnerships differ in their ability as well as profitability.

Let us assume that investment banks hire employees of different abilities, generating surplus V to clients, which has a distribution $F(V)$. Investment banks know the ability of their employees. We further assume that the quality of the service can only be assessed by clients with probability p; in other cases, the market infers the value of the service from the incentives the investment bank has in hiring employees.

If clients have no market power, then the price clients are willing to pay for investment banking services is equal to its expected surplus V. Incorporated investment banks only hire employees with an ability of at least V^* and V^{**} the minimum ability for investment banks organised as partnerships. Hence, the price of the service that clients pay is given by

$$P^* = E\left[V|V > V^*\right] = \frac{1}{1 - F\left(V^*\right)} \int_{V^*}^{+\infty} V dF\left(V\right) \tag{17.14}$$

$$P^{**} = E\left[V|V > V^{**}\right] = \frac{1}{1 - F\left(V^{**}\right)} \int_{V^{**}}^{+\infty} V dF\left(V\right)$$

for corporations and partnerships, respectively. We can now determine the profits of incorporated investment banks and partnerships as well as their hiring threshold for employees.

Abilities in Incorporated Investment Banks Corporations make profits of

$$\Pi_C = \left(1 - F\left(V^*\right)\right)\left(pP^* + (1-p)\hat{P}^* - w\right) - E \tag{17.15}$$

where the first term in brackets denotes the revenue received from those knowing the value of the services to be P^*, which is revealed with probability p. The following term denotes the revenue from those only inferring the value $\hat{P}^*$, the remaining fraction $1 - p$, less the wages w paid to employees. Only a fraction of $1 - F\left(V^*\right)$ are employed to generate these profits and E denotes the equity the bank needs to raise in order to operate.

The optimal hiring threshold is given from the first-order condition, which, using the Leibniz integral rule after inserting for the price P^* from Eq. (17.14), is given by

$$\frac{\partial \Pi_C}{\partial V^*} = -pV^* f\left(V^*\right) - f\left(V^*\right)\left((1-p)\hat{P}^* - w\right) = 0$$

where $f(\cdot)$ denotes the density of the employee ability. We can solve this equation easily for

$$w = pV^* + (1-p) P^* \tag{17.16}$$

where we use that in equilibrium the ability threshold of employees hired by the investment bank is correctly anticipated and hence the price correctly inferred, such that $P^* = \hat{P}^*$. Inserting this first-order condition back into Eq. (17.15), the profits of the investment bank become

$$\Pi_C = p\left(1 - F\left(V^*\right)\right)\left(P^* - V^*\right) - E. \tag{17.17}$$

Having established the profits of incorporated investment banks, we can now continue to determine the profits partnerships make.

Abilities in Partnerships In a partnership, each partner contributes the equity. As only $1 - F(V^{**})$ partners are employed, they have to raise equity of E; thus, each partner needs to raise $\frac{E}{1-F(V^{**})}$. However, each partner generates surplus $pP^{**} + (1-p)\hat{P}^{**}$ from those that identify the quality of the service and those that can only infer the quality of the service provided. Thus, for each partner, the profits are given by

$$\Pi_P = pP^{**} + (1-p)\hat{P}^{**} - \frac{E}{1-F(V^{**})} \tag{17.18}$$
$$= \frac{1}{1-F(V^{**})}\left(\left(1-F\left(V^{**}\right)\right)\left(pP^{**} + (1-p)\hat{P}^{**}\right) - E\right)$$

We note that partners do not receive a salary, but their entire remuneration is obtained from the profits of the investment bank.

In this case the optimal hiring threshold is given from the first condition derived using the Leibniz integral rule. After using the expression for P^{**} from Eq. (17.14), the first-order condition reads

$$\frac{\partial \Pi_P}{\partial V^{**}} = \frac{f(V^{**})}{(1-F(V^{**}))^2}\left(1-F\left(V^{**}\right)\right)\left(pP^{**} + (1-p)\hat{P}^{**} - E\right)$$
$$+\frac{1}{1-F(V^{**})}\left(-pf\left(V^{**}\right)V^{**} - f\left(V^{**}\right)(1-p)\hat{P}^{**}\right) = 0$$

which solves for

$$pP^{**} + (1-p)\hat{P}^{**} - \frac{E}{1-F(V^{**})} = pV^{**} + (1-p)P^{**} \tag{17.19}$$

using that expected and actual price are identical in equilibrium; thus, $\hat{P}^{**} = P^{**}$. This again arises from the equilibrium assumption that clients correctly infer the hiring threshold for partners and hence infer the surplus provided, which the investment bank charges their clients.

Inserting this result into the profits of Eq. (17.18), we get the expected profits of a partnership as

$$\Pi_P = P^{**} - \frac{E}{1-F(V^{**})} = pV^{**} + (1-p)P^{**} \tag{17.20}$$

Having derived the hiring thresholds and profits of incorporated investment banks and partnerships, we can now proceed to compare these results.

Comparing Skills of Employees We can solve the first-order conditions for optimal hiring thresholds in Eq. (17.17) for $\frac{\Pi_C+E}{1-F(V^*)} = p(P^* - V^*)$ and then Eq. (17.16) for pV^*. Inserting these expressions into the stated result, we get the price charged by incorporated investment banks as

$$P^* = \frac{\Pi_C + E}{1 - F(V^*)} + w \tag{17.21}$$

Let us now assume that the hiring thresholds for partnerships and corporations are the same; hence, we have $V^* = V^{**}$. This then also implies from Eq. (17.14) that both investment banks charge the same price, $P^{***} = P^*$. Inserting Eq. (17.21) into the first part of Eq. (17.20), we easily get that

$$\Pi_P = \frac{\Pi_C}{1 - F(V^*)} + w.$$

If V^* is optimal for Π_C, then the first-order condition $\frac{\partial \Pi_C}{\partial V^*} = 0$ is fulfilled. We then have

$$\frac{\partial \Pi_P}{\partial V^*} = \frac{\partial \Pi_C}{\partial V^*}\frac{1}{1 - F(V^*)} + \frac{\Pi_C f(V^*)}{(1 - F(V^*))^2} = \frac{\Pi_C f(V^*)}{(1 - F(V^*))^2} > 0, \tag{17.22}$$

where the final inequality emerges if $\Pi_C > 0$, which we assume here. Thus, at a threshold of V^* the marginal profits of partnerships are positive, implying that their optimal threshold must be higher; hence, $V^{**} > V^*$. Therefore, partnerships employ more highly skilled employees than incorporated investment banks. The reason for this higher level of skills is that partnerships hold more equity, E for incorporated investment banks against $\frac{E}{1-F(V^{**})}$ for partnerships. In partnerships, all employees bring in their own equity, rather than the existing equity being spread out amongst the employees; this provides incentives to increase the quality of services and be able to charge higher prices to obtain higher profits.

Attractiveness of Partnerships For the partnership to be attractive, we need that the profits a partner can obtain, exceed the wages of employees in incorporated investment banks, and thus, we need $\Pi_P \geq w$, as otherwise employees would prefer working for the incorporated investment bank. Using Eqs. (17.16) and (17.20) this requirement implies that

$$pV^{**} + (1 - p) P^{**} \geq pV^* + (1 - p) P^* \tag{17.23}$$

Differentiating the right-hand side of this inequality with respect to V^*, we get using equation the definition of P^* from Eq. (17.14) using the Leibniz integral rule that

$$\begin{aligned} & p + \frac{(1-p) f(V^*)}{(1-F(V^*))^2} \int_{V^*}^{+\infty} V dF(V) - \frac{(1-p) V^* f(V^*)}{1-F(V^*)} \\ & > p + \frac{(1-p) f(V^*)}{(1-F(V^*))^2} \int_{V^*}^{+\infty} V^* dF(V) - \frac{(1-p) V^* f(V^*)}{1-F(V^*)} \\ & = p > 0 \end{aligned} \tag{17.24}$$

In the second line we have replaced V in the integral with its lower boundary V^*, making the expression smaller, and to obtain the final line, we note that $\int_{V^*}^{+\infty} V^* dF(V) = V^* \int_{V^*}^{+\infty} dF(V) = V^*(1-F(V^*))$. This result implies that the right-hand side of Eq. (17.23) is increasing in V^*. As Eq. (17.23) is fulfilled with equality for $V^* = V^{**}$, as this implies $P^* = P^{**}$, and this expression increases as we increase V^*, the left-hand side must be larger if $V^{**} > V^*$. Thus, we find that for $V^{**} > V^*$, $\Pi_P > w$, and partnerships are preferred by employees. As we have found that $V^{**} > V^*$, we have established that becoming a partner is preferred to being an employee in an incorporated investment bank.

Using Eq. (17.19) to replace E in Eq. (17.15) and replacing w from Eq. (17.16), we get the profits of the incorporated investment bank as

$$\Pi_C = p\left(\left(1-F\left(V^*\right)\right)\left(P^* - V^*\right) - \left(1-F\left(V^{**}\right)\right)\left(P^{**} - V^{**}\right)\right) \tag{17.25}$$

Differentiating this relationship with respect to V^{**}, we get

$$\begin{aligned} \frac{\partial \Pi_C}{\partial V^{**}} &= -p\left(-V^{**} f\left(V^{**}\right) - \left(1-F\left(V^{**}\right)\right) + V^{**} f\left(V^{**}\right)\right) \\ &= p\left(1-F\left(V^{**}\right)\right) > 0, \end{aligned}$$

and hence, if $V^{**} > V^*$, then $\Pi_C \geq 0$. This follows from the fact that for $V^* = V^{**}$, and hence, $P^* = P^{**}$, we easily have $\Pi_C = 0$ and increasing V^{**} will increase the profits of corporations. As we also have $\Pi_P \geq w$ if $V^{**} > V^*$, we see that both corporations are profitable and partnerships are attractive to employees.

We have assumed thus far that $\Pi_C > 0$ and in Eq. (17.22) depended on this assumption to derive that $V^{**} > V^*$. Let us now make this assumption less strict by only assuming that for $p = 1$, $\Pi_C > 0$. Thus, if all clients can identify the ability of investment banks, incorporated investment banks are profitable. For $p = 0$ we have from Eq. (17.17) that the profits of incorporated investment banks are $\Pi_C = -E < 0$, and as we can easily show that $\frac{\partial \Pi_C}{\partial p} > 0$, there exists a $\hat{p}$ such that for $p > \hat{p}$, incorporated investment banks are viable.

Let us now focus on conditions under which partnerships are more profitable than incorporated investment banks; thus, $\Pi_P - w \geq \Pi_C$. We consider here the profits of the partnership after they have paid the equivalent to the wages their partners could have earned in an incorporated investment bank. Inserting from Eqs. (17.16), (17.20), and (17.25), we easily get that this condition is fulfilled if

$$p \leq \hat{\hat{p}} = \frac{P^{**} - P^{*}}{F(V^{**})(P^{**} - V^{**}) - F(V^{*})(P^{*} - V^{*})} \tag{17.26}$$

Therefore, if $p \leq \hat{\hat{p}}$ partnerships are more profitable than incorporated investment banks. It might be that $\hat{\hat{p}} \leq \hat{p}$ as partnerships are more profitable than incorporated investment banks, and hence, in some situations partnerships are the only investment bank type that is viable.

We thus see that partnerships are more profitable if clients find it difficult to identify the ability of investment banks. It is the incentive of partnerships to have higher employment thresholds than incorporated investment banks that allows them to charge higher prices as clients will infer their higher ability.

Summary We have seen that partnerships provide higher profits and are therefore preferred by investors if the identification of the quality of services is difficult; if the quality is more easily identifiable, incorporated investment banks are more profitable. In some markets, service quality might be more difficult to assess, either because it is less well regulated, or the tasks required are more complex or the products offered are new. Also in situations where clients are operating in markets they have no or very little experience in, they will find it difficult to assess the quality of services offered. In these situations we would expect to find investment banks organised as partnerships rather than being incorporated. In more transparent markets, however, incorporated investment banks should dominate. Another aspect of partnership banks is that the average quality of their services is better, because they employ more able staff.

Reading Levin and Tadelis (2005).

Conclusions

Investment banks might want to organise as partnerships if it is difficult for the quality of their advice to be assessed. This will be in situations where investment banks have advised in areas that have significant uncertainties, making it more difficult to see whether the advice given in the past has been good, or the outcome the result of factors not known at the time or luck in an uncertain environment. Investment banks overcome this problem by hiring staff that are, on average, more skilled than those of shareholder-owned banks. This increases the quality of the advice given overall and will make the investment bank more profitable as higher fees can be charged. This higher profitability will then allow partnerships to serve markets where their advice is less easily verified, while for shareholder-owned banks the low price they can charge in such situations will either preclude them from offering any advice or they are less profitable and investment banks would prefer a partnership for operating in these markets. Partnerships do not only need to be more profitable than shareholder-owned banks in these situations; they must also be able to recruit the necessary staff having such high skills. It therefore must be profitable for employees to join partnerships and subsequently become partners, while at the same time, the partnership must ensure that only highly skilled associates are promoted to become partners. As long as the difference between highly and lowly skilled employees is sufficiently high, partnerships would not make lowly skilled associates partner as the reduction in value due to their low skills is too high. If the costs of being partner is not too high, arising from additional duties, such as mentoring associates or other duties as a partner, are not too high, it is profitable for associates to join rather than seek alternative employment. Thus, partnerships are viable.

The demise of many partnerships in investment banking by transforming into shareholder-owned investment banks can be the result of increased costs in maintaining partnerships as an attractive alternative to being employed in shareholder-owned investment banks. Increasing workloads makes it more difficult to mentor associates on their path to becoming partners, and thus, joining a partnership is becoming less attractive. Technological advances might also even the differences between highly skilled and low-skilled employees, given once again rise to less incentives to join a partnership and engage in the ever more costly mentoring. Clients having access to more information about markets and products, but also the performance of investment banks in providing advice, will make it easier to identify the quality of advice an investment bank provides. Even though partnerships provide a better-quality service than shareholder-owned banks, they will also be more expensive. While with little transparency on the quality provided, the price might be seen as an indicator of the unknown quality, the increased transparency has reduced this benefit. It is thus that partnerships in investment banks are becoming less and less common, mainly maintained by smaller specialised boutique investment banks, who operate often in niche markets. In such markets, transparency to clients will still be limited and the workload be lower to allow the mentoring of associates.

18 The Decision-Making Process

A characteristic of investment banks is that they give great autonomy to individual employees, often with minimal interference by managers. Managers are often only involved in managing the relationship with clients to give them a feeling of being important to the investment bank as senior managers are engaging with them; they are often not much involved in decisions made on the advice their clients receive, but merely present the advice prepared by more junior staff to the client. This leads to a situation in which decision-making is delegated to a large extent to relatively junior employees. The organisational structure of investment banks also reflects such delegated decision-making, with only a small number of management levels present, and these often being more formal than of any practical relevance in the daily work of investment banks. This is commonly referred to as a flat organisational structure. Granting employees such autonomy to use their expertise and make independent decisions is not common in other industries, including commercial banking, and probably to the same extent only found in management consulting.

To explain these observations, we will look at the decision-making process in investment banks and how the characteristics of investment banks give rise to flat organisational structures in Sect. 18.1 as well as the delegation of decision-making to employees in Sect. 18.2. Any differences in the knowledge and expertise of employees and managers, or lack thereof, will be the main driving force behind these results, along with motivating employees to apply their knowledge diligently.

18.1 The Impact of the Organisational Structure

Investment banks advise a large number of clients with different requirements across a wide range of products and services. Most investment banks give their staff significant degrees of freedom to provide clients with such advice and investment banks' organisational structure commonly reflects this freedom. Typically, investment banks show a flat organisational structure that allows specialists for each

A. Krause, *Theoretical Foundations of Investment Banking*, Springer Texts in Business and Economics, https://doi.org/10.1007/978-3-031-58060-4_18

service to advise their clients with minimal oversight by more senior managers. Such senior managers will typically have responsibility over a range of specialists and therefore might lack the detailed knowledge required to interfere in the process. On the other hand, their experience might well put the manager in a favourable position to add value to the advice the client is provided with.

We assume that managers have the ability to provide their ideas to clients and the more senior a manager is in the organisation, the higher the seniority in having their suggestions heard by clients. Let us assume that a manager, regardless of the level of its seniority, has his ideas accepted by the client with probability π_M and then generates a surplus to the investment bank of V_M. A specialist is only heard after managers have provided their ideas and the specialists' ideas are accepted with probability π_S, generating surplus V_S to the investment bank. The likelihood of having an idea accepted from a specialist, π_S, might be higher than that of a manager, π_M, if the specific knowledge of the specialist is of importance; but it might also be lower if the experience of the manager has a high weight. Similarly, the surplus generated by the specialist to the investment bank, V_S, may be above or below that of the manager, V_M, depending on the relative importance of experience and expertise knowledge.

Possible Organisational Forms Let us assume that there are two clients with different requirements that seek advice and we consider the revenue to the bank using different organisational structures. Throughout, we assume that across these two clients, four investment bankers are involved in the advice, either managers or specialists. At first, let us assume that an investment bank is organised very hierarchical as depicted in Fig. 18.1a. Here all investment bankers are classified as managers in that they are not having specialist knowledge and are the only ones making decisions on client advice. We assume that there are four layers of such management, each layer in turn will seek to provide a solution to the clients' problems, that is then accepted with probability π_M and generates a surplus V_M to the investment bank. For a single client, the probability that no solution of any of the four managers is accepted is $(1-\pi_M)^4$ and that this is the case for both clients gives us a probability of $\left((1-\pi_M)^4\right)^2$. In this case no advice is accepted and no surplus is generated. With probability $1-(1-\pi_M)^4$, the investment bank provides a solution to their client that is accepted. The probability that both clients accept the advice given to them is $\left(1-(1-\pi_M)^4\right)^2$, generating a surplus of $2V_M$ from both clients jointly. The advice is accepted by one of the clients only with probability $2\left(1-(1-\pi_M)^4\right)(1-\pi_M)^4$, generating a surplus V_M from the client accepting the advice. The expected profits to the investment bank are thus given by

$$\begin{aligned}\Pi_H &= 2\left(1-(1-\pi_M)^4\right)^2 V_M \\ &\quad +2\left(1-(1-\pi_M)^4\right)(1-\pi_M)^4 V_M \\ &= 2\left(1-(1-\pi_M)^4\right) V_M\end{aligned} \tag{18.1}$$

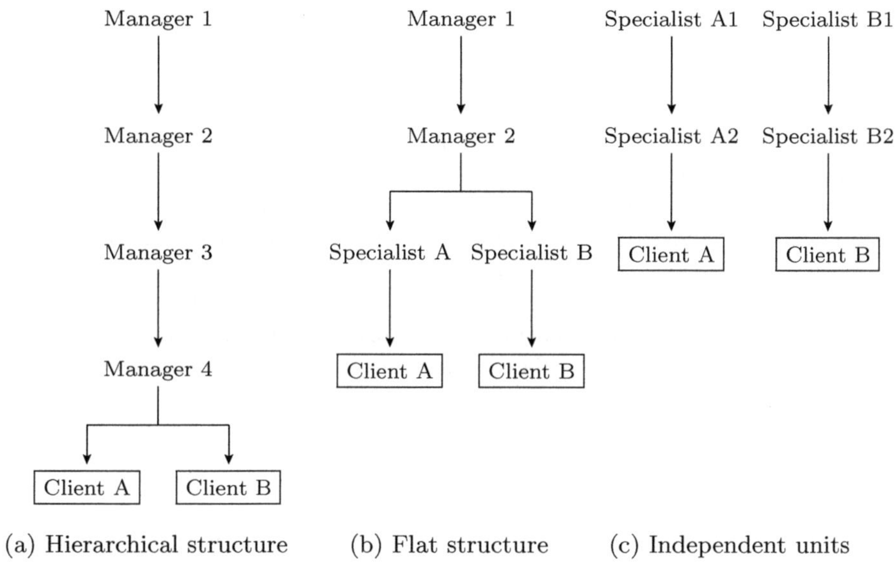

Fig. 18.1 Possible organisational structures

An alternative organisational structure is to include specialists into the hierarchy. A flat structure is obtained if we involve only two layers of management and at the lowest level employ two specialists, one for each of the client's needs, as depicted in Fig. 18.1b. With managers given priority in determining the advice given to clients, we will consider their advice first. With a probability of $(1-\pi_M)^2$ neither manager suggests an acceptable solution to a client. Hence, with probability $1-(1-\pi_M)^2$ they suggest a solution the client accepts, and with probability $\left(1-(1-\pi_M)^2\right)^2$ both clients accept the advice suggested and the surplus generated to the investment bank is $2V_M$. As both clients have accepted the suggestions of the managers, specialists do not get involved. With probability $2\left(1-(1-\pi_M)^2\right)(1-\pi_M)^2$ only one of the clients accepts the suggestion by one of the managers and from this client the investment bank generates surplus V_M. For the client having not accepted any of the two managers suggestions, the specialist makes a final suggestion, which is accepted with probability π_S and generates a surplus of V_S to the investment bank. Finally, with probability $(1-\pi_M)^4$, both clients reject the suggestions of all managers and leave the two specialists to make separate suggestions to their respective clients that are each accepted with probability π_S and each generates V_S for the investment bank. This gives expected profits of

$$\Pi_F = 2\left(1-(1-\pi_M)^2\right)^2 V_M \qquad (18.2)$$

$$+2\left(1-(1-\pi_M)^2\right)(1-\pi_M)^2\left(V_M+\pi_S V_S\right)$$

$$+2\left(1-\pi_M\right)^4\pi_S V_S$$
$$=2\left(1-\left(1-\pi_M\right)^2\right)V_M+2\pi_S\left(1-\pi_M\right)^2 V_S$$

Finally, we might consider an organisational structure that allows specialists to operate independently of any managerial oversight to advise their clients. In this case, the advice is exclusively given by specialists as indicated in Fig. 18.1c. As both clients are advised independently by different groups of specialists, we can focus on the advice given to one of these clients. That both specialists do not provide an acceptable solution to their client is $(1 - \pi_S)^2$, and hence, with probability $1 - (1 - \pi_S)^2$, at least one of the specialists will provide acceptable advice and generate surplus V_S for either of the two clients. Thus, the profits of the investment bank are given by

$$\Pi_I = 2\left(1-\left(1-\pi_S\right)^2\right)V_S. \tag{18.3}$$

Optimal Organisational Form We can now compare the profits for each organisational form to determine the one that is most profitable to investment banks. We easily obtain that

$$\Pi_H > \Pi_F \text{ if } \frac{V_M}{V_S} > \frac{\pi_S}{1-\left(1-\pi_M\right)^2}, \tag{18.4}$$
$$\Pi_H > \Pi_I \text{ if } \frac{V_M}{V_S} > \frac{1-\left(1-\pi_S\right)^2}{1-\left(1-\pi_M\right)^4},$$
$$\Pi_F > \Pi_I \text{ if } \frac{V_M}{V_S} > \frac{1-\pi_S\left(1-\pi_M\right)^2-\left(1-\pi_S\right)^2}{1-\left(1-\pi_M\right)^2}$$

We can see that the final relationship can never be fulfilled if $\frac{V_M}{V_S} < 1$, and hence, for $V_M < V_S$, the flat structure is never optimal. Depending on the values for π_S and π_M, the likelihood the suggestions of specialists and managers are accepted, different optimal organisational structures emerge as shown in Fig. 18.2. We firstly see that if $V_M > V_S$ and managers provide a higher surplus, a hierarchical structure is always optimal as long as $\pi_M > \pi_S$. In this case, the managers are better than specialists in the amount of surplus they generate as well as the likelihood of their advice being accepted. Thus, it is optimal to involve as many managers as possible in the process, which is given by the hierarchical structure.

As the probability of specialists' advice being accepted increases, they become more and more valuable to the investment bank. Despite providing a lower surplus, specialists can increase profits to the investment bank by having their advice more commonly accepted than that of managers. Balancing the surplus generated against the likelihood of having the advice accepted will eventually make the employment of specialists in the flat structure more attractive. If this difference is high enough in having the likelihood of having the advice accepted, employing only specialists in

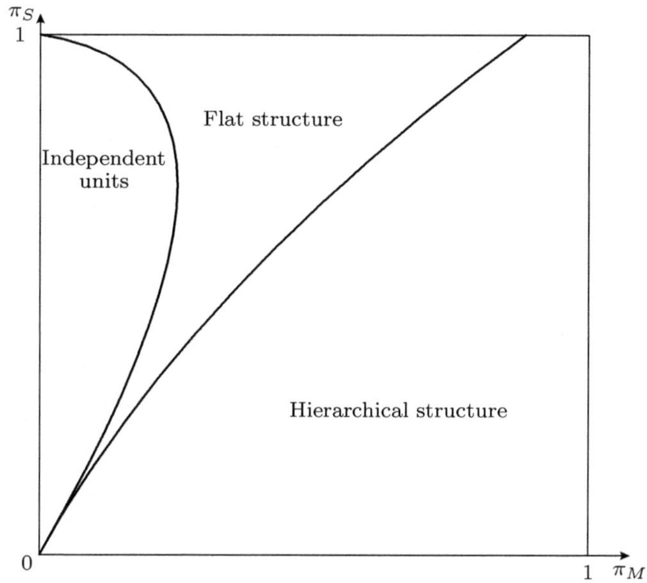

(a) Managers providing higher surplus than specialists ($V_M > V_S$)

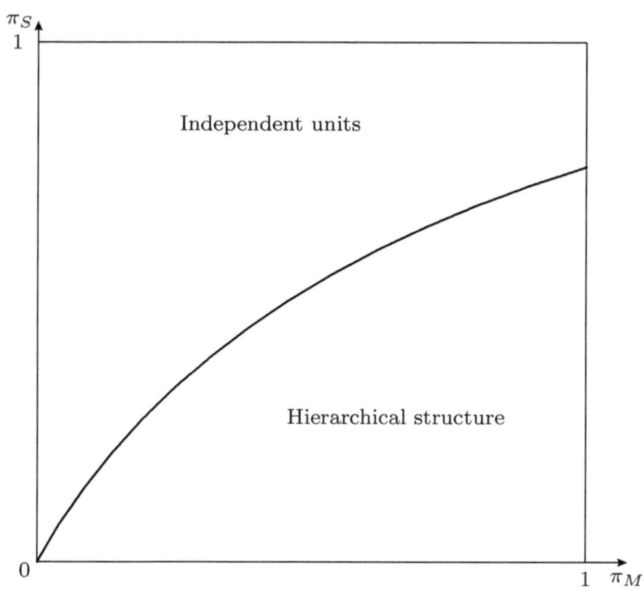

(b) Managers providing lower surplus than specialists ($V_M < V_S$)

Fig. 18.2 Optimal organisational structure

independent units becomes more attractive. The less likely the advice of managers is accepted, the more beneficial the reliance on specialists alone in the independent units become.

If specialists provide a higher surplus than managers, the benefits of the hierarchical structure is that more managers are involved in the provision of advice as there are four layers of managers, compared to three in the flat structure and only two in the independent units. Hence, choosing a hierarchical structure is optimal if these benefits outweigh the lower surplus managers generate. Once these benefits are eroded, either through specialists having a higher acceptance rate of the suggested advice or the likelihood of advice being accepted is already sufficiently high, the higher surplus specialists provide will make independent units optimal. The flat structure is never optimal as a partial involvement of managers does not outweigh the benefits of specialists generating higher surplus and having higher acceptance rates in independent units.

Summary More senior managers might involve themselves in the provision of advice given to clients. Having multiple layers of management involved in the advice might add value in that among the many ideas that get developed, there is an idea that clients might find favourable, while if only engaging with specialists for their immediate needs, the ideas generated might be better, but there are also fewer of them, which will affect the overall quality of advice given. We can assume that in many cases managers, as not being privy to the detailed knowledge that specialists might have and that clients might find attractive, produce ideas that generate more surplus to the investment bank, but are less likely accepted by clients. This might arise from their experience, where they balance the needs of clients and the profits generated to investment banks. Leaving more surplus to the investment bank might also leave the client with less surplus for themselves and makes them therefore less willing to accept advice. These considerations have given rise to flat organisational structures in investment banks. Other organisations, commercial banks included, rely much less on specific knowledge and the probability of specialists and managers producing surplus might well be much closer aligned, and with the experience of managers to produce surplus, more hierarchical structures are optimal.

Reading Hart and Moore (2005).

18.2 Delegation of Decision-Making

Investment banks commonly give employees a large degree of independence in their decision-making; this can be observed not only when advising clients, but also in accepting clients in the first place. Such practices would clearly be beneficial if employees have better information than their managers, but it can be that even if the manager is slightly better informed, employees are given the opportunity to make their own decisions.

Let us assume that an investment bank faces the situation that it can accept a new client. Ex ante, the probability that this client will generate surplus to the investment bank is $p = \frac{1}{2}$, but employees and managers obtain a signal whether the client is likely to produce this surplus. This signal has precision $\rho_E > \frac{1}{2}$ for the employee and $\rho_M > \frac{1}{2}$ for the manager. This precision is defined as the probability that the signal the employee and manager, respectively, have obtained is correct. Using Bayesian learning, we then have the probability that the client will generate a surplus to the investment bank, given by

$$\hat{p}_i = \frac{p\rho_i}{p\rho_i + (1-p)(1-\rho_i)} = \rho_i \tag{18.5}$$

where we have used the ex ante assumption that $p = \frac{1}{2}$. Hence, based on their signal, the employee and manager believe the likelihood of generating a surplus to be ρ_i. If the client produces a surplus to the investment bank, it takes the value of V.

Employees are rewarded through wages that are w_S if the client produces a surplus and w_F if it fails to do so. We assume here that $w_F \leq 0$, implying a penalty to the employee if the no surplus is generated; such a penalty might arise from a reduction in agreed bonuses. They also face costs C of exerting effort if conducting work for the client; without such effort, no surplus can be generated. If effort is exerted, then the surplus is generated with probability ρ_E from the perspective of the employee. Managers do not receive a wage, but we assume that they are motivated by the profits the investment bank generates and from which they obtain a fraction. Managers do not exert effort as all work is conducted by their employees.

The decision to accept a new client can now be made by the manager in a centralised decision or the decision can be delegated to the employee.

Delegated Decision-Making Employees are paid a wage w_S if surplus is generated and w_F if no surplus is generated. Their assessment of the probability of success is ρ_E, giving an expected wage of $w = \rho_E w_S + (1-\rho_E) w_F$. Facing costs of effort C, the employee will exert such effort if the expected wage, net of costs, exceeds the remuneration if no effort is exerted. Without exerting effort, no surplus is generated, and hence, the employee receives w_F. Hence, we need $w - C \geq w_F$ for the employee to exert effort. Taking w_F as given, we thus obtain that

$$w_S \geq w_F + \frac{C}{\rho_E} \tag{18.6}$$

In order to become an employee with the investment bank, the employee needs to expect to obtain a wage in excess of his effort costs, and thus, we require that $w - C \geq 0$, or

$$w_S \geq -\frac{1-\rho_E}{\rho_E} w_F + \frac{C}{\rho_E} \tag{18.7}$$

As $w_F \leq 0$, we see that this constraint is more binding than the constraint to exert effort in Eq. (18.6); hence, the wage in case of success will be set according to Eq. (18.7), giving $w = C$, and the employee covers his effort costs.

The profits of the investment bank are now given by the expected revenue from the client, less the wages paid to the employee. Thus, we have

$$\Pi_D = \rho_E V - w = \rho_E V - C \tag{18.8}$$

As the employee makes the decision whether to accept or reject the client, the relevant probability of success to consider is that of the employee, ρ_E.

Centralised Decision-Making If the manager decides whether to go ahead accepting a client, the employee takes this information into account to update his beliefs on the probability of success. The manager will only proceed with accepting the client if the signal received is positive. The employee is aware of this positive signal and hence can now consider two signals, his own and that of his manager. We have two possible scenarios for the employee: he might have obtained the same positive signal as the manager or he might have received a negative signal. The probabilities of success are then given by

$$\begin{aligned}\pi_H &= \frac{\rho_E \rho_M}{\rho_E \rho_M + (1-\rho_E)(1-\rho_M)} \\ \pi_L &= \frac{\rho_M (1-\rho_E)}{\rho_M (1-\rho_E) + (1-\rho_M)\rho_E}\end{aligned} \tag{18.9}$$

To obtain these probabilities, we used Bayesian learning. Here $\rho_E \rho_M$ denotes the probability of receiving the same correct signal for the employee and the manager, while another way of succeeding in this case is if both signals are wrong, $(1-\rho_E)(1-\rho_M)$. If the signals received are different, success is obtained if the manager's signal was correct and the employee's signal wrong, $\rho_M (1-\rho_E)$. This has to be balanced against the possibility that different signals might also be obtained if the manager's signal is wrong and that of the employee correct. We can easily see that $\pi_H \geq \pi_L$ and both, the employee and his manager, obtaining a positive signal results in the employee inferring a higher probability of success than if the employee had obtained a negative signal.

Using these success probabilities, the employee will then exert effort if $\hat{w} - C \geq w_F$, where $\hat{w} = \pi_i \hat{w}_S + (1-\pi_i) w_F$. This condition requires

$$\hat{w}_S \geq w_F + \frac{C}{\pi_i} \tag{18.10}$$

If the manager wants to ensure the employee exerts effort regardless of their own signal and knowing that $\pi_H \geq \pi_L$, we will set the wage in case of success such that this condition is fulfilled for $\pi_i = \pi_L$. As we can easily see that $\pi_L < \rho_E$, the condition to join the investment bank from Eq. (18.7) is less restrictive. We have to note that at the time of joining the investment bank, the employee does not know the signal yet.

This decision to ensure that employees exert effort, regardless of their own signal, then implies that when making the decision to accept the client, the manager expects to pay the employee a wage of $\hat{\hat{w}} = \rho_M \hat{w}_s + (1 - \rho_M) w_F = w_F + \frac{\rho_M}{\pi_L} C$, based on his own assessment as he is unaware of the signal the employee has received. This then gives us the profits of the investment bank, as seen by the manager, as

$$\Pi_C = \rho_M V - \hat{\hat{w}} = \rho_M \left(V - \frac{C}{\pi_L} \right) - w_F \tag{18.11}$$

We can compare these profits with those from delegated decision-making in Eq. (18.8) and obtain that we have $\Pi_D \geq \Pi_C$ if

$$\rho_M \leq \rho_M^* = \frac{\rho_E (1 - \rho_E) V - (1 - 2\rho_E) C + (1 - \rho_E) w_F}{(1 - \rho_E) V - (1 - 2\rho_E) C} \tag{18.12}$$

Hence, the signal managers receive cannot be too precise to make delegation of decisions to employees optimal. We can compare the maximum precision signals to managers can have with the precision of the signal received by employees, ρ_E, and we see that managers might have a more precise signal than employees if $\rho_M^* > \rho_E$. This requires that

$$w_F > (1 - 2\rho_E) C \tag{18.13}$$

or alternatively that $\rho_E > \frac{1}{2} - \frac{w_F}{2C}$. Thus, if the signal of the employee is sufficiently precise, noting that $w_F < 0$, delegation is optimal, even if the manager has a slightly more precise signal. If $\rho_E < \rho_M \leq \rho_M^*$, the information the manager has is more precise than that of his employee, but he nevertheless delegates decision-making to his employee. This difference in the precision of the signal must not be too large to be viable.

The reason for this result is that if the employee receives a different signal to that of the manager, the probability he assigns to the surplus being realised is low, falling below his original signal ρ_E, and hence, it is costly for the investment bank to induce the employee to exert effort, requiring a higher wage. This in turn reduces the profits of the investment bank, making centralised decisions by managers less attractive. In delegation, no such different signals can be observed; hence, the incentive to exert effort is less costly to the investment bank as the employee will base his decision solely on his own signal.

Summary We see that delegation of decisions to employees is not only beneficial if the employee is better informed, but in some instances it can also be beneficial if the manager is better informed. The motivation of the employee to exert effort in cases where their assessment differs from that of the manager will require higher wages to be paid, reducing the profits if managers make decisions centrally. As long as the differences between the manager and the employee is not too large, investment banks would delegate decisions to employee so that they remain motivated to exert efforts without having to be paid significantly higher wages.

With employees often similarly well informed as their managers, it will commonly be beneficial for investment banks to delegate decision-making to employees and thereby minimise the conflict of interest in exerting effort to generate the surplus by employees. We therefore find delegation of decision-making in investment banks to be much more widespread than in most other industries. The importance of knowledge and the difficulty in monitoring whether employees apply their knowledge diligently require investment banks to rely on incentives to motivate employees. By delegating decision-making, employees will be involved in tasks they find beneficial from their own assessment, requiring less incentives to motive them to exert efforts, reducing the costs of investment banks.

Reading Zábojník (2002).

Conclusions

Investment banks rely to a large extent on the knowledge and expertise of their staff to advise clients and thus generate surplus. With larger responsibilities comes also the requirement to spread the knowledge over a wider area, often at the cost of specialist knowledge. Partly this can be compensated for by the inherent ability of managers, which got them promoted into more senior positions, but it may well be that lower-ranked employees have a better understanding of the specific needs of clients and can thus generate more profits for the investment bank. Interference by senior managers might dilute their effort as the suggestions of more senior staff will more likely be implemented, even if they do not represent the most profitable solution for the investment bank. While having senior managers provides additional input into decisions, the risk of implementing suboptimal suggestions might favour the use of flatter hierarchies to reduce the influence of senior managers on the decision-making process. Similarly, requiring staff to work on the implementation of ideas they do not support will be costly as the motivation of staff will be lower and higher incentives will have to be paid. With the importance of information and the difficulty in monitoring the effort of any staff member, delegating decision-making to reduce any conflicts of interest can well be optimal, even if the decisions of managers are superior.

With such delegated decision-making processes in a flat organisation, investment bank managers are often in the role of presenting ideas to clients that have been generated by more junior staff members. They can be seen as relationship managers who leave all key decisions to junior staff. Such arrangements are most profitable to investment banks as long as the differences in the ability to generate surplus between managers and employees are not too large. If managers are much more capable than their junior staff, then traditional forms of centralised decision-making in steep hierarchies should prevail. The fact that investment banks are commonly not operating such a model suggests that differences in abilities across levels of seniority within investment banks are less prominent than in most other industries.

Relationship Banking

19

Clients frequently use the same investment bank for advice on different deals, even in very different areas of expertise. Maintaining such relationships might be costly to investment banks as they have to maintain a workforce that has sufficient capacity to work on the requirements of their clients, while it is not known if they are actually requiring any advice and in which area. Hence, investment banks might run staff levels that are at times too high and who could work on other deals to generate additional income, while at other times staffing levels might be too low to work on all the deals clients seek advice on. This would require staff to work long hours, which is compensated by investment banks with high salaries, adding to their costs.

To analyse relationship banking in the context of investment banks, let us assume that each client has a relationship with a total of M of the N banks in the economy. These banks charge a fraction f of the deal value V as a fee for their services. Companies may switch relationship banks at a cost of c. In order to engage in relationship banking, banks face a fixed cost of C for each deal they are involved in, covering the abovementioned additional costs or the lost income from not working other deals.

Investment Bank Profits Any deal a client needs advice on is randomly assigned to one of the M investment banks the client has a relationship with, such that for each deal the expected surplus of the investment bank is $\frac{fV}{M} - C$. This consists of the revenue from the deal to the investment bank, fV, which it receives with probability $\frac{1}{M}$, less the costs of relationship banking C. This surplus must be positive, which implies that a relationship is only entered if

$$V \geq \underline{V} = \frac{CM}{f} \tag{19.1}$$

A. Krause, *Theoretical Foundations of Investment Banking*, Springer Texts in Business and Economics, https://doi.org/10.1007/978-3-031-58060-4_19

Only clients which have deals of a minimum size $\underline{V}$ can enter relationships with investment banks.

If we assume that the deal volume is distributed across clients with some distribution $F(V)$, then the average deal size in relationship banking will be

$$\overline{V} = \frac{1}{1 - F(\underline{V})} \int_{\underline{V}}^{+\infty} V dF(V) \tag{19.2}$$

This gives average profits of $\frac{f\overline{V}}{M} - C$ per deal. The fraction of clients able to engage in relationship banking is given by all those whose deal value exceeds $\underline{V}$; thus,

$$\gamma = 1 - F(\underline{V}) \tag{19.3}$$

Banks have relationships with a fraction $\frac{M}{N}$ of clients as each client has M relationships that are randomly distributed among the N banks.

Banks discount future profits with a discount factor of $\rho > 1$ and we assume that profits are realised in each time period. The expected profits are then given by

$$\Pi_B = \frac{\gamma \frac{M}{N}\left(\frac{f\overline{V}}{M} - C\right)}{1 - \frac{1}{\rho}} \tag{19.4}$$

capitalising the profits of each time period. These profits consist of the profits for each deal the investment bank completes, $\frac{f\overline{V}}{M} - C$, in which it has a market share of $\frac{M}{N}$ and a fraction γ of all clients that are accepted into relationship banking.

Undercutting Fees Rather than charging their clients a fee f, investment banks could seek to expand their market share by undercutting these fees. The consequence is that this triggers a price war between investment banks such that after this move by a single investment bank from the next time period onwards, investment banks do not make any profits and we have $\Pi_B = 0$. For their own clients, an investment bank could charge marginally less than the fee f and it would receive the revenue it normally obtains in that time period from this client, $\gamma \frac{M}{N}\left(\frac{f\overline{V}}{M} - C\right)$. In addition, this investment bank will receive the business of all the other investment banks this client has a relationship with; the additional revenue is $\gamma \frac{M}{N}\left(f\overline{V} - \frac{f\overline{V}}{M}\right) = \gamma \frac{M}{N} f \left(1 - \frac{1}{M}\right)\overline{V}$. As the client is already with the bank, the additional costs C are not incurred again. By charging $f - c$, this investment bank can also attract clients of other investment banks to switch, overcoming the switching costs c, and get additional revenue of $\left(1 - \frac{M}{N}\right)\gamma (f - c)\overline{V}$. As this does not involve building a relationship, no costs C are incurred for this revenue. Thus to ensure banks cooperate, what in the literature is often referred to as tacit collusion to sustain high fees, we need

$$\frac{\gamma\frac{M}{N}\left(\frac{f\overline{V}}{M}-C\right)}{1-\frac{1}{\rho}} \geq \gamma\frac{M}{N}\left(\frac{f\overline{V}}{M}-C\right) + \gamma\frac{M}{N}f\left(1-\frac{1}{M}\right)\overline{V} + \left(1-\frac{M}{N}\right)\gamma\left(f-c\right)\overline{V} \tag{19.5}$$

which can be rewritten as

$$\Psi = \frac{M}{\rho}\left(\frac{f\overline{V}}{M}-C\right) - \left(\left(N-1\right)f-\left(N-M\right)c\right)\overline{V} \geq 0 \tag{19.6}$$

If competition between banks is such that they will erode any excess profit that can be made from sustaining the fee f, this relationship holds with equality. Let us now assume that competition between investment banks is fierce and they make zero profits when charging the fee f; thus, $\Pi_B = \frac{f\overline{V}}{M} - C = 0$. In this case we have $\overline{V} = \frac{CM}{f}$ and thus $\frac{\partial\overline{V}}{\partial M} = \frac{C}{f}$. If we finally define $\varepsilon = -\frac{\partial V}{\partial f}\frac{f}{V}$ as the elasticity of demand for services of the investment bank, we can get

$$\begin{aligned}
\frac{\partial\Psi}{\partial N} &= -\left(f-c\right)\overline{V} < 0 \\
\frac{\partial\Psi}{\partial c} &= \left(N-M\right)\overline{V} > 0 \\
\frac{\partial\Psi}{\partial M} &= \frac{\partial\overline{V}}{\partial M}\left(\frac{f}{\rho}-\left(N-1\right)f+\left(N-1\right)c\right)+c\overline{V}-\frac{C}{\rho} \\
&= \frac{C}{f}\left(Nc-\left(N-1\right)f\right) < 0 \\
\frac{\partial\Psi}{\partial f} &= \left(\frac{1}{\rho N}-\left(N-1\right)\right)\left(V+f\frac{\partial V}{\partial f}\right)-c\left(N-M\right)\frac{\partial V}{\partial f} \\
&= \left(\frac{1}{\rho N}-\left(N-1\right)\right)\left(1-\varepsilon\right)\overline{V}-\frac{c}{f}\left(N-M\right)\varepsilon\overline{V} > 0
\end{aligned} \tag{19.7}$$

where the inequalities in the final two derivatives arise for switching costs c being sufficiently small.

Using the implicit function theorem, we now get

$$\frac{\partial N}{\partial f} = -\frac{\frac{\partial \Psi}{\partial f}}{\frac{\partial \Psi}{\partial N}} > 0 \qquad (19.8)$$

$$\frac{\partial M}{\partial N} = -\frac{\frac{\partial \Psi}{\partial N}}{\frac{\partial \Psi}{\partial M}} < 0$$

$$\frac{\partial c}{\partial N} = -\frac{\frac{\partial \Psi}{\partial N}}{\frac{\partial \Psi}{\partial c}} > 0$$

$$\frac{\partial f}{\partial M} = -\frac{\frac{\partial \Psi}{\partial M}}{\frac{\partial \Psi}{\partial f}} > 0$$

$$\frac{\partial f}{\partial c} = -\frac{\frac{\partial \Psi}{\partial c}}{\frac{\partial \Psi}{\partial f}} < 0$$

$$\frac{\partial M}{\partial c} = -\frac{\frac{\partial \Psi}{\partial c}}{\frac{\partial \Psi}{\partial M}} > 0$$

From these results we see that lower costs to switch investment banks, c, would imply more competition for clients between investment banks seeking to attract them to switch. Higher competition (lower switching costs c) leads to fewer relationships for each client (lower M) as changing investment banks becomes less costly, and hence, retaining a large number of relationships to induce competition between investment banks to be awarded the deal is less beneficial; investment banks cannot sustain their business if too many relationships are sought by each client as the revenue is split between these banks and they cannot recover their fixed costs C to maintain the relationship. Nevertheless, the fee f will increase as fewer relationship banks means there is less competition for any deal between relationship banks and attracting clients to switch investment banks is less costly; hence, profits increase from starting a bidding war as the fee charged is $f - c$ and hence higher. Similarly, more relationships (a higher M) make it less likely for an investment bank to obtain the deal; hence, the incentives to undercut the fee f are higher, necessitating a higher fee f to increase the costs of doing so from lost future revenue. As there are also less deals per investment bank, there is less chance to recover any costs C and hence less investment banks become relationship banks, N reduces.

Summary Relationship banking is only available to those clients that are generating large enough deals or a sufficiently large number of smaller deals for investment banks to recover the additional costs such relationships cause, such as higher staffing costs. For those clients that can access relationship banking, investment banks will compete with each other. Firstly, there will be competition between all investment banks a client has relationships with, meaning they only recover their additional costs. In addition, there will be competition between investment banks to induce clients to switch investment banks. This competition will only go so far that banks do not undercut each other and trigger a price war, which would erode any future profits. This has implications for the pricing structure and the number of banks that are sustainable in a market. If the costs of switching investment banks are reduced, thereby increasing competition between investment banks as inducing clients to switch is easier, clients will see less need to maintain a large number of relationships due to the lower cost of switching if pricing is not competitive. This, however, increases the fees investment banks can charge. The lower number of relationship banks increases the share of deals from each client an investment bank handles, reducing competition between investment banks as the incentives to undercut each other are smaller due to the higher future profits from such an arrangement. Having less relationship banks increases the number of investment banks sustainable in the market as each investment bank obtains a larger share of the deals available.

If competition between investment banks is encouraged, for example, by regulatory interventions that reduce the switching costs for clients, relationship banking will reduce in importance. The number of relationships each client has will reduce as will the number of investment banks engaging in relationship banking. This in turn might increase the concentration of investment banks if the market cannot sustain the number of investment banks currently operating.

Reading Anand and Galetovic (2006).

Optimal Investment Banks 20

Investment banks offer different services at different levels of expertise that will result in different surplus to clients seeking their advice. Clients needs to seek out the investment bank that is most suitable to their needs and investment banks position themselves in the market such that they maximise their own profits. This involves a decision on their level of expertise, but also whether to specialise in certain services or offer all investment banking activities. Section 20.1 will address the question of specialisation of investment banks and how this relates to the level of expertise they acquire. While there the client base of investment banks is assumed to be homogenous, we will assume in Sect. 20.2 that the surplus generated by investment bank advice differs across clients and will establish how investment banks and clients are optimally matched.

20.1 Specialisation of Investment Banks

Clients require a range of services from investment banks, each requiring specialist knowledge, where the demands of each client will vary and each client will have different demands over time. It is not possible to have high expertise in all areas clients might have demand for advice; hence, investment banks will specialise in certain areas and have a higher expertise there than in other areas. The degree of specialisation will vary across investment banks. They might not specialise much and therefore serve a wider range of areas and thus clients, but as their knowledge is limited, they will not be able to provide clients with a high surplus; on the other hand, investment banks might specialise and then provide clients with services that generate clients a high surplus, but this will be limited to a small area of expertise.

Let us assume that the areas of expertise investment banks have are located on an interval of unit length and that the services a client requires are also located in this interval. In this sense the model we are developing is built on the Hotelling model. Investment banks build their expertise e_i, which gives clients benefits V_i and

A. Krause, *Theoretical Foundations of Investment Banking*, Springer Texts in Business and Economics, https://doi.org/10.1007/978-3-031-58060-4_20

costs the investment bank C_i to maintain. With $\frac{\partial V_i}{\partial e_i} > 0$ and $\frac{\partial^2 V_i}{\partial e_i^2} < 0$, the marginal benefits to clients of such expertise are diminishing, while the marginal costs of investment banks are increasing, as we assume that $\frac{\partial C_i}{\partial e_i} > 0$ and $\frac{\partial^2 C_i}{\partial e_i^2} > 0$. Thus, the more expertise an investment bank has, the higher the benefits to clients, but these increases are reducing the higher the level of expertise is, while the costs to investment banks are increasing ever faster. We assume there are two investment banks competing for clients and they can freely choose their location on the interval as well as their level of expertise.

Investment banks select a location d_i, representing their point of highest expertise and the benefits to clients seeking advice on a service located at d are then reducing with the distance to this location d_i at a rate c. Thus, the net benefits to clients of seeking advice from investment bank i located at d_i for a service d are $V_i - c|d - d_i|$. If we let $d_1 \leq d \leq d_2$ for convenience, then a client is indifferent between the two investment banks if

$$V_1 - c(d - d_1) = V_2 - c(d_2 - d)$$

or the service required is located at

$$d^* = \frac{d_1 + d_2}{2} + \frac{V_1 - V_2}{2c} \tag{20.1}$$

If a service is located at $d < d^*$, the client would seek advice from investment bank 1, and if $d > d^*$, advice is sought from investment bank 2. If $d < d_1$ or $d > d_2$, the client will choose the investment nearest to them, investment bank 1 or 2, respectively.

Let us assume that the services needed are uniformly distributed across the range of the interval (normalised to unity); then we have the expected profits of using investment banks 1 and 2, respectively, as

$$\begin{aligned}
\Pi_C^1 &= \int_0^{d^*} (V_1 - c|d_1 - d|)\, dd \qquad (20.2)\\
&= \int_0^{d^*} V_1 dd - c\left(\int_0^{d_1} (d_1 - d)\, dd + \int_{d_1}^{d^*} (d - d_1)\, dd\right)\\
&= d^* V_1 - \frac{1}{2}c\left(d_1^2 + (d^* - d_1)^2\right)\\
\Pi_C^2 &= \int_{d^*}^{1} (V_2 - c|d_2 - d|)\, dd\\
&= \int_{d^*}^{1} V_2 dd - c\left(\int_{d^*}^{d_2} (d_2 - d)\, dd + \int_{d_2}^{1} (d - d_2)\, dd\right)\\
&= (1 - d^*)\, V_2 - \frac{1}{2}c\left((1 - d_2)^2 + (d_2 - d^*)^2\right)
\end{aligned}$$

The initial term represents the clients located below (above) d^* for investment bank 1 (investment bank 2) and hence choosing this investment bank, obtaining benefits V_i, from which we need to subtract the reduction in value due to the investment bank not having the right expertise as required, which will depend on the distance to the investment bank.

We can now investigate the degree of specialisation and expertise of investment banks. We might interpret a location of investment banks at either $d_i = 0$ or $d_i = 1$ as fully specialised and a location $d_i = \frac{1}{2}$ as not specialised. Being located at the extremes implies that only a very narrow range of services will provide clients with close to the full benefits V_i; there will only be demand for their services above d_1 or below d_2. If the investment bank is located in the middle of the interval, this allows many more clients to benefit from a wider range of services as there will be demand for their services above and below d_i. The level of expertise e_i can indirectly be measured through the level of surplus the investment bank generates, V_i.

Social Optimum We can now obtain the socially optimal location by maximising $\Pi_W = \Pi_C^1 + \Pi_C^2 - C_1 - C_2$. The social welfare consists of the surplus generated for the clients, less the costs investment banks faced from having to build up their expertise. After inserting d^* from Eq. (20.1) into Eq. (20.2), the first-order conditions for the optimal locations are given by

$$\frac{\partial \Pi_W}{\partial d_1} = \frac{1}{2}(V_1 - V_2) - \frac{1}{2}c(3d_1 - d_2) = 0 \tag{20.3}$$

$$\frac{\partial \Pi_W}{\partial d_2} = \frac{1}{2}(V_1 - V_2) - \frac{1}{2}c(3d_2 - d_1 - 2) = 0$$

which solves for

$$d_1 = \frac{1}{4} + \frac{V_1 - V_2}{2c} \tag{20.4}$$

$$d_2 = \frac{3}{4} + \frac{V_1 - V_2}{2c}$$

Inserting this result into Eq. (20.2) to obtain the surplus of the clients and noting that $d^* = \frac{1}{2} + \frac{V_1 - V_2}{c}$, we can now in a second step determine the optimal level of expertise, e_i, through the following first-order conditions:

$$\frac{\partial \Pi_W}{\partial e_1} = \frac{1}{2}\frac{\partial V_1}{\partial e_1}\left(1 + 2\frac{V_1 - V_2}{c}\right) - \frac{\partial C_1}{\partial e_1} = 0 \tag{20.5}$$

$$\frac{\partial \Pi_W}{\partial e_2} = \frac{1}{2}\frac{\partial V_2}{\partial e_2}\left(1 + 2\frac{V_2 - V_1}{c}\right) - \frac{\partial C_2}{\partial e_2} = 0$$

As the first-order conditions for both investment banks are symmetric, and there are no inherent differences between investment banks, we can focus on symmetric equilibria in which their level of expertise, e_i, will be identical, and hence, the level of surplus generated, V_i, will also be identical. Using $V_1 = V_2$, we get the social equilibrium characterised by

$$d_1 = \frac{1}{4} \tag{20.6}$$
$$d_2 = \frac{3}{4}$$
$$\frac{\partial V_i}{\partial e_i} = 2\frac{\partial C_i}{\partial e_i}$$

We use this social optimum as a benchmark to analyse a situation in which the investment banks determine their optimal locations and level of expertise independently by maximising their respective profits. We will consider the case of relationship banking and transaction banking.

Relationship Banking Let us now assume that investment banks charge a fee F_i for their services, such that they participate in the value they generate, by setting

$$F_i = f_0 + f_1 \Pi_C^i$$

An investment bank charging a fraction of the profits their clients make from using its services can be interpreted as relationship banking. The investment bank and their client share some of the benefits created; thus, their profits are interlocked.

Investment banking profits are then given by $\Pi_B^i = F_i - C_i$. Inserting for F_i and then for Π_C^i from Eq. (20.2), as well as for d^* from Eq. (20.1), we get as first-order conditions for the optimal location that

$$\frac{\partial \Pi_B^1}{\partial d_1} = \frac{1}{2} f_1 \left(V_1 - c\left(3d_1 - d^*\right)\right) = 0 \tag{20.7}$$
$$\frac{\partial \Pi_B^2}{\partial d_2} = -\frac{1}{2} f_1 \left(V_2 - c\left(2 + d^* - 3d_2\right)\right) = 0$$

which easily solves for

$$d_1 = \frac{1}{6} + \frac{2}{3}\frac{V_1}{c} - \frac{1}{3}\frac{V_2}{c} \tag{20.8}$$
$$d_2 = \frac{5}{6} + \frac{1}{3}\frac{V_1}{c} - \frac{2}{3}\frac{V_2}{c}$$

Inserting these results back into the investment bank profits $\Pi_B^i = F_i - C_i$, using Π_C^i from Eq. (20.2) and noting that $d^* = \frac{1}{2} + \frac{V_1 - V_2}{c}$, we get the first-order conditions for the optimal level of expertise as

$$\frac{\partial \Pi_B^1}{\partial e_1} = f_1 \frac{\partial V_1}{\partial e_1}\left(\frac{5}{18} + \frac{13}{9c}V_1 - \frac{7}{9c}V_2\right) - \frac{\partial C_1}{\partial e_1} = 0 \tag{20.9}$$

$$\frac{\partial \Pi_B^2}{\partial e_2} = f_1 \frac{\partial V_2}{\partial e_2}\left(\frac{5}{18} + \frac{13}{9c}V_2 - \frac{7}{9c}V_2\right) - \frac{\partial C_2}{\partial e_2} = 0$$

Given the symmetry of these first-order conditions and the fact that investment banks are ex ante identical, we focus again on symmetric equilibria such that $e_1 = e_2$ and consequently $V_1 = V_2$. This gives us the properties of the equilibrium with relationship banking as

$$d_1 = \frac{1}{6} + \frac{1}{3}\frac{V_1}{c} \tag{20.10}$$

$$d_2 = \frac{5}{6} - \frac{1}{3}\frac{V_1}{c}$$

$$\frac{\partial V_i}{\partial e_i} = \frac{f_1}{\frac{5}{18} + \frac{2}{3c}V_1}\frac{\partial C_i}{\partial e_i}$$

If $\frac{V_1}{c} > \frac{1}{4}$, which we assume here as this allows investment banks to cover the entire area of services between them without giving any client a negative surplus, we easily see that $d_1 > \frac{1}{4}$ and $d_2 < \frac{3}{4}$. Thus, compared to the social optimum in Eq. (20.6), the distance of the two investment banks is reduced, which implies they do not specialise as much as they would in the social optimum.

Furthermore, if $f_1 < \frac{8}{9}$, that is, the investment bank does not charge too much of the surplus generated, we have $\frac{f_1}{\frac{5}{18}+\frac{2}{3c}V_1} < 2$, which is the term used in the first-order condition in the social optimum on the level of expertise. This implies that with relationship banking, investment banks invest more than the social optimum into their expertise. This is because with the marginal costs $\frac{\partial C_i}{\partial e_i}$ increasing and the marginal benefits of expertise $\frac{\partial V_i}{\partial e_i}$ reducing, these marginal costs and benefits will move closer together for larger values of expertise e_i. As the first-order condition in relationship banking needs costs and surplus to be closer to together, the level of expertise needs to be higher. We can interpret this increased expertise as a way the investment banks compensate clients for their under-specialisation.

In relationship banking, the investment banks' choice of location is identical to where clients would like the investment banks to be located. To see this, note that the client profits, after the investment bank's fee has been deducted, is $\hat{\Pi}_V^i = \Pi_C^i - F_i = (1 - f_1)\,\Pi_C^i - f_0$, while for investment banks it is $\Pi_B^i = f_0 + f_1\Pi_C^i - C_i$. With neither f_0 nor C_i being affected by the location of the investment banks, the first-order conditions for the optimal locations are identical for investment banks and clients, and hence, the optimal locations are identical.

Transaction Banking Let us now consider an investment bank that only charges a fee proportional to the additional value gained from its services, relative to the other investment banks. Here investment banks do not participate in the surplus of the transaction, but merely take a fraction f_1 of the surplus compared to using the other investment banks. We can interpret such an approach as transaction banking, because the investment bank does not participate in the surplus their client obtains from the advice they provide. Hence, the fee income of the investment banks would be given by

$$\begin{aligned} F_1 &= f_0 + f_1 \int_0^{d^*} \left((V_1 - c|d - d_1|) - (V_2 - c(d_2 - d)) \right) dd \\ &= f_0 + f_1 \left(\Pi_C^1 - \left(d^* V_2 - \frac{1}{2} c d^* (2d_2 - d^*) \right) \right) \\ F_2 &= f_0 + f_1 \int_{d^*}^{1} \left((V_2 - c|d_2 - d|) - (V_1 - c(d - d_1)) \right) dd \\ &= f_0 \\ &\quad + f_1 \left(\Pi_C^2 - \left((1 - d^*) V_1 - \frac{1}{2} c (1 - d^*) (d^* - 2d_1 + 1) \right) \right) \end{aligned} \tag{20.11}$$

Here the first term denotes the surplus from seeking advice from the investment bank and the second term that of using the other investment bank. Of the difference, the investment bank charges a fraction f_1 and the total profits of the investment bank is $\Pi_B^i = F_i - C_i$. We then get the first-order conditions for the optimal investment bank locations as

$$\begin{aligned} \frac{\partial \Pi_B^1}{\partial d_1} &= \frac{1}{2} f_1 \left((V_1 - V_2) + c(d_2 - 3d_1) \right) = 0 \\ \frac{\partial \Pi_B^2}{\partial d_2} &= -\frac{1}{2} f_1 \left((V_1 - V_2) + c(3d_2 - d_1 - 2) \right) = 0 \end{aligned} \tag{20.12}$$

These conditions can be solved for

$$\begin{aligned} d_1 &= \frac{1}{4} + \frac{V_1 - V_2}{2c} \\ d_2 &= \frac{3}{4} - \frac{V_1 - V_2}{2c} \end{aligned} \tag{20.13}$$

Inserting these relationships into the fees of Eq. (20.11) and noting that $d^* = \frac{1}{2} + \frac{V_1 - V_2}{2c}$, we get the conditions for the optimal expertise as

$$\frac{\partial \Pi_B^1}{\partial e_1} = f_1 \frac{\partial V_1}{\partial e_1} \left(\frac{1}{2} - \frac{V_1 - V_2}{2c} \right) - \frac{\partial C_1}{\partial e_1} = 0 \tag{20.14}$$

$$\frac{\partial \Pi_B^2}{\partial e_2} = f_2 \frac{\partial V_2}{\partial e_2} \left(\frac{1}{2} - \frac{V_1 - V_2}{2c} \right) - \frac{\partial C_2}{\partial e_2} = 0$$

As these conditions are identical, we obtain identical levels of expertise, e_i, and hence identical surplus for clients, V_i. Thus, the equilibrium with transaction banking is characterised by

$$d_1 = \frac{1}{4} \tag{20.15}$$

$$d_2 = \frac{3}{4}$$

$$\frac{\partial V_i}{\partial e_i} = \frac{2}{f_1} \frac{\partial C_i}{\partial e_i}$$

As $f_1 \leq 1$ we have $\frac{2}{f_1} \geq 2$, and hence, investment banks invest less than the social optimum into expertise. This is because the increasing marginal costs and decreasing marginal benefits of expertise, $\frac{\partial C_i}{\partial e_i}$ and $\frac{\partial V_i}{\partial e_i}$, are further apart, which implies a lower level of expertise. Therefore, with transaction banking, the investment banks are located at the social optimum, but invest not sufficiently into their expertise.

From the clients' perspective, the profits are maximised if the first-order conditions, using $\hat{\Pi}_C = \Pi_C^i - F_i$, are met such that with $V_1 = V_2$ we have

$$\frac{\partial \hat{\Pi}_C^1}{\partial d_1} = \frac{1}{2} \left(V_1 - c \left(\frac{5d_1 - d_2}{2} + f_1 (d_2 - 3d_1) \right) \right) = 0 \tag{20.16}$$

$$\frac{\partial \hat{\Pi}_C^2}{\partial d_2} = \frac{1}{2} \left(V_1 - c \left(\frac{d_1 - 5d_2}{2} + 2 + f_1 (3d_2 - d_1 - 2) \right) \right) = 0$$

Solving for their respective locations, we get

$$d_1 = \frac{\frac{2V_1}{c} + \frac{1}{2} - f_1}{3 - 4f_1} \geq \frac{1}{4} \tag{20.17}$$

$$d_2 = \frac{\frac{-2V_1}{c} + \frac{5}{2} - 3f_1}{3 - 4f_1} \leq \frac{3}{4}$$

where the final inequalities emerge using the condition that $\frac{V_1}{c} > \frac{1}{8}$ and each investment bank covers the entire market. We thus see that from the clients' perspective, investment banks have specialised too much.

Summary In relationship banking, investment banks under-specialise and over-invest into their expertise, compared to the social optimum, although from their clients' perspective, investment banks specialise optimally. In contrast, with transaction banking, investment banks specialise appropriately but underinvest into their expertise, if comparing to the social optimum. Here, their clients feel that investment banks do not have sufficient expertise. Thus, in relationship banking we should find banks that are covering a wider range of services, while in transaction banking they tend to be overly specialised. If covering a wide range of services with a high level of expertise is the characteristics of relationship banking, we would expect such investment banks to be larger to be able to cover adequately all areas, while transaction banks should be smaller and more focused on their area of expertise.

Reading Das and Nanda (1999).

20.2 Matching Banks and Clients

Investment banks are seen as offering different quality of advice. Some investment banks are generally seen as being more capable of understanding market conditions, investors, and clients needs than others. As much as there are differences in the ability of investment banks, there are differences between clients on how much they would benefit from the advice investment banks provide. These differences might arise from the complexity of the advice that is required or, more often, the size of the client being correlated with the benefits investment banks can generate. We here explore how investment banks and clients should be matched efficiently.

Let us assume that there are N investment banks with abilities η_j ordered such that $\eta_j > \eta_{j+1}$ and N groups of clients with qualities γ_i, ordered such that $\gamma_i > \gamma_{i+1}$. Hence, a smaller index i or j indicates a higher quality or ability; it is therefore akin to a ranking of clients and banks. We furthermore assume that the surplus the engagement of bank j by client i generates, $\Pi_{i,j}$, is affected positively by these qualities; thus, we find that $\frac{\partial \Pi_{i,j}}{\partial \eta_j} > 0$ and $\frac{\partial \Pi_{i,j}}{\partial \gamma_i} > 0$. These surpluses are now such that

$$\Pi_{i,j} - \Pi_{i,j+1} \geq \Pi_{i+1,j} - \Pi_{i+1,j+1} \tag{20.18}$$

This implies that an investment bank with higher ability j has a larger impact on clients with higher quality i. This assumption can be justified if high-quality clients would only gain from advice by banks that have a high ability as the advice that lower-ranked banks could provide has already been addressed by the client. In other words, the value added by lower-ranked investment banks would be smaller than that of higher-ranked investment banks and this difference is widening the higher the quality of the client. Rearranging Eq. (20.18), we also see that a higher-quality client affects the surplus more, the higher the ability of the investment bank. Thus, the two qualities of investment banks and their clients are complements.

Let us now assume that $\Pi_{i,i} < \Pi_{i,i+1}$ and $\Pi_{i+1,i+1} < \Pi_{i+1,i}$, i.e., banks and clients are not matched by the rank of their ability. Then $\Pi_{i,i} - \Pi_{i,i+1} < 0$ and $\Pi_{i+1,i} - \Pi_{i+1,i+1} > 0$, thus violating equation (20.18) for $i = j$. Therefore, banks and clients are matched by the rank of their ability and quality.

The surplus $\Pi_{i,i}$ that investment banks generate needs to be distributed between the bank and their client. For a client i, the additional surplus generated compared to choosing investment bank $i + 1$ is $\Pi_{i,i} - \Pi_{i,i+1}$. The client would require this surplus as otherwise a lower-ranked investment bank could offer the client a larger share of the (smaller) joint surplus that makes the client better off. In addition, the client would require the surplus it would get if it was lower ranked; thus,

$$\Pi_C^{i,i} = \Pi_C^{i+1,i+1} + \left(\Pi_{i,i} - \Pi_{i,i+1}\right) \tag{20.19}$$

It would need this surplus of the lower-ranked client as it could always pretend to be of lower quality.

We have $\Pi_C^{N,N} = 0$ as the lowest-ranked client has no opportunity to pretend to be of lower quality and would not obtain any surplus by seeking advice from an investment bank. Similarly, for the investment bank, its surplus would be determined such that

$$\Pi_B^{i,i} = \Pi_B^{i+1,i+1} + \left(\Pi_{i,i} - \Pi_{i+1,i}\right) \tag{20.20}$$

We are continuously adding positive terms as the ability of investment banks and the quality of clients are increasing, and the minimum surpluses allocated to investment banks and their clients are also increasing. This implies that more able investment banks will be more profitable, and if higher-quality clients in terms of surplus generation imply larger clients, the best investment banks will attract these larger clients. Similarly, high-quality clients are obtaining increasing benefits from seeking investment banking advice from seeking out more able investment banks. The surplus can be distributed through investment banking fees, but also the effort a bank exerts to provide the advice.

Summary The ability of investment banks is matched by the amount of surplus the investment bank's advice can generate for the client. More able investment banks attract clients that benefit more from investment bank advice. As the benefits of advice will often increase with size or the complexity of a client, we should find that the most able investment banks attract the largest clients and those clients with the most complex needs. The surplus generated is divided such that it is increasing for both clients and investment banks as the ability of banks and quality of clients increases, thus implying that banks with higher ability are more profitable and higher quality clients gaining more from advice and lower-quality clients.

Reading Fernando, Gatchev, and Spindt (2005).

Conclusions

We observe investment banks that offer advice across the entire range of investment banking activities, while other investment banks specialise in certain areas and are often known as boutique investment banks. This specialisation allows boutique investment banks to serve their clients well in their area of specialisation, while any services outside their area of expertise, if even offered, will be of less value to their client. Generalist investment banks, on the other hand, may not be able to serve their clients well in specific circumstances as they lack the expertise and boutique investment banks might provide better advice. There is trade-off that between serving a client with all their needs, but maybe lacking the level of expertise overall, or providing high-quality advice only in specific areas and serving the interest of their clients less well in other areas. Clearly there is room for both types of investment banks to coexist and all investment banks will have some degree of specialisation, although some are more focused than others. The degree of specialisation will also depend on the business model the investment bank employs. If engaged in relationship banking, thus seeking to advice clients for the long term and participating in the value of their advice, investment banks will specialise less to capture the wider needs of their clients than investment banks mainly engaged in transaction banking. Here they primarily serve the needs of their clients in the current circumstances and clients would benefit from their high level of expertise in the specific area.

Some investment banks are able to attract more able employees and thus provide advice that generates more surplus to their client. Similarly, some clients will benefit more from the advice of investment banks than others, be it due to the nature of the area they seek advice in or their own level of knowledge. Given such surplus, investment banks and their clients need to find together such that the surplus across investment banks and clients is maximised. By bringing together the most able investment banks with those that benefit most from their advice, not only is the welfare maximised, but also the surpluses available to investment banks and clients.

Review of Part V

The wide range of services investment banks offer comes with a diverse requirement for skills of staff and diverse employment practices necessitated by the specific demands of the roles that are filled. The tasks employees have to cover range from valuing companies and devising bidding strategies in mergers and acquisitions advisory to obtaining information from investors about the willingness to purchase securities in underwriting. In order to develop new products and services, market demands need to be analysed and then appropriate products and services be developed and priced, while in other tasks, investment strategies need to be developed in order to manage the wealth of their clients, or they have to identify profitable trading strategies if investment banks are using their own funds in proprietary trading.

Many of these roles lead to conflicts of interest between investment banks and clients, but they manifest themselves in many different ways, specific to the service provided. Contractual arrangements have been established to address these conflicts of interest and for each service a unique solution has been found. For example, in mergers and acquisitions advice contingent contracts are commonly used to align the interests of the investment bank and the client, while in securities underwriting, book building has been established to solicit information from investors. Financial analysts might bias their recommendation in order to gain access to more accurate information from companies they cover and brokers are providing advice to their clients on suitable investments, but only charge for this advice through a fee on the amount that is actually traded by their client.

We thus see that as much as the responsibilities vary across different services, so do contractual arrangements to mitigate any conflicts of interest that might arise. However, despite these differences, we are able to distinguish a number of common characteristics that are observed consistently across the services offered and also across investment banks. These commonalities are sufficiently general, however, to enable the investment bank to operate efficiently in each area it is operating in.

One common observation is that investment banks pay consistently higher salaries than comparable positions in many other industries, maybe with the exception of management consulting. Combined with the high salaries are high responsibilities given to employees already at an early stage in their career. In most other industries, employees have to gain significant experience before being given wide-ranging responsibilities, while in investment banks such responsibilities are allocated from the very start. Salaries and also the promotion to more senior positions are very much based on performance and seniority in terms of the time spent with an investment bank or within the industry is of secondary importance at most. Employees that are not meeting the performance requirements are often dismissed. Such arrangements provide strong incentives for employees to acquire the requisite skills for their roles and exert a high level of effort. In an industry where the outcomes to a significant amount are driven by random exogenous events, establishing the skill level and the amount of effort an employee exerts would be very difficult and time-consuming. Having the practice of paying well, while providing significant responsibilities, will ensure there is an intrinsic motivation to acquire the skills and exert effort, such that the employee performs well. Rather than relying on monitoring of employee activities, investment banks use incentives to avoid the difficulty and costs of monitoring employees.

In the same way do partnership provide incentives to existing partners to support the training and development of more junior staff. They do so to maintain the quality of their services and thus the value of their partnership. Given the co-ownership of the investment bank in a partnership, high rewards are available for those performing well enough to being invited into such a position, providing incentives to exert high levels of efforts and acquiring the requisite knowledge. The pressure on partners to be more actively involved in client work limits their time spent on developing junior staff, making it more difficult for partnerships to be sustained. The reliance on the expertise of staff members has led to small differences in the ability across different levels of seniority, favouring local decision-making. This makes optimal use of the expertise that staff working with clients have and minimises suggestions of senior staff members who, despite all good intentions, might lack the specific knowledge for the client, but whose suggestions cannot be dismissed by junior staff given their relative positions. Similarly, motivating staff to work on solutions they do not agree on can lead to poor implementation of otherwise good advice, making the delegation of decisions to those tasked with their implementation optimal.

Despite competing fiercely for any deal originating from clients, investment banks have remained highly profitable with fees showing substantial profit margins. They limit competition for new deals by competing only with a small number of investment banks, all of which have an existing relationship with a client. This way, high investment banking fees can be sustained through tacit collusion. Maintaining the relationship, and thus limiting competition, requires investment banks to retain capacity within their staffing levels to ensure that any of their existing clients can be advised if and as needed. This will lead to higher staffing than necessary or excessive workload for existing staff, both of which will be costly.

Finally, we observe the coexistence of small boutique investment banks, specialising in specific services, with bulge-bracket investment banks, that offer the full range of services. Bulge-bracket investment banks offer all services at a good level of expertise; they will be able to serve their clients across their demands, while boutique investment banks will provide high-quality services only for specific needs that bulge-bracket investment banks cannot provide at that quality. The choice of investment bank will be such that it optimises the joint surplus of the investment banks and their clients, which is then distributed between them. This results in the investment bank providing the highest-quality service being the most profitable and the clients they serve usually being the one seeking the most services or having the most complex requirements.

Investment banks invest heavily into the expertise of their staff and the focus on performance in pay and promotion provides strong incentives for staff to acquire such expertise, in addition to exert high levels of effort. The high quality of their staff allows investment banks to produce high-quality advice that adds surplus to their client, allowing them to charge high fees and be very profitable. While such characteristics are widely spread, they mask substantial differences in each service provided where these principles are applied to suit the local needs. There are not only differences in the detail of practices across different services provided by investment banks, but different services are also seen differently by employees, clients, and the general public. It is commonly asserted that working on mergers and acquisitions is most prestigious, while brokerage is interpreted as being much less desirable. However, in most areas, the salaries as well as the level of expertise are high.

Epilogue: Ethical Considerations

On first sight, economic models seem to not make any judgments on whether an action taken is just. A typical chain or arguments is that an action A induced a utility change Δu_i in individual i. If we find that for all N individuals together $\sum_{i=1}^{N} \Delta u_i \geq 0$, the action A is beneficial. Should there be an individual j for who $\Delta u_j < 0$, then at least one individual must have $\Delta u_i > 0$, and it would be possible to transfer utility from such individual i to individual j to ensure that $\Delta u_j \geq 0$ while maintaining that $\Delta u_i \geq 0$; such a transfer usually takes the form of monetary compensation. After this transfer, all individuals are gaining from taking action A and are willing to participate. In many of the models we discussed, such transfers were not explicitly conducted, but a constraint imposed that all individuals must be better off. Such a constraint is then enforced by the use of a specific type of contract that ensures certain decisions are made by individuals that ensure action A improves the utility of all individuals.

Many different choices, apart from A, can be made, and which action is chosen will depend on who makes this choice, as this individual would choose the action that increases its utility the most while ensuring that no one is worse off. The aim of the decision-making process is to maximise the utility of the decision-maker while ensuring that other individuals that have to participate in the action are willing to participate. This is ensured by requiring that their utility levels are not reducing. Despite all individuals increasing their utility level from taking action A, this action might be seen as unjust and morally not acceptable.

In ethics, a number of fundamental theories of just behaviour have been developed that can give additional insights into a moral assessment of any decisions that are made, in our context especially the decisions of investment banks with respect to the advice they provide clients with, but also the compensation of employees. Making decisions that are just, we here call ethical behaviour.

Teleology One can argue that an action is just if it makes everyone better off. The end of the decision, an increase in utility, justifies the means, the action taken. This teleological approach to identifying just actions is the common technique used in economics to identify acceptable actions and then the best action to choose. More specifically, economics is using utilitarianism in its assessment of actions and

A. Krause, *Theoretical Foundations of Investment Banking*, Springer Texts in Business and Economics, https://doi.org/10.1007/978-3-031-58060-4

decisions; utilitarianism specifically suggests that actions should be maximising the happiness (utility) of all individuals affected by an action.

Taking such a teleological approach is not without its critics, and its conclusions on just actions have often been questioned. Consider the model from Sect. 8.1, where a financial analyst obtains more precise information from companies, provided he provides an excessively positive assessment of the company. With access to the additional information, the financial analyst is able to produce a forecast that has smaller errors than if he had no access to the additional information; this is despite the fact the forecast is biased. Being able to make better forecasts will benefit the financial analyst itself as it will improve its reputation, while investors using the information will benefit from a more precise forecast, and the company will benefit from the positive coverage and the likely increased share price. Thus, all individuals affected by the decision of the company to give access to additional information only if the forecast of analysts is biased in their favour are better off. Using teleological ethics, the end of a better forecast justifies the means, the provision of information only in return for biased forecasts. As we will see below, using alternative criteria that might include the honesty of advice given, this decision will no longer be seen as just.

Another criticism that might arise is that while teleology may ensure that every individual is better off and that contracts are set up such that this key property is ensured, how these gains are distributed might not be seen as just. It is often that one of the individuals involved, often the investment bank, can use these contracts to extract all benefits from other individuals, such as the company advised, and themselves gain the most from providing advice. It could also be possible that due to competition between investment banks, companies might be able to extract all benefits of the advice investment banks provide and gain most, while investment banks make no net gain. Teleology (in general) and utilitarianism (specifically) do not provide criteria to decide whether such extraction of all surplus from other individuals can be seen as just.

Another concern when using teleology is that what might be individually rational in the sense of increasing the utility of an individual might be a waste of resources. While using this approach can be used to justify the high compensation investment bankers obtain, be it due to their high productivity or the need to provide incentives to exert effort, the reliance on bonuses in this framework can also lead to morally questionable behaviour. If bonuses are determined subjectively on the basis of an assessment managers make regarding the individual contribution to profits, investment bankers might be tempted to spend resources and effort on presenting themselves in the best light. This is not only using resources, such as time, that could be used to provide advice to clients, but might also affect the advice given as we have demonstrated in Chap. 9. There, financial analysts changed their forecasts to improve the perception of their ability, rather than provide the advice they believe to be best for their client. If only considering those individuals that are involved in the decision-making, here the financial analyst, the effect on other individuals can easily be overlooked.

A situation in which the effect of an action on individuals that are not part of the decision-making is ignored is often referred to as an external effect. The ethics literature often refers to stakeholders as all those individuals, or groups of individuals, that are affected by any decision, whether they have been involved in the process or not. While teleology would require the assessment of an action to consider the effect of all stakeholders to assess whether it is a just action, the reality is that often only those are considered who are involved in the decision-making and in some instances those who the decision is directed at. The wider range of stakeholders is commonly ignored. While this is not a limitation of the teleological approach in itself, but more the way this is often implemented, particularly in economics, alternative ethical theories might provide an approach that puts the need to consider the wider impact of decisions at the forefront.

Deontology While teleology focused on the outcome to assess whether an action is just, deontology investigates the action itself. Rather than assessing an action based on its just ends, hence that an action is just if all individuals affected benefit, the means to obtain an end itself should be just. An action is considered just if it complies with a set of rules that have been judged to lead to just actions.

The most widely known set of such rules has been proposed by Immanuel Kant and is generally known as Kant's categorical imperative, Kant (1783). The tests proposed to judge an action can be formulated in different ways, one of which states that each individual has a duty to look after all other individuals. Implied in this formulation is that when taking an action, the decision-maker should consider the impact this action has on others and not take this action if they are affected negatively, or do not participate sufficiently in any gains. This criterion for a just action, and hence what is generally interpreted as ethical behaviour, addresses the limitation of the teleological approach that an individual could extract all surplus for their own benefit. While no one is worse off and the teleological criterion of a just action would be fulfilled, it would fall foul of this interpretation of Kant's categorical imperative.

An alternative formulation of Kant's categorical imperative proposes to assess that if everyone took this action or behaved in this way would the outcome still be beneficial. It might be beneficial for an individual financial analyst to change their forecast to be seen as having higher ability, but if every financial analyst would be doing this, then no one would provide an assessment that is truthful. Whether such an outcome is desirable and beneficial for investors seeking advice is doubtful. Hence, while changing the forecast to appear having higher ability is ethical in the assessment of teleological criteria, it would not be an ethical behaviour using the deontological approach.

The so-called Golden Rule, which can be stated as "do only what you others want to do to you", is not based on Kant's categorical imperative, but largely compatible with his suggested criterion. A direct implication of the Golden Rule in our context is that if an investment bank seeks to obtain surplus from giving advice, their clients should also obtain some surplus; thus investment banks would not extract all surplus for their own benefit and instead share the surplus generated. This would suggest that all stakeholders of an action are considered and their respective interests balanced against each other. Only if the allocation of surplus across all stakeholders is generally accepted is an action deemed to be just and the behaviour ethical.

Apart from Kant's categorical imperative, John Rawls (1971), focuses directly on the action taken. Considering the context of investment banking, he proposes that all individuals should have equal opportunities to achieve surplus from any decisions and not be excluded from it by their role in the economy. This would imply a negotiation between all individuals affected by an action, taking into account the specific circumstances of each individual as equally valid. All employees should have the same criteria applied to gain promotions or bonuses, and this should be based on merit alone, not on their ability for self-promotion, unless this is part of the criterion, or their personal connections with more senior managers.

Furthermore, the least-advantaged individual should also participate in any surplus. In terms of the compensation policy of investment banks, this implies that all employees should be benefitting from the bonuses available, not only those employees who have directly contributed to the profits; other employees will have made their contribution more indirectly through cleaning offices, providing secretarial support, maintaining the IT infrastructure, or supplying food in the canteen and should also be rewarded for their roles.

In addition, Rawls also required that all this is achieved with minimal restrictions on the decisions that individuals make, implying that regulatory interference by governments in achieving moral aims should be minimal, but also constraints imposed on employees by investment banks should be limited. Therefore, imposing ethical behaviour through restrictions is not in itself an ethical action; ethical behaviour should be coming out of the individuals own values and not be the result of constraints that are followed.

Virtue Ethics While teleology assesses ethical behaviour from the outcome of actions, deontology focuses on whether the way actions are determined follows a just process. Virtue ethics goes one step further and judges the motivations for such actions. The outcomes of actions or whether they are actually just by some criteria are irrelevant for the assessment whether an action is classified as just and hence represents ethical behaviour. Virtues that should be reflected in any action go back to the Ancient Greek times of Aristotle and include honesty and modesty, among many others. In modern times, such virtues have been extended to include the support for equality rights.

The same action can be seen as virtuous and hence ethical, and unethical, depending on the context in which it is taken. Consider the competition between investment banks; it can be ethical if the investment banks compete with the aim of providing the best advice for their clients or provide this advice at the lowest possible cost. The same competition would be judged unethical in virtue ethics if the motivation for such competition was to harm a competitor, for example, by driving him out of the market. Dishonest behaviour, such as misrepresenting outcomes by traders as discussed in Sect. 15.3, would be unethical in any circumstances, but we note that in the framework of the model, a teleological approach would judge fraud as ethical as it benefits the trader and its manager, neglecting here the external effects on the shareholders of the investment bank. Similarly, the award of bonuses can be unethical if the aim is not to reward contributions to the profits of the investment bank, but if they are the result of employees not criticising their managers or if this allows managers to promote their own goals by claiming to have managed their staff so successfully that they have earned large bonuses, and therefore he himself deserves being awarded a large bonus.

Rights and Duties As has become clear in the previous discussion, the different approaches to assessing ethical behaviour—teleology, deontology, and virtue ethics—can give rise to different results. Teleology seeks a desirable outcome and deontology a just cause, and virtue ethics assesses the right motives for the action taken. As the arbitrary examples in Table 1 show, it is possible to identify actions that meet all the criteria for ethical behaviour, but in many cases an action would be judged ethical by some criteria, but not by others. As the criteria for assessing ethical behaviour are not generally agreed and investment banks are exposed to many different stakeholders, with often conflicting ethical assessments, it will be easy to accuse investment banks of acting unethical by violating one of the criteria.

Table 1 Examples of conflicting ethical assessments

Action	Teleology (desirable outcome)	Deontology (just cause)	Virtue ethics (just motive)
Obtain information from investors on their assessment of a company	Investors obtain profits from underpricing, company raises funds, investment banks obtains fee income	Allow the company to raise capital at low costs	Grow the economy through investment
Develop a new security that allows banks to transfer risks between them	**Risks become concentrated and banks may require bailouts**	Move risks from banks who do not want to take it	Allow risks to be distributed according to preferences
Lowering fees and initiating a price war	After banks merge economies of scale reduce costs and fees	Lower the costs to clients by concentrating investment banks	**Cause losses to competitors to cause them to fail or merge with them at low costs**
Advise company in distress to merge with another company	Loan is repaid and company survives	**Investment bank seeks to secure its own loans, not the company's survival**	Ensure the company survives

Entries in **bold** indicate that the assessment suggests unethical behavior

Investment banks are often criticised for their unethical behaviour, and the behaviour that is criticised is changing according to the circumstances of the time. Investment banks have been criticised for making excessive profits and paying large bonuses to their employees during recessions, for example, in the aftermath of the 2007/2008 financial crisis. At other times, they have been criticised for publishing overly positive assessments of companies and misleading investors; this happened in the aftermath of the 2001 dotcom crash. Before that, in the 1980s, they have been criticised for their focus on generating profits through MBOs and LBOs, often at the expense of the viability of industrial companies. The reaction to such accusations is often that regulation is imposed on investment banks that seek to limit such behaviour. It was in reaction to the dotcom crash that financial analysts were required to become more independent from the other investment banking activities to limit any conflicts of interest that lead to overly positive recommendations. As a consequence of the criticism of high bonus payments during the financial crisis 2007/2008 bonus payments were restricted in some jurisdictions, with the aim to limit pay, but also curb excessive risk taking that had contributed to that crisis. Losses arising from the trading in stock markets in the aftermath of the 1929 stock market crash lead to the separation of investment and commercial banking in the USA with the Glass-Steagall Act 1933.

Such regulatory interventions are seeking to address what is seen at that time as unethical behaviour and thereby impose more ethical behaviour on investment banks through the requirement to comply with the imposed regulation. As I have pointed out above, this in itself might not be ethical behaviour as it imposes additional constraints on decisions individuals make. Especially virtue ethics can be very restrictive on what constitutes ethical behaviour as it imposes a strict set of norms on the motivation of decisions that cannot easily be mitigated. In contrast, teleology allows to offset any losses to some individuals by sharing the surplus other individuals obtain and is therefore more flexible in what constitutes ethical behaviour.

Whenever multiple goals and criteria should be met, compromises have to be found; this compromise could be classified as a balance of rights and duties. In the context of investment banking, there is the right of the investment bank to benefit from their expertise and knowledge by generating profits. This is covered by teleology as the investment bank benefits from these profits, but also deontology where generating profits to maintain the services in the future could be regarded as ethically desirable. Unless profits themselves are seen as unethical, virtue ethics would also allow for investment banks to make profits, although the size of these profits should not be too high to comply with the virtue of modesty. These rights, however, have to be balanced against the duties of investment banks, most notably that of acting in their clients' best interest by giving the best possible advice. With clients as stakeholders, the teleological approach suggests that they also need to obtain benefits from seeking investment bank advice, which is also covered by a deontological approach, and similarly virtue ethics would not object to clients benefitting. The ethical judgment comes into finding the right balance between investment banks and their clients, and other stakeholders, as appropriate. Ideally investment banks would seek to comply with all three approaches of assessing ethical behaviour, but as we have seen, while some criteria can easily be met, an action might fall short of another criterion and be judged as unethical by those applying this theory.

Ethical behaviour cannot be imposed by regulation; whether from politics or internal ethics codes, it must be internalised by employees and be applied as a matter of course.

Reading Liaw (2012, Ch. 16), Reynolds and Newell (2011, Chs. 3, 5, 7–8)

Final Reflections

Investment banks offer a wide variety of services to their clients. Each of these services addresses a specific need the client has, and the investment bank will be able to offer a tailor-made solution, taking into account the client's specific situation. Given the differences in the type of services provided to clients, it has been difficult to provide a single coherent theory of investment banking activities. Each service provided has its own unique characteristics and this manifests itself in conflicts of interest between the investment bank and their client in different ways. The reaction to address such conflicts of interest through the contract between the investment bank and their client, predominantly regarding the way payment for the service is determined, has therefore also been a local solution that cannot easily be transferred to other services.

Key Lessons Despite such variety, some common themes can be observed when looking across the spectrum of services offered. A key feature of investment banking activities is that in most cases investment banks provide advice to their client and this advice is mostly followed. While following this advice has tangible consequences for their clients, the investment bank is in most cases not affected by the outcome of their advice. The advice has only direct consequences for investment banks if the contract with their client links the fee income they receive to the outcome the advice has. Such contracts are designed to align the interests on investment banks and their clients. Given the differences in services provided, the contractual arrangement addressing the conflict of interest between investment banks and their clients, will vary considerably.

A key characteristic of the relationship between investment banks and their clients is that of asymmetric information. Commonly investment banks either have better information than their clients, can access such information more easily, or have a better ability to interpret the information obtained. This informational asymmetry is the key reason investment banks are sought as advisors. In some instances, they are also used to reduce the asymmetric information between a well-informed client and investors; here the investment bank is used to corroborate the information the clients claims to have. Investment banks can exploit their informational advantage by maximising their own profits rather than providing the

A. Krause, *Theoretical Foundations of Investment Banking*, Springer Texts in Business and Economics, https://doi.org/10.1007/978-3-031-58060-4

best advice to the benefit of their clients. This conflict of interest is, as mentioned, at the heart of the relationship between investment banks and their clients.

Investment banks also need to obtain information. While some information can be collected from specialist providers and past experience, other information can only be obtained from investors directly; this might include assessing the market perception of a security or merger proposal. Investors will give up their informational advantage to the investment bank if providing such information and consequently require incentives to truthfully report the information they hold. Compensating investors will either cost the investment bank by having to provide compensation to these investors, or they are compensated indirectly by their clients, for example, by underpricing securities.

The contracts negotiated between investment banks and their clients seek to align their interests and provide incentives for investment banks to obtain the requisite information. The aim is to provide clients with advice that is in their best interest while also giving the investment bank the highest profits. The models discussed in this book were either pointing out the conflict of interest and how it manifests itself in the advice investment banks provide, and in many cases I also discussed models that showed how contractual arrangements can be used to mitigate these conflicts of interest. Given the variety of services investment banks provide, it has, however, not been possible to develop a general framework to analyse and address the conflict of interest inherent in the relationship between investment banks and their clients.

Investment Banking Business Not Considered While I have covered the most common services investment banks provide, there are still some areas that require further research. Many investment banking activities not covered in this book, however, have applications in other areas of finance and can be investigated with these tools. Investment into private equity, hedge funds, investment into companies, or the retention of securities issued for investment purposes have not been addressed. These are, however, investment decisions by the investment bank and can therefore be addressed with common theories on the valuation of securities and portfolio theory. Similarly have I not covered the areas of prime brokerage and securities lending. Prime brokerage, apart from providing brokerage services, also involves securities lending to the client as well as the investment bank borrowing securities to cover short positions. The lending of securities is similar to the provision of loans in commercial banks, even though the terms are quite different, and can be addressed with the tools developed there. Similarly, borrowing securities will be part of a trading strategy and as such is best analysed in that context.

I have also not covered the role of the middle and back offices, who are both not generating revenue and not client-facing. The middle office concerns itself with the clearing and settlement of securities, ensuring all trades are conducted properly, the securities allocated, and payments made and received. This is mostly an administrative task that has very limited influence on the services provided—brokerage, asset management, securities underwriting, market making, and proprietary trading. Where it can have an impact in the settlement of trades, the concerns are similar to the settlement in the payments network between commercial banks and the tools developed there can be used to analyse this issue. Risk management is also located in the middle office, and it affects mainly proprietary trading and any long-term investments the investment bank has made and should be addressed as part of trading and investment strategies. Risks also arise in derivatives markets through counterparty risk from open positions; the analysis of these risks is very similar to that of interbank lending between commercial banks. Finally, treasury management seeks the optimal investment of short-term funds belonging to the investment bank and the raising of any additional funds. The decisions in this area can be addressed using techniques from working capital management and investment theory.

The back office supports investment banking activities by providing general administrative support, including facilities management and human resource management. The back office is also responsible for the strategic direction of the investment bank, be it in expanding their business, its focus, or the merger with other investment or commercial banks. Developing strategies to improve the profitability of investment banks are also developed here. Like the middle office, there is no direct interaction with the clients of investment banks, and most decisions in both offices can be analysed with tools developed in other areas of finance and strategy.

Regulatory aspects I have only considered in specific circumstances where they might affect the advice given, such as Chinese Walls for financial analysts or dual capacity in proprietary trading. Compared to commercial banks, investment banks are lightly regulated in many ways. While they face many regulatory constraints, these are often concerning specific activities and involve disclosure requirements or constraints on the provision of information to selected investors only. Where such constraints have a meaningful impact on the relationship between an investment bank and its clients, these aspects have been included in the model assumptions and are therefore not specifically considered.

Open Questions The theories presented in this book address individual services investment banks provide. A holistic view of investment banking activities is not possible. It is, for example, unclear, how investment banks should allocate resources internally. As all institutions are facing resource constraints, and investment banks are no exemption, it is important to allocate the existing resources efficiently. However, having to take into account that activities are often complementary, standard allocation techniques developed in management accounting might not be appropriate. It is expected that investment banks provide analyst coverage of clients whose securities they have underwritten or who they have advised on mergers. It would therefore not be possible to remove resources completely from financial analysts. These interdependencies of different services investment banks provide make the question of resource allocation very difficult.

With universal banking having been the norm in Continental Europe since before the Second World War, and a clear trend in this direction in many other countries since the 1990s, it has not been much investigated how lending to clients might affect the advice given. While some models exist that address this concern, the research is merely in its infancy. We also know very little about the risk exposure investment banks have to their clients from providing financial innovations. It is often necessary to retain significant proportions of securities that have been created or act as the counterparty to clients purchasing such securities. How this affects incentives to provide such innovations remains unclear, as much as concerns about such risks might affect advice given in mergers and acquisitions or the issuance of other securities.

A final, less well-understood problem is the interconnection of investment banks with other financial institutions and shadow banks. Having widespread interactions with institutional investors, such as insurance companies, pension funds, hedge funds, or mutual funds, their exposure in terms of revenue, but also counterparty risk, might affect not only systemic risk in the financial sector as a whole but also the relationship with these clients.

While we have a good understanding about the relationship of investment banks with their clients and how contractual arrangements are used to mitigate the effect conflicts of interest have, there are many aspects of investment banking that we so not know well enough. With much of the theoretical research focused on commercial banks, it might prove to be beneficial to also increase our understanding of investment banking further, especially focusing on the interactions of the services provided with each other and also across different clients.

Problem Sets

Problems Sets for Part I

Problem 1

Tenggara is a developing country which has started to develop a stock market that seeks to attract local companies to list their shares. Accounting and disclosure standards are still not comparable to those of more advanced economies, although there are plans to enhance them in the future. Listings have so far been sought directly, making use of the latest online technology for buyers to subscribe to the issues brought to market. This was done as investment banks showed little interest and no support for the introduction of the local stock market, having proposed to list on other stock markets in the region instead. Having rejected this proposal, Tenggara's government has sought the current arrangement to reduce the costs of engaging investment banks, who charge considerable fees for the usually small offers in the country, if they are even interested. While a small number of companies have successfully listed, these were mostly local subsidiaries of larger international companies, and local companies were very limited in securing a listing. Many companies had started the process of registering with the online platform, but the interest of buyers has been very low. Critics of the current approach to developing the stock market blame the exclusion of investment banks in the process for this lack of success and consequently demand that Tenggara takes the more conventional route to issue new shares through investment bank underwriting.

Is this the only way to make listings of local companies on the stock exchange easier for companies?

A. Krause, *Theoretical Foundations of Investment Banking*, Springer Texts in Business and Economics, https://doi.org/10.1007/978-3-031-58060-4

Problem 2

In Samia, Makka Holinen is the head of new listings at the local stock exchange. Looking back over the past few years, she finds new listings in the technology sector have overall performed disappointingly, while those in more traditional sectors have been more successful. Having taken into account the higher risks in the technology sector, this effect still persists and has led to discussions whether the listing requirements for technology stocks should be tightened. Makka points out that while this would obviously improve the quality of listings, it would mainly be achieved by reducing the number of listings in these sectors, rather than improve the quality of companies itself. She points out that improving the prospects of technology companies is generally more difficult than for traditional sectors, not least due to rapid technological progress and uncertain demand structures for new products. Instead, she suggests to look at how listings are conducted and see whether the processes contribute to this development. The role of investment banks should be looked at in particular.

Why would investment banks distort the listing of companies such that technology stocks are faring worse than traditional stocks?

Problem 3

Carlos Severiano has recently taken early retirement in lieu of redundancy and received a significant lump sum in compensation. He seeks to invest this money into the stock market for long-term returns, but has not the requisite knowledge to evaluate the prospects of companies. Therefore, he seeks to acquire relevant information from a small investment bank to aid his decision-making. Upon reviewing the files he received, covering a wide range of companies, he notices that information on many companies seems to be missing and any information provided in the pack is negative in that they suggest the companies will be performing worse than expected. He complains to his contact at the investment bank that they have not provided him with information on the other companies. They respond that he has received the full set of reports they have available and only been charged for those companies he has received information on.

Why is there no information on many companies and what is the likely outlook for those companies not included?

Problem 4

Nusinia has strict regulations on financial services, any activities are strictly controlled: any public statements require government approval and banks are generally not allowed to buy or sell securities. As the government sees any activity by banks with suspicion and against the national interest, not many banks have entered the market in Nusinia. This has resulted in virtually non-existing capital markets for bonds or stocks. Businesses gently pressure the government to allow capital markets to develop in order that they can finance future investments more easily and attract some foreign capital. The government is hesitant and claims that investment banks offer no real benefits as they just take a slice of any capital raised, adding little value in the process. Using online platforms allows investors to buy and sell stocks or bonds, so investment banks are no longer needed.

Do investment banks add any value beyond distributing stocks and shares?

Problem 5

Aliena Vikolova has inherited a significant amount of money from a relative, and she approached her bank, Agricultural Bank plc., for advice on its investment for a period of a few months to consider the best options for her future. She is directed towards the asset management division, but her short-term plans are not suitable for their business model, and she is instead referred to an advisor working with this division to cover instances like hers. Seeking a higher return than deposit accounts, this advisor directs her to a range of investment funds and talks her through the options that are available. Finally he firmly recommends a number of funds by a small but well-respected investment company. Having followed this advice, a few months later she seeks advice from another bank that positions itself as being strong in advising individuals with considerable but not very high wealth. In a first meeting, her advisor tells her bluntly that the advice she had been given previously was bad. She has invested in funds that are among the most expensive in the market for initial fees and are not really suitable for her needs. Instead he proposes another range of products that he says is more in line with her needs. Although they charge a higher management fee, they are cheaper in the long run and overall suit her profile better.

Aliena Vikolova asks herself whether she can trust the advice given by her new advisor. She does not know whether one or both advisors are providing good advice or why they might differ so much in their recommendations. Can you explain some of the motivations of her advisors?

Problem 6

Carsten Stockl has been advising clients on suitable investments for many years and achieved a high satisfaction rate with his customers. His advice has always been free of charge as he was paid a fee for referring business to them by the investment providers, mutual funds, real estate companies, insurances, and others. More than other colleagues, he used to have a customer base that usually had quite specific needs on their investments. His customers were highly satisfied with the advice given, such that he usually had the highest ranking. As these rankings are made public to customers, more and more customers have sought to switch advice to him. Over time his satisfaction scores have reduced and are now only marginally above that of colleagues.

Carsten Stockl blames this development on the high workload due to all the additional customers he has to cover. Is there an alternative explanation?

Problem 7

Chandapoon Ramaswamy is a well-known trader who has made a name for himself through frequent appearances on television, mostly on programs concerning stock market developments, but also in mainstream news reports to answer questions on significant events in the stock market. Given his status as a well-known and highly successful trader, he has set up his own company that allows subscribers to receive regular trading tips through email prior to the start of the trading day. The number of subscribers to his newsletter has been very low and not improved significantly over time, despite being given effectively free advertising opportunities during his television appearances. A common response he has heard from the public when asked why they do not subscribe to his newsletter was that if the tips he gives are that good, he surely has used them already, and it will now be too late to make profits. The fortunes of his newsletter significantly improve once Chandapoon Ramaswamy starts to publish his trading records in nearly real-time format and changes the focus of his newsletters on warnings of stocks that he believes will be underperforming in the short run. The number of subscribers significantly increases in a short period of time.

How can you explain the sudden success of the newsletter?

Problem 8

Winslow Financial Advisors Ltd. recommends financial products to its clients. Many clients, however, think that the recommendations often turn out to be wrong when looked at retrospectively. Clients find that the way Winslow Financial

Advisors Ltd. makes its recommendations is akin to a "black box", and they do not understand the basis for their recommendations and how this is suitable for their specific needs. Many clients have therefore requested that they are given the information itself, and it is explained to them clearly how this information gives rise to the recommendations they provide. Winslow Financial Advisors Ltd., however, refuses to do so with the argument that information is not easily conveyed, and it would therefore not help their clients.

Would providing the information as requested improve the advice given by Winslow Financial Advisors Ltd.?

Problem 9

A talk show on Radio Capital asks for opinions on the importance of the financial sector relative to manufacturing and other services in the economy. The discussion quickly turns on the role of investment banks in particular, and one listener calls in to say that in her view investment banks do not add any value to the economy and their demise would not make any difference for anyone, except for those working in them. She elaborates that they are similar to retailers in that they just bring people together and that could be done much cheaper and faster using online platforms.

Do you agree with this assessment of the role of investment banks?

Problems Sets for Part II

Problem 10

Rolltech plc. has made an offer to buy their competitor Glide Inc. from its current owner. Both companies are well established with their main business focusing on ball-bearings for a wide range of applications. After months of negotiation, the deal fell through as the current owner did not accept the direction the business would take, with a stronger focus on energy generation rather than transport solutions. A few days after the negotiations had been terminated, the investment bank of Rolltech plc. sends its invoice for the termination fee that had been agreed and at the same time offers a detailed debrief for senior management to discuss ways forward. The CEO is livid about being presented with such a bill as he has come out of the negotiations with no benefits for the company. While he accepts that this was part of the contract they signed and was thus payable, he continues to rant in the debrief the coming week that now he understands why the investment bank did not really advise him well. He claims that as they were being paid anyway, they had no interest in the outcome whatsoever and should have put more effort in advising him better.

How would you as a member of the team advising Rolltech plc. react to this allegation?

Problem 11

Hortman plc. is a large construction company specialising in the erection of warehouses and storage facilities. It is considering to acquire Groundworks Ltd., with which they have worked together on many projects and who focus on the preparation of work sites such that construction can commence, for example, levelling sites, ensuring adequate drainage, and similar tasks. To facilitate the acquisition and due to the lack of financial expertise in the top management of Hortman plc., they have approached an investment bank to advise them on the acquisition, even though they are confident to know the other company and their owners well enough to ensure the acquisition proceeds. After initial discussions went well, they are presented with a standard contract that specifies that Hortman plc. pays 1.2% of the value of the acquisition to its investment bank on completion of the acquisition. If the acquisition does not go ahead, the investment bank is paid a nominal amount for its time and expenses. While other board members are pleased with the detailed terms and condition, Philip Hortman, the CEO and largest shareholder, is critical of it. He points out that if they only pay on completing the acquisition, the investment bank will pressure them to pay any price or accept any conditions Groundworks Ltd. might want.

How would you convince Philip Hortman that his fears are unfounded?

Problem 12

General Holdings plc. is a large globally active conglomerate with a wide range of interests in many industries and sectors. As such it is constantly looking for opportunities to add companies to its portfolio and integrating them into their business. Having wide ranging experience, their success rate on completing acquisitions is consistently high, but the number and size of acquisitions vary widely over time. As long-standing clients of Winner & Winner, an investment bank specialising in acquisition advice, they have negotiated a global contract in which they pay a fee of $5,000,000 for each acquisition they successfully complete using their advice. Due to disclosure requirements from their listings, this contract is well-known in the industry. When negotiating a contract with Winner & Winner for an upcoming acquisition of a supplier, CarPay plc., providing solutions for road charging, questions why they are not offered a similar contract to General Holdings plc. Instead they are offered a contract where they have to pay a fee of 0.78% of the deal value on its completion only. When raising their concerns about the terms of their contract, their contact at Winner & Winner says that in their circumstances this is the better contract as they do not even know if their target is willing to engage in talks, even though the company is confident about its success.

Is this claim correct?

Problem 13

PrecGlass Inc. has been bought by PrecisionMeasure plc., both supplying laboratories with highly specialised glass and measurement products, respectively. Both, having taken advice from investment banks during the acquisition, are subsequently unhappy about the advice given. While not agreeing on much as the acquisition was not entirely friendly and tension between the business are still high, both feel they have been pressured by their investment banks into a deal that could have been much better. PrecGlass Inc. mainly complains about the way its main shareholders and senior managers have been integrated into the management structure of the joint company, and PrecisionMeasure plc. thinks it has overpaid. Both blame their advisors for this situation. After the investment banks both suggested to reject the initial offer, in both cases they wanted to continue to negotiate and hope for a better offer, but the investment bank strongly suggested to accept the deal they finally agreed on after the first revision.

Can it be that both parties can be aggrieved into accepting deals that could have been improved?

Problem 14

SpaceDrive Ltd. has been founded by a leading space scientist collaborating with an engineer, previously working in the defence industry on missile development, with the aim of developing new forms of providing propulsion for space exploration. Their ideas and prototypes have often been dismissed as not realistic, wishful thinking or not feasible in practice, but they also had some significant successes in improving the efficiency of existing propulsion mechanisms. Having been backed by a small number of venture capitalists, these seek to exit their investment and plan on floating the company on the stock exchange. The rather mixed success of their developments and many questions on commercial reliability have made finding an underwriter a challenge. After having been turned down as having no prospect of succeeding in attracting sufficient interest by investors, they finally find a newly formed investment bank that is willing to underwrite the issue. They are, however, making it clear that given SpaceDrive Ltd.'s past record, they will not guarantee to sell the full stake the venture capitalist are seeking to sell, nor will they commit to a minimum price, but will let the market decide what they are willing to pay.

Why are no major investment banks willing to underwrite SpaceDrive Ltd.'s Initial Public Offering and the investment finally found offering only to attempt to sell the shares, but not guaranteeing success?

Problem 15

The CEO of Hammond plc., a national house builder, has been in very preliminary talks with the CEO of Paring plc., a competitor, about a possible merger. Both have signalled interest and decided to take things to the next level. Presenting this state of discussions to the board of Hammond plc., the board is critical about employing an investment bank for advice. Some members state that of course the investment bank will advise us to go ahead with the merger; it's how they make money, whether it's good for the company or not.

Are they correct in their criticism of investment banks' incentives?

Problem 16

Modern Antiques Ltd. buys and restores used furniture and sells these online and in a small number of stores around the country. They have been a family business since they were founded over 30 years ago, but now some family members want to leave the business, and in order to prepare for an envisaged expansion of their business, they seek a listing on the stock exchange. They are a well-recognised name in the furniture business with a solid outlook, steady income, and their expansion of the business is generally seen as a positive move. In preparing their forthcoming public offering, they have been meeting with their investment bank and been told the usual procedure is to gauge the market interest through book building and, based on the feedback returned there, set an offer price. This offer price would then be guaranteed by the investment bank. Thomas Asburton, the majority shareholder and CEO, is surprised by this procedure. Sounding a little bit annoyed he says to the investment banking team he meets with: "So, I pay you a lot of money to underwrite these shares, but you do only do so once you know that it will sell at that price? This sounds like a great business model for you, buy what you already sold and then charge a big fee on top. If you just sound out the market, you are not doing anything, I cannot see why that is good for us".

Being in the investment banking team, how would you respond?

Problem 17

BioPharm plc. has recently listed their shares at the stock exchange through an initial public offering, that generally was deemed a success by market observers. On listing, the price quickly stabilised at $56, after having been issued at $45. At a debrief meeting a week after the listing, the investment banking team presents to the board of BioPharm plc. how the entire process worked and where some challenges lay. They report in particular on the process leading up to the book-building where they thought they require a substantial number of meetings with potential investors, but this was not necessary as investors were more quickly sold on the merits of the company than anticipated. The board is of course pleased with this information, but also points out that they were confident about the prospects of their company as they had lots of interest from competitors to acquire them or to merge. In hindsight the board thinks that the underpricing was quite high and the value added by the investment bank in determining an adequate offer price was low. One board member goes even so far to suggest that they should have agreed a much cheaper best efforts contracts as the investment bank did pretty much nothing of value and they probably would have achieved a higher price on top of that.

Is the board member correct in his claim that a best effort contract would have been better?

Problem 18

ACorn Ltd. is seeking a listing on the stock exchange and to that effect looks into appointing an underwriter. For its CEO, Stanley Hope, it is obvious that they will contact a few investment banks and then choose the best offer among those bids, similar to any other procurement decision. Julianna Timbourgh, who attends the board meeting in her capacity as future head of investor relations, says that this move would be counterproductive. All the companies she has worked for previously had only approached one investment bank at a time and usually taken the first offer that was made. For that reason she thinks Acron Ltd. should follow a similar approach. On being asked how this way of appointing an underwriter can be better, she is not able to give a straight answer.

What should she have replied?

Problem 19

Hoffmann Ltd. has appointed a lead underwriter who now seeks to assemble a syndicate to ensure a wider investors base can be reached. To this effect, members of the team at Hoffmann Ltd. pressure their lead underwriter to increase the size of the syndicate from the proposed five investment banks. They argue that by including more banks, they could reach a wider range of investors, making the issue more successful, even if it costs them a bit more to compensate for the larger number of investment banks involved. The lead underwriter resists this move and points out that this would be counterproductive to the issue. Hoffmann Ltd. is accusing their investment bank of refusing to increase the syndicate size so they can obtain a larger share of the fees, and it is purely for the investment banks' own benefit, rather than improving the success of the issue.

Is the lead underwriter right in suggesting to limit the syndicate size to five members?

Problem 20

Ramsey Inc. is a family-owned business mainly specialising in the production of pipes for chemical plants and power stations. Having grown significantly in recent years and seeking to expand overseas, they have decided to raise capital through a listing on the stock exchange. In preparing for the first steps in the process, the board, consisting of seven family members, has to decide on the approach to appoint an investment bank as underwrite for their issue. Having very little knowledge of the procedures involved, never having had dealings with investment banks before, and a relationship with a commercial bank that does not offer underwriting services, they do not know how to approach an investment bank. During the discussion, quickly two factions emerge, one wants to appoint a single underwriter but have them compete for this business through a tendering process, while the other faction wants to approach an investment bank exclusively, which they have heard lots of good comments about, but, because of their limited size, suggest this investment bank should form a syndicate with other banks.

Which approach is preferable?

Problem 21

Michael Learing is a wealthy but not very sophisticated investor, and he relies on his broker giving him investment advice and is often participating in IPOs. However, he complains to his broker that whenever an IPO is not going well, he obtains a larger allocation of shares, making very little profit on a large investment, while in very successful IPOs, he is allocated only a small amount, even though he makes a lot of profits in these cases. He feels cheated in that his loyalty is not rewarded.

Is Michael Learing right to suggest his broker exploits his willingness to participate in IPOs?

Problem 22

Longsoft plc. has recently gone public, and generally the offering has been judged a success with high investor demand and a price realised at the upper end of the initial estimate. At the debriefing a week after the listing, Longsoft plc.'s team complains about the high level of underpricing. Having seen the allocation, they see that the investment bank benefitted a range of long-standing clients that have a known allegiance with their lead underwriter. Their stance is that those investors should have paid more and the investment bank has been giving them free money at their expense. The underwriter points out that while these investors are loyal clients of theirs, they are well informed and would not participate if they do not obtain adequate returns. On being prompted to justify how a return of nearly 30% would be adequate rather than excessive in a market where annual returns are about 10–15%, the investment bank representative looks around his team in search for an answer.

How would the lead underwriter justify the underpricing?

Problem 23

Sterling & Co. is a boutique investment bank specialising in the issuing of fixed income instruments to issuers from smaller and emerging countries. It has a range of investor contacts, ranging from highly sophisticated hedge fund managers to wealthy, but not very informed, individuals. One such wealthy individual, Jorge Sobrano, has recently changed his broker to Sterling & Co. and on this broker's advice participated in a zero-bond issue by a large government-backed road construction company in a developing country, and he was allocated a large amount, his full subscription. Shortly after the bond starts trading, it falls below its issue price, and Jorge Sobrano complains to his broker about being used by Sterling & Co. as a dumping ground for bad issues. Also, he adds, he had never his full subscription being honoured, only now when he makes a loss.

How can you convince Jorge Sobrano that this is an unfortunate start to their relationship and how will you seek to maintain his custom?

Problem 24

Trianos LLP is a wealth management company set up with the sole purpose of managing the wealth of the Olawemu family. Having made forays into venture capital provision and not been very successful, it has been decided to withdraw from those activities and instead seek to invest into young companies as they are being listed. The aim is to take advantage of the underpricing of IPOs to generate good returns and then support the company for a time afterwards as a long-term, but rather passive, investor. Looking into the IPO market, an analyst at Trianos LLP makes the observation that in Waading, the underpricing typically stands at 12–15%, while for comparable companies in Reinging, the underpricing is 17–20%. Reinging is well-known for its very strict investor protection rules, resulting in stringent disclosure requirements and many adverse court rulings if requirements have not been followed meticulously, causing losses to investors. In contrast, Waading takes a much more business-friendly approach; while the rules are only slightly less strict than in Reinging, courts are much more hesitant to rule in favour of investors if they are broken.

The analyst believes that the stricter enforcement of rules in Reinging results in investors requiring much higher returns, and hence underpricing is higher. Is this a correct assessment?

Problem 25

SayIt Ltd. provides a popular online platform for discussions and sharing of information, covering all areas of interest. Since it was announced that the company seeks to list their shares on the stock exchange, a large publicity campaign has been started by some activists seeking larger control of the contents that is posted. Backed by a number of prominent figures, a movement has formed that seeks to buy shares in the IPO and then very quickly dump the shares in the market to make sure the stock price falls well below the issue price. While a target price has already been made public at the early stages of the IPO process, the investment bank seeks an urgent meeting with the aim to lower the target price. SayIt Ltd. is surprised and correctly remarks that this campaign does not affect the value of their shares and any drop in the price would only be temporary as they would soon run out of shares to sell.

While the investment bank agrees that any drop in stock price would probably be only temporary, why do they want to reduce the offer price?

Problem 26

ControlRobo plc. has just been taken public. It was seen as the hottest IPO for quite a long time as the company holds a number of highly desired patents in producing and navigating nano-robots with potential medical applications, among many other areas. The company is generally seen as not being well run as it is controlled by two brothers, both of whom are specialists in robotics rather than business. After the IPO they have retained a share of 67% in the company. Despite these shortcomings in the management of the company, the IPO was highly successful and had a larger-than-average underpricing of 47%. Many professional investors in such businesses sought to buy shares in the IPO, but most were not allocated any shares. It emerges that a stake of at least 15% has been allocated to Alpha LLP, a hedge fund that is well-known for its pro-active approach to companies it invests in. Its attempts to interfere in the running of the business are not much liked by companies, but the companies they invest in all perform exceptionally well. The other investors complain that the high underpricing has been chosen such that Alpha LLP could be allocated a large part of the shares and as they are the favourite clients of the lead underwriter, they have been given preferential treatment. ControlRobo plc. has also complained about this allocation as it had hoped for a more widespread shareholder base. Furthermore, they consider the underpricing to be too high and causing them significant losses, especially as the stock price is now higher than the top end of the initial valuation of the investment bank.

Has ControlRobo plc. been given a bad service by the investment bank?

Problem 27

PharmDev plc. is a small pharmaceutical company that produces and develops medicines for use in developing countries. Their products are modified from main medicines such that storage and transport are less critical to maintain their effectiveness, such as the need for cooling or short shelf lives. To finance their research, they raised capital in an IPO. They agreed to have the issue underpriced by about 20% in order to ensure the success of the issue, and the return on the first day was in line with that agreement. They had also agreed to allocate a sizeable fraction of the shares to a long-standing partner in research to fortify their strategic alliance. Once all documents have been disclosed, the stock price jumps by another 15%. The investment by their strategic partner has been interpreted very positively by the market. As this has always been the plan, PharmDev plc. feels that the underpricing was not 20% as agreed, but rather 35%, which they feel is rather excessive.

Are they correct to complain about this large underpricing?

Problem 28

The IPO of GreenGas plc., a producer of biogas, was significantly oversubscribed, and many investors were disappointed to not receive an allocation at all or an allocation significantly below their subscription. Comments in the financial press during the days following the IPO show widespread dissatisfaction with the lead underwriter. It had secured a greenshoe option of 10% of the offer, but did not exercise their discretion on providing more investors with an allocation. In their defence, the lead underwriter says they were surprised by the level of oversubscription, but would not want to increase the price above the initially announced target range as a fairness to all investors. They also claim that exercising the greenshoe option would not have made a material difference and therefore had decided against it.

Is this explanation of the lead underwriter believable?

Problem 29

Looking at the trading in the first few days after an IPO, you observe that more underpricing is commonly associated with more trading volume, but also with stock prices that fluctuate less. As you work in the newly setup department for investor relations of Abbott Ltd. and prepare for the upcoming IPO of the company, you suggest in a meeting with senior management that they should aim for very little underpricing. The benefits in terms of trading volume and less fluctuations for the stock price do not really affect the company at all, while underpricing costs money. In addition, you question how there can be a relationship between underpricing and trading, as stock markets are difficult to predict. The investment banks that have joined the meeting look down on their papers as you make this remark and hold back laughing.

Why are you wrong in your assertion?

Problem 30

After an IPO, many investors have sold their shares very quickly to realise their gains from underpricing. Afterward, many of these investors are claiming that the underwriters selling more shares than they had initially claimed in the IPO have reduced their profits and only benefitted the underwriters.

Is this assessment correct?

Problem 31

You are an assistant to the CEO of Greenhill Ltd. and as the company considers a listing on the stock exchange, you have been asked to look into the characteristics of a wide range of investment banks with the aim to see which investment bank is most suitable for Greenhill Ltd. You observe that investment banks that are commonly regarded as being the best have higher success rates in IPOs, but they also charge much higher fees than less prestigious competitors. You present this finding as being the result of good companies being able to afford the high fees charged by the leading investment banks. An experienced board member challenges this interpretation and says that given his experience, it is that all companies want to be underwritten by top investment banks, but it is investment banks that turn down less good companies. No one worries about the fees.

Who is correct in their assessment?

Problem 32

Working for the investment bank of Harding & Son, Slavia Mycheslav talks at the opening of a new museum in the banking district to Heino Nymarken, who has recently joined Kleinmann Bank plc., a large lender with a small investment banking division, in which he works. Jokingly, Slavia Mycheslav says that of course her bank gets the much higher quality companies to underwrite; all Kleinmann Bank plc. will care about is how the increased capital will affect their loans; they do not look at the quality of the company they underwrite, and hence many IPOs will be of moderate success. Surely, everyone realises that and hence Kleinmann Banks plc. can only charge small fees, while Harding & Son provide a better service and charge the appropriate fee for that.

Is Slavia Mycheslav's brutal assessment of Kleinmann Bank's incentives accurate?

Problem 33

Baking Brothers Inc. is a leading bakery chain operating nationally, and it has begun into expand in other countries as well. Its rapid expansion is seen critically by many market observers, but the management is convinced of its strategic planning. To finance a major expansion of shops and factories overseas, they seek to issue a bond. Having approached some reputable investment banks to manage the issue of this bond, they have been politely refused. Their long-standing lender, who has provided them with loans in the last few years, directs them to their small underwriting team for further consideration. It is only after they have consulted with their corporate lending department to exchange information on Baking Brothers Inc. that they indicate a willingness to underwrite the bond issue.

How can you explain these different decisions by the investment banks on the one hand and their lender on the other hand?

Problem 34

The Sameda Stock Exchange seeks to make itself more attractive to new listings, especially for innovative smaller companies. These companies had previously complained about finding it difficult to secure the services of an approved underwriter for their stocks, which used to be a prerequisite for obtaining a listing. The new listing regulations now allow for a direct listing of a company, and Sameda Stock Exchange has provided an auction-style platform that can be used to sell stocks to those investors willing to pay the highest price. To the surprise of the Sameda Stock Exchange and many of the companies seeking a listing through this new mechanism, investor demand has been low, and the few companies that successfully listed their stocks were soon delisted again; either taken private because of their poor performance or taken over by other companies. The delistings usually occurred at prices well below the initial offer price.

Why was the innovation of a direct listing on the Sameda Stock Exchange not successful?

Problem 35

George Cooper frequently seeks to participate in IPOs and subscribes to issues underwritten by some of the leading investment banks. He does not get an allocation of shares often, and if he does obtain an allocation of shares, the returns are usually lower than in other IPOs he has not been successful in. A friend suggests that he seeks financial advice from an investment bank instead of subscribing to any IPO, such that he can avoid those that perform poorly.

Would such advice improve his returns from subscribing to IPOs?

Problem 36

Spice & More plc. has recently acquired a competitor, and while integrating this company into their own operations, they discover that there are significant problems with the ability of their customers to pay outstanding invoices. The wide customer base was one of the main reasons for the acquisition. Given they have made it clear to the investment bank advising them that this was their main objective, they are unhappy with the advice given by the investment bank to proceed once they had conducted a due diligence assessment of their competitor in confidence. The CEO of Spice & More plc. in particular points out that the way the investment bank is paid provides the investment bank with strong incentives for the acquisition to be completed. He points in particular to a clause where the majority of the fee is payable to the investment bank only if the acquisition is completed, while only a small break-up fee would be payable otherwise. He argues that the investment bank was driven by their desire to complete the acquisition such that they could obtain their fee, but instead should have either advised on abandoning the acquisition or negotiated a much lower price.

How would the investment bank respond to this complaint?

Problem 37

Gerhard Bank AG has been hired by Inform GmbH to manage their initial public offering. During the first meeting between the investment banking team and the working group from Inform GmbH managing the process internally, the investment bankers explain in detail the process of going public from this point until the shares are listed on the local stock exchange. When explaining the book-building mechanism they seek to employ, the Chief Financial Officer of Inform GmbH interjects that this sounds way too complicated to him. Why does Gerhard Bank AG go to such great lengths of determining the price and share allocation if all that is needed is an auction platform for investors to submit bids? Similarly, banks buying the shares first and then selling them on just a few days later seems to be an unnecessary step.

How would you explain the advantages of the processes typically followed in underwriting?

Problem 38

The Competition Commission investigates the behaviour of investment banks in IPOs. They have heard the view of companies who have recently gone public that underpricing to them is equivalent to an additional fee they have to pay and which is not detailed in the underwriting contract. One company director suggested that investment banks should issue the stocks at their full value and instead charge a higher fee for their services. This way the costs of going public would become more transparent to companies.

Would this suggested transparency work?

Problem 39

The merger of Hamamoto plc. and Seco Industries plc. was hailed as the biggest and most important merger of an American and Japanese company. Having been widely promoted by the advising investment banks as a milestone for the future development of both companies, the merger turned out to be a failure. After only a few months, it became clear that the different corporate cultures could not be reconciled and the newly formed joined company is considering splitting along its original lines. Many commentators now see this failure, as well as many others before, as evidence of investment banks pushing for mergers to go ahead, presumably as they are then paid high fees for their services.

Is this a fair assessment of the motivations of investment banks?

Problem 40

"If the money is right, investment banks will underwrite any stock, however bad its prospects are".

Is this statement true?

Problems Sets for Part III

Problem 41

John Neumann is a fund manager, whose fund is a long-term client of your investment bank. As part of the agreement the fund has with us, he is given access to analyst reports. At a meeting to renew the agreement, John Neumann is highly critical of the quality of the reports provided. He points out that each and every report has been overly optimistic about the prospects of the company concerned, evidenced by the fact that the returns in nearly all cases are less than those implied by the analyst report. Representing the investment bank, you point out that this positive bias is inevitable and he should simply account for this in his decision-making. John Neumann replies that if you know about this problem, why don't you simply correct for this distortion.

How would you reply?

Problem 42

Contex plc. is a leading provider of technology for contactless payments. Their business is going strongly and they have attracted a number of analysts providing positive coverage of their prospects. The head on the investor relations team that is also the first point of contact for financial analysts seeking information about the company is overall very satisfied with the reports published by the analysts. There is, however, one analyst whose reports, although overall positive, are consistently much less upbeat than any other analyst report. He puts this down to some bad blood between the investment bank this analyst works for and the CEO of Contex plc. After a dispute over advice received in an acquisition a few years ago, he has made it clear to that bank that, as long as he has any say, they will never again advise the company on any transactions.

Is it correct to attribute the less positive coverage to the dispute on previous advice?

Problem 43

Looking across analyst reports and comparing their recommendations as well as forecasts, you notice when comparing the affiliation of analysts with investment banks that if investment banks had been advising a company on any transaction in the last few years, the reports were usually more positive than those that did not advise the company, even though these were still more positive than would be justified by subsequent performance.

Are you right to attribute this observation to the fact they have been advising the company recently and the overall positive, although less positive, coverage of all the other analysts to their hope of advising the company in the future?

Problem 44

ConTech plc. has been found to fraudulently increase its revenue numbers over the last few years. While many had suspected that their financial reporting and disclosure statements were too good to be true, none of the financial analysts has taken up these rumours and even questioned their disclosures. All analysts had published positive reports, but it now transpires that some, mainly junior, analysts had raised some concerns in internal discussions, but did not make them public. At an inquiry into the failing of ConTech Plc. and the role financial analysts played in covering their misconduct up, one member of the inquiry panel quotes John Maynard Keynes, a financial analyst, who said: "Worldly wisdom teaches that it is better for reputation to fail conventionally than to succeed unconventionally".

How does this quote relate to the position the financial analyst found himself in?

Problem 45

Priska Romain is the CEO of SwissMade Plc., a holding company with a portfolio of Swiss-based producers covering the high-end of the market, such as mechanical watches, medical equipment, and specialist construction machines. During a rather informal meeting with financial analysts and journalists at the reception held for the opening of a new headquarter, she responds to questions how it is that her company is consistently underperforming the predictions of analysts. In her reply she embarrasses the present analysts by stating that if their employers would not tout for business by trying to please her with ever more upbeat public statements, they might be a bit more realistic in what can be achieved. Another problem, she says, is not only that they try to be unnecessarily positive but that many analysts seem to have very little understanding of the company and do not understand much of the industry she operates in. So going back to study, those finance and strategy book might improve things. A junior analyst says that they are not paid for the business she gives to his bank, but his and other pay packages are purely based on the quality of their reports. Priska Romain laughs and says that in that case he probably should pay the bank to work there. Before turning away, she says in the old days it was analysts like you openly vying for business and I am sure you were on a bonus if I signed up, but things have not really changed since then.

Can you explain why the quality of reports seems unchanged despite the changes that have occurred?

Problem 46

During a meeting to discuss the extension of brokerage contracts, Adelphi Funds Group, managing a large number of individual investment funds, discuss the conditions for access to analyst reports to their individual fund managers. Ita Vayassani, as the CEO of the group, finds the price that has been charged in the past as too high. He points out that all he gets, more or less, are reports that say what everyone else already in the business knows. There have been many instances of events that have not been picked up in these reports, even just mentioning them as possible scenarios would have helped investment decisions. He thinks the reports are overall of poor quality. Leading the brokerage division, Vaclav Racinski says that they have overhauled their analyst division and now he can get more detailed information on the remuneration of each analyst and as clients are now more informed how they are viewed internally, they have more incentives to improve the quality of their reports as that will be reflected in higher pay and a wider recognition of the quality they produce. Ita Vayassani points out that improving quality is good, but if he just gets more detailed analysis of things he already knows, there is hardly a point as he will not learn anything new; he wants to hear alternative views. Therefore he does not think that the reports will become more valuable to him just because they changed some contract terms.

Is Ita Vayassani correct to dismiss the changes the analyst contract has undergone as being of limited value to him?

Problem 47

As head of a group of junior analysts your role is to assess their performance over the last few years and make recommendations for promotions. Part of the assessment is to determine the quality of those reports they completed alone or under supervision, but also the contributions each has made to joint reports. Although not the only criterion, one aspect is to look at how their recommendations and target prices compare to the actual events. While the results naturally will be mixed, you spot that in most cases junior analysts' report were consistent with what most reports from competitors showed, even if this turned out to be very wrong. You find only a few instances in which deviating opinions were voiced, and in many cases these were shown to be correct. The same analysts, though, in most other reports were not deviating from the consensus, even if this was shown to be wrong. You find that where the consensus was wrong, sometimes internal notes suggested that different scenarios had been considered, but then dismissed without further explanations.

How can you explain that in some cases the deviating scenarios are included, while in other cases they are not?

Problem 48

Constantin Bulgakin is a financial analyst providing coverage for a range of companies in the pharmaceutical industry. Due to regulatory changes, his employment contract has been amended and rather than obtaining a fraction of the revenue the companies generate for his employer, he will only be rewarded for the accuracy of his reports. He fears that this new arrangement will lead to a reduction in his remuneration, and he will lose access to companies that he relies on to provide him with information for his reports.

Are these concerns justified?

Problem 49

Joyce Banowolo has been accused of providing low-quality reports on companies she covers as financial analyst. A number of clients of the investment bank that employs her have mentioned that her reports are all overly optimistic if compared to the actual outcomes and she never anticipates any unexpected developments, even though in retrospect it is obvious that with access to information she has been provided with, this should have been possible.

Given this negative feedback from clients, Joyce Banowolo is asked to meet her manager to explain the quality of her reports. After this meeting, she has to write a brief note to him addressing the concerns. What would she put into this note?

Problem 50

Hiroki Mayosama has obtained excellent contacts with companies that he covers as financial analyst. His contacts have allowed his employer to gain numerous advising contracts in mergers and acquisitions these companies have been involved in. The price for his ability is that his analyst reports are seen as being of questionable quality by his clients in the investor community. They seem to mostly ignore his reports and see them as not much more than an advert for the company subject to the report.

With Chinese Walls being introduced, will this affect his recommendations and remuneration?

Problems Sets for Part IV

Problem 51

Computech Inc. has grown considerably over the last few years. It has acquired many subsidiaries in various countries and partnerships across the globe, requiring ever more sophisticated processes and structures to navigate the often complex local regulations and tax rules. These more complex needs have lead Computech Inc. to review its policy with respect to investment banking relationships. Thus far they have sought ad hoc advice from the investment bank that seemed most appropriate for their specific needs, such as investment banks that specialise in specific countries or types of transactions, such as hostile takeovers. To this effect they have relied on small and specialised investment banks, who would not be suitable for a wider range of advice that is needed. One drawback they have using this strategy is, while specific advice on transactions is of high quality, they would often require solutions that require the development of securities with specific features to meet regulatory constraints. In many cases they are only aware of this after the transaction has been completed, but the investment bank advising them does not provide them with such securities.

Would changing to a mainstream investment bank for all their needs be beneficial?

Problem 52

Jérôme Cheniers is the head of the treasury department of an internationally operating company. In response to ever more restrictive practices in many countries to increase the tax businesses pay, he has relied on new financial instruments developed by their investment banks to shift revenue and profits between jurisdictions and across different time periods legally. As the company has grown considerably in the last few years, thought is given to establish a link with larger investment banks to reflect the wider needs of the company. Jérôme Cheniers objects to this suggestion, remarking that the smaller investment bank they currently deal with are providing them with excellent service for his department. In his experience, larger investment banks are much less innovative, having less of a big vision, and instead develop any innovations only slowly and in a piecemeal fashion in many steps, depriving them of a lot of the benefits the full innovation would have had.

From his perspective, is Jérôme Cheniers right to object to engaging larger investment banks?

Problem 53

Nisa Chanda has taken over the family business, EduChan Ltd., providing outsourcing solutions to education providers, such as schools and colleges, but in some cases also universities. To improve knowledge of local requirements, EduChan Ltd. has set up a network of subsidiaries in its main markets. This has complicated the management of the company considerably as now many rules and regulations have to be followed, but it also allows innovative ways to finance their business by tapping into local resources that had thus far not been available. Given the complexity of the issues on hand, advice would be required on these issues. For this reason and an immediate need to hedge the revenue from a large new contract, Nisa Chanda has thought about seeking more advice with an investment bank. From her family, many sitting on the board of EduChan Ltd., she gets conflicting advice. Some suggest that she should always go to the investment bank that is best for the specific circumstances as they all have different expertises; others say that having a single investment bank to go for is better. There are also those advocating to use a small boutique investment bank as they provide better service and EduChan Ltd. is not big enough to be of interest to the market leaders, while others suggest to at least try the market leaders as they have better all-round knowledge.

Focusing on the current needs of EduChan Ltd. in the area of seeking innovative solutions in managing the financial and regulatory aspects of their expansion, how would you advise Nisa Chanda?

Problem 54

Having inherited a considerable amount of cash from a relative, Anders Andersson seeks to invest these into shares. He has some experience and knowledge of the stock market and is confident that with some basic advice from an advisor of his bank, he can manage his new-found wealth independently. As he looks for some advice on his investments, he is not considering discount brokers, but instead focuses on the brokerage divisions of some reputable local banks. Just by investigating their standard fee structure, he is quite amazed how they differ between banks, but also the different schedules banks have for different types of stocks. Looking at the European stock market only, he finds the following information for two banks he picked out:

	Trade size	Grimu Bank	Flora Bank
Main index	$0-$10,000	2%	1.8%
	$10,000-$100,000	1%	1%
	$100,000 +	0.5%	0.6%
Wider index	$0-$10,000	2.5%	4%
	$10,000-$100,000	1.5%	3%
	$100,000 +	1%	2%
Small caps	$0-$10,000	5%	2.3%
	$10,000-$100,000	3%	1.5%
	$100,000 +	2%	1.2%
Other	$0-$10,000	2.5%	2.5%
	$10,000-$100,000	1.5%	1.3%
	$100,000 +	1%	1.3%

"Main index" includes all companies that are in the lead index of a European country, such as the FTSE100, DAX30, CAC40, SMI, and similar. "Wider index" includes all shares that are not included in the leading indices but wider indices, such as the FTSE 250, or in leading industry indices, while "small caps" includes all stocks that are included in small cap indices.

Anders Andersson is puzzled by the fee structure. While he understands that for larger trades the fees are reduced, the differences between the stocks in a wider index and small caps seem to make no sense. Can you explain these brokerage fees?

Problem 55

Connor Strange has grown up in a family of considerable fortune from a number of businesses. Having shown neither aptitude nor interest in running these businesses, he has happily agreed for his sister to take over once their father retires. In return for this arrangement, he has been given a lump sum to provide him with a good living. Having no experience of investing and on the advice of his father, he has instructed Forlong & Sons with the management of his wealth. Having his annual meeting to discuss the arrangements Forlong & Sons has made and any changes for the future that might become necessary, Connor Strange is surprised to hear that the last year had been rather difficult in investment terms and while his wealth did not decline, the return generated was very low. When questioning that, he is told that in the interest of long-term growth, they had invested into some more risky stocks, and this did not pay off as many lost value this year, but, so the advisor reassures him, this is likely to reverse. Connor Strange looks at him puzzled and says that he remembers well from last year that they agreed to not take any unnecessary risks as that was not to his liking. He tells his advisor to reduce the risk for the coming year, but is assured that his perception of the risk is exaggerated as they have much better information on these stocks and it appears much more risky to him than it actually is.

Unconvinced, Connor Strange leaves the meeting to think about his response. Is it that the higher risk he perceives is due to him having less information or does the bank take excessive risks?

Problem 56

Having taken responsibility for the investment of the family trust from his uncle, Sibolu Arassawake considers next steps. His uncle had over many decades managed the investments successfully and had considerable knowledge in such investments, but his ill-health does not allow him to continue this role, nor to teach his nephew the required skills. Therefore, Sibolu Arassawake's first thought is to seek out an experienced asset manager to perform most of the duties, allowing him to focus on developing the general principles on which investments should be based, such as the family's commitment to environmental concerns and human rights. In a discussion with his uncle on handing over the role, he remarks that Sibolu Arassawake could instead manage the investments himself; he always got tips from his bank when buying or selling assets. That way he would retain much more control, and it would be cheaper, too, as the advice comes free.

Investigating the brokerage fees a full-service broker would charge, and comparing this with the fees of asset managers, shows that based on average returns, the asset manager is actually cheaper. Why are the broker fees more expensive and is it therefore better to engage the asset manager?

Problem 57

Your investment bank has agreed to be added as market maker for a few well-established but small stocks and has assigned you to set up the processes to enable quoting prices from next month. Looking into the stocks concerned, you observe that the spreads quoted in the market are surprisingly narrow and prices move very little over a trading day. Looking at the costs you would face as market maker you quickly come to the conclusion that given the spreads quoted in the market, it is impossible to cover the costs. You feed your assessment back to your manager and ask if he is willing to go ahead even if this would incur losses to the investment bank.

Your manager replies that market making is not very profitable but never loses money. Is your manager right and you have assessed the costs wrongly?

Problem 58

You are overhearing two junior traders at a fund management company complaining about the price setting of market makers in some of the major stocks listed on the stock exchange. They specifically complain that in times before major announcement, when rumours are rife and not many facts are known, the spread increases significantly. Often the increase is such that profitable trading opportunities are rare until after the announcement. They quickly agree that this must be the greed of investment banks and their market makers that increases the spread to make more profits as they know traders are keen to adjust their positions.

Are market makers increasing spreads to raise their profits?

Problem 59

Looking to expand the scope of your investment banking business, you consider entering market making. While acknowledging that it is not a highly profitable business, it seems to be safe and a good diversification to your other business lines. Considering a range of stocks, you think that the business might be more profitable than you had initially believed. You observe market spreads that seem to be rather higher than what you expect them to be when trying to balance the order flow and not building up a large position in the stocks. In addition, prices seem to move more than you would expect them to achieve such a balance.

Are these observations an indication of market making not being competitive?

Problem 60

You are working at the trading desk of a leading investment bank and have performed well for many years. During your annual review, the topic of additional training requirements comes up. Having gone through lots of training since starting in your role many years ago, you have not seen that your performance has increased. Nor is there evidence that traders at other banks have caught up with your skills. Therefore you suggest that no training is required, benefitting the bank in saving money for these expensive courses and gives you a few more days to generate profits for the bank.

Your manager rejects your suggestion and says that if you do not maintain your skills, you will soon generate less profits for the bank. Is he right?

Problem 61

Peter Hillier and Nijs van Steen are traders and were hired together by Bell Bros. after graduating from university. While Nijs van Steen has been specialising in trading small companies in emerging markets, Peter Hillier has been allocated to trade US bonds. Having both been successful in their careers, Nijs van Steen has been moved to a contract that sees him receiving a much lower base salary, but also a much higher component of performance-related pay, mostly based on the returns he generates. Peter Hillier, however, has not seen a change to his contract and remains on a largely fixed wage with a small-performance component only. During one of their after-work meets, Nijs van Steen quips that he is clearly much better than his friend and therefore given a better contract.

Is Nijs van Steen right to claim that he must have superior performance to be moved to his new contract?

Problem 62

Constantin Navonin has received extensive training over the last 3 years to change trading desks from trading exotic derivatives to fixed income. His move was motivated by being able to adhere to better working hours after the birth of his first child. After a year in his new role, his existing contract is renewed, as agreed, but he is surprised to find that his new contract only has a small bonus component related to his trading performance, while this was previously a main part of his salary. He feels that during his first year, his performance was comparable to his previous role, even though profits generated were less, but he feels the market environment is much more difficult. In addition he has extensive training even during his year, and he feels this has improved his skills. He sees his new contract as a punishment for seeking to change trading desks.

Is he right in his assessment of the motivations of his employer?

Problem 63

Selkirk & Co is a long-standing investment bank that has suffered a substantial loss due to the losses accumulated by a rogue trader. It had secretly accumulated losses that were for a time threatening the survival of the bank, but through a lucky turn in the market, this could be avoided with some losses recovered as positions were liquidated. The banking regulator has asked for a complete audit of the internal processes of the trading desks at Selkirk & Co, but nothing was found to suggest that controls were more lax than at other investment banks. The regulator is quite surprised by these findings as they expected to find deficits in the internal processes and in response suggests that banks overall should improve their monitoring of traders by their managers. Having put the suggested improvements out for consultation, the overwhelming response is that the new rules are mainly burdensome but would not change the risk of future rogue traders emerging.

Why is focusing on the monitoring of traders unlikely to succeed and what would have been a better approach?

Problem 64

As the head of Internal Audit at Halfing Bank plc., you have seen through internal communications at trading desks and followed up many leads of potential rule breaking at your trading desks. You found a number of occasions where the heads of trading desks have turned a blind eye to breaking rules and in other cases helping to cover up the consequences of such rule breaks. There was no evidence that the bank suffered any losses arising from these violations of rules and so in individual meetings with the relevant managers, they pointed out that no harm was done. Putting together their findings in a report, the committee you are heading gets into an argument about the proposed remedies. You propose to tighten the rules for those heading the trading desks, effectively ruling out that they could interfere with any decisions after the fact. Making sure they cannot cover up any rules breaking should ensure that they happen less is your thinking. Another group on the committee, tough, suggests that rather than changing rules, the committee should appoint a group of staff from their department to closely monitor the activities of traders instead. You dismiss this being too costly and just duplicating the work that the heads of the trading desks should do anyway.

Is there a better proposal to improve the compliance of traders with rules?

Problem 65

Looking at the market, you notice a peculiarity in price movements. After each trade, orders in the market are updated, and bid and ask prices change in line with the order just executed; thus, prices tend to increase after a buy order and decrease after a sell order. However, you notice that the extent of these price adjustments are different and seem to cluster around two values. They tend to move either by \$0.02 or \$0.04 for the most common order sizes of 1000 shares. The larger movement is more common than the smaller movement, and other movements, like \$0.03, are very rare.

You wonder whether these movements are just randomly or is there a reason for it?

Problem 66

The Raminga Stock Exchange, together with the Financial Supervisory Board as regulator of securities firms, has introduced stringent new rules on the activities of investment banks. A particular concern of many institutional investors has been that investment banks use information on their trading plans that they share with them to optimally submit orders to the market, to benefit their own traders. Stringent rules have been put into place that prevent any communication between traders and any other parts of investment banks. Since this rule has been brought in, the market has become overall more volatile, which has raised concerns about the market quality. Institutional investors are pleased with the decision, as they report higher profits than before, which they attribute to banks not being able to siphon off some of their profits.

How can you explain these findings?

Problem 67

Colerne Agricultural Bank has developed a bond whose interest payments depend on the average crop yield across the county they are mainly operating in. Being a bank which specialises in providing services to the agricultural sector, as well as those working in it, their new offering has received widespread interest from farmers in particular. The development of the bond was triggered by the Department for Agriculture seeking out Colerne County as an area in which they monitor the impact of weather and climate change on crop yields. As part of this monitoring, they collect data on the harvest of all farms in the county, which is then published as an index using the year 2020 as the base year. The bond has proven to be very popular with farmers, but also in other areas of agriculture. Farmers in neighbouring counties have also expressed their interest in such bonds, but as due to their location, no information on crop yields is available and they fall outside of the geographical area covered by Colerne Agricultural Bank, they have been referred to their own banks. While one other bank has introduced a similar bond recently, banks in other areas are reluctant to support the issuance of such bonds. They cite the uncertainty that investors would be willing to subscribe to such bonds. Indeed, Colerne Agricultural Bank had to approach investors in more urban areas to sell the bonds, and while they have managed, they found it challenging to sell them completely, although they were successful in the end.

Colerne Agricultural Bank finds it strange that their innovation has not been copied more widely, especially by banks that have more and better contact with investors. How can you explain this reluctance to copy the innovative bond developed by Colerne Agricultural Bank?

Problem 68

A few years ago, Hameed Bank has developed a new method to authenticate large payments between companies, governments, and institutional investors. Many such transactions are often held up for considerable time by banks or government agencies to investigate the potential for fraud, corruption, money laundering, tax evasion, and many other possible criminal acts. The new authentication system allows the money transferred to be traced at any time and the government has agreed to not put payments on hold if this system is used by the bank sending and receiving the money. While the authentication system would be highly beneficial to all payers and payees, it was initially very slow to be taken up by other banks, even though the protocols required were made available for free. Other banks cited the costs in setting up a parallel system for making payments, in addition to the conventional payment system, and reported that customers saw the requirement of monies to be sent on having to use the same protocol as overly restrictive. They thus doubted that it would be profitable for them to introduce this system. It was only after Hameed Bank and a small number of other banks were successfully operating this protocol with high demand by customers that most banks followed very quickly the lead of Hameed Bank to introduce this protocol. Now there are only a small number of banks left that have not adopted this protocol.

How can you explain the sudden adoption of the protocol after the initial reluctant uptake?

Problem 69

Jerôme Hinault is head of trading at Legrande Banque SA and noticed that those trading in securities of countries that allow dual capacity seem to anticipate investor behaviour better than those in markets without dual capacity, but have a lower understanding of the market dynamics itself.

How can you explain this observation?

Problem 70

Leman & Cie have developed a new security that allows clients to reallocate financing costs across different jurisdictions through the use of innovative interest rate swap agreements. This security has been offered to clients for a while, and the uptake has been slow. Initially clients were not convinced about the benefits and whether the arrangements would be accepted by national tax authorities. With no ban of this security in sight, the uptake of this security has increased recently and it becomes more widely known in the field. Given the slow uptake of the innovation, Leman & Cie is reluctant to support the development of another innovative security. It anticipates that it would be more popular with clients, but is likely to be looked at negatively by regulators with a high possibility of it being banned after a short period of time.

Is Leman & Cie right to shelf the further development of the latest innovation?

Problem 71

Kalimantan Bank is unusual in its approach to compensating their proprietary traders. They pay them a fixed wage, which is supplemented by only a small amount of performance-related pay; this is very much in contrast to all other banks who pay most of the compensation based on the performance of a proprietary trader. Kalimantan Bank has been justifying their approach with the fact that they are very good at identifying able traders and for that reason can afford to pay high fixed remuneration. Furthermore, their engagement mostly in markets with low volatility does not generate large profits to individual traders that can be used to pay them according to their performance, thus making a fixed wage easier to administer. Their remuneration policy has become more widely known when a number of competitors were exposed to significant losses in their proprietary trading as the result of traders hiding losses from their employers. Subsequent investigations showed that traders were able to hide their losses mainly due to poor oversight by managers and a failure of internal control measures.

It is now suggested by the financial regulators that all banks follow the remuneration policy of Kalimantan bank to eliminate incentives to defraud the bank with the aim of obtaining larger bonuses. Would such a compensation policy be optimal for all banks or should other measures be employed to prevent any future losses from fraudulent proprietary traders?

Problem Sets for Part V

Problem 72

Olesa and Jorge have known each other since becoming neighbours during their school years and have attended the same school and studied the same subject at university. Even though they attended different universities, both were seen as providing an education of similar quality. Having lost contact during their student days, they are very surprised to see each other again on their first day at work at the same bank. Olesa had secured a role within the investment banking division, while Jorge was assigned to corporate clients in the lending division of the bank. Having both successfully completed the graduate training program in different locations, they find themselves once again working in the same building, just four floors apart. Catching up after work, it becomes very obvious that Olesa must earn significantly more than Jorge, judging by the flat she rents, the car she owns, and the holidays she has taken in the last year. As the evening progresses, Jorge complains that he believes the bank does not really value him and his work, he feels he contributes much more than what he is paid. And while it is good pay, so he concludes, and others are unlikely to be paid much more than him, he is looking to find employment elsewhere. Olesa suggests he might want to join her side of the business. While she thinks that the hours can be long and the pressure extremely high, the pay more than makes up for that. During this conversation they have been joined by a common acquaintance, who has completed training as a lawyer and been advising banking clients. He throws in that investment bankers do not do really much; they merely take money away from each other or their clients, not adding much value. In corporate lending, there is, however, a lot of skills involved to manage the loans and indirectly the investments of companies that generate actual profits for the company and bank, without taking it away from someone else. So he cannot understand why banks pay investment bankers so much more.

What is an explanation for this discrepancy of pay between investment bankers and other parts of the bank?

Problem 73

Andrea Salieri has been appointed as the head of Human Resources of TLC Bank LLP, a small but well-established investment bank. Having started his career in the banking industry, but for a leading lender, before moving into positions in car manufacturing and lately energy generation, he is rather surprised to notice that recent graduates have been given leading roles in large deals or allowed to trade large positions in securities. Despite them having limited experience and more established colleagues having a higher performance, this practice seems to be widespread as he discovers while looking through the employment practices of the bank. At a regular meeting with heads of division to discuss plans for recruitment, retention, and redundancies, he suggests to look at these practices and make sure all employees are sufficiently trained before taking on responsibilities while at the same time ensuring that those with more experience and better performance take a more leading role. He finds it unusual that recent graduates are located routinely in the front office rather than the back office or middle office to gain experience. After voicing this suggestion, the division heads look at each other half in disbelief, half in contempt for their new colleague. Finally, the head of trading says: "This is how we do things here and everywhere else". It is clear that this point is not to be discussed, but Andrea Salieri is puzzled by their response.

Back in his office, he meets other senior members of the human resources team and asks why his suggestion has received such a dismissive response. What are the responses he should receive?

Problem 74

"Whether you make a career in investment banks is more down to luck than ability and hard work. I know of many people that work very hard and very quickly were side-lined from the well-paying client-facing roles, while others seem to be doing the bare minimum and are rewarded with ever higher positions and salaries. I agree that those who made a career have all performed well, while those that did not get promoted were at the lower end of expectations. In both groups, though, are some that worked hard while others did not put a lot of effort in. It therefore just comes down to luck, being involved in the right deal or avoiding deals that later turn out to be bad".

This statement is made during a careers talk at university given by a student and addressed to a recruiter from a leading investment bank. Apart from luck, is there another explanation for the observations the student reports?

Problem 75

Facing a downturn of the economy, trade unions in Thuringistan demand legislation to protect employees from redundancies, unjustified pay cuts, and generally a fairer treatment of all staff. Special attention has been given to investment banks, who serve the entire region as a financial hub and thus are an important part of the economy. Trade unions bemoan the differences between those directly involved in banking activities and other staff in banks and elsewhere. They notice that, compared to their productivity, investment bankers are paid more than other professions and get paid such salaries from an early stage in their career. They feel their pay should be limited in line with their productivity as in other sectors and the money the investment banks save be used for a pay rise of those who are paid less. Investment bankers are also, however, easily made redundant if the bank feels they are not performing sufficiently well. The trade unions suggest that this is due to a lack of training in the early stages of their career and demand enhanced training in all aspects of their future roles, combined with protection from redundancy for underperformance. Only once employees have shown that they are capable of performing tasks should they be allowed to take these up.

Representatives of investment banks dismiss the demand by trade unions and point out that it would make them unable to compete with investment banks elsewhere and in general harm the performance of the banks and ultimately their ability to provide jobs. What is the basis for their claim?

Problem 76

Jinpeng Hwang has been a highly successful investment banker with over 20 years of experience at various global investment banks. Building on his extensive network of contacts to companies he has advised over the years, he has decided to set up his own investment bank with the help of a number of financial backers. While his initial plan had been to take an entire team of people with him to his bank, this proved more difficult than he thought. He has worked with a number of very able colleagues over the years and always had a good working relationship with them, often collaborating on deals, even across banks if this was allowed. However, very few of these colleagues were willing to follow him to his bank, and so he had to rely on younger and less experienced colleagues instead. Having had particular success in deals that many colleagues would turn down due to many difficulties, such as complex regulatory requirements, hostile shareholders, or industries in challenging circumstances, he is confident that his reputation will allow him to recruit these former clients and clients in similar circumstances to his bank. This proved, however, to be as much of a challenge as convincing his former colleagues to join him at his bank. While his reputation has allowed him to attract a number of low-profile clients in the first few months, none of the more profitable clients of past deals have sought his bank's advice, and his profitability is significantly lower than he and his financial backers anticipated.

Jinpeng Hwang is surprised by these difficulties in starting his own bank. What might be the problem he faces?

Problem 77

Senior members in the treasury department of GardenTools Ltd. are discussing ways to finance overseas expansion plans and their financing with Hoover Brothers, a leading investment bank they have not dealt with previously. Previous interactions with investment banks have been very limited as the financing of their business in a domestic setting had always been straightforward, although with the overseas expansion that has now changed. During lunch break, the team by chance come across another treasury team from Metallurga plc., who are also at Hoover Brothers to discuss financing options. As the heads of Treasury know each other well from attending meetings at industry conventions and conferences, the teams share a table in the restaurant. Of course, the conversation quickly drifts towards their experience with the Hoover Brothers. It transpires that those with GardenTools Ltd. find the bankers they are dealing with have rather limited knowledge, in depth and breadth. The Metallurga plc. team, on the other hand, think the team they are interacting with has an adequate breadth of knowledge, admitting they do not know everything, but that overall they know more than merely their primary area, and, in addition, their specialist knowledge is really good. They point out that they have dealt with various teams over many years and the experience has been pretty consistent. GardenTools Ltd. hopes that they have not just been given access to a less knowledgeable team as they are a new customer that might not have much future business.

Assuming the investment banking teams the two companies have been assigned to are not uncharacteristic for Hoover Brothers, how can you explain the differences in opinions by two highly experienced treasury teams?

Problem 78

Technological advances have made the collection and processing of information much more efficient and less reliant on the work of junior analysts. In addition, the outsourcing of routine work such as the preparation of reports, filing of documents, and drawing up of contracts has reduced the burden of these duties in investment banks, who now buy these in as services if they are needed. At the same time, the homogenisation and increased accuracy of reporting standards and requirements, as well as the availability of most information a company would provide to investment banks in standardised electronic form, facilitate the work of investment banks and require less specialist knowledge about specific industries or companies. These increased efficiencies had only a very limited impact on the fees charged by investment banks, who have remained stable throughout and the number of investment banks has reduced. Those critical of investment banks see this as evidence of collusion among investment banks to maintain their high profits and demand a tighter regulation of the sector.

Other than banks colluding, how can these observations be explained?

Problem 79

EmployTech Ltd. is a recruiting specialist for roles in the technology sector, mostly covering computer specialists. Over the last few years, they have seen a significant increase in their business and have acquired a number of smaller competitors. Now they have reached a size that makes them a serious player in the recruitment sector, and a further expansion of the company is expected to diversify their offerings and be a partner of companies in the technology sector for a wider range of recruitment. During past acquisitions, they have employed the same investment bank, but have had mixed feelings about the quality of service they offered. They found that often the investment bankers were not that well informed about their market and competitors as they would have expected and their expertise was often rather narrow, having been working with teams that did not offer a good breadth of knowledge. In the recent merger with a competitor, this has changed, though. Their impression was that the team they worked with was very knowledgeable and the team members did complement each other well, offering a broad spectrum of knowledge.

During the drinks reception celebrating the merger, some board members reflect on the recent experience and come to the conclusion they were either just lucky for once with the investment banking team or it is because now they are bigger and investment banks take them more seriously. Were they merely lucky or is there a good explanation for the improved experience?

Problem 80

Norris & Partners is one of the oldest investment banks, having been established in 1758 as a merchant house importing tea, coffee, and spices from all over the world. It quickly expanded to finance the import of such goods by other merchants and in the early nineteenth century gave up the importing of goods focusing on financing other merchants. In the mid-1800s, their business changed again in light of the industrialisation, and they commenced activities that today would be described as investment banking. It was not until about five decades ago that the bank was reorganised as a partnership to include non-family members in an expansion drive. This era has now come to an end, and it has been decided to transform Norris & Partners into Norris Bank Ltd., abandoning the partnership structure. This move has surprised many industry insiders as Norris & Partners has not been expanding its business and is thus not in need of fresh capital to require this move. The reason they give is that recently they have struggled to attract high-caliber applicants to their bank, despite having an excellent name in the industry and offering competitive salaries for these more junior roles. While applicants are in no short supply and many of these looking promising recruits, very few fulfilled the high expectations, despite additional support and training put into place. In addition, of the five staff members that were offered partnerships, only two accepted the offer, both of which were not their first choice candidates. In light of these problems, they decided to abandon the partnership structure.

What is the rationale for Norris & Partners to abandon the partnership?

Problem 81

Remo Suter is the CEO of Suter Mechanics Ltd., a specialist provider of precision-machined parts used in a wide variety of applications requiring low tolerances, including space exploration, submarines, but also medical apparatuses. Over the years he has expanded his business through the acquisition of a few competitors but also bought into suppliers of tools his company needs. The specialist nature of his business is not well understood by many, and the small market in which he very successfully operates in is often not considered to be sufficiently different from other markets that provide specialist parts to industries like train or car manufacturers. Having sought advice on structuring and financing previous acquisitions, he has become frustrated by their lack of skills and knowledge that he needs to make most of the advice they provide. He appreciates that in his line of business, a lot of random factors might influence decisions that are generally not foreseeable, and any advice might easily be outdated by events. When he approached some of the leading and even second-tier investment banks, he often has been turned down with the unconvincing argument that his business does not fit their expertise. A friend suggests to try a boutique investment bank instead; he would deal with senior partners who actually own the business rather than employees generating money for anonymous shareholders. Remo Suter points out that he has heard that these types of banks are usually more expensive and he doubts they will be any better, if they even take him on.

How would you argue that he nevertheless gives these boutique investment banks serious consideration?

Problem 82

Laura Sanchez had been in charge of completing the acquisition of two major competitors of Warehouse Inc., a logistics firm that provides temporary storage space for companies, who require additional storage due to seasonal fluctuations, renovations, or damage to existing facilities. When given the chance to enter a new business that provides self-storage facilities to individuals and small firms, she left Warehouse Inc. and joined the new company Store4Me Ltd. as CEO. Under her leadership, the company has grown considerably and is now in a position to take over other, similar, companies. Even though the assessment of competitors is much easier in the self-storage business than at Warehouse Inc., she uses her contacts from that time and approaches the same two investment banks that she had been dealing with while in her previous role. Both investment banks turn her down, citing that they are too busy at this time. With both investment banks being market leaders, she is forced to approach lower-ranked investment banks to provide her with advice on the acquisition. During the first meeting with an investment bank that has indicated its willingness in principle to advice on the acquisition, Laura Sanchez quips that clearly her business is too small for the bigger investment banks to bother with her. In a surprise response, one investment banker shoots back and says that when she was working at Warehouse Inc., she would not bother with small investment banks like his. Only then does she realize that the investment bank she is now negotiating with had offered their services in her last acquisition at Warehouse Inc. but she had turned them down rather briskly.

Can you explain the rationale for each decision?

Problem 83

Commercial Bank plc. has in recent years expanded its business by acquiring a number of smaller investment banks and has grown this part of the business through promoting their use with its existing borrowers. Part of the investment banking business is a trading desk that has been the backbone of the investment banking division by providing the majority of profits as the business grew. Now, however, it has accumulated large losses that, although not threatening the survival of Commercial Bank plc., have led to the board questioning the strategy of engaging in investment banking at all. While many arguments for and against this strategy have been made during this discussion, a nonexecutive director without any meaningful banking experience, Constantin Ionu, remarked that banks in any case should not be run in this form. On receiving looks that show no one understands what he means by that, he elaborates that he thinks banks should not be owned by shareholders, but senior management should take more personal responsibility for their actions. He continues that the biggest mistake was that in the mid-nineteenth centuries, banks were allowed to be set up as joint stock companies rather than as partnerships run by senior managers with significant stakes in the bank. After all, he kind of concludes, investment banks used to be run like this until recently and were very successful with that model. His remarks are mostly ignored, and the discussion carries on.

Would a return to partnerships for commercial banks be a good step?

Problem 84

Tomas Nagy has for a few years worked in his role as a credit analyst assessing the risks of borrowers of Antal Bank, a commercial bank. He has recently been hired by Horvath Bank, a leading investment bank, to fill a similar role in its underwriting division, which is newly expanding into bond underwriting. During his time at Antal Bank, Tomas Nagy had achieved two promotions and was considered highly skilled in his role. He worked closely with his head of department, and they frequently exchanged views on the assessment of borrowers, but when making changes to the way credit risk was assessed, he had always to get approval from his head of department. Looking at the procedures that exist at Horvath Bank, he finds them to be deficient in many ways. Seeking a meeting with his team leader, his effective supervisor, he is briskly told to "do it then, that's your job", and no further discussion is entered into. He finds this surprising and very different to his experience at Antal Bank, where his suggestions would be scrutinised by his superiors and often dismissed or significantly amended, sometimes against his explicit wishes. Initially Tomas Nagy puts this approach of his team leader down to the fact that he is not much more experienced in corporate bond underwriting than him, having moved from equity underwriting into his new role just months before. In contrast, his superiors were vastly experienced with deep knowledge of credit risk assessment in theory and practice. On the one hand he enjoys the freedom to work on his own ideas at Horvath Bank, but is also concerned about the lack of checks and balances of his proposed approach.

How can you explain the differences in the management style between Antal Bank and Horvath Bank?

Problem 85

Siversky Bank, an investment bank specialising in companies in the defence industry, has lost a number of senior managers on the back of a few years making significant losses in proprietary trading operations and the subsequent lack of bonuses at higher levels. The departure of the most senior managers, who were all highly regarded in their areas of expertise, has also led to many less senior managers leaving the bank. With the injection of fresh capital, Siversky Bank has been able to hire a number of new senior managers; however, they are much less experienced overall and have less knowledge about the markets that Siversky Bank mainly operates in. One of the first tasks of the new management is to reorganise the bank's management structure. They replace the old system in which at all levels, managers were highly involved in any decisions and deals, to one in which teams of employees work together with clients and senior management does not interfere in the process. Many intermediate management positions are not being replaced in the process and the new senior management team sees itself as ambassadors of Siversky Bank and their role as that of acquiring new clients.

What might have caused this reorganisation of Siversky Bank?

Problem 86

Angeley Bank Ltd. is a new investment bank that has been set up by a small group of investment bankers from various leading investment banks. They have assembled teams of staff that have been selected carefully from the owners' previous roles and that largely share their outlook as they have been former or very recent mentors of the staff they hired. In the industry, Angeley Bank is very quickly highly regarded in their niche of advising clients in developing countries due the standing of their owners as well as the similar caliber of the more junior staff they could convince to join them. Despite their outstanding reputation from the start, the number of deals they advise on in the first months after setting up is relatively low. At various stages of advising the few clients, the founders and other employees appointed to more senior positions at Angeley Bank are all involved in developing such advice. Having been carefully selected, junior staff respect senior managers and the founders highly, keen to learn from their suggestions and ideas to improve their own skills. Seeking to recruit more widely and expand their expertise, potential junior staff are reluctant to apply once they learn more about the way Angeley Bank operates.

Why is Angeley Bank less attractive to junior staff than other investment banks?

Problem 87

Walton plc. is a mid-sized investment bank that until recently enjoyed a good reputation in advising smaller companies in going public. Companies seeking their advice always liked the close involvement of a number of senior managers in the development of their IPO strategy. However, over time clients became less and less satisfied with the outcome of their IPO, often citing that the advice given by senior managers was not good and many have been recorded mentioning that more junior staff members were often overheard discussing alternatives that, in retrospect, would have been preferred. In receiving such feedback, Walton plc. changed their business practice and have since removed the active involvement of senior staff in most cases. Since then, the satisfaction of clients has increased. Staff were allocated into teams, and great care was given to ensure that each team is balanced in terms of their expertise and the team leader is supposed to act as primus-inter-pares rather than a manager and this role should rotate regularly. There are, however, two teams that show consistently low satisfaction by clients. In both cases you find that the team leader takes a much more dominant position, imposing its suggestions on the team. It is generally accepted that the suggestions made by these two team leaders are slightly better than those developed in other teams, but the implementation of this advice is often lacking quality.

How can you explain this result?

Problem 88

Helen Søberg is the CEO of Aften AB and about to embark on a major expansion through the planned acquisition of a few companies. To facilitate this process, she seeks to appoint an investment bank as advisor. During a board meeting to discuss this appointment, some board members suggest to use one of the largest investment banks as they must be the best, given that everyone uses them. On the other hand, an alternative proposal is to appoint a small investment bank, ideally a small partnership, as they are always better because the owners themselves put their reputation on the line.

Which strategy of appointing an investment bank as advisor would be best?

Problem 89

Perot & Cie is a small investment bank specialising in advising companies operating in mechanical engineering, organised as a partnership. They find it increasingly difficult to identify suitable future partners of high caliber and bemoan the lack of quality in applicants they receive for entry positions. Larger investment banks do not report such problems. On discussing the attractiveness of their investment bank with newly recruited staff, Perot & Cie discover that the extremely high workload as partner is unattractive, especially the requirement to not only work on investment banking deals but mentoring staff and general administrative responsibilities. At a meeting of partners, it has been suggested to restructure the investment bank by introducing one or two additional layers of management and only mentor staff that have been promoted to such senior positions.

Would this proposed restructuring improve the recruitment of high-caliber staff at entry-level positions?

Problem 90

During a discussion on employment rights, the discussion has drifted towards the level of compensation employees receive, especially in the financial services industry. Simon Baker, advocating the rights of manual workers, cites a study in which investment banking pay is highest for those working in mergers and acquisitions advisory as well as proprietary trading, while the lowest pay is in underwriting, when measured against the revenue generated. He uses this finding as evidence that pay in investment banks is heavily skewed in favour of those adding no value but just buying and selling companies, while value-enhancing roles are not rewarded accordingly.

How could a representative of the financial industry justify this difference in pay?

Problem 91

You observe that in recent years, companies maintain a smaller number of relationships with investment banks. While previously it was common for larger companies to maintain relationships with four or five investment banks and using their services either concurrently or rotating the award of business between them, this has now reduced to two or three investment banks. An experienced investment banker tells you that over the last decades the rules on information disclosure have been tightened and generally the transparency of market as well as companies has improved significantly.

How can this statement explain your observation?

Problem 92

Conrad & Co has suffered substantial losses from its trading desk that have endangered the survival of the investment bank. They were eventually bought by a competitor to avoid its potential collapse. During a parliamentary inquiry into the circumstances of the demise of Conrad & Co, members of parliament are questioning Georgios Saragiannis as a representative of an investment banking lobby group. It is put to him that investment banks are taking excessive risks and that this is the result of a practice that gives high responsibilities to inexperienced staff, giving them high pay to incentivise them to take such risks, and generally providing very little oversight of their activities.

How would Georgios Saragiannis defend the practices of investment banks?

Problem 93

Salcombe Ltd. is looking at a listing on the stock exchange and seek to appoint an investment bank as advisor for this transaction. The CEO of Salcombe Ltd., Carl Salcombe, suggests to investigate only boutique investment banks as they are usually providing better advice. He links this to the fact that the senior managements are commonly partners in the investment bank and as such have an inherent interest in providing high-quality advice. Furthermore, their small size makes it necessary for them to specialise in a specific area, such that their level of expertise will be more focused than that of the larger bulge-bracket investment banks. His son, Simon Salcombe, is against this suggestion and argues to foremost consider larger investment banks as they are able to provide them with not only advice in the planned listing, but in most other future needs they might have.

Whose argument can you support?

Problem Sets for the Prologue and Epilogue

Problem 94

You work for an investment bank and at a family gathering get to sit next to your uncle, who has a very negative view of investment banks. After a few beers, he tells you that investment banks are simply money-making machines for those working there, extracting any money out of ordinary people and good manufacturing companies alike. They attract the most ruthless individuals that are only caring about making as much money as possible for themselves and to get this money they exploit that the average person knows very little about the financial world.

How would you politely try to counter his negative views of investment banks?

Problem 95

A comment put to you as an investment banker at a recent meeting with old school friends was "Investment banks work for large companies and their shareholders, but the general public sees no benefits from their presence".

What would you have answered to counter this view?

Problem 96

The government of Kampania seeks to promote competition in the economy in general and the financial sector specifically. To this effect it has established a working group addressing competition between investment banks. During the deliberations, it has been suggested that investment banks should be broken up along their business lines. The argument brought forward was that investment banks offer a number of different services that have very little common grounds and by breaking up investment banks, cross-selling these distinct services would be prevented, making clients more aware of alternative investment banks offering these services and thereby enhancing competition.

What arguments can be brought up against breaking up investment banks?

Problem 97

"Talk with me" is a weekly talk show that seeks out controversial individuals and invites them for a moderated discussion of their opposing views. At times these discussions are very polemic, but other discussions are conducted at a high level of sophistication, using arguments soundly based in science or philosophy. The discussion in a recent edition of this show drifted towards investment banks. One participant in the discussion said that investment banks do not follow any ethical rules at all; they only care about making money at the expense of their clients and any other person affected by their actions.

Can you argue that this behaviour is ethical?

Problem 98

During an interview with a newspaper, the retiring CEO of Volkert AB, a leading investment bank, is accused of exploiting his clients by charging them exorbitant fees that provide the investment bank with huge profits. In a flipping remark, he responds "If they agree to pay it, it must be worth it". In comments appearing in the online edition of the newspaper, his reply is seen as an example for the unethical behaviour of investment banks.

Is the approach taken by the retiring CEO unethical?

Problem 99

"Our investment bank should focus on its traditional core business of corporate finance, which is also highly profitable, and not expand into other areas and provide additional services". This statement comes from a nonexecutive board member of

Banca Pezzoli SpA, a highly respected but small investment bank, during a meeting discussing the further development of their business strategy.

What arguments can be brought in favour of expanding into other business lines that many competitors already cover?

Problem 100

After the financial crisis 2007/2008, the blame for the spread of the initial failure of Lehman Brothers has been put on the widespread use of mortgage-backed security and derivatives on these. In an essay, a student analyzes the financial crisis from the perspective of ethical behaviour. In the student's view, it was obvious that financial innovations have contributed to the fragility of the financial system. She acknowledges that these innovations, such as collateralized debt obligations, met the demands by investors and issuers alike, but argues that their development and sale was nevertheless unethical.

What would be the argument in favour of this view?

Appendix

In this book I assume that readers are familiar with the economic ideas, and the associated mathematics, as is covered in typical first year programs of economics degrees. I therefore assume that readers are aware of utility functions and the concept of equilibrium, along with budget constraints. It is also necessary to be aware of perfect and imperfect competition in markets, specifically, competitive equilibria, oligopolistic models of competition, and monopolies. Strategic interaction as introduced with basic non-cooperative game theory is also required, along with the concept of the Nash equilibrium.

The mathematical tools associated with such basic economic ideas include the rules of differentiation and integration as well as the maximisation and minimisation of functions. Knowledge of linear algebra, in particular the use of matrices and vectors, is also beneficial. I also assume that readers have elementary knowledge of statistics. They should be aware of the properties of probabilities and probability distributions, including specific knowledge of normal, binomial, and uniform distributions, along with an understanding of means, variances, covariances, and correlations. Knowledge of basic linear multivariate regressions is also helpful.

While most models in investment banking do not go beyond such basic concepts, on occasions, I require more advanced knowledge of some specific economic theories as well as mathematical tools. While a detailed understanding of these is not necessary to appreciate the models and their results, it is unavoidable to require such knowledge for the derivation of the results and sometimes their interpretation. Those economic theories and mathematical tools that are not commonly taught at an introductory level but needed in model here are included in this appendix. The treatment will be such that economic theories are not presented overly mathematical; instead the focus will be on gaining an understanding of the basic idea. For mathematical tools, mainly the results are stated without formal derivations or proofs.

For reference, this appendix also includes some basic notations of the valuation of securities and assessment of credit risk, which is a key expertise required for investment bankers.

A. Krause, *Theoretical Foundations of Investment Banking*, Springer Texts in Business and Economics, https://doi.org/10.1007/978-3-031-58060-4

Mathematical Tools

A

A.1 Implicit Functions

Let us assume we have a function f of $n \geq 2$ variables, x_i, with $f(x_1, x_2, \ldots, x_n) = 0$. Such a function might emerge in our context mainly from a first-order condition, in which case f would be the first derivative of the objective function or a constraint to an optimisation problem. We would often be interested in the trade-off between two variables, x_i and x_j, that allows this function to remain at zero; we would thus would seek to find $\frac{\partial x_i}{\partial x_j}$.

To achieve this goal, consider the total differential of the function f, which is given by

$$df(x_1, x_2, \ldots, x_n) = \sum_{i=1}^{n} \frac{\partial f(x_1, x_2, \ldots, x_n)}{\partial x_i} dx_i, \tag{A.1}$$

where $\frac{\partial f(x_1, x_2, \ldots, x_n)}{\partial x_i}$ denotes the partial derivative with respect to x_i. The total differential can be interpreted as a linear approximation of the change of the function f, represented by $df(x_1, x_2, \ldots, x_n)$, through the changes of all the variables, dx_i, who have a marginal influence of $\frac{\partial f(x_1, x_2, \ldots, x_n)}{\partial x_i}$, which can be interpreted as the slope of the function f in the direction of variable x_i.

Let us now assume that we are only interested in two variables, x_i and x_j. We set all the other changes of variables in Eq. (A.1) equal to zero and obtain

$$\begin{aligned} df(x_1, x_2, \ldots, x_n) = & \frac{\partial f(x_1, x_2, \ldots, x_n)}{\partial x_i} dx_i \\ & + \frac{\partial f(x_1, x_2, \ldots, x_n)}{\partial x_j} dx_j. \end{aligned} \tag{A.2}$$

A. Krause, *Theoretical Foundations of Investment Banking*, Springer Texts in Business and Economics, https://doi.org/10.1007/978-3-031-58060-4

From the condition that $f(x_1, x_2, \ldots, x_n) = 0$, we know that its value cannot change; thus we need $df(x_1, x_2, \ldots, x_n) = 0$. If we insert for $df(x_1, x_2, \ldots, x_n)$ from Eq. (A.2), we can solve this expression for

$$\frac{dx_i}{dx_j} = -\frac{\frac{\partial f(x_1, x_2, \ldots, x_n)}{\partial x_j}}{\frac{\partial f(x_1, x_2, \ldots, x_n)}{\partial x_i}}. \tag{A.3}$$

This expression, known as the *implicit function*, now provides us with the relationship between x_i and x_j, namely, how x_i needs to change if we change x_j (marginally). The implicit function gives us therefore the trade-off between these two variables such that $f(x_1, x_2, \ldots, x_n) = 0$.

A.2 Constrained Optimisation

In many cases we will face constraints when maximising or minimising our objective function. We might have to apply a constraint due to limited resources available (budget constraint) or have to meet other constraints to induce certain behaviour (incentive constraint). There might also be limits on the maximum number of units of a good available from production, that the demand for a good cannot be negative, or if seeking an optimal probability that the solution must be between 0 and 1. We therefore face a constrained optimisation.

The most common form of constrained optimisation in economic theory is that the constraint is an equality, and we apply the Lagrange multiplier, as detailed in Appendix A.2.1. A less common and more general case arises if the constraints consist of equalities and inequalities, requiring the use of the Karush-Kuhn-Tucker conditions in Appendix A.2.2. The Lagrange multiplier can be seen as a special case of the Karush-Kuhn-Tucker conditions where no inequalities exist. Nevertheless, we treat these two approaches separately as many of the interpretations of Lagrange multipliers also apply to the Karush-Kuhn-Tucker conditions and this therefore facilitates its treatment and interpretation.

A.2.1 Lagrange Multiplier

Let us assume we have n decision variables x_i that we need to choose optimally by maximising or minimising an objective function $f(x_1, x_2, \ldots, x_n)$, such as profits, costs, or utility. In addition, we have m constraints that need to be fulfilled with equality, denoted $g_k(x_1, x_2, \ldots, x_n) = c_k$. We can add these constraints to the objective function without changing its value if we deduct c_k. When doing so, we multiply them with a constant ζ_k and obtain

$$\mathcal{L} = f(x_1, x_2, \ldots, x_n) + \sum_{k=1}^{m} \zeta_k (c_k - g_k(x_1, x_2, \ldots, x_n)). \tag{A.4}$$

This function is commonly referred to as the *Lagrangian* and ζ_k as the *Lagrange multipliers*. We now need to find the maximum for this Lagrangian and the variables to be determined are the decision variables x_i and the Lagrange multipliers ζ_k. The first-order conditions are then given by

$$\begin{aligned}\forall i = 1, \ldots, n : \frac{\partial \mathcal{L}}{\partial x_i} = & \frac{\partial f(x_1, x_2, \ldots, x_n)}{\partial x_i} \\ & - \sum_{k=1}^{m} \zeta_k \frac{\partial g_k(x_1, x_2, \ldots, x_n)}{\partial x_i} = 0, \\ \forall k = 1, \ldots, m : \frac{\partial \mathcal{L}}{\partial \zeta_k} = & c_k - g_k(x_1, x_2, \ldots, x_n) = 0.\end{aligned} \tag{A.5}$$

The second set of equations recovers the constraints, and we can solve the resulting equation system for the x_i, which will provide us with the solution(s) to the optimisation problem, subject to the constraints imposed.

We can also provide an interpretation of the Lagrange multipliers as the marginal effect the constraints have on the optimal value of the objective function $f(x_1, x_2, \ldots, x_n)$. We easily have that $\frac{\partial \mathcal{L}}{\partial c_k} = \frac{\partial f(x_1, x_2, \ldots, x_n)}{\partial c_k} + \zeta_k = 0$ and hence

$$\frac{\partial f(x_1, x_2, \ldots, x_n)}{\partial c_k} = -\zeta_k. \tag{A.6}$$

We can interpret the (negative) Lagrange multiplier as the marginal product of changing the constraint. If we were to increase the value of the constraint, c_k, the effect on the objective function $f(x_1, x_2, \ldots, x_n)$ is given by $-\zeta_k$. In economic terms, the marginal product would be the price of a good. We can therefore interpret the Lagrange multipliers as the shadow prices of the constraint.

A.2.2 Karush-Kuhn-Tucker Conditions

As before, let us assume we have n decision variables x_i that we need to choose optimally by maximising or minimising an objective function $f(x_1, x_2, \ldots, x_n)$, such as profits, costs, or utility. In addition, we have m constraints that need to be fulfilled with equality, denoted $g_k(x_1, x_2, \ldots, x_n) = c_k$, and now additionally l inequality constraints $h_s(x_1, x_2, \ldots, x_n) \leq c_s$. If the actual constraint requires non-negative solutions, a multiplication by -1 will transform the inequality as shown here.

Let us now treat these inequalities the same way as equalities and apply the Lagrange multiplier, such that

$$\mathcal{L} = f(x_1, x_2, \ldots, x_n) + \sum_{k=1}^{m} \zeta_k (c_k - g_k(x_1, x_2, \ldots, x_n)) + \sum_{s=1}^{l} \zeta_{m+s} (c_{m+s} - h_s(x_1, x_2, \ldots, x_n)) \tag{A.7}$$

and the first-order conditions become

$$\begin{aligned}
\forall i = 1, \ldots, n : \frac{\partial \mathcal{L}}{\partial x_i} &= \frac{\partial f(x_1, x_2, \ldots, x_n)}{\partial x_i} \\
&\quad - \sum_{k=1}^{m} \zeta_k \frac{\partial g_k(x_1, x_2, \ldots, x_n)}{\partial x_i} \\
&\quad - \sum_{l=1}^{s} \zeta_{m+l} \frac{\partial h_l(x_1, x_2, \ldots, x_n)}{\partial x_i} = 0 \\
\forall k = 1, \ldots, m : \frac{\partial \mathcal{L}}{\partial \zeta_k} &= c_k - g_k(x_1, x_2, \ldots, x_n) = 0, \\
\forall s = 1, \ldots, l : \frac{\partial \mathcal{L}}{\partial \zeta_{m+s}} &= c_s - h_s(x_1, x_2, \ldots, x_n) = 0.
\end{aligned} \tag{A.8}$$

In deviation from the solution of this equation system for Lagrange multipliers as explained above, we need to consider whether the condition $h_s(x_1, x_2, \ldots, x_n) \leq c_s$ is binding in that $h_s(x_1, x_2, \ldots, x_n) = c_s$. In this case we treat ζ_{m+s} as a Lagrange multiplier. If this constraint is not binding, then $\zeta_{m+s} = 0$ and the constraint can be dropped from the solution.

A solution concept would thus be to determine the value of all ζ_{m+s}. If $\zeta_{m+s} > 0$, then the constraint is binding, and if $\zeta_{m+s} = 0$, then it is not binding, and the constraint as well as ζ_{m+s} can be eliminated from the solution. Negative values for ζ_{m+s} cannot be observed. Using the interpretation of the Lagrange multipliers as shadow prices, we see that if this shadow price is positive, it affects the value of the objective function, implying that the constraint is binding. If the constraint is not binding, changing the constraint does not affect the outcome; hence the shadow price is $\zeta_{m+s} = 0$.

The remaining positive ζ_{m+s} are treated like Lagrange multipliers and the associated constraints as binding equalities, giving rise to solving an equation system akin to that emerging from using Lagrange multipliers.

A.3 Bayesian Learning

Many models in banking involve incomplete information about the structure of the economy, causing outcomes to be perceived as random from the perspective of the bank, borrower, or depositor. It is, however, often that some additional information is available to these market participants that will affect the distribution of such random outcomes. Assume we have an outcome H that has some probability of $Prob\,(H)$ to occur; alternatively an outcome L is observed. If we now get some signal s on the outcome for H, we are interested in the conditional probability of H occurring, given the signal s has been received. Conditional probabilities are defined as

$$Prob\,(H|s) = \frac{Prob\,(H \cap s)}{Prob\,(s)}, \tag{A.9}$$

where $Prob\,(\cdot)$ denotes the probability of the outcome, $Prob\,(\cdot|s)$ the probability of an outcome conditional on observing the signal s, and $\cap$ denotes that both outcome and signal have to be observed. Similarly we have

$$Prob\,(s|H) = \frac{Prob\,(H \cap s)}{Prob\,(H)}. \tag{A.10}$$

Solving Eqs. (A.9) and (A.10) for $Prob\,(H \cap s)$, and setting these equal, we get what is often referred to as *Bayes' Theorem*:

$$Prob\,(H|s) = \frac{Prob\,(s|H)\,Prob\,(H)}{Prob\,(s)}. \tag{A.11}$$

We call $Prob\,(H|s)$ the posterior probability, i. e., the probability after observing the signal s, while $Prob\,(H)$ is the prior probability as it denotes the initial belief for the likelihood of H occurring. If we set $s = H$, the signal indicates that outcome H will be obtained, then $Prob\,(s|H)$ can be interpreted as the probability that the signal s is correct. Furthermore, we have that

$$Prob\,(s) = Prob\,(s|H)\,Prob\,(H) + Prob\,(s|L)\,Prob\,(L)\,. \tag{A.12}$$

Using the expression in Eq. (A.9), we see that the first term is equal to $Prob\,(H \cap s)$ and the second term is $Prob\,(L \cap s)$. Adding these two probabilities means the probability that it is either the signal s is observed with H (first term) or with L (second term), and as H and L are the only possible outcomes, it must be the probability that the signal s is observed. Using these conditional probabilities, we can now also determine conditional expected values and other moments of the distribution.

If the distributions of two variables are normally distributed, then Bayesian learning allows us to obtain an explicit expression for the distribution of the posterior probability. Let us assume that $Y = X + \varepsilon$, where X has a normal distribution with mean μ and variance σ_X^2 and ε a normal distribution with mean zero and variance σ_ε^2. X and ε are independent of each other. We can interpret Y as a noisy signal of X; if X is the true outcome and we can only observe Y, then Y will reflect the value of X, but with an added fluctuation ε, which is commonly referred to as noise. We can now use our observation of Y to make inferences about the true value of X. We then can show that the distribution of X given Y, denoted $X|Y$, is a normal distribution with mean and variance

$$E\left[X|Y\right] = \mu + \frac{\sigma_X^2}{\sigma_X^2 + \sigma_\varepsilon^2}\left(Y - \mu\right), \tag{A.13}$$

$$Var\left[X|Y\right] = \frac{1}{\frac{1}{\sigma_X^2} + \frac{1}{\sigma_\varepsilon^2}},$$

respectively. Thus in the case of having normal distributions, the analysis of expected values and variances can be conducted much more easily than in the general case, where no such analytical solutions are easily available.

A.4 Leibniz Integral Rule

In some instances, we need to optimise a function Π, where the decision variable is the boundaries of an integral. This can be the case, for example, if the payoff Ψ depends not only on this value V but also a random variable s, and, in addition, the value V determines the range on which this function Π can be achieved. we denote the lower limit by $\underline{\lambda}\left(V\right)$ and the upper limit by $\overline{\lambda}\left(V\right)$. Let now

$$\Pi\left(V\right) = \int_{\underline{\lambda}(V)}^{\overline{\lambda}(V)} \Psi\left(V, s\right) ds \tag{A.14}$$

be our objective function. The Leibniz integral rule now specifies that the derivative of the function with respect to the value V is given by

$$\begin{aligned} \frac{\partial \Pi\left(V\right)}{\partial V} &= \frac{\partial \overline{\lambda}\left(V\right)}{\partial V}\Psi\left(V, \overline{\lambda}\left(V\right)\right) \\ &\quad - \frac{\partial \underline{\lambda}\left(V\right)}{\partial V}\Psi\left(V, \underline{\lambda}\left(V\right)\right) \\ &\quad + \int_{\underline{\lambda}(V)}^{\overline{\lambda}(V)} \frac{\partial \Psi\left(V, s\right)}{\partial V} ds. \end{aligned} \tag{A.15}$$

If either $\underline{\lambda}\left(V\right)$ or $\overline{\lambda}\left(V\right)$ are constants or $\pm\infty$, then the associated derivative in Eq. (A.15) is zero, and the term can be eliminated.

A.5 Statistical Tools

A.5.1 Conditional Moments

Let us assume we have two variables, X and Y, and have obtained information on the value of Y. We now want to predict the value of X given our information on Y and limit ourselves to a linear prediction. Hence, we seek to find the expected value of X, given our observation of Y, such that

$$E\left[X|Y\right] = \alpha_0 + \alpha_1 Y. \tag{A.16}$$

We now seek to minimise the prediction error $\mathfrak{E} = E\left[(X - E\left[X|Y\right])^2\right]$ over the parameters α_0 and α_1. The first-order conditions after inserting for $E\left[X|Y\right]$ from Eq. (A.16) are given by

$$\begin{aligned}\frac{\partial \mathfrak{E}}{\partial \alpha_0} &= 2\alpha_0 - 2E\left[X\right] + 2\alpha_1 E\left[Y\right] = 0, \\ \frac{\partial \mathfrak{E}}{\partial \alpha_1} &= 2\alpha_1 E\left[Y^2\right] - 2E\left[XY\right] + 2\alpha_0 E\left[Y\right] = 0.\end{aligned} \tag{A.17}$$

These two equations can be solved for

$$\begin{aligned}\alpha_0 &= E\left[X\right] - \alpha_1 E\left[Y\right], \\ \alpha_1 &= \frac{E\left[XY\right] - E\left[X\right]E\left[Y\right]}{E\left[X^2\right] - E\left[X\right]^2} = \frac{Cov\left[X,Y\right]}{Var\left[X\right]},\end{aligned} \tag{A.18}$$

where $E\left[\cdot\right]$ denotes the expected value, $Var\left[\cdot\right]$ the variance, and $Cov\left[\cdot,\cdot\right]$ the covariance. Inserting this result into Eq. (A.16), we get for our prediction of X, given the value for Y, that

$$E\left[X|Y\right] = E\left[X\right] + \frac{Cov\left[X,Y\right]}{Var\left[X\right]}\left(Y - E\left[Y\right]\right). \tag{A.19}$$

From Eq. (A.16), we also obtain that

$$\begin{aligned}Var\left(E\left[X|Y\right]\right) &= \alpha_1^2 Var\left[Y\right] \\ &= \frac{Cov\left[X,Y\right]^2}{Var\left[X\right]^2} Var\left[Y\right].\end{aligned} \tag{A.20}$$

This expression represents the ex ante variance of the conditional expected value that prior to observing the value for Y, we know the conditional expected value, which we will obtain, has a variance as indicated here.

A.5.2 Order Statistics

The Mth largest value out of N total values is called the Mth order statistic. The cumulative distribution function is given by

$$F_M(V) = \sum_{i=M}^{N} \binom{N}{M} F(V)^i \left(1 - F(V)\right)^{N-i}, \tag{A.21}$$

where $F(\cdot)$ denotes the cumulative distribution function and $\binom{\cdot}{\cdot}$ the binomial coefficient. The order statistic is determined by M observations being below V and $N - M$ above the value of V. $F(V)$ then denotes the probability of making an observation below V. Seeking the Mth largest value, we require to have at least M observations above V, with the remainder below.

In general the resulting distribution F_M cannot be determined analytically, except for the case that V itself is uniformly distributed on the interval $[0; 1]$. In this case the Mth largest value is distributed like a beta distribution with parameters M and $N + 1 - M$. Such a distribution has a mean of $\frac{M}{M+N+1-M} = \frac{M}{N+1}$ and a variance of $\frac{M(N+1-M)}{(M+N+1-M)^2(M+N+1-M+1)} = \frac{M(N+1-M)}{(N+1)^2(N+2)}$. For other distributions, no further results are generally available analytically.

Economic Models

B

B.1 Nash Bargaining

Consider two individuals negotiating a price, for example, a bank and borrower negotiating the loan rate, a bank and depositor negotiating the deposit rate, or an investment bank negotiating its fee for providing advice with a client. Both parties in this negotiation will have the option of terminating the negotiation and falling back on alternative solutions, the so-called outside option, which we assume provides utility $\hat{u}_i$ to individual i. Such alternative solution might be to not obtain a loan, not deposit monies, or not seek advice, but could also include taking their custom to another bank. The utility of individual i derived from agreeing a price p is denoted by $u_i(p)$. The surplus from concluding the negotiation is then $u_i(p) - \hat{u}_i$. In many models we will assume that either the bank or their client have market power; in this case the price would be set such that $u_i(r) - \hat{u}_i = 0$ for the individual lacking market power.

An alternative modelling assumption is that both individuals seek to share the joint surplus fairly. Nash (1953) proposes that maximising

$$\mathcal{L} = \left(u_1(p) - \hat{u}_1\right)\left(u_2(p) - \hat{u}_2\right) \tag{B.1}$$

is optimal, and both parties obtain the same surplus beyond their outside option. The maximisation of this expression is called the *Nash bargaining* solution. The first-order condition is

$$\frac{\partial \mathcal{L}}{\partial p} = \frac{\partial u_1(p)}{\partial p}\left(u_2(p) - \hat{u}_2\right) + \frac{\partial u_2(p)}{\partial p}\left(u_1(p) - \hat{u}_1\right) = 0. \tag{B.2}$$

A. Krause, *Theoretical Foundations of Investment Banking*, Springer Texts in Business and Economics, https://doi.org/10.1007/978-3-031-58060-4

The joint surplus is $\mathcal{S} = \left(u_1(p) - \hat{u}_1\right) + \left(u_2(p) - \hat{u}_2\right)$ and hence the maximum is obtained if

$$\frac{\partial \mathcal{S}}{\partial p} = \frac{\partial u_1(p)}{\partial p} + \frac{\partial u_2(p)}{\partial p} = 0. \tag{B.3}$$

We now see from Eq. (B.2) that if $u_1(p) - \hat{u}_1 = u_2(p) - \hat{u}_2$, i. e. the surpluses both parties obtain are identical, then the first-order conditions from maximising $\mathcal{L}$ and $\mathcal{S}$ are identical; therefore maximising Eq. (B.1) gives the outcome that maximises the joint surplus.

We are now left to show that an unequal distribution of surpluses is not optimal. The first-order conditions for maximising the objective functions $\mathcal{L}$ and $\mathcal{S}$, Eqs. (B.2) and (B.3), can be rewritten at the optimal price p^* as

$$\frac{\partial u_1(p^*)}{\partial u_2(p^*)} = -1, \tag{B.4}$$

$$\frac{\partial u_1(p^*)}{\partial u_2(p^*)} = -\frac{u_1(P^*) - \hat{u}_1}{u_2(p^*) - \hat{u}_2}.$$

The first equation represents the total differential $d\mathcal{L} = 0$ at the optimal price p^* and the second the total differential of $d\mathcal{S} = 0$. Suppose now the surplus is not allocated equally; thus for the second equation, we have $\frac{\partial u_1(p^*)}{\partial u_2(p^*)} \neq -1$. Figure B.1 illustrates this situation. The lines denoted by $d\mathcal{L}_0 = 0$ and $d\mathcal{S} = 0$ (colored black in the online version) illustrate the situation in which the Nash bargaining solution is optimal. Now suppose that the surplus is not allocated equally, in which case the slopes of the curve $d\mathcal{L}_i = 0$ will be either below or above -1 at the point where the slope of $d\mathcal{S} = 0$ is equal to -1, as indicated by the lines annotated $d\mathcal{L}_1 = 0$ (colored red in the online version) and $d\mathcal{L}_2 = 0$ (colored blue in the online version). We now see that in the hatched areas, the utility of both parties could be increased; thus the solution p^* would no longer be optimal, contradicting the optimality of p^* from maximizing the joint surplus. Hence the surplus must be divided equally, and the Nash bargaining solution is optimal.

B.2 Tacit Collusion

Let us consider two individuals i setting prices strategically. If both set high prices and do not aggressively compete with each other, they will both make high profits, Π^i_{CC}. This is often referred to as "cooperate". Alternatively they could both compete with each other and set lower prices such that their profits are $\Pi^i_{DD} < \Pi^i_{CC}$, something commonly referred to as "defect". Another scenario is that only one of the two individuals seeks to compete by undercutting their competitor marginally, taking a larger share of the market and thus making higher profits $\Pi^i_{DC} > \Pi^i_{CC}$. Taking a higher markets share leaves less or nothing for the competitor, and we

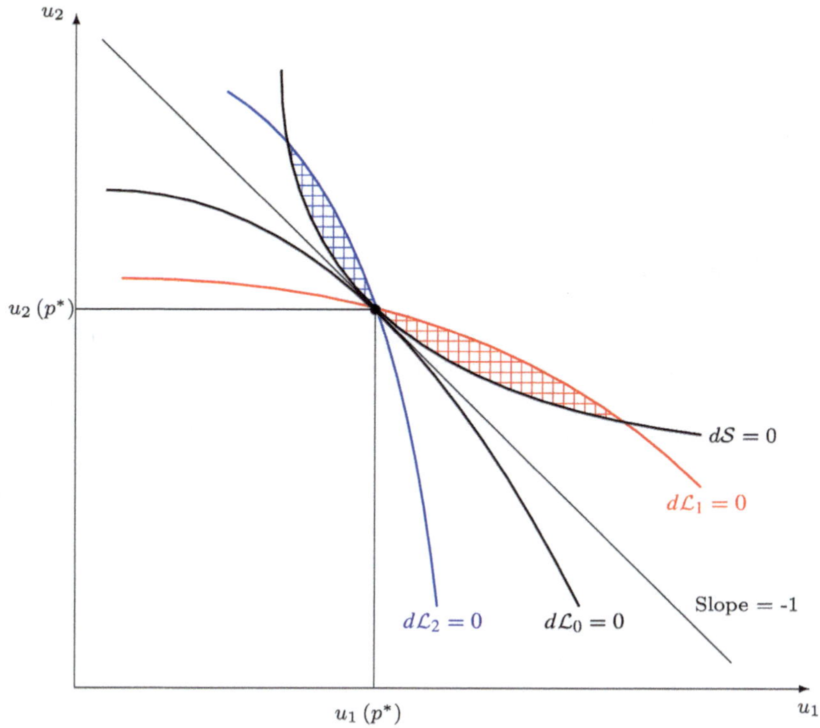

Fig. B.1 Optimality of the Nash bargaining solution

assume that $\Pi^i_{CD} < \Pi^i_{DD}$. Hence, we have $\Pi^i_{DC} > \Pi^i_{CC} > \Pi^i_{DD} > \Pi^i_{CD}$. This is the situation of the prisoner's dilemma, and the only Nash equilibrium is for both individuals to defect and hence obtain Π^i_{DD}, even though cooperating and obtaining Π^i_{CC} would be preferred by both individuals.

Let us now assume that these two individuals interact repeatedly over time. If they always cooperate, they would obtain Π^i_{CC} in each time period, and with a discount factor ρ_i, the total value obtained would be $\frac{\Pi^i_{CC}}{1-\rho_i}$. If one of the individuals would defect, they would obtain Π^i_{DC} for that time period. We then assume that in reaction to the defection, the other individual will from then onward defect, too. Thus from the subsequent time periods, both individuals obtain Π^i_{DD}, giving total value $\Pi^i_{DC} + \rho_i \frac{\Pi^i_{DD}}{1-\rho_i}$. Individuals will cooperate if $\frac{\Pi^i_{CC}}{1-\rho_i} \geq \Pi^i_{DC} + \rho_i \frac{\Pi^i_{DD}}{1-\rho_i}$, or

$$\rho_i \geq \frac{\Pi^i_{DC} - \Pi^i_{CC}}{\Pi^i_{DC} - \Pi^i_{DD}}. \tag{B.5}$$

Hence, if individuals are sufficiently patient, that is have a sufficiently high discount factor, the cooperative outcome is an equilibrium. The Nash equilibrium of the prisoner's dilemma of course remains an equilibrium, but will be inferior for both individuals. As both individuals charge higher than competitive prices, which would be the Nash equilibrium of the prisoner's dilemma, and make higher profits, this outcome is of referred to as *tacit collusion* or *implicit collusion*, even though no agreement on the behaviour has been reached; it is purely driven by economic incentives.

B.3 Risk Aversion

Individuals prefer an investment with a certain outcome to an investment that has the same expected outcome but whose realised outcomes are uncertain. This is referred to as *risk aversion*. Pratt (1964) has developed a measure that allows us to quantify the strength of this risk aversion, also known as the Arrow-Pratt measure of risk aversion.

Let us assume that the outcome of an investment is V, which is random with some probability distribution and has expected value $E[V]$. If individuals are risk averse, they would prefer to receive a certain amount $E[V]$ to the random amount V. With utility function $u(\cdot)$, we can now determine a value π that makes a consumer indifferent between these two choices. Hence we need the expected utilities to be equal

$$E[u(E[V]-\pi)] = u(E[V]-\pi) = E[u(V)], \tag{B.6}$$

where the first equality arises from the observation that no random terms are included in the arguments of the utility function.

The term $E[V]-\pi$ is also called the *cash equivalent* or *certainty equivalent* of V and π is called the *risk premium*. Approximating the right-hand side of Eq. (B.6) by a second-order Taylor series expansion around $E[V]$, we get

$$\begin{aligned} E[u(V)] &= E\left[u(E[V]) + \frac{\partial u(E[V])}{\partial V}(E[V])(V-E[V]) \right. \\ &\quad \left. + \frac{1}{2}\frac{\partial^2 u(E[V])}{\partial V^2}(V-E[V])^2\right] \\ &= u(E[V]) + \frac{1}{2}\frac{\partial^2 u(E[V])}{\partial V^2} Var[V], \end{aligned} \tag{B.7}$$

where the second term in the original approximation vanishes as $E[V-E[V]] = 0$ and for the final expression we used that $E\left[(V-E[V])^2\right] = Var[V]$ is the definition of the variance.

In a similar way, we can approximate the left-hand side of Eq. (B.6) by a first-order Taylor series around $E[V]$ and get

$$u(E[V]-\pi) = u(E[V]) + \frac{\partial u(E[V])}{\partial V}\pi. \tag{B.8}$$

Inserting Eqs. (B.7) and (B.8) into Eq. (B.6), we get after solving for the risk premium π that

$$\pi = -\frac{1}{2}\frac{\frac{\partial^2 u(E[V])}{\partial V^2}}{\frac{\partial u(E[V])}{\partial V}} Var\,[V]. \tag{B.9}$$

We now define

$$z = -\frac{\frac{\partial^2 u(E[V])}{\partial V^2}}{\frac{\partial u(E[V])}{\partial V}} \tag{B.10}$$

as the *absolute local risk aversion.* This can be justified by noting that the risk premia π has to be larger, the more risk averse an individual is, and the higher the risk. The risk is measured by the variance of V, $Var\,[V]$; hence the other term in Eq. (B.9) can be interpreted as risk aversion. By inserting Eq. (B.10) into Eq. (B.9), we get

$$\pi = \frac{1}{2} z Var\,[V]. \tag{B.11}$$

If we assume that individuals are risk averse we need $\pi > 0$, implying $z > 0$. It is reasonable to assume positive marginal utility, i. e. $\frac{\partial u(E[V])}{\partial V} > 0$, which then implies that we require $\frac{\partial^2 u(E[V])}{\partial V^2} < 0$ to obtain $z > 0$. This property of diminishing marginal utility is a common assumption about utility functions in economic theories. The assumption of risk aversion is therefore in line with the standard assumptions about utility functions in microeconomic theory.

These conditions imply a concave utility function, whose concavity (radius) is determined by the risk aversion. Figure B.2 visualises these findings for the simple case of two possible outcomes, V_1 and V_2, having equal probability of occurrence.

We can now insert Eq. (B.11) into Eq. (B.6) and obtain

$$E\,[u\,(V)] = u\,(E\,[V] - \pi) = u\left(E\,[V] - \frac{1}{2} z Var\,[V]\right). \tag{B.12}$$

To simplify the analysis even further, as $\frac{\partial u(E[V])}{\partial V} > 0$, we can use $E\,[V] - \frac{1}{2} z Var\,[V]$ as our objective function.

B.4 Monopolistic Competition

Goods are often similar and close substitutes, but not identical. There might be small differences in certain qualities such as its design or the combination of features it offers that make a consumer to prefer one over the other. We assume that each

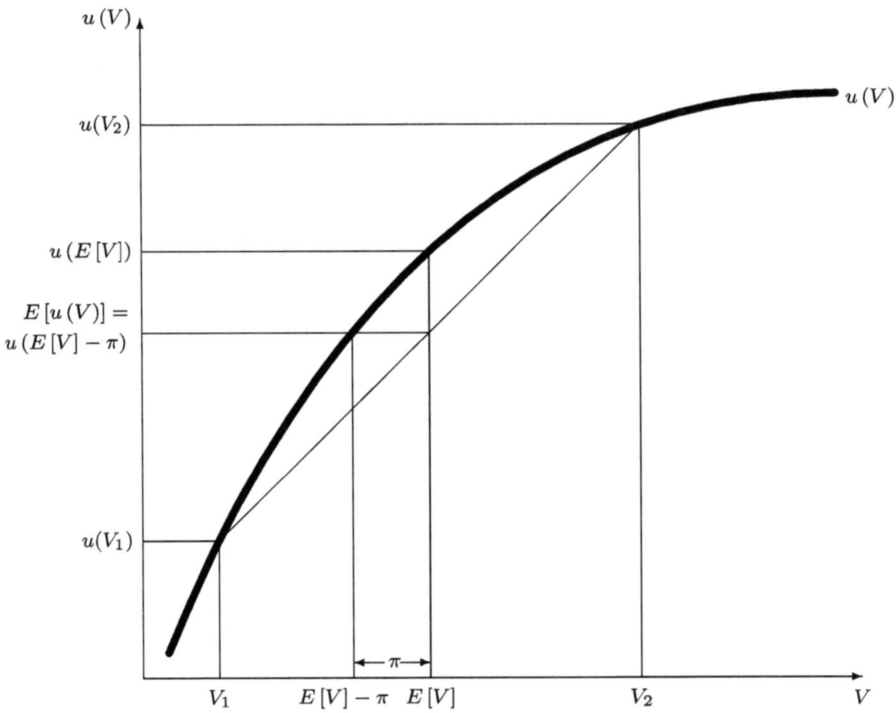

Fig. B.2 The Arrow-Pratt measure of risk aversion

consumer has a preference for these qualities and that each company produces a good with a given set of such qualities. The more differences there are between the preferences of the consumer and the good offered by the company, the less these goods are worth to the consumer. With each unit of difference, we assume that the value of the good, V, reduces by c.

Consumers are assumed to be evenly distributed on a line of length 1, where the location indicates their preferences for a specific quality and each company is located in a single position on this line, representing the qualities of their good. Consumers located at the some point as the company would be offered a good that exactly meets their preferences, and the further the consumer is located from the company, the lower the value to the consumer would be.

We now investigate the competition between companies in such a market for differentiated goods, in terms of prices set but also the location of the companies themselves.

B.4.1 Hotelling Model

Hotelling (1929) assumes that consumers are located on a straight line of length 1 and indicates their location by the distance d from the start of the line, hence $0 \leq d \leq 1$. There are two companies offering a good for which they charge a price P_i, and they are located in positions d_1 and d_2, respectively. Without loss of generality, we assume that $0 \leq d_1 \leq d_2 \leq 1$.

The value of the good to a consumer buying from company i will be

$$\Pi_C^i = V - P_i - c\,|d - d_i|\,, \tag{B.13}$$

where $|\cdot|$ denotes the absolute value and hence the distance of the consumer to the company. The consumer who is indifferent between buying from the two companies will be located at the point where $\Pi_C^1 = \Pi_C^2$. As $d_1 \leq d_2$, we will have that $|d - d_1| = d - d_1$ and $|d - d_2| = d_2 - d$ for any $d_1 \leq d \leq d_2$. Inserting this into Eq. (B.13), we obtain the location of the indifferent consumer as

$$d^* = \frac{d_1 + d_2}{2} + \frac{P_2 - P_1}{2c}. \tag{B.14}$$

If $d < d_1$ or $d > d_2$, the consumer will choose the nearest company, company 1 and company 2, respectively.

Company 1 will now obtain the business of all consumers $d \leq d^*$, which given the uniform distribution of consumers, gives us a demand for their good of d^*. The demand for company 2 will be the remainder of consumers, thus $1 - d^*$, and the profits of the companies, assuming they have no further costs, are thus

$$\begin{aligned} \Pi_B^1 &= P_1 d^* \\ &= \frac{cP_1\,(d_1 + d_2) + P_1P_2 - P_1^2}{2c}, \\ \Pi_B^2 &= P_2\left(1 - d^*\right) \\ &= \frac{cP_2\,(2 - d_1 - d_2) + P_1P_2 - P_2^2}{2c}. \end{aligned} \tag{B.15}$$

Both companies maximise their respective profits, assuming that the location has been chosen previously, and the first-order conditions are given by

$$\begin{aligned} \frac{\partial \Pi_C^1}{\partial P_1} &= \frac{c\,(d_1 + d_2) + P_2 - 2P_1}{2c} = 0, \\ \frac{\partial \Pi_C^2}{\partial P_2} &= \frac{c\,(2 - d_1 - d_2) + P_1 - 2P_2}{2c} = 0, \end{aligned} \tag{B.16}$$

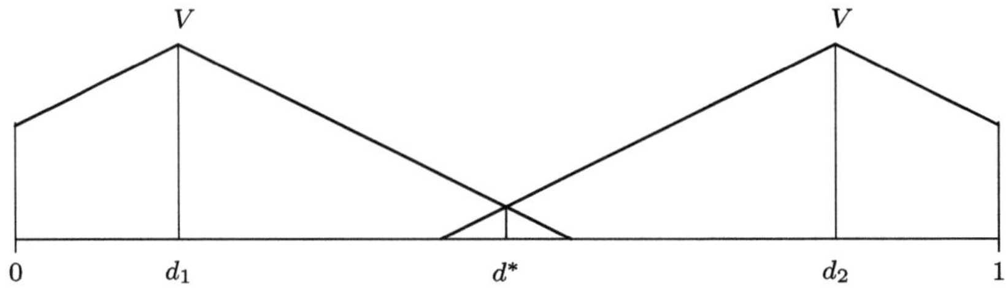

Fig. B.3 The Hotelling model

which can be solved for

$$P_1 = \frac{c}{3}(2 + d_1 + d_2), \qquad (B.17)$$
$$P_2 = \frac{c}{3}(4 - d_1 - d_2).$$

Inserting these prices into Eqs. (B.14) and (B.15), we get the company profits as

$$\Pi_B^1 = \frac{c}{18}(2 + d_1 + d_2)^2, \qquad (B.18)$$
$$\Pi_B^2 = \frac{c}{18}(4 - d_1 - d_2)^2.$$

As both companies are inherently equal, we are only looking at symmetric equilibria in which $\Pi_B^1 = \Pi_B^2$ and thus companies have no desire to switch positions. Solving for this relationship using Eqs. (B.18), we easily get that $d_1 + d_2 = 1$. Thus all locations that are symmetric from the end of the line are giving symmetric equilibria with $P_1 = P_2 = c$ and $\Pi_B^1 = \Pi_B^2 = \frac{c}{2}$.

With us being interested in the competition between companies for consumers, we will normally choose $d_1 = 0$ and $d_2 = 1$ such that all consumers are subjected to the competitive forces between the two companies. Figure B.3 illustrates the Hotelling model with arbitrarily chosen (symmetric) locations of the two companies.

B.4.2 Salop Circle

Rather than assuming that consumers and companies are located on a straight line of length 1, Salop (1979) assumes the line to form a circle; thus, the start and end of the line are connected. In addition, there are now $N \geq 2$ companies offering differentiated goods, and the distance between bank i and companies $i+1$ is denoted d_i, where $\sum_{i=1}^{N} d_i = 1$. Of course, if $i = N$, then we set $i + 1 = 1$ to complete the circle. The distance of a consumer to company i is denoted by $\hat{d}_i$. We have $\hat{d}_i + \hat{d}_{i+1} = d_i$ as the distance of a consumer located between companies i and $i+1$

to company i and company $i+1$ together, which must equal the distance between the companies.

The profits to a consumer selecting different companies are then given by

$$\begin{aligned}\Pi_C^i &= V - P_i - c\hat{d}_i, \\ \Pi_C^{i+1} &= V - P_{i+1} - c\left(d_i - \hat{d}_i\right), \\ \Pi_C^{i-1} &= V - P_{i-1} - c\left(d_{i-1} - \hat{d}_i\right).\end{aligned} \tag{B.19}$$

Consumers being indifferent between companies i and $i+1$ require $\Pi_C^i = \Pi_C^{i+1}$ and being indifferent between companies i and $i-1$ requires $\Pi_C^i = \Pi_C^{i-1}$. This implies that the distance to banks $i+1$ and $i-1$, respective, must be at least

$$\begin{aligned}\hat{d}_{i+1}^* &= \frac{cd_i + P_{i+1} - P_i}{2c}, \\ \hat{d}_{i-1}^* &= \frac{cd_{i-1} + P_{i-1} - P_i}{2c}\end{aligned} \tag{B.20}$$

for the consumer to prefer company i.

The company profits are then given by the demand of consumers located closer than $\hat{d}_{i-1}^*$ to company $i-1$ and closer than $\hat{d}_{i+1}^*$ to company $i+1$, hence

$$\Pi_B^i = \left(\hat{d}_{i-1}^* + \hat{d}_{i+1}^*\right) P_i = \frac{c\left(d_i + d_{i-1}\right) + P_{i+1} + P_{i-1} - 2P_i}{2c} P_i, \tag{B.21}$$

such that for given locations, the optimal price P_i has to fulfill the first-order condition

$$\frac{\partial \Pi_B^1}{\partial P_i} = \frac{c\left(d_i + d_{i-1}\right) + P_{i+1} + P_{i-1} - 4P_i}{2c} = 0. \tag{B.22}$$

This solves for

$$P_i = \frac{1}{4}\left(c\left(d_i + d_{i-1}\right) + P_{i+1} + P_{i-1}\right). \tag{B.23}$$

As this condition is identical for all companies, we again look only at symmetric equilibria and assume that all prices are equal, thus $P = P_{i-1} = P_i = P_{i+1}$, solving for

$$P = \frac{c}{2}\left(d_i + d_{i-1}\right). \tag{B.24}$$

Inserting this result into Eqs. (B.20) and (B.21), we find that $\Pi_B^i = \frac{c}{4}\,(d_i + d_{i-1})^2$ and requiring all companies to have equal profits to avoid swapping locations as they are inherently identical, we get from $\Pi_B^i = \Pi_B^{i+1}$ that $d_{i-1} = d_{i+1}$. Thus, the distance between any companies $i-1$ and i is the same as between companies $i+1$ and $i+2$. While the distance between companies i and $i+1$ could be different, the symmetry would imply that there is no reason for this to be so; hence, all distances between companies are identical and $d_i = \frac{1}{N}$. This implies then from Eqs. (B.23) and (B.24) that $P_i = \frac{c}{N}$ and $\Pi_B^i = \frac{c}{N^2}$.

We note that in this model for $N = 2$ companies, the prices the companies charge for the good is identical to the case of consumers and companies being located on a line, while the profits are lower as comparison with the final results of the Hotelling model in Appendix B.4.1 shows. The reason is that in the circular model here, companies face competition from both sides, while in the linear model this competition is only in the direction of the other company.

Credit Risk Assessment

C

Credit risk is the possibility of a bank making losses from borrowers not repaying their loans or a counterparty in a transaction not meeting their obligations in full. Such a situation is referred to as default. If the probability of default is given by p and the loss given default, the losses that are made if default occurs are denoted λ, then for an exposure to such a risk of size L, we have the expected losses as

$$\Pi_L = p\lambda L. \tag{C.1}$$

Rather than loss given default, it also common to use the recovery rate $1-\lambda$, which denotes the fraction of the exposure that the lender is able to obtain in the case of a default.

In terms of loans, there is a simple relationship between the loan rate r_L that should be charged and the default rate. The loan of size L is supposed to be repaid including interest r_L, giving us an exposure of $(1+r_L)\,L$. This is repaid with probability p, while with probability $1-p$, default occurs and the lender obtains a fraction $1-\lambda$ of their exposure. This gives us an expected repayment of

$$\begin{aligned}\hat{\Pi}_L &= p\,(1+r_L)\,L + (1-p)\,(1-\lambda)\,(1+r_L)\,L \\ &= (p\lambda + (1-\lambda))\,(1+r_L)\,L.\end{aligned} \tag{C.2}$$

An investment of the initial loan L into a risk-free asset yielding a return of r would give us $(1+r)\,L$. In equilibrium, the returns from two investments must be equal, yielding

$$1+r_L = \frac{1+r}{p\lambda + (1-\lambda)}. \tag{C.3}$$

In most practical cases, we find that upon default the bank will not obtain any payments from the borrowers once the liquidation process is completed, thus $\lambda = 1$,

A. Krause, *Theoretical Foundations of Investment Banking*, Springer Texts in Business and Economics, https://doi.org/10.1007/978-3-031-58060-4

and hence upon default the entire loan is lost. This simplifies Eq. (C.3) to $1 + r_L = \frac{1+r}{p}$, and if we use the approximation that for small values of x we have $\ln(1+x) \approx x$, we can rewrite this expression as

$$r_L \approx r + p. \tag{C.4}$$

The loan rate r_L is the risk-free rate r adjusted by the probability of default p. Hence the probability of default is a key parameter that credit risk assessment seeks to determine. Different methods of obtaining the probability of default have been proposed and many banks generally apply their own methodology, informed by data from past lending. The most common theoretical approaches are based on the idea of Merton (1974).

C.1 The Merton Model

The total assets of a company at time t, A_t, are financed by debt L and equity E_t, such that $A_t = L + E_t$. Default occurs if at maturity of the loan, T, the assets are not sufficient to repay the debt, thus if $A_T < L$, ignoring for convenience the accumulated interest in the exposure of the bank. The probability of default is then given by $p = \text{Prob}(A_T < L)$. We now assume that assets grow at an expected rate of μ_A and the growth rate has a volatility of σ_A. We can then write the development of the asset price over time as a stochastic process. The change of the asset value over Δt time periods is ΔA_t and the growth rate therefore $\frac{\Delta A_t}{A_t}$. We thus have $\frac{\Delta A_t}{A_t} = \mu_A \Delta t + \varepsilon_t$, where ε_t is normally distributed with a mean of zero and variance of σ_A^2. If we take the time period becoming ever smaller, this approaches continuous time, and we obtain the Brownian motion

$$\frac{dA_t}{A_t} = \mu_A dt + \sigma_A dz_t, \tag{C.5}$$

where dz_t represents a standard Wiener process that only adds noise of variance 1 to the realised return. We can now use statistics to obtain that

$$p = \text{Prob}(A_T < L) = \Phi\left(\frac{\ln \frac{A_t}{L} + \left(\mu_A - \frac{1}{2}\sigma_A^2\right)(T-t)}{\sigma_A \sqrt{T-t}}\right), \tag{C.6}$$

where $\Phi(\cdot)$ denotes the cumulative standard normal distribution. This probability of default is the probability of default that by the end of time period T, i. e., in $T-t$ time periods, the company cannot repay the loan. If we assume that the actual default can happen at any point until time period T, then the probability of default per time period is $\frac{p}{T-t}$.

It has to be noted that in order to apply this approach, the volatility of the assets, σ_A and their growth rate need to be known. While a connection to the volatility of the observable volatility of stock prices can be made, this will only be of assistance in the determination of the credit risk from listed companies that have sufficient liquidity to ensure that prices are efficient. For the vast majority of lending decisions, no stock prices exist and therefore estimates of the asset volatility need to be obtained. This might be possible to be obtained from accounting data or other sources.

The expression $\frac{\ln\frac{A_t}{L}+\left(\mu_A-\frac{1}{2}\sigma_A^2\right)(T-t)}{\sigma_A\sqrt{T-t}}$ is also referred to as distance-to-default. With $\Phi(\cdot)$ denoting the cumulative standard normal distribution, the distance-to-default can be interpreted as the number of standard deviations the assets need to fall to trigger default. The distance to default represents the same information as the probability of default and is only a different way to express this information.

C.2 The KMV Model

Building on the Merton model, the risk consultancy KMV has simplified the distance-to-default expression. Empirically we find that $\mu_A - \frac{1}{2}\sigma_A^2 \approx 0$ and hence the distance-to-default simplifies to $\frac{\ln\frac{A_t}{L}}{\sigma_A\sqrt{T-t}}$. If we only consider the probability of default during the next time period, thus setting $T = t+1$, we only need to consider the short-term liabilities $\hat{L}$ that become due within the next year and can replace this expression in the distance to default. We can now make a further approximation that $\ln\frac{A_t}{\hat{L}} = \ln\left(1+\left(\frac{A_t}{\hat{L}}-1\right)\right) \approx \frac{A_t}{\hat{L}} - 1 = \frac{A_t-\hat{L}}{\hat{L}}$ and obtain

$$\frac{\ln\frac{A_t}{\hat{L}}}{\sigma_A} \approx \frac{A_t-\hat{L}}{\sigma_A\hat{L}}. \tag{C.7}$$

Using this distance to default and then applying $p = \Phi\left(\frac{A_t-\hat{L}}{\sigma_A\hat{L}}\right)$ from the Merton model, or a modified distribution that fits the actual observations better than the standard normal distribution, have the advantage that short-term defaults are considered, rather than long-term defaults that allow companies to make management decisions to avoid such default. This approach is widely used by banks.

C.3 The Vasicek Model

What is unsatisfactory in the Merton model, and by extension, the KMV model, is that defaults are driven purely by a stochastic process of the assets of a company. Often we can, however, identify determinants that will affect default rates, such a macroeconomic conditions, industry-specific developments, or even company-specific factors. As in Vasicek (2002), let us therefore assume that the value of the assets of a company, A_t, are determined by

$$\ln A_t = \mu_A + \sigma_A \Psi_t, \tag{C.8}$$

where Ψ_t represents such factors and we assume that this variable is normally distributed with mean zero and variance 1. The logarithm of the assets thus has a mean of μ_A and a variance of σ_A^2. With a loan of L, neglecting interest payments in the exposure, we observe a default if at any time the assets are not sufficient to cover the loan amount, hence we require $A_t < L$. Thus

$$\begin{aligned} p &= \text{Prob}\left(A_t < L\right) = \text{Prob}\left(\ln A_t < \ln L\right) \\ &= \text{Prob}\left(\Psi_t < \frac{\ln L - \mu_A}{\sigma_A}\right) \\ &= \Phi\left(\frac{\ln L - \mu_A}{\sigma_A}\right) \end{aligned} \tag{C.9}$$

and default is caused by the variable Ψ_t being sufficiently low. $\Phi(\cdot)$ denotes the cumulative normal distribution as we had assumed that Ψ_t is standard normally distributed. This variable Ψ_t is used here to represent the underlying factor driving the default of a company. Let us now assume that

$$\Psi_t = \rho \Upsilon_t + \sqrt{1-\rho^2}\varepsilon_t, \tag{C.10}$$

where Υ_t is a normalised variable that is a common factor for defaults to occur in an economy and ε_t is an idiosyncratic factor that is unique and unpredictable to the company considered. We assume Υ_t and ε_t to be standard normally distributed and to be independent of each other. In this case, we easily see that the Ψ_t is standard normally distributed as we had assumed in Eq. (C.9). Let us now assume that we know the value of Υ from observation. Such a factor might also be an aggregate of a variety of factors that we have considered to be relevant for the default of companies; banks will usually employ models that use a variety of factors to determine such values and obtain a credit score like Υ_t. Inserting Eq. (C.10) into Eq. (C.9), we obtain

$$\begin{aligned} \hat{p} &= \text{Prob}\left(\varepsilon_t < \frac{\frac{\ln L - \mu_A}{\sigma_A} - \rho\Upsilon_t}{\sqrt{1-\rho^2}}\right) \\ &= \Phi\left(\frac{\frac{\ln L - \mu_A}{\sigma_A} - \rho\Upsilon_t}{\sqrt{1-\rho^2}}\right) \\ &= \Phi\left(\frac{p - \rho\Upsilon_t}{\sqrt{1-\rho^2}}\right). \end{aligned} \tag{C.11}$$

We can now interpret p as the average probability of default of the company and $\hat{p}$ as the probability of default adjusted to the current economic conditions. A value of $\Upsilon_t = 0$ corresponds to this average value, given that we assumed this variable to have a mean of zero. The actual probability of default $\hat{p}$ will be higher than p, because the risk of the common factor Υ_t to move adversely makes a default more likely than if default was purely driven by an idiosyncratic stochastic element.

Security Valuation

D

Securities give the owner the right to future payments as specified in the conditions of the security. The challenge in determining the value of such a security is to firstly estimate these future payments and then to use an appropriate discount rate to determine the present value of these future payments. This methodology, also referred to as the discounted cash flow methodology, is the theoretically correct methodology to use, but practitioners have developed alternative methods as outlined in Rosenbaum and Pearl (2009, Chs. 1-3).

D.1 Discounted Cash Flow

A security promises to pay the expected amount of C_t at time t. The present value of such future payments will then be

$$V_0 = \sum_{t=0}^{+\infty} \rho^t C_t, \tag{D.1}$$

where $\rho \leq 1$ denotes the discount factor. If the future payments were guaranteed, then the risk-free rate r would be used to discount future payments, and we set $\rho = \frac{1}{1+r}$. Commonly, though, payments are not guaranteed, and we have to form expectations about these payments C_t. This is most prominent with shares, where C_t are the dividends the company will pay in the future. As these dividends are not guaranteed, the resulting risk for any deviations from the expectations needs to be compensated; this is achieved by applying a lower discount factor. It is common to use the Capital Asset Pricing Model (CAPM) to determine appropriate discount factors by applying the required rate of return obtained from this model, $\mu = r + \beta(\mu_M - r)$, and set $\rho = \frac{1}{1+\mu}$. Here μ_M denotes the market return and $\beta = \frac{\sigma_{iM}}{\sigma_M^2}$ the

A. Krause, *Theoretical Foundations of Investment Banking*, Springer Texts in Business and Economics, https://doi.org/10.1007/978-3-031-58060-4

systematic risk of the shares, calculated as the ratio of the covariance of the stock with the market, σ_{iM}, and the market variance, σ_M^2.

Expectations about future dividends will be based on information the investment banker has about the prospects of the company. A common simplification is to assume that dividends remain constant, $C_t = C$, resulting in Eq. (D.2) to simplify to $V_0 = \frac{C}{1-\rho}$, Alternatively, a constant growth rate of g is assumed, such that $C_t = (1+g)\, C_{t-1}$. This assumption, known as the Gordon Growth Model, gives us a value of $V = \frac{1+r}{r-g} C_0$. Of course, more specific estimates can, and commonly are, used by investment banks when valuing companies. They will in particular take into account any synergies arising from mergers, but also their costs; for IPOs they would determine the impact the additional capital raised has due to the increased investment the company can make.

Discounted cash flow analysis is not only applicable to the valuation of shares, but can also be applied to bonds. The regular payments of a bond are the coupons C, and the last payment at maturity T consists of this coupon payment and the repayment of the bond, L. Thus Eq. (D.2) becomes

$$V_0 = \sum_{t=0}^{T} \rho^t C + \rho^T L. \tag{D.2}$$

The appropriate discount factor will have to take into account the default risk of a bond. With a probability of default p and a risk-free rate r, we can set $\rho = \frac{1}{1+r_L} = \frac{1}{1+r+p}$. Here the expertise of the investment banker is required to determine the appropriate probability of default as part of their credit risk assessment.

D.2 Comparable Companies Analysis

Rather than relying on their own valuation of a company, investment banks might make use of market data available from other companies or bonds. For the valuation of shares and bonds, it is common to identify other companies or bond issuers that have similar characteristics to the one to be considered. Investment banks look for companies that are active in the same sector and jurisdiction and have a similar size, comparable capital structure, as well as a similar market position within their industry. Having identified such companies, the investment bank then compares so-called trading multiples. These often include the price-earnings-ratio or the ratio of the price and the earnings before interest, taxes, depreciation, and amortisation (EBITDA). Applying the same ratio to the company to be valued will then give its value. Underlying this methodology is the assumption that the future dividends of companies that are currently similar will develop in a similar way and that the risks involved are also comparable; hence the same discount factor can be applied. For bonds, the comparison is easier in that the yield of bonds should be identical for otherwise comparable issuers; the only addition for bonds is that bonds of similar time to maturity have to be chosen.

The comparable company analysis is often used in addition to the discounted cash flow methodology and might provide some insights into the assumptions the market makes about other companies' growth potential and risks that might inform the valuation of the company concerned. Investment banks might want to adjust the risks or growth prospects from those of comparable companies if this is justified by the circumstances of the company or issuer.

D.3 Precedents Transactions Analysis

In particular if the valuation of a company is made for a specific purpose, such as a merger or an IPO, the valuation might deviate from that of comparable companies. Such a deviation maybe the result of synergies having to be taken into account in mergers, or an acquirer might be willing to pay more for a target company as he believes he can change the prospects of the company and thus add value. This would, of course, not be included in the market price of comparable companies. In an IPO it is common to underprice the issue, which would also not be included in the price of companies already listed on an exchange. In this case, investment banks would look at similar trading multiples as in the comparable companies analysis, but select companies that recently have undergone similar transactions to the company they seek to analyse. This gives investment bankers information on how high merger premia might be and how this would translate into appropriate transaction prices in the case they are advising on. Similarly, it would give them an initial indication of a reasonable price for an IPO or a reasonable estimate for the yield of a bond, even before any book-building would commence to gain more information on the market perception of the security.

Again, similar to the comparable companies analysis, the precedents transactions analysis would serve as a benchmark to analyse the company or issuer, and the results would then be compared to that of a discounted cash flow analysis for a more complete evaluation of the security.

D.4 Derivatives Pricing

The valuation of derivatives is usually conducted very differently from that of shares or bonds. Most derivatives have a time to maturity, similar to bonds, and the payments made from owning derivatives often depend on the value of other securities, such as in options, futures, and swaps. However, it can be that derivatives are not based on other securities, but events happening to other entities, such as the default of companies triggering payments from credit default swaps. There are two basic methodologies to value derivatives. The first methodology seeks to balance the present value of future payments that these derivatives make with the payments the owner has to make. In the case of an option, this would mean that the payments received from exercising the option, if it is profitable to exercise the option, discounted to its present value, should equal the option premium the buyer has to pay. In the case of credit default swaps, the payments triggered by the default of the underlying entity have to the balanced against the regular payments the owner of this derivative has to make. The value would then be the amount that is regularly paid.

An alternative approach is to form a replicating portfolio. In this methodology, the value of the derivative is determined by a portfolio of securities that are available in the market and for which market prices are observable. A portfolio is constructed such that whenever the derivative makes a payment to its owner, often, but not always, at maturity, the portfolio makes the same payment or has an identical value. The market prices of the components of this portfolio are then added to give the value of the security. Often the portfolio includes short positions of securities.

Both methodologies should provide the same value of the derivative, but often one methodology is chosen in preference over the other for convenience of calculating the value. In other cases, one methodology, in most cases the replicating portfolio, is not available as securities required in such a portfolio are not traded. In other instances the reason for a specific methodology might be historical in that a certain methodology was first used to determine the value in the literature and has been maintained since.

Of central importance in derivatives pricing is the modelling of the payments the derivative makes and/or the payments the buyer makes. These payments are often assumed to have distributions that arise from stochastic processes; commonly the timing of such payments are also the result of the same or a different stochastic process. Solving for the expected payments or obtaining a replicating portfolio uses advanced mathematical and statistical methods, making the valuation of derivatives a task which is commonly left to specialists rather than investment bankers in direct contact with their clients.

Glossary

Acquisition See *Mergers and acquisitions*

Adverse selection Adverse selection refers to a situation in which one or more market participants have more or better information than other market participants and can exploit this advantage to increase their profits at the expense of the less well-informed market participants

Allocation See *Security allocation*

Ask See *Ask price*

Ask price In → *market making*, the price at which the → *market maker* is willing to sell a security. See also *Bid-ask spread*

Asset management In asset management, an investment bank will make investment decisions on behalf of their client. The funds invested will remain in their clients, name and any profits or losses will accrue to the client and not the investment bank.

Associate An employee in a → *partnership*, who may be promoted to become a → *partner*.

Back office The back office of an investment bank ensures that the infrastructure on which employees rely on when advising clients is working efficiently, such as the access to and maintenance of databases. They are also responsible for the → *clearing* and → *settlement* of trades and → *security allocation*, that is, ensuring that monies are collected from buyers to pay sellers, and securities are transferred from sellers to buyers. See also *Front office*, *Middle office*

Beauty parade Companies inviting investment banks to offer their services in → *mergers and acquisitions*.

Best efforts contract In → *security underwriting*, a contract in which the investment bank does not guarantee the sale of all securities nor the price at which they are sold to investors. See also *firm-commitment contract*

Biased advice Advice given to a client by an investment bank that is not consistent with the investment bank's information.

Bid 1. The offer a → *bidder* in → *mergers and acquisitions* makes to acquire the → *target*. 2. In → *security underwriting*, the price an investor is willing to pay for a security. 3. See *Bid price*

A. Krause, *Theoretical Foundations of Investment Banking*, Springer Texts in Business and Economics, https://doi.org/10.1007/978-3-031-58060-4

Bid price In → *market making*, the price at which the → *market maker* is willing to buy a security. See also *Bid-ask spread*

Bid-ask spread In → *market making*, the difference between the → *ask price* and the → *bid price* a → *market maker* sets.

Bidder The company that seeks to purchase the shares of another company in → *mergers and acquisitions*. See also *Target*

Bonus The part of an investment banker's → *compensation* that is based on their performance.

Book-building In → *security underwriting*, the process during which investment banks solicit indicative bids from selected investors.

Boutique investment bank An investment bank that specialises in a small number of business lines in investment banking. See also *Bulge-bracket investment bank*

Break-up fee In → *mergers and acquisitions*, a fee that is payable if the transaction is not completed. See also *Retainer fee*

Broker See *Brokerage* See also *Discount broker*, *Full-servive broker*

Brokerage A broker allows the general public to trade securities on an exchange by taking their orders and transmitting these to the exchange for execution.

Bulge-bracket investment bank An investment bank that provides a full range of services. See also *Boutique investment bank*

Buy-side analyst A → *financial analyst* providing information to the investment bank's own asset managers and proprietary traders. See also *Sell-side analyst*

Chinese Walls The separation of → *financial analyst*s from the influence of → *corporate finance* in their analyst reports.

Clearing The transfer of monies following the transfer of securities. See also *Settlement*

Client In investment banking, a client is the person or company the investment bank advises in a specific → *deal*. For this specific deal, the client seek advice exclusively from one investment bank or a syndicate.

Co-underwriter In → *security underwriting*, a member of a → *syndicate* not taking a major role in the underwriting process. See also *Lead underwriter*

Commercial bank A financial institution taking deposits from and giving loans to the public. See also *Investment banking*, *Universal banking*

Compensation In investment banks, the salary employees receive is commonly referred to as compensation; it encompasses fixed salaries as well as performance-related components, such as a → *bonus*.

Conditional fee contract In → *mergers and acquisitions*, a contract in which the investment bank is paid a fixed fee only if the merger is completed. See also *Contingent fee contract*

Contingent fee contract In → *mergers and acquisitions*, a contract in which the fee paid to the investment bank is dependent on the value of the transaction and is only due if the merger is completed. See also *Conditional fee contract*

Controlling stake An investor or company has a controlling stake in another company if it obtains a fraction of the ownership such that no decisions can be made against its will. Depending on the level of control desired and the legistlative framework, a controlling stake can be obtained if a quarter or a third of the company is owned, as for major decisions, often a qualified majority of at least two-thirds or three-quarters is required. Obtaining more than half the ownership usually allows control of most operations of the company.

Corporate finance In investment banking, corporate finance encompasses the business lines of providing advice in → *merges and acquisitions* and → *underwriting*

Counterparty When selling (buying) a security, the buyer (seller) taking the opposite side of the trade is referred to as the counterparty.

Deal The transaction an investment bank advises a client on.

Dealer See *Market maker*

Discount broker A → *broker* that does not provide any advice to clients on trading and investment opportunities. See also *Full-service broker*

Dual capacity An investment bank acting as a → *broker* to clients and engaged in → *proprietary trading* with the ability to pass information between these two business lines.

Due diligence The detailed investigation of a company to establish the value of its securities by the investment bank in → *mergers and acquisitions* and → *security underwriting*.

Exchange listing A security that can be traded on an exchange.

Execution-only broker See *Discount broker*

Financial Analyst A financial analyst conducts → *research* into the future prospects of securities, most commonly shares and bonds, but also on general macroeconomic conditions and commodities.

Financial innovation The development of new securities or new processes in banking.

Firm-commitment contract In → *security underwriting*, a contract in which the investment bank guarantees the issuer to sell all securities at a given price. See also *Best efforts contract*

Front office The front office of an investment bank is client-facing, provides the advice to their clients, and is the origin of most revenue an investment bank generates. See also *Middle office*, *Back office*

Full-service broker A → *broker* that also provides advice to clients on trading and investment opportunities. See also *Discount broker*

Full-service investment bank *see* Bulge-bracket investment bank

Going public See *Initial Public Offering*

Greenshoe option In → *security underwriting*, the right of an investment bank to purchase additional securities from the issuer at the → *offer price*.

Hedge funds Hedge funds invest money obtained from investors into securities and other financial instruments, including commodities, foreign exchange, or cryptocurrencies.

Informed trader A trader in financial markets that has received additional information on the value of a security and takes this information into consideration for their trading decision. See also *Uninformed trader*, *Noise trader*

Initial public offering An initial public offering (IPO) is the offer of shares from a company to the general public for the first time with the aim of → *listing* these shares on an exchange for trading.

Investment bank A financial institution advising clients on capital markets transactions. See also *Commercial banking*, *Universal banking*

IPO See *Initial public offering*

LBO See *Leveraged buy-out*

Lead underwriter In → *security underwriting*, a member of a → *syndicate* taking major responsibility in the underwriting process by completing → *due diligence* investigations and organising the → *roadshow* and with a → *firm-commitment contract* underwriting the largest share of the securities issued. See also *Co-underwriter*

Leveraged buy-out A leveraged buy-out is a transaction in which investors seek to acquire a → *controlling stake* in a company and finance the purchase using debt.

Liquidity The ability to trade instantly in a market without affecting the price of this trade.

Listing See *Exchange listing*

M&A See *Mergers and acquisitions*

Management buy-out A management buy-out is a transaction in which senior managers of a company seek to purchase its shares to gain a → *controlling stake*

Market maker A market maker will at any time quote prices at which he is willing to buy and sell a security up to a given quantity.

Market making See *Market maker*

MBO See *Management buy-out*

Merger See *Mergers and acquisitions*

Mergers and acquisitions Mergers and acquisitions refers to a situation in which ownership of an entire company or a → *controlling stake* of a company is transferred to another party, usually another company. If the ownership of a company is transferred to another party and subsumed into its organization with most key management position in its control, this is commonly referred to as an acquisition. If both companies are combined as equals with key management positions shared between managers of both companies, this is referred to as a merger. Typically, in acquisitions, the acquired company is significantly smaller than the acquiring company, while for mergers the two companies are of comparable size.

Middle office The middle office of an investment bank is concerned with the running of the investment bank. It encompasses tasks like the development of a business strategy; the → *compensation* policy of the investment bank exerts internal controls such as performance assessment and the management of risks, as well as the investment of internal funds in what is generally called treasury management. See also *Front office*, *Back office*

Moral hazard Moral hazard describes a situation in which a market participant may not act as agreed or desired without facing adverse consequences resulting from their choice of action.

Noise trader A trader in financial markets that is assumed to trade for exogenous reasons and does not maximise an objective function. It is common to assume that noise traders submit orders of random size. See also *Informed trader*, *Uninformed trader*

Offer price In → *security underwriting*, the price at which the security is sold to investors.

Partner A senior manager in a → *partnership* who is also an equity holder. See also *Associate*

Partnership An investment bank in which all equity holders are also senior managers. See also *Associate*, *Partner*

Primary market In a primary market, securities are sold directly from the issuer for the first time. See *Secondary market*, *Secondary offering*

Primary offer See *Primary market*

Private equity Private equity is a company set up for the purpose of investing any funds obtained into the equity of listed or private companies.

Private placement A private placement occurs if securities are not sold to the general public but only to selected investors on invitation. See also *Initial pulic offering*

Proprietary trading The trading of securities by investment banks on their own account.

Relationship banking An investment bank seeking to meet the needs of their clients across the range of services they offer and over a longer period of time. See also *Transaction banking*

Research In investment banking, research refers to the provision of information by → *financial analysts* on the future prospects of securities to investors, commonly combined with investment recommendations. Research may also include the provision of information on macroecoonomic conditions or commodities.

Retainer fee In → *mergers and acquisitions*, a fee that is paid to secure the services of an investment bank. The retainer fee can either be a fixed amount or be based on the time length the investment bank advises their client on the → *deal*.

Rights offer Shares offered by a company offered exclusively to its existing shareholders, commonly at a discount to the current market price.

Roadshow Presentations made to potential investors and financial analysts about a company by an investment bank, usually in connection with → *security underwriting*.

Seasoned equity offer The offering of shares to the general public by a company whose shares are already listed on an exchange.

Secondary market In a secondary market, securities are traded among investors that have previously been sold by an issuer in the → *primary market*. See also *Primary market*

Secondary offer The sale of existing securities to the general public.

Secondary offering A secondary offering refers to the issuing company increasing the number shares already held by investors and traded on an exchange. See also *primary market*

Security A security is a right to the proceeds from a financial asset. How these proceeds are calculated will be determined by the type of security. Securities can usually be traded between investors.

Security allocation In → *security underwriting*, the distribution of securities to investors by investment banks.

Security Underwriting See *Underwriting*

Sell-side analyst A → *financial analyst* providing information to the investment bank's clients. See also *Buy-side analyst*

SEO See *Seasoned equity offer*

Settlement The allocation of securities to the new owners after a transaction. See also *Clearing*

Soft commission The payment for → *financial analyst* reports through inflated brokerage commissions.

Spread 1. See *Underwriting spread* 2. See *Bid-ask spread*

Success fee See *Conditional fee contract*, *Contingent fee contract*

Syndicate In → *security underwriting*, a group of investment banks advising the issuer.

Target The company that is purchased by a → *bidder* in → *mergers and acquisitions*

Trading and sales In investment banking, trading and sales commonly refers to the business lines that facilitate the trading of and investment in securities. It includes → *brokerage*, → *market makers*, → *asset management*, → *proprietary trading*, → *financial innovation*

Transaction banking An investment bank seeking to meet the needs of their clients for the specific service they are currently advising on only. See also *Relationship banking*

Trapped bidders In → *security underwriting*, an investor that would want to buy the security at issue, but is prevented from doing so by not having access to sufficient information due the investment bank he as a relationship with, not being part of the → *syndicate*.

Underpricing In → *security underwriting*, the difference between the market price once trading on an exchange commences and the → *offer price*.

Underwriter See *Underwriting*

Underwriting Underwriting is the process of issuing securities in the → *primary market*, facilitated by investment banks, called underwriters.

Underwriting See *Security underwriting*

Underwriting Underwriting is the process of issuing securities in the → *primary market*, facilitated by investment banks.

Underwriting spread In → *security underwriting*, the difference between the → *offer price* and the price the investment banks pays the issuer for their securities.

Uninformed trader A trader in financial markets that does not have additional information on the value of a security, but seeks to maximise an objective function. See also *Informed trader*, *Noise trader*

Universal bank A financial institution offering → *commercial banking* and → *investment banking.*

Wealth management See *Asset management*

Winner's curse In → *security underwriting*, a situation in which an investor obtaining a security will be paying a price above its true value.

References

Allen, F. (1990). The market for information and the origin of financial intermediation. *Journal of Financial Intermediation, 1*(1), 3–30.

Anand, B. N., & Galetovic, A. (2006). Relationships, competition and the structure of investment banking markets. *Journal of Industrial Economics, 54*(2), 151–199.

Axelson, U., & Bond, P. (2015). Wall street occupations. *Journal of Finance, 70*(5), 1949–1996.

Benveniste, L. M., & Busaba, W. Y. (1997). Bookbuilding vs. fixed price: An analysis of competing strategies for marketing IPOs. *Journal of Financial and Quantitative Analysis, 32*(4), 383–403.

Bhattacharya, S., & Pfleiderer, P. (1985). Delegated portfolio management. *Journal of Economic Theory, 36*(1), 1–25.

Bhattacharyya, S., & Nanda, V. (2000). Client discretion, switching costs, and financial innovation. *Review of Financial Studies, 13*(4), 1101–1127.

Biglaiser, G. (1993). Middlemen as experts. *RAND Journal of Economics, 24*(2), 212–223.

Biglaiser, G. & Li, F. (2018). Middlemen: The good, the bad, and the ugly. *RAND Journal of Economics, 49*(1), 3–22.

Boehmer, E., & Fishe, R. P. H. (2000). *Do underwriters encourage stock flipping? A new explanation for the underpricing of IPOs*. Working Paper, Coral Gables: University of Miami.

Boot, A. W. A., & Thakor, A. V. (1997). Banking scope and financial innovation. *Review of Financial Studies, 10*(4), 1099–1131.

Brennan, M. J., & Chordia, T. (1993). Brokerage commission schedules. *Journal of Finance, 48*(4), 1379–1402.

Caselli, S., Gigante, G., & Tortoroglio, A. (2021). *Corporate and Investment Banking*. Milan: Bocconi University Press.

Chemmanur, T. J., & Fulghieri, P. (1994). Investment bank reputation, information production, and financial intermediation. *Journal of Finance, 49*(1), 57–79.

Chen, M. A., & Marquez, R. (2009). Regulating securities analysts. *Journal of Financial Intermediation, 18*(2), 259–283.

Dana, J. D. Jr, & Spier, K. E. (1993). Expertise and contingent fees: The role of asymmetric information in attorney compensation. *Journal of Law, Economics, and Organization, 9*(2), 349–367.

Das, S. R., & Nanda, A. (1999). A theory of banking structure. *Journal of Banking & Finance, 23*(6), 863–895.

Davis, S. I. (2003). *Investment Banking*. New York: Palgrave Macmillan.

Emons, W. (2006). Playing it safe with low conditional fees versus being insured by high contingent fees. *American Law and Economics Review, 8(1)*, 20–32.

Emons, W. (2007). Conditional versus contingent fees. *Oxford Economic Papers, 59*(1), 89–101.

Fernando, C. S., Gatchev, V. A., & Spindt, P. A. (2005). Wanna dance? How firms and underwriters choose each other. *Journal of Finance, 60*(5), 2437–2469.

Fishe, R. P. H. (2002). How stock flippers affect IPO pricing and stabilization. *Journal of Financial and Quantitative Analysis, 37*(2), 319–340.

A. Krause, *Theoretical Foundations of Investment Banking*, Springer Texts in Business and Economics, https://doi.org/10.1007/978-3-031-58060-4

Glode, V., & Lowery, R. (2016). Compensating financial experts. *Journal of Finance, 71*(6), 2781–2808.
Glode, V., Green, R. C., & Lowery, R. (2012). Financial expertise as an arms race. *The Journal of Finance, 67*(5), 1723–1759.
Glosten, L. R., & Milgrom, P. R. (1985). Bid, ask and transaction prices in a specialist market with heterogenously informed traders. *Journal of Financial Economics, 14*(1), 71–100.
Gravelle, H., & Waterson, M. (1993). No win, no fee: Some economics of contingent legal fees. *The Economic Journal, 103*(420), 1205–1220.
Hansen, R. S., & Khanna, N. (1994). Why negotiation with a single syndicate may be preferred to making syndicates compete: The problem of trapped bidders. *Journal of Business, 67*(3), 423–457.
Hart, O., & Moore, J. (2005). On the design of hierarchies: Coordination versus specialisation. *Journal of Policical Economy, 113*(4), 675–702.
Ho, T., & Stoll, H. R. (1980). On dealer markets under competition. *Journal of Finance, 35*, 259–268.
Hotelling, H. (1929). Stability in competition. *Economic Journal, 39*(153), 41–57.
Hughes, P. J., & Thakor, A. V. (2015). Litigation risk, intermediation, and the underpricing of initial public offerings. *Review of Financial Studies, 5*(4), 709–742.
Iannotta, G. (2010). *Investment Banking*. Berlin: Springer.
Inderst, R., & Ottaviani, M. (2012). Competition through Commissions and Kickbacks. *American Economic Review, 102*(2), 780–809.
Instefjord, N., & Sasaki, K. (2007). Proprietary trading losses in banks: Do banks invest sufficiently in control? *Annals of Finance, 3*(3), 329–350.
Instefjord, N., Jackson, P., & Perraudin, W. (2014). Securities fraud. *Economic Policy, 13*(27), 586–623.
Kant, I. (1783). *Prolegomena zu einer jeden künftigen Metaphysik, die als Wissenschaft wird auftreten können*. Riga: Johann Friedrich Hartknoch.
Levin, J., & Tadelis, S. (2005). Profit sharing and the role of professional partnerships. *Quarterly Journal of Economics, 120*(1), 131–171.
Liaw, K. T. (2012). *The business of investment banking*, (3rd ed.). Hoboken: Wiley.
Lim, T. (2001). Rationality and analysts' forecast bias. *Journal of Finance, 56*(1), 369–385.
Mandelker, G., & Raviv, A. (1977). Investment banking: An economic analysis of optimal underwriting contracts. *Journal of Finance, 32*(3), 683–694.
Merton, R. C. (1974). On the pricing of corporate debt: The risk structure of interest rates. *Journal of Finance, 29*(2), 449–470.
Morrison, A. D., & Wilhelm Jr., W. J. (2008). The demise of investment banking partnerships: Theory and evidence. *Journal of Finance, 63*(1), 311–350.
Nash, J. (1953). Two-person cooperative games. *Econometrica, 21*(1), 128–140.
Persons, J. C., & Warther, V. A. (1997). Boom and bust patterns in the adoption of financial innovations. *Review of Financial Studies, 10*(4), 939–967.
Pichler, P., & Wilhelm, W. (2001). A theory of the syndicate: Form follows function. *Journal of Finance, 56*(6), 2237–2264.
Pratt, J. W. (1964). Risk aversion in the small and in the large. *Econometrica, 32*(1/2), 122–136.
Puri, M. (1999). Commercial banks as underwriters: implications for the going public process. *Journal of Financial Economics, 54*(2), 133–163.
Rawls, J. (1971). *A theory of justice*. Cambridge: Harvard University Press.
Reynolds, J. N., & Newell, E. (2011). *Ethics in investment banking*. New York: Palgrave MacMillan.
Rock, K. (1986). Why new issues are underpriced. *Journal of Financial Economics, 15*(1), 187–212.
Rosenbaum, J., & Pearl, J. (2009). *Investment banking*. Hoboken: Wiley.
Röell, A. (1990). Dual-capacity trading and the quality of the market. *Journal of Financial Intermediation, 1*(2), 105–124.

Salop, S. C. (1979). Monopolistic competition with outside goods. *Bell Journal of Economics, 10*(1), 141–156.
Sherman, A. E. (2015). IPOs and long-term relationships: An advantage of book building. *Review of Financial Studies, 13*(3), 697–714.
Spulber, D. F. (1999). *Market microstructure: intermediaries and the theory of the firm*. Cambridge: Cambridge University.
Stoll, H. R. (1978). The supply of dealer services in securities markets. *Journal of Finance, 33*(4), 1133–1151.
Stoughton, N. M., & Zechner, J. (1998). IPO-mechanisms, monitoring and ownership structure. *Journal of Financial Economics, 49*(1), 45–77.
Stowell, D. P. (2018). *Investment banks, hedge funds, and private equity* (3rd ed.). London: Academic Press.
Teo, M. (2000). *Strategic interactions between sell-side analysts and the firms they cover*. Working paper, Singapore: Singapore Management University.
Trueman, B. (1994). Analyst forecasts and herding behavior. *Review of Financial Studies, 7*(1), 97–124.
Vasicek, O. A. (2002). Loan portfolio value. *Risk*, pp. 160–162.
Welch, I. (1992). Sequential sales, learning, and cascades. *Journal of Finance, 47*(2), 695–732.
Zábojník, J. (2002). Centralized and decentralized decision making in organisation. *Journal of Labor Economics, 20*(1), 1–22.

Index

A. Krause, *Theoretical Foundations of Investment Banking*, Springer Texts in Business and Economics, https://doi.org/10.1007/978-3-031-58060-4

MIX
Papier aus verantwortungsvollen Quellen
Paper from responsible sources
FSC® C105338

If you have any concerns about our products,
you can contact us on
ProductSafety@springernature.com

In case Publisher is established outside the EU,
the EU authorized representative is:
Springer Nature Customer Service Center GmbH
Europaplatz 3, 69115 Heidelberg, Germany

Printed by Libri Plureos GmbH
in Hamburg, Germany